2000 Supplement
to Ninth Editions

MODERN CRIMINAL PROCEDURE

Cases — Comments — Questions

BASIC CRIMINAL PROCEDURE

Cases — Comments — Questions

and

ADVANCED CRIMINAL PROCEDURE

Cases — Comments — Questions

By

Yale Kamisar

Clarence Darrow Distinguished University Professor of Law, University of Michigan

Wayne R. LaFave

Professor Emeritus in the College of Law and Center for Advanced Study, University of Illinois

Jerold H. Israel

Ed Rood Eminent Scholar in Trial Advocacy and Procedure, University of Florida, College of Law
Alene and Allan F. Smith Professor of Law, University of Michigan

Nancy J. King

Professor of Law and Associate Dean, Vanderbilt University School of Law

AMERICAN CASEBOOK SERIES®

WEST GROUP

ST. PAUL, MINN., 2000

610 Opperman Drive
P.O. Box 64526
St. Paul, MN 55164–0526
1–800–328–9352

Printed in the United States of America

ISBN 0–314–24748–3

TEXT IS PRINTED ON 10% POST CONSUMER RECYCLED PAPER

Preface

This Supplement contains all significant United States Supreme Court cases decided during the second half of the 1999-2000 Term. It also contains a number of state court and lower federal court cases and various secondary materials. Finally, this volume contains selected provisions of the U.S. Constitution (App. A); selected federal statutory provisions, e.g., the Bail Reform Act, the Speedy Trial Act and the habeas corpus provisions of Title 28 (App. B); the Federal Rules of Criminal Procedure (including recent amendments)(App. C); and proposed amendments to the Rules (App. D).

City of Chicago v. Morales, the 1999 "gang ordinance" case, does not fit easily into a standard course on criminal procedure. But the case dramatically illustrates the tension between the need of the police to perform their peace-keeping responsibilities satisfactorily (in this instance, to combat gang crime and intimidation) and the need of a democratic society to provide the police with sufficient guidelines to prevent arbitrary or discriminating law enforcement. We have included *Morales* in this Supplement on the premise that some instructors may want to assign it, or at least refer to it at one or more points in the course.

YALE KAMISAR
WAYNE LAFAVE
JEROLD H. ISRAEL
NANCY J. KING

July, 2000

*

Acknowledgments

Excerpts from the following articles appear with the kind permission of the copyright holders.

Kennedy, Randall, Suspect Policy, New Republic, Sept. 13–20, 1999. Copyright © 1999 by the New Republic. Reprinted with permission.

*

Table of Contents

Table of Cases

The principal cases are in bold type. Cases cited or discussed in the text are roman type. References are to pages. Cases cited in principal cases and within other quoted materials are not included.

2000 Supplement
to Ninth Editions

MODERN CRIMINAL PROCEDURE

Cases — Comments — Questions

BASIC CRIMINAL PROCEDURE

Cases — Comments — Questions

and

ADVANCED CRIMINAL PROCEDURE

Cases — Comments — Questions

*

Part One
INTRODUCTION

Chapter 3
THE RIGHT TO COUNSEL, TRANSCRIPTS AND OTHER AIDS

SECTION 1. THE RIGHT TO APPOINTED COUNSEL AND RELATED PROBLEMS

B. THE "BEGINNING" OF THE RIGHT TO COUNSEL: HEREIN OF "CRIMINAL PROSECUTIONS" AND "CULTURAL STAGES"

9th ed., p. 83; after extracts from *Gouveia* case:

In *United States v. Moody* (discussed in Supp. at p. 80), the Sixth Circuit relied on *Gouveia* to hold that the Sixth Amendment right to counsel does not "attach" during preindictment plea bargaining. Thus, defendant could not be given the benefit of the plea bargain he rejected due to the ineffective assistance of counsel.

Part Two
POLICE PRACTICES

Chapter 4
SOME GENERAL REFLECTIONS ON THE POLICE, THE PROSECUTORS, THE LEGISLATURES AND THE CRIMINAL PROCESS

9th ed., p. 121; after extract from Prof. Kennedy's book, add:

Consider, too, Randall L. Kennedy, *Suspect Policy: Racial profiling by the police isn't necessarily motivated by bigotry. In fact, it's quite rational. But whatever benefits it may produce in the war against crime are outweighed by the damage it does to the very legitimacy of law enforcement*, New Republic, Sept. 13 & 20, 1999, pp. 30, 33–34:

"* * * For the sake of better law enforcement, we need to be mindful of the deep reservoir of anger toward the police that now exists within many racial minority neighborhoods. Racial profiling is a big part of what keeps the pool of accumulated rage filled to the brim.

"* * * Racial profiling undercuts a good idea that needs more support from both society and the law: that individuals should be judged by public authority on the basis of their own conduct and not on the basis—not even *partly* on the basis—of racial generalization. Race-dependent policing retards the development and spread of such thinking; indeed, it encourages the opposite tendency.

"* * * [R]acial equality, like all good things in life, costs something; it does not come for free. [Americans] must be willing to demand equal treatment before the law even under circumstances in which unequal treatment is plausibly defensible in the name of nonracist goals. They must be willing to do so when their effort will be costly.

"Since abandoning racial profiling would undeniably raise the information costs of policing to some extent, with some attendant potential loss in effective crime control, those of us who would do away with it must advocate a responsible alternative. Mine is simply to spend more on other means of enforcement—and then spread the cost on some nonracial basis. This is hardly infeasible. One possibility is hiring more police officers. Another is subjecting everyone to closer surveillance. A benefit of the second option would be to acquaint more whites with the burden of police intrusion, the knowledge of which might prompt more whites to insist upon reining the police in."

9th ed., p. 121; end of chapter, add:

In CITY OF CHICAGO v. MORALES, set forth below, a sharply divided Court struck down Chicago's Gang Congregation Ordinance, which prohibited "criminal street gang members" from "loitering" in public places. Under the Ordinance, a police officer observing a person he or she "reasonably believes" to be a gang member "loitering" in any public place with one or more other persons "shall order all such persons to disperse and remove themselves from the area." A person failing to obey such an order promptly is in violation of this section. "Loiter" is defined by the ordinance as "remain[ing] in any one place with no apparent purpose."

Few cases better illustrate the tension between the need and desire of the police to perform their peace-keeping responsibilities satisfactorily (in this instance, to combat gang crime and intimidation) and the need and desire to provide sufficient guidelines for police officers to prevent arbitrary or discriminatory law enforcement (and adequate notice to the ordinary citizen of what is forbidden and what is permitted).

CITY OF CHICAGO v. MORALES

527 U.S. 41, 119 S.Ct. 1849, 144 L.Ed.2d 67 (1999).

Justice STEVENS announced the judgment of the Court and delivered the opinion of the Court with respect to Parts I, II, and V, [in which O'Connor, Kennedy, Souter, Ginsburg, and Breyer, JJ., joined], and an opinion with respect to Parts III, IV, and VI, in which SOUTER and GINSBURG JJ., joined. * * *

III

The basic factual predicate for the city's ordinance is not in dispute. As the city argues in its brief, "the very presence of a large collection of obviously brazen, insistent, and lawless gang members and hangers-on on the public ways intimidates residents, who become afraid even to leave their homes and go about their business. That, in turn, imperils community residents' sense of safety and security, detracts from property values, and can ultimately destabilize entire neighborhoods." The findings in the ordinance explain that it was motivated by these concerns. We have no doubt that a law that directly prohibited such intimidating conduct would be constitutional, but this ordinance broadly covers a significant amount of additional activity. Uncertainty about the scope of that additional coverage provides the basis for respondents' claim that the ordinance is too vague.

[As] the United States recognizes, the freedom to loiter for innocent purposes is part of the "liberty" protected by the Due Process Clause of the Fourteenth Amendment. We have expressly identified this "right to remove from one place to another according to inclination" as "an attribute of personal liberty" protected by the Constitution. Indeed, it is apparent that an individual's decision to remain in a public place of his choice is as much a part of his liberty as the freedom of movement inside frontiers that is "a part of our heritage" or the right to move "to whatsoever place one's own inclination may direct" identified in Blackstone's Commentaries.

There is no need, however, to decide whether the impact of the Chicago ordinance on constitutionally protected liberty alone would suffice to support a facial challenge under the overbreadth doctrine. For it is clear that the vagueness of this enactment makes a facial challenge appropriate. This is not an ordinance that "simply regulates business behavior and contains a scienter requirement." It is a criminal law that contains no *mens rea* requirement, and infringes on constitutionally protected rights When vagueness permeates the text of such a law, it is subject to facial attack.

Vagueness may invalidate a criminal law for either of two independent reasons. First, it may fail to provide the kind of notice that will enable ordinary people to understand what conduct it prohibits; second, it may authorize and even encourage arbitrary and discriminatory enforcement. See *Kolender v. Lawson*, [9th ed., p. 328]. Accordingly, we first consider whether the ordinance provides fair notice to the citizen and then discuss its potential for arbitrary enforcement.

IV * * *

Since the city cannot conceivably have meant to criminalize each instance a citizen stands in public with a gang member, the vagueness that dooms this ordinance is not the product of uncertainty about the normal meaning of "loitering," but rather about what loitering is covered by the ordinance and what is not. The Illinois Supreme Court emphasized the law's failure to distinguish between innocent conduct and conduct threatening harm.

[The] city's principal response to this concern about adequate notice is that loiterers are not subject to sanction until after they have failed to comply with an officer's order to disperse. * * * We find this response unpersuasive for at least two reasons.

First, the purpose of the fair notice requirement is to enable the ordinary citizen to conform his or her conduct to the law. [Although] it is true that a loiterer is not subject to criminal sanctions unless he or she disobeys a dispersal order, the loitering is the conduct that the ordinance is designed to prohibit. If the loitering is in fact harmless and innocent, the dispersal order itself is an unjustified impairment of liberty. If the police are able to decide arbitrarily which members of the public they will order to disperse, then the Chicago ordinance becomes indistinguishable from the law we held invalid in *Shuttlesworth v. Birmingham*, 382 U.S. 87, 90, 86 S.Ct. 211, 15 L.Ed.2d 176 (1965).[29] Because an officer may issue an order only after prohibited conduct has already occurred, it cannot provide the kind of advance notice that will protect the putative loiterer from being ordered to disperse. Such an order cannot retroactively give adequate warning of the boundary between the permissible and the impermissible applications of the law.

Second, the terms of the dispersal order compound the inadequacy of the notice afforded by the ordinance. It provides that the officer "shall order all such persons to disperse and remove themselves from the area." This vague phrasing raises a host of questions. After such an order issues, how long must the loiterers remain apart? How far must they move? If each loiterer walks around the block and they meet again at the same location, are they subject to arrest or merely to being ordered to disperse again? * * *

V

The broad sweep of the ordinance also violates " 'the requirement that a legislature establish minimal guidelines to govern law enforcement.' " *Kolender v. Lawson*. There are no such guidelines in the ordinance. In any public place in the city of Chicago, persons who stand or sit in the company of a gang member may be ordered to disperse unless their purpose is apparent. The mandatory language in the enactment directs the police to issue an order without first making any inquiry about their possible purposes. It matters not whether the reason that a gang member and his father, for example, might loiter near Wrigley Field is to rob an unsuspecting fan or just to get a glimpse of Sammy Sosa leaving the ballpark; in either event, if their purpose is not apparent to a nearby police officer, she may—indeed, she "shall"—order them to disperse. * * *

It is true, as the city argues, that the requirement that the officer reasonably believe that a group of loiterers contains a gang member does place a limit on the authority to order dispersal. That limitation would no doubt be sufficient if the ordinance only applied to loitering that had an apparently harmful purpose or effect,[33] or possibly if it only applied to loitering by persons reasonably believed to be criminal gang members. But this ordinance, for reasons that are not explained in the findings of the city council, requires no harmful purpose and applies to non-gang members as well as suspected gang members. It applies to everyone in the city who may remain in one place with one suspected gang member

29. "Literally read ... this ordinance says that a person may stand on a public sidewalk in Birmingham only at the whim of any police officer of that city. The constitutional vice of so broad a provision needs no demonstration."

33. Justice Thomas' dissent overlooks the important distinction between this ordinance and those that authorize the police "to order groups of individuals who threaten the public peace to disperse."

as long as their purpose is not apparent to an officer observing them. Friends, relatives, teachers, counselors, or even total strangers might unwittingly engage in forbidden loitering if they happen to engage in idle conversation with a gang member.

Ironically, the definition of loitering in the Chicago ordinance not only extends its scope to encompass harmless conduct, but also has the perverse consequence of excluding from its coverage much of the intimidating conduct that motivated its enactment. As the city council's findings demonstrate, the most harmful gang loitering is motivated either by an apparent purpose to publicize the gang's dominance of certain territory, thereby intimidating nonmembers, or by an equally apparent purpose to conceal ongoing commerce in illegal drugs. As the Illinois Supreme Court has not placed any limiting construction on the language in the ordinance, we must assume that the ordinance means what it says and that it has no application to loiterers whose purpose is apparent. The relative importance of its application to harmless loitering is magnified by its inapplicability to loitering that has an obviously threatening or illicit purpose.

VI

* * * We recognize the serious and difficult problems testified to by the citizens of Chicago that led to the enactment of this ordinance. "We are mindful that the preservation of liberty depends in part on the maintenance of social order." However, in this instance the city has enacted an ordinance that affords too much discretion to the police and too little notice to citizens who wish to use the public streets. * * *

Justice O'CONNOR, with whom Justice BREYER joins, concurring in part and concurring in the judgment. * * *

As it has been construed by the Illinois court, Chicago's gang loitering ordinance is unconstitutionally vague because it lacks sufficient minimal standards to guide law enforcement officers. In particular, it fails to provide police with any standard by which they can judge whether an individual has an "*apparent* purpose." Indeed, because any person standing on the street has a general "purpose"—even if it is simply to stand—the ordinance permits police officers to choose which purposes are *permissible*. * * * Any police officer in Chicago is free, under the Illinois Supreme Court's construction of the ordinance, to order at his whim any person standing in a public place with a suspected gang member to disperse. Further, as construed by the Illinois court, the ordinance applies to hundreds of thousands of persons who are *not* gang members, standing on any sidewalk or in any park, coffee shop, bar, or "other location open to the public, whether publicly or privately owned."

[It] is important to courts and legislatures alike that we characterize more clearly the narrow scope of today's holding. As the ordinance comes to this Court, it is unconstitutionally vague. Nevertheless, there remain open to Chicago reasonable alternatives to combat the very real threat posed by gang intimidation and violence. For example, the Court properly and expressly distinguishes the ordinance from laws that require loiterers to have a "harmful purpose," from laws that target only gang members, and from laws that incorporate limits on the area and manner in which the laws may be enforced.

[In] my view, the gang loitering ordinance could have been construed more narrowly. The term "loiter" might possibly be construed in a more limited fashion to mean "to remain in any one place with no apparent purpose other than to establish control over identifiable areas, to intimidate others from entering those areas, or to conceal illegal activities." Such a definition would be consistent with the Chicago City Council's findings and would avoid the vagueness problems of the ordinance as construed by the Illinois Supreme Court. [So] would limitations that restricted the ordinance's criminal penalties to gang members or that more carefully delineated the circumstances in which those penalties would apply to nongang members. * * *

Justice KENNEDY, concurring in part and concurring in the judgment.

I join Parts I, II, and V of Justice Stevens' opinion.

I also share many of the concerns he expresses in Part IV with respect to the sufficiency of notice under the ordinance. As interpreted by the Illinois Supreme Court, the Chicago ordinance would reach a broad range of innocent conduct. For this reason it is not necessarily saved by the requirement that the citizen must disobey a police order to disperse before there is a violation. * * *

Justice BREYER, concurring in part and concurring in the judgment.

The ordinance before us creates more than a "*minor* limitation upon the free state of nature." (Scalia, J., dissenting) (emphasis added). The law authorizes a police officer to order any person to remove himself from any "location open to the public, whether publicly or privately owned," *i.e.*, any sidewalk, front stoop, public park, public square, lakeside promenade, hotel, restaurant, bowling alley, bar, barbershop, sports arena, shopping mall, etc., but with two, and only two, limitations: First, that person must be accompanied by (or must himself be) someone police reasonably believe is a gang member. Second, that person must have remained in that public place "with no apparent purpose."

The first limitation cannot save the ordinance. Though it limits the number of persons subject to the law, it leaves many individuals, gang members and nongang members alike, subject to its strictures. Nor does it limit in any way the range of conduct that police may prohibit. The second limitation is, as Justice Stevens and Justice O'Connor point out, not a limitation at all. Since one always has some apparent purpose, the so-called limitation invites, in fact requires, the policeman to interpret the words "no apparent purpose" as meaning "no apparent purpose except for. . . ." And it is in the ordinance's delegation to the policeman of open-ended discretion to fill in that blank that the problem lies. To grant to a policeman virtually standardless discretion to close off major portions of the city to an innocent person is, in my view, to create a major, not a "minor," "limitation upon the free state of nature." * * *

Justice SCALIA, dissenting. * * *

Until the ordinance that is before us today was adopted, the citizens of Chicago were free to stand about in public places with no apparent purpose—to engage, that is, in conduct that appeared to be loitering. In recent years, however, the city has been afflicted with criminal street gangs. As reflected in the record before us, these gangs congregated in public places to deal in drugs, and to terrorize the neighborhoods by demonstrating control over their "turf." Many residents of the inner city felt that they were prisoners in their own homes. Once again, Chicagoans decided that to eliminate the problem it was worth restricting some of the freedom that they once enjoyed. * * * Loitering was not made unlawful, but when a group of people occupied a public place without an apparent purpose and in the company of a known gang member, police officers were authorized to order them to disperse, and the failure to obey such an order was made unlawful. The minor limitation upon the free state of nature that this prophylactic arrangement imposed upon all Chicagoans seemed to them (and it seems to me) a small price to pay for liberation of their streets.

The majority today invalidates this perfectly reasonable measure by ignoring our rules governing facial challenges, by elevating loitering to a constitutionally guaranteed right, and by discerning vagueness where, according to our usual standards, none exists. * * *

When our normal criteria for facial challenges are applied, it is clear that the Justices in the majority have transposed the burden of proof. Instead of requiring the respondents, who are challenging the Ordinance, to show that it is invalid in all its applications, they have required the petitioner to show that it is valid in all its applications. Both the plurality opinion and the concurrences display a lively imagination, creating hypothetical situations in which the law's application would (in their view) be ambiguous. But that creative role has been usurped from the petitioner, who can defeat the respondents' facial challenge by conjuring up *a single valid application* of the law. My contribution would go something like this: Tony, a member of the Jets criminal street gang, is standing alongside and chatting with fellow gang members while staking out their turf at Promontory Point on the South Side of Chicago; the group is flashing gang signs and displaying their distinctive tattoos to passersby. Officer Krupke, applying the Ordinance at issue here, orders the group to disperse. After some speculative discussion (probably irrelevant here) over whether the Jets are depraved because they are deprived, Tony and the other gang members break off further conversation with the statement—not entirely coherent, but evidently intended to be rude—"Gee, Officer Krupke, krup you." A tense standoff ensues until Officer Krupke arrests the group for failing to obey his dispersal order. Even assuming (as the Justices in the majority do, but I do not) that a law requiring obedience to a dispersal order is impermissibly vague unless it is clear to the objects of the order, before its issuance, that their conduct justifies it, I find it hard to believe that the Jets would not have known they had it coming. That should settle the matter of respondents' facial challenge to the Ordinance's vagueness.

Of course respondents would still be able to claim that the Ordinance was vague as applied to them. But the ultimate demonstration of the inappropriateness of the Court's holding of *facial* invalidity is the fact that it is doubtful whether some of these respondents could even sustain an *as-applied* challenge on the basis of the majority's own criteria. For instance, respondent Jose Renteria—who admitted that he was a member of the Satan Disciples gang—was observed by the arresting officer loitering on a street corner with other gang members. The officer issued a dispersal order, but when she returned to the same corner 15 to 20 minutes later, Renteria was still there with his friends, whereupon he was arrested. In another example, respondent Daniel Washington and several others—who admitted they were members of the Vice Lords gang—were observed by the arresting officer loitering in the street, yelling at passing vehicles, stopping traffic, and preventing pedestrians from using the sidewalks. The arresting officer issued a dispersal order, issued another dispersal order later when the group did not move, and finally arrested the group when they were found loitering in the same place still later. Finally, respondent Gregorio Gutierrez—who had previously admitted to the arresting officer his membership in the Latin Kings gang—was observed loitering with two other men. The officer issued a dispersal order, drove around the block, and arrested the men after finding them in the same place upon his return. Even on the majority's assumption that to avoid vagueness it must be clear to the object of the dispersal order *ex ante* that his conduct is covered by the Ordinance, it seems most improbable that any of these as-applied challenges would be sustained. Much less is it possible to say that the Ordinance is invalid in *all* its applications.

The plurality's explanation for its departure from the usual rule governing facial challenges is seemingly contained in the following statement: "[This] is a criminal law that contains no *mens rea* requirement ... and infringes on constitutionally protected rights.... When vagueness permeates the text of *such* a law, it is subject to facial attack." (emphasis added). The proposition is set forth with such assurance that one might suppose that it repeats some well-accepted formula in our jurisprudence: (Criminal law without *mens rea* requirement) + (infringement of constitutionally protected right) + (vagueness) = (entitlement to facial invalidation). There is no such formula; the plurality has made it up for this case, as the absence of any citation demonstrates.

But no matter. None of the three factors that the plurality relies upon exists anyway. I turn first to the support for the proposition that there is a constitutionally protected right to loiter—or, as the plurality more favorably describes it, for a person to "remain in a public place of his choice." * * *

Of course every activity, even scratching one's head, can be called a "constitutional right" if one means by that term nothing more than the fact that the activity is covered (as all are) by the Equal Protection Clause, so that those who engage in it cannot be singled out without "rational basis." But using the term in that sense utterly impoverishes our constitutional discourse. We would then need a *new* term for those activities—such as political speech or religious worship—that cannot be forbidden even *with* rational basis.

The plurality tosses around the term "constitutional right" in this renegade sense, because there is not the slightest evidence for the existence of a genuine constitutional right to loiter. Justice Thomas recounts the vast historical tradition of criminalizing the activity. It is simply not maintainable that the right to loiter would have been regarded as an essential attribute of liberty at the time of the framing or at the time of adoption of the Fourteenth Amendment. For the plurality, however, the historical practices of our people are nothing more than a speed bump on the road to the "right" result. * * *

It would be unfair, however, to criticize the plurality's failed attempt to establish that loitering is a constitutionally protected right while saying nothing of the concurrences. The plurality at least makes an attempt. The concurrences, on the other hand, make no pretense at attaching their broad "vagueness invalidates" rule to a liberty interest. As far as appears from Justice O'Connor's and Justice Breyer's opinions, *no* police officer may issue *any* order, affecting *any* insignificant sort of citizen conduct (except, perhaps, an order addressed to the unprotected class of "gang members") unless the standards for the issuance of that order are precise. No modern urban society—and probably none since London got big enough to have sewers—could function under such a rule. There are innumerable reasons why it may be important for a constable to tell a pedestrian to "move on"—and even if it were possible to list in an ordinance all of the reasons that are known, many are simply unpredictable. Hence the (entirely reasonable) Rule of the City of New York which reads: "No person shall fail, neglect or refuse to comply with the lawful direction or command of any Police Officer, Urban Park Ranger, Parks Enforcement Patrol Officer or other [Parks and Recreation] Department employee, indicated by gesture or otherwise." * * *

I turn next to that element of the plurality's facial-challenge formula which consists of the proposition that this criminal ordinance contains no *mens rea* requirement. The first step in analyzing this proposition is to determine what the *actus reus*, to which that *mens rea* is supposed to be attached, consists of. The majority believes that loitering forms part of (indeed, the essence of) the offense, and must be proved if conviction is to be obtained. [That] is not what the Ordinance provides. The only part of the Ordinance that refers to loitering is the portion that addresses, not the punishable conduct of the defendant, but what the police officer must observe before he can issue an order to disperse; and what he must observe is carefully defined in terms of what the defendant *appears* to be doing, not in terms of what the defendant is *actually* doing. * * *

The *only* act of a defendant that is made punishable by the Ordinance—or, indeed, that is even mentioned by the Ordinance—is his failure to "promptly obey" an order to disperse. The question, then, is whether that *actus reus* must be accompanied by any wrongful intent—and of course it must. As the Court itself describes the requirement, "a person must *disobey* the officer's order." (emphasis added). No one thinks a defendant could be successfully prosecuted under the Ordinance if he did not hear the order to disperse, or if he suffered a paralysis that rendered his compliance impossible. The willful failure to obey a police order is wrongful intent enough.

Finally, I address [the] plurality's facial-challenge formula: the proposition that the Ordinance is vague. It is not. Even under the ersatz overbreadth standard applied in *Kolender v. Lawson*, which allows facial challenges if a law reaches "a substantial amount of constitutionally protected conduct," respondents' claim fails because the Ordinance would not be vague in most or even a substantial number of applications. * * *

The criteria for issuance of a dispersal order under the Chicago Ordinance could hardly be clearer. First, the law requires police officers to "reasonably believ[e]" that one of the group to which the order is issued is a "criminal street gang member." This resembles a probable-cause standard, and the Chicago Police Department's General Order 92–4 (1992)—promulgated to govern enforcement of the Ordinance—makes the probable cause requirement explicit. Under the Order, officers must have probable cause to believe that an individual is a member of a criminal street gang, to be substantiated by the officer's "experience and knowledge of the alleged offenders" and by "specific, documented and reliable information" such as reliable witness testimony or an individual's admission of gang membership or display of distinctive colors, tattoos, signs, or other markings worn by members of particular criminal street gangs.

Second, the Ordinance requires that the group be "remain[ing] in one place with no apparent purpose." Justice O'Connor's assertion that this applies to "any person standing in a public place" is a distortion. The Ordinance does not apply to "standing," but to "remain[ing]"—a term which in this context obviously means "[to] endure or persist," see American Heritage Dictionary 1525 (1992). There may be some ambiguity at the margin, but "remain[ing] in one place" requires more than a temporary stop, and is clear in most of its applications, including all of those represented by the facts surrounding the respondents' arrests.

As for the phrase "with no apparent purpose": Justice O'Connor again distorts this adjectival phrase, by separating it from the word that it modifies. "[A]ny person standing on the street," her concurrence says, "has a general 'purpose'—even if it is simply to stand," and thus "the ordinance permits police officers to choose which purposes are permissible." But Chicago police officers enforcing the Ordinance are not looking for people with no apparent purpose (who are regrettably in oversupply); they are looking for people who "remain in any one place with no apparent purpose"—that is, who remain there without any apparent reason *for remaining there*. That is not difficult to perceive. * * *

The fact is that the present ordinance is entirely clear in its application, cannot be violated except with full knowledge and intent, and vests no more discretion in the police than innumerable other measures authorizing police orders to preserve the public peace and safety. As suggested by their tortured analyses, and by their suggested solutions that bear no relation to the identified constitutional problem, the majority's real quarrel with the Chicago Ordinance is simply that it permits (or indeed requires) too much harmless conduct by innocent citizens to be proscribed. As Justice O'Connor's concurrence says with disapprobation, "the ordinance applies to hundreds of thousands of persons who are not gang members, standing on any sidewalk or in any park, coffee shop, bar, or other location open to the public."

But in our democratic system, how much harmless conduct to proscribe is not a judgment to be made by the courts. So long as constitutionally guaranteed rights are not affected, and so long as the proscription has a rational basis, *all sorts* of perfectly harmless activity by millions of perfectly innocent people can be forbidden—riding a motorcycle without a safety helmet, for example, starting a campfire in a national forest, or selling a safe and effective drug not yet approved by the FDA. All of these acts are entirely innocent and harmless in themselves, but because of the risk of harm that they entail, the freedom to engage in them has been abridged. The citizens of Chicago have decided that depriving themselves of the freedom to "hang out" with a gang member is necessary to eliminate pervasive gang crime and intimidation—and that the elimination of the one is worth the deprivation of the other. This Court has no business second-guessing either the degree of necessity or the fairness of the trade. * * *

Justice THOMAS, with whom THE CHIEF JUSTICE and Justice SCALIA join, dissenting.

The duly elected members of the Chicago City Council enacted the ordinance at issue as part of a larger effort to prevent gangs from establishing dominion over the public streets. By invalidating Chicago's ordinance, I fear that the Court has unnecessarily sentenced law-abiding citizens to lives of terror and misery. The ordinance is not vague. "[A]ny fool would know that a particular category of conduct would be within [its] reach." *Kolender v. Lawson* (White, J., dissenting). Nor does it violate the Due Process Clause. The asserted "freedom to loiter for innocent purposes," is in no way " 'deeply rooted in this Nation's history and tradition.' "

The human costs exacted by criminal street gangs are inestimable. * * * Gangs fill the daily lives of many of our poorest and most vulnerable citizens with a terror that the Court does not give sufficient consideration, often relegating them to the status of prisoners in their own homes. * * *

The city of Chicago has suffered the devastation wrought by this national tragedy. Last year, in an effort to curb plummeting attendance, the Chicago Public Schools hired dozens of adults to escort children to school. The youngsters had become too terrified of gang violence to leave their homes alone. The children's fears were not unfounded. In 1996, the Chicago Police Department estimated that there were 132 criminal street gangs in the city. Between 1987 and 1994, these gangs were involved in 63,141 criminal incidents, including 21,689 nonlethal violent crimes and 894 homicides. Many of these criminal incidents and homicides result from gang "turf battles," which take place on the public streets and place innocent residents in grave danger. * * *

As part of its ongoing effort to curb the deleterious effects of criminal street gangs, the citizens of Chicago sensibly decided to return to basics. The ordinance does nothing more than confirm the well-established principle that the police have the duty and the power to maintain the public peace, and, when necessary, to disperse groups of individuals who threaten it. The plurality, however, concludes that the city's commonsense effort to combat gang loitering fails constitutional scrutiny for two separate reasons—because it infringes upon gang members' constitutional right to "loiter for innocent purposes," and because it is vague on its face. A majority of the Court endorses the latter conclusion. I respectfully disagree. * * *

* * * [It] is important to note that the ordinance does not criminalize loitering per se. Rather, it penalizes loiterers' failure to obey a police officer's order to move along. A majority of the Court believes that this scheme vests too much discretion in police officers. Nothing could be further from the truth. Far from according officers too much discretion, the ordinance merely enables police officers to fulfill one of their traditional functions. Police officers are not, and have never been, simply enforcers of the criminal law. They wear other hats—importantly, they have long been vested with the responsibility for preserving the public peace. [Nor] is the idea that the police are also *peace officers* simply a quaint anachronism. In most American jurisdictions, police officers continue to be obligated, by law, to maintain the public peace. * * *

In order to perform their peace-keeping responsibilities satisfactorily, the police inevitably must exercise discretion. Indeed, by empowering them to act as peace officers, the law assumes that the police will exercise that discretion responsibly and with sound judgment. That is not to say that the law should not provide objective guidelines for the police, but simply that it cannot rigidly constrain their every action. By directing a police officer not to issue a dispersal order unless he "observes a person whom he reasonably believes to be a criminal street gang member loitering in any public place." Chicago's ordinance strikes an appropriate balance between those two extremes. Just as we trust officers to rely on their experience and expertise in order to make spurof-the-moment determinations about amorphous legal standards such as "probable cause" and "reasonable suspicion," so we must trust them to determine whether a group of loiterers contains individuals (in this case members of criminal street gangs) whom the city has determined threaten the public peace. [In] sum, the Court's conclusion that the ordinance is impermissibly vague because it " 'necessarily entrusts lawmaking to the moment-to-moment judgment of the policeman on his beat,' " cannot be reconciled with common sense, longstanding police practice, or this Court's Fourth Amendment jurisprudence. * * *

The plurality's conclusion that the ordinance "fails to give the ordinary citizen adequate notice of what is forbidden and what is permitted" is similarly untenable. There is nothing "vague" about an order to disperse. While "we can never expect mathematical certainty from our language," it is safe to assume that the vast majority of people who are ordered by the police to "disperse and remove themselves from the area" will have little difficulty understanding how to comply. * * *

Today, the Court focuses extensively on the "rights" of gang members and their companions. It can safely do so—the people who will have to live with the consequences of today's opinion do not live in our neighborhoods. Rather, the people who will suffer from our lofty pronouncements are people like Ms. Susan Mary Jackson; people who have seen their neighborhoods literally destroyed by gangs and violence and drugs. They are good, decent people who must struggle to overcome their desperate situation, against all odds, in order to raise their families, earn a living, and remain good citizens. As one resident described, "There is only about maybe one or two percent of the people in the city causing these problems maybe, but it's keeping 98 percent of us in our houses and off the streets and afraid to shop." By focusing exclusively on the imagined "rights" of the two percent, the Court today has denied our most vulnerable citizens the very thing that Justice Stevens elevates above all else—the "freedom of movement." And that is a shame. * * *

Chapter 5

ARREST, SEARCH AND SEIZURE

SECTION 1. THE EXCLUSIONARY RULE

9th ed., p. 145; after Note 10, add:

10a. What if a police officer at the time of his search or seizure had relied upon law then authorizing such action, but that law was not in a statute (as in *Krull*) but rather in an appellate court decision since disapproved by a Supreme Court case which, per the Court's current retroactivity doctrine (see 9th ed., Ch. 2, § 3), relates back to the time of the officer's conduct? Such was the situation in *State v. Ward*, 604 N.W.2d 517 (Wis. 2000), where the court concluded that because the officer's Fourth Amendment violation was "not due to negligence, a mistake of law, or willful or malicious misconduct," but rather because of reliance upon the case law then existing, such "good faith reliance upon the pronouncements of this court" is on a par with the "good faith reliance upon an apparently valid statute" in *Krull*, meaning that here as there "excluding the evidence seized by the police [would not] serve any remedial objective."

SECTION 2. PROTECTED AREAS AND INTERESTS

9th ed., p. 168; after Note 4, add:

4A. *Effects.* During a lawful stop of a Greyhound bus, federal agents walked through the bus and squeezed the soft luggage passengers had placed in the overhead storage spaces. An agent noticed thereby that one bag contained a brick-like object; passenger Downs admitted the bag was his and allowed the agent to open it, revealing a brick of methamphetamine. In BOND v. UNITED STATES, 529 U.S. ___, 120 S.Ct. 1462, 146 L.Ed.2d 365 (2000), the Court, per REHNQUIST, C.J., preliminarily noted: (1) that a "traveler's personal luggage is clearly an 'effect' protected by the Fourth Amendment"; (2) that the government's reliance on such cases as *Riley* was misplaced because "[p]hysical invasive inspection is simply more intrusive than purely visual inspection"; and (3) that while Bond's "bag was not part of his person," "travelers are particularly concerned about their carry-on luggage; they generally use it to transport personal items that, for whatever reason, they prefer to keep close at hand." The Court then concluded:

"When a bus passenger places a bag in an overhead bin, he expects that other passengers or bus employees may move it for one reason or another. Thus, a bus passenger clearly expects that his bag may be handled. He does not expect that other passengers or bus employees will, as a matter of course, feel the bag in an exploratory manner. But this is exactly what the agent did here. We therefore hold that the agent's physical manipulation of petitioner's bag violated the Fourth Amendment."

BREYER and SCALIA, JJ., dissenting, objected: (1) that the squeezing did not "differ from the treatment that overhead luggage is likely to receive from strangers in a world of travel that is somewhat less gentle than it used to be"; (2) that whether "tactile manipulation * * * is more intrusive or less intrusive than visual observation * * * necessarily depends on the particular circumstances"; and (3) that "the decision will lead to a constitutional jurisprudence of 'squeezes,' thereby complicating further already complex Fourth Amendment law."

What is the significance of *Bond* with respect to tactile examination of the carry-on luggage of train and airplane passengers, and of the checked luggage of passengers on various forms of public transportation?

SECTION 4. SEARCH WARRANTS

9th ed., p. 211; after Note 4, add:

5. *Purpose of search warrants.* Usually, as in the cases in the preceding Notes, search warrants are issued to authorize a search for and seizure of evidence of criminal activity. But search warrants sometimes have other purposes, as was highlighted in the celebrated Elián González case. When a law professor charged that the entry of premises to remove Elián violated the Fourth Amendment because it was essentially warrantless, because the search warrant the agents had was "not a warrant to seize the child" and because, any way, "the seizure of evidence . . . is what a search warrant is for," N.Y. Times, p. A31, col.2, April 25, 2000, the INS General Counsel responded that the warrant obtained authorized the agents to search "the residence of Lázaro González" and to seize "the person of Elián González," as authorized by Fed.R.Crim.P 41(b), which provides that a warrant may be issued to search for and seize any person "who is unlawfully restrained." N.Y. Times, p. A30, col. 4, April 27, 2000.

As for use of a search warrant to search for and seize a person to be arrested, see *Steagald v. United States*, 9th ed., p. 273.

9th ed., p. 219; before subsection C, add:

7. *Presence of third parties.* Police executing search warrants are sometimes accompanied by other persons. The most common situation was noted in *Wilson v. Layne*, 526 U.S. 603, 119 S.Ct. 1692, 143 L.Ed.2d 818 (1999): "Where the police enter a home under the authority of a warrant to search for stolen property, the presence of third parties for the purpose of identifying the stolen property has long been approved by this Court and our common-law tradition." But in *Wilson*, which involved execution of an *arrest* warrant within premises, the police were accompanied by a reporter and a photographer from the Washington

Post. Citing such cases as *Summers*, 9th ed., p. 216, and *Horton*, 9th ed., p. 217, in support of the proposition that the Fourth Amendment requires "that police actions in execution of a warrant be related to the objectives of the authorized intrusion," a unanimous Court concluded the presence of members of the media was unconstitutional because it "was not in aid of the execution of the warrant." Had the media representatives been present during execution of a *search* warrant, would any evidence first discovered by them be inadmissible? Would all the evidence found by the police be inadmissible? In *Wilson*, which was a § 1983 case, the Court, speaking of the media presence, dropped this footnote: "Even though such actions might violate the Fourth Amendment, if the police are lawfully present, the violation of the Fourth Amendment is the presence of the media and not the presence of the police in the home. We have no occasion here to decide whether the exclusionary rule would apply to any evidence discovered or developed by the media representatives."

SECTION 6. WARRANTLESS SEARCHES OF PREMISES, VEHICLES, AND CONTAINERS

9th ed., p. 265; at the end of Note 5, add:

In *Flippo v. West Virginia*, 528 U.S. ___, 120 S.Ct. 7, 145 L.Ed.2d 16 (1999), after defendant's 911 call that he and his wife had been attacked at a cabin in a state park, police arrived at the scene and found defendant outside wounded and his wife inside dead. The contents of a briefcase near the body, found upon a warrantless police reentry and search several hours later, were held admissible by the trial judge because found "within the crime scene area," a position the Court unanimously concluded "squarely conflicts with *Mincey*." As for the state's contention "that the trial court's ruling is supportable on the theory that petitioner's direction of the police to the scene of the attack implied consent to search as they did," the Court expressed no opinion because this "factual" issue had not been raised below.

9th ed., p. 280; before Note 2, add:

1a. In *Maryland v. Dyson*, 527 U.S. 465, 119 S.Ct. 2013, 144 L.Ed.2d 442 (1999), the Court, per curiam, summarily reversed a state court decision holding "that in order for the automobile exception to the warrant requirement to apply, there must not only be probable cause to believe that evidence of a crime is contained in the automobile, but also a separate finding of exigency precluding the police from obtaining a warrant." That holding, the Court declared, "rests upon an incorrect interpretation of the automobile exception to the Fourth Amendment's warrant requirement," which "does not have a separate exigency requirement."

1b. In *Florida v. White*, 526 U.S. 559, 119 S.Ct. 1555, 143 L.Ed.2d 748 (1999), upholding the warrantless *seizure* of a car on probable cause that the vehicle was contraband under the state forfeiture law, the Court took note of "the special considerations recognized in the context of movable items" in the *Carroll-Carney* line of cases, and then concluded the need was "equally weighty when the *automobile*, as opposed to its contents, is the contraband that the police seek to secure." The Court also emphasized that "our Fourth Amendment jurisprudence has consistently accorded law enforcement officials greater latitude in exercising their duties in public places," and deemed the instant case "nearly indistinguishable" in this respect from *G.M. Leasing Corp. v. United States*, 429 U.S. 338, 97 S.Ct. 619, 50 L.Ed.2d 530 (1977), upholding the warrantless seizure from a public area of automobiles in partial satisfaction of income tax assessments. Two dissenting Justices in *White* objected (i) that an exigent circumstances rationale has no application "when the seizure is based upon a belief that the automobile may have been used at some time in the past to assist in illegal activity and the owner is already in custody," and (ii) that a warrant requirement "is bolstered by the inherent risks of hindsight at post-seizure hearings and law enforcement agencies' pecuniary interest in the seizure of such property."

9th ed., p. 281; before *Acevedo*, add:

WYOMING v. HOUGHTON

526 U.S. 295, 119 S.Ct. 1297, 143 L.Ed.2d 408 (1999).

Justice SCALIA delivered the opinion of the Court. * * *

In the early morning hours of July 23, 1995, a Wyoming Highway Patrol officer stopped an automobile for speeding and driving with a faulty brake light. There were three passengers in the front seat of the car: David Young (the driver), his girlfriend, and respondent. While questioning Young, the officer noticed a hypodermic syringe in Young's shirt pocket. He left the occupants under the supervision of two backup officers as he went to get gloves from his patrol car. Upon his return, he instructed Young to step out of the car and place the syringe on the hood. The officer then asked Young why he had a syringe; with refreshing candor, Young replied that he used it to take drugs.

At this point, the backup officers ordered the two female passengers out of the car and asked them for identification. Respondent falsely identified herself as "Sandra James" and stated that she did not have any identification. Meanwhile, in light of Young's admission, the officer searched the passenger compartment of the car for contraband. On the back seat, he found a purse, which respondent claimed as hers. He removed from the purse a wallet containing respondent's driver's license, identifying her properly as Sandra K. Houghton. When the officer asked her why she had lied about her name, she replied: "In case things went bad."

Continuing his search of the purse, the officer found a brown pouch and a black wallet-type container. Respondent denied that the former was hers, and claimed ignorance of how it came to be there; it was found to contain drug paraphernalia and a syringe with 60 ccs of methamphetamine. Respondent admitted ownership of the black container, which was also found to contain drug paraphernalia, and a syringe (which respondent acknowledged was hers) with 10 ccs of methamphetamine—

an amount insufficient to support the felony conviction at issue in this case. The officer also found fresh needle-track marks on respondent's arms. He placed her under arrest.

The State of Wyoming charged respondent with felony possession of methamphetamine in a liquid amount greater than three-tenths of a gram. After a hearing, the trial court denied her motion to suppress all evidence obtained from the purse as the fruit of a violation of the Fourth and Fourteenth Amendments. The court held that the officer had probable cause to search the car for contraband, and, by extension, any containers therein that could hold such contraband. A jury convicted respondent as charged.

The Wyoming Supreme Court, by divided vote, reversed the conviction and * * * held that the search of respondent's purse violated the Fourth and Fourteenth Amendments because the officer "knew or should have known that the purse did not belong to the driver, but to one of the passengers," and because "there was no probable cause to search the passengers' personal effects and no reason to believe that contraband had been placed within the purse."

The Fourth Amendment protects "[t]he right of the people to be secure in their persons, houses, papers, and effects, against unreasonable searches and seizures." In determining whether a particular governmental action violates this provision, we inquire first whether the action was regarded as an unlawful search or seizure under the common law when the Amendment was framed. Where that inquiry yields no answer, we must evaluate the search or seizure under traditional standards of reasonableness by assessing, on the one hand, the degree to which it intrudes upon an individual's privacy and, on the other, the degree to which it is needed for the promotion of legitimate governmental interests.

It is uncontested in the present case that the police officers had probable cause to believe there were illegal drugs in the car. *Carroll v. United States*, [9th ed., p. 275], similarly involved the warrantless search of a car that law enforcement officials had probable cause to believe contained contraband—in that case, bootleg liquor. The Court concluded that the Framers would have regarded such a search as reasonable in light of legislation enacted by Congress from 1789 through 1799—as well as subsequent legislation from the Founding era and beyond—that empowered customs officials to search any ship or vessel without a warrant if they had probable cause to believe that it contained goods subject to a duty. Thus, the Court held that "contraband goods concealed and illegally transported in an automobile or other vehicle may be searched for without a warrant" where probable cause exists.

We have furthermore read the historical evidence to show that the Framers would have regarded as reasonable (if there was probable cause) the warrantless search of containers within an automobile. In [*United States v.*] *Ross*, [9th ed., p. 281], we upheld as reasonable the warrantless search of a paper bag and leather pouch found in the trunk of the defendant's car by officers who had probable cause to believe that the trunk contained drugs. Justice STEVENS, writing for the Court, observed:

> "It is noteworthy that the early legislation on which the Court relied in *Carroll* concerned the enforcement of laws imposing duties on imported merchandise.... Presumably such merchandise was shipped then in containers of various kinds, just as it is today. Since Congress had authorized warrantless searches of vessels and beasts for imported merchandise, it is inconceivable that it intended a customs officer to obtain a warrant for every package discovered during the search; certainly Congress intended customs officers to open shipping containers when necessary and not merely to examine the exterior of cartons or boxes in which smuggled goods might be concealed. During virtually the entire history of our country—whether contraband was transported in a horse-drawn carriage, a 1921 roadster, or a modern automobile—it has been assumed that a lawful search of a vehicle would include a search of any container that might conceal the object of the search."

Ross summarized its holding as follows: "If probable cause justifies the search of a lawfully stopped vehicle, it justifies the search of *every part of the vehicle and its contents* that may conceal the object of the search" (emphasis added). And our later cases describing *Ross* have characterized it as applying broadly to all containers within a car, without qualification as to ownership. * * *

To be sure, there was no passenger in *Ross*, and it was not claimed that the package in the trunk belonged to anyone other than the driver. Even so, if the rule of law that *Ross* announced were limited to contents belonging to the driver, or contents other than those belonging to passengers, one would have expected that substantial limitation to be expressed. And, more importantly, one would have expected that limitation to be apparent in the historical evidence that formed the basis for *Ross*'s holding. In fact, however, nothing in the statutes *Ross* relied upon, or in the practice under those statutes, would except from authorized warrantless search packages belonging to passengers on the suspect ship, horse-drawn carriage, or automobile.

Finally, we must observe that the analytical principle underlying the rule announced in *Ross* is fully consistent—as respondent's proposal is not—with the balance of our Fourth Amendment jurisprudence. *Ross* concluded from the historical evidence that the permissible scope of a warrantless car search "is defined by the object of the search and the places in which there is probable cause to believe that it may be found." The same principle is reflected in an earlier case involving the constitutionality of a search warrant directed at premises belonging to one who is not suspected of any crime: "The critical element in a reasonable search is not that the owner of the property is suspected of crime but that there is reasonable cause to believe that the specific 'things' to be searched for and seized are located on the property to which entry is sought." *Zurcher v. Stanford Daily*, [9th ed., p. 177]. * * *

In sum, neither *Ross* itself nor the historical evidence it relied upon admits of a distinction among packages or containers based on ownership. When there is probable cause to search for contraband in a car, it is reasonable for police officers—like customs officials in the Founding era—to examine packages and containers without a showing of individualized probable cause for each one. A passenger's personal belongings, just like the driver's belongings or containers attached to the car like a glove compartment, are "in" the car, and the officer has probable cause to search for contraband in the car.

Even if the historical evidence, as described by *Ross*, were thought to be equivocal, we would find that the balancing of the relative interests weighs decidedly in favor of allowing searches of a passenger's belongings. Passengers, no less than drivers, possess a reduced expectation of privacy with regard to the property that they transport in cars, which "trave[l] public thoroughfares," "seldom serv[e] as ... the repository of personal effects," are subjected to police stop and examination to enforce "pervasive" governmental controls "[a]s an everyday occurrence," and, finally, are exposed to traffic accidents that may render all their contents open to public scrutiny.

In this regard—the degree of intrusiveness upon personal privacy and indeed even personal dignity—the two cases the Wyoming Supreme Court found dispositive differ substantially from the package search at issue here. *United States v. Di Re*, [9th ed., p. 222], held that probable cause to search a car did not justify a body search of a passenger. And *Ybarra v. Illinois*, [9th ed., p. 215], held that a search warrant for a tavern and its bartender did not permit body searches of all the bar's patrons. These cases turned on the unique, significantly heightened protection afforded against searches of one's person. "Even a limited search of the outer clothing ... constitutes a severe, though brief, intrusion upon cherished personal security, and it must surely be an annoying, frightening, and perhaps humiliating experience." *Terry v. Ohio*, [9th ed., p. 304]. Such traumatic consequences are not to be expected when the police examine an item of personal property found in a car.[34]

34. The dissent begins its analysis with an assertion that this case is governed by our decision in *United States v. Di Re*, which held, as the dissent describes it, that the automobile exception to the warrant requirement did not justify "searches of the passenger's pockets and the space between his shirt and underwear." It attributes that holding to "the settled distinction between drivers and passengers," rather than to a distinction between search of the person and search of property, which the dissent claims is "newly minted" by today's opinion—a "new rule that is based on a distinction between property contained in clothing worn by a passenger and property contained in a passenger's briefcase or purse."

In its peroration, however, the dissent quotes extensively from Justice Jackson's opinion in *Di Re*, which makes it very clear that it is precisely this distinction between search of the person and search of property that the case relied upon: "The Government says it would not contend that, armed 'with a search warrant for a residence only, it could search all persons found in it. But an occupant of a house could be used to conceal this contraband on his person quite

Whereas the passenger's privacy expectations are, as we have described, considerably diminished, the governmental interests at stake are substantial. Effective law enforcement would be appreciably impaired without the ability to search a passenger's personal belongings when there is reason to believe contraband or evidence of criminal wrongdoing is hidden in the car. As in all car-search cases, the "ready mobility" of an automobile creates a risk that the evidence or contraband will be permanently lost while a warrant is obtained. In addition, a car passenger—unlike the unwitting tavern patron in *Ybarra*—will often be engaged in a common enterprise with the driver, and have the same interest in concealing the fruits or the evidence of their wrongdoing. A criminal might be able to hide contraband in a passenger's belongings as readily as in other containers in the car—perhaps even surreptitiously, without the passenger's knowledge or permission. (This last possibility provided the basis for respondent's defense at trial; she testified that most of the seized contraband must have been placed in her purse by her traveling companions at one or another of various times, including the time she was "half asleep" in the car.)

To be sure, these factors favoring a search will not always be present, but the balancing of interests must be conducted with an eye to the generality of cases. To require that the investigating officer have positive reason to believe that the passenger and driver were engaged in a common enterprise, or positive reason to believe that the driver had time and occasion to conceal the item in the passenger's belongings, surreptitiously or with friendly permission, is to impose requirements so seldom met that a "passenger's property" rule would dramatically reduce the ability to find and seize contraband and evidence of crime. Of course these requirements would not attach (under the Wyoming Supreme Court's rule) until the police officer knows or has reason to know that the container belongs to a passenger. But once a "passenger's property" exception to car searches became widely known, one would expect passenger-confederates to claim everything as their own. And one would anticipate a bog of litigation—in the form of both civil lawsuits and motions to suppress in criminal trials—involving such questions as whether the officer should have believed a passenger's claim of ownership, whether he should have inferred ownership from various objective factors, whether he had probable cause to believe that the passenger was a confederate, or to believe that the driver might have introduced the contraband into the package with or without the passenger's knowl-

as readily as can an occupant of a car.'" Does the dissent really believe that Justice Jackson was saying that a house-search could not inspect property belonging to persons found in the house—say a large standing safe or violin case belonging to the owner's visiting godfather? Of course that is not what Justice Jackson meant at all. He was referring precisely to that "distinction between property contained in clothing worn by a passenger and property contained in a passenger's briefcase or purse" that the dissent disparages. This distinction between searches of the person and searches of property is assuredly not "newly minted." And if the dissent thinks "pockets" and "clothing" do not count as part of the person, it must believe that the only searches of the person are strip searches.

edge.[35] When balancing the competing interests, our determinations of "reasonableness" under the Fourth Amendment must take account of these practical realities. We think they militate in favor of the needs of law enforcement, and against a personal-privacy interest that is ordinarily weak.

Finally, if we were to invent an exception from the historical practice that *Ross* accurately described and summarized, it is perplexing why that exception should protect only property belonging to a passenger, rather than (what seems much more logical) property belonging to anyone other than the driver. Surely Houghton's privacy would have been invaded to the same degree whether she was present or absent when her purse was searched. And surely her presence in the car with the driver provided more, rather than less, reason to believe that the two were in league. It may ordinarily be easier to identify the property as belonging to someone other than the driver when the purported owner is present to identify it—but in the many cases (like *Ross* itself) where the car is seized, that identification may occur later, at the station-house; and even at the site of the stop one can readily imagine a package clearly marked with the owner's name and phone number, by which the officer can confirm the driver's denial of ownership. The sensible rule (and the one supported by history and caselaw) is that such a package may be searched, whether or not its owner is present as a passenger or otherwise, because it may contain the contraband that the officer has reason to believe is in the car.

We hold that police officers with probable cause to search a car may inspect passengers' belongings found in the car that are capable of concealing the object of the search. The judgment of the Wyoming Supreme Court is reversed.

It is so ordered.

Justice BREYER, concurring.

I join the Court's opinion with the understanding that history is meant to inform, but not automatically to determine, the answer to a Fourth Amendment question. I also agree with the Court that when a police officer has probable cause to search a car, say, for drugs, it is reasonable for that officer also to search containers within the car. If the police must establish a container's ownership prior to the search of that

35. The dissent is "confident in a police officer's ability to apply a rule requiring a warrant or individualized probable cause to search belongings that are ... obviously owned by and in the custody of a passenger." If this is the dissent's strange criterion for warrant protection ("obviously owned by and in the custody of") its preceding paean to the importance of preserving passengers' privacy rings a little hollow on rehearing. Should it not be enough if the passenger says he owns the briefcase, and the officer has no concrete reason to believe otherwise? Or would the dissent consider that an example of "obvious" ownership? On reflection, it seems not at all obvious precisely what constitutes obviousness—and so even the dissent's on-the-cheap protection of passengers' privacy interest in their property turns out to be unclear, and hence unadministrable. But maybe the dissent does not mean to propose an obviously-owned-by-and-in-the-custody-of test after all, since a few sentences later it endorses, simpliciter, "a rule requiring a warrant or individualized probable cause to search passenger belongings." For the reasons described in text, that will not work.

container (whenever, for example, a passenger says "that's mine"), the resulting uncertainty will destroy the workability of the bright-line rule set forth in *United States v. Ross*. At the same time, police officers with probable cause to search a car for drugs would often have probable cause to search containers regardless. Hence a bright-line rule will authorize only a limited number of searches that the law would not otherwise justify.

At the same time, I would point out certain limitations upon the scope of the bright-line rule that the Court describes. Obviously, the rule applies only to automobile searches. Equally obviously, the rule applies only to containers found within automobiles. And it does not extend to the search of a person found in that automobile. As the Court notes, and as *United States v. Di Re*, relied on heavily by Justice STEVENS' dissent, makes clear, the search of a person, including even " 'a limited search of the outer clothing,' " is a very different matter in respect to which the law provides "significantly heightened protection."

Less obviously, but in my view also important, is the fact that the container here at issue, a woman's purse, was found at a considerable distance from its owner, who did not claim ownership until the officer discovered her identification while looking through it. Purses are special containers. They are repositories of especially personal items that people generally like to keep with them at all times. So I am tempted to say that a search of a purse involves an intrusion so similar to a search of one's person that the same rule should govern both. However, given this Court's prior cases, I cannot argue that the fact that the container was a purse automatically makes a legal difference, for the Court has warned against trying to make that kind of distinction. But I can say that it would matter if a woman's purse, like a man's billfold, were attached to her person. It might then amount to a kind of "outer clothing" which under the Court's cases would properly receive increased protection. In this case, the purse was separate from the person, and no one has claimed that, under those circumstances, the type of container makes a difference. For that reason, I join the Court's opinion.

Justice STEVENS, with whom Justice SOUTER and Justice GINSBURG join, dissenting. * * *

In all of our prior cases applying the automobile exception to the Fourth Amendment's warrant requirement, either the defendant was the operator of the vehicle and in custody of the object of the search, or no question was raised as to the defendant's ownership or custody. In the only automobile case confronting the search of a passenger defendant—United States v. Di Re—the Court held that the exception to the warrant requirement did not apply. In *Di Re*, as here, the information prompting the search directly implicated the driver, not the passenger. Today, instead of adhering to the settled distinction between drivers and passengers, the Court fashions a new rule that is based on a distinction between property contained in clothing worn by a passenger and property contained in a passenger's briefcase or purse. In cases on both sides of the Court's newly minted test, the property is in a "container" (whether a pocket or a pouch) located in the vehicle. Moreover, unlike the Court, I think it quite plain that the search of a passenger's purse or briefcase involves an intrusion on privacy that may be just as serious as was the intrusion in *Di Re*.

Even apart from *Di Re*, the Court's rights-restrictive approach is not dictated by precedent. For example, in *United States v. Ross* we were concerned with the interest of the driver in the integrity of "his automobile," and we categorically rejected the notion that the scope of a warrantless search of a vehicle might be "defined by the nature of the container in which the contraband is secreted." "Rather, it is defined by the object of the search and the places in which there is probable cause to believe that it may be found." We thus disapproved of a possible container-based distinction between a man's pocket and a woman's pocketbook. Ironically, while we concluded in *Ross* that "[p]robable cause to believe that a container placed in the trunk of a taxi contains contraband or evidence does not justify a search of the entire cab," the rule the Court fashions would apparently permit a warrantless search of a passenger's briefcase if there is probable cause to believe the taxi driver had a syringe somewhere in his vehicle.

Nor am I persuaded that the mere spatial association between a passenger and a driver provides an acceptable basis for presuming that they are partners in crime or for ignoring privacy interests in a purse. Whether or not the Fourth Amendment required a warrant to search Houghton's purse, at the very least the trooper in this case had to have probable cause to believe that her purse contained contraband. The Wyoming Supreme Court concluded that he did not.

Finally, in my view, the State's legitimate interest in effective law enforcement does not outweigh the privacy concerns at issue. I am as confident in a police officer's ability to apply a rule requiring a warrant or individualized probable cause to search belongings that are—as in this case—obviously owned by and in the custody of a passenger as is the Court in a "passenger-confederate[']s" ability to circumvent the rule. Certainly the ostensible clarity of the Court's rule is attractive. But that virtue is insufficient justification for its adoption. Moreover, a rule requiring a warrant or individualized probable cause to search passenger belongings is every bit as simple as the Court's rule; it simply protects more privacy.

I would decide this case in accord with what we have said about passengers and privacy, rather than what we might have said in cases where the issue was not squarely presented. What Justice Jackson wrote for the Court fifty years ago is just as sound today:

> "The Government says it would not contend that, armed with a search warrant for a residence only, it could search all persons found in it. But an occupant of a house could be used to conceal this contraband on his person quite as readily as can an occupant of a car. Necessity, an argument advanced in support of this search,

would seem as strong a reason for searching guests of a house for which a search warrant had issued as for search of guests in a car for which none had been issued. By a parity of reasoning with that on which the Government disclaims the right to search occupants of a house, we suppose the Government would not contend that if it had a valid search warrant for the car only it could search the occupants as an incident to its execution. How then could we say that the right to search a car without a warrant confers greater latitude to search occupants than a search by warrant would permit?

"We see no ground for expanding the ruling in the *Carroll* case to justify this arrest and search as incident to the search of a car. We are not convinced that a person, by mere presence in a suspected car, loses immunities from search of his person to which he would otherwise be entitled." *Di Re.*[2]

Instead of applying ordinary Fourth Amendment principles to this case, the majority extends the automobile warrant exception to allow searches of passenger belongings based on the driver's misconduct. Thankfully, the Court's automobile-centered analysis limits the scope of its holding. But it does not justify the outcome in this case.

I respectfully dissent.

SECTION 7. STOP AND FRISK

9th ed., p. 311; before subsection A, add:

For an exhaustive assessment of *Terry* by over 30 analysts, reflecting an interesting variety of viewpoints, see Symposium, *Terry v. Ohio 30 Years Later*, 72 St.John's L.Rev. 721–1524 (1998). Especially intriguing is John Q. Barrett, *Deciding the Stop and Frisk Cases: A Look Inside the Supreme Court's Conference*, id. at 749, which uses the available papers of former Justices to illuminate the role of individual members of the Court in resolving these cases.

9th ed., p. 320; In lieu of Note 3, add:

3. In FLORIDA v. J. L., 529 U.S. ___, 120 S.Ct. 1375, 146 L.Ed.2d 254 (2000), an anonymous caller reported to police than a young black male standing at a particular bus stop and wearing a plaid shirt was carrying a gun; officers went there and saw such a person but did not see a firearm or any unusual movements, and had no reason to suspect him apart from the tip. A frisk of the suspect, which produced a firearm, was held by the Court, per GINSBURG, J., to be unreasonable: "Unlike a tip from a known informant whose reputation can be assessed and who can be held responsible if her allegations turn out to be fabricated, 'an anonymous tip alone seldom

2. In response to this dissent the Court has crafted an imaginative footnote suggesting that the *Di Re* decision rested, not on Di Re's status as a mere occupant of the vehicle and the importance of individualized suspicion, but rather on the intrusive character of the search. That the search of a safe or violin case would be less intrusive than a strip search does not, however, persuade me that the *Di Re* case would have been decided differently if Di Re had been a woman and the gas coupons had been found in her purse. * * *

demonstrates the informant's basis of knowledge or veracity,' *Alabama v. White*, [496 U.S. 325, 110 S.Ct. 2412, 110 L.Ed.2d 301 (1990)]. As we have recognized, however, there are situations in which an anonymous tip, suitably corroborated, exhibits 'sufficient indicia of reliability to provide reasonable suspicion to make the investigatory stop.' The question we here confront is whether the tip pointing to J.L. had those indicia of reliability.

"In *White*, the police received an anonymous tip asserting that a woman was carrying cocaine and predicting that she would leave an apartment building at a specified time, get into a car matching a particular description, and drive to a named motel. Standing alone, the tip would not have justified a *Terry* stop. Only after police observation showed that the informant had accurately predicted the woman's movements, we explained, did it become reasonable to think the tipster had inside knowledge about the suspect and therefore to credit his assertion about the cocaine. Although the Court held that the suspicion in *White* became reasonable after police surveillance, we regarded the case as borderline. Knowledge about a person's future movements indicates some familiarity with that person's affairs, but having such knowledge does not necessarily imply that the informant knows, in particular, whether that person is carrying hidden contraband. We accordingly classified *White* as a 'close case.'

"The tip in the instant case lacked the moderate indicia of reliability present in *White* and essential to the Court's decision in that case. The anonymous call concerning J.L. provided no predictive information and therefore left the police without means to test the informant's knowledge or credibility. That the allegation about the gun turned out to be correct does not suggest that the officers, prior to the frisks, had a reasonable basis for suspecting J.L. of engaging in unlawful conduct: The reasonableness of official suspicion must be measured by what the officers knew before they conducted their search. All the police had to go on in this case was the bare report of an unknown, unaccountable informant who neither explained how he knew about the gun nor supplied any basis for believing he had inside information about J.L. If *White* was a close case on the reliability of anonymous tips, this one surely falls on the other side of the line. * * *

"An accurate description of a subject's readily observable location and appearance is of course reliable in this limited sense: It will help the police correctly identify the person whom the tipster means to accuse. Such a tip, however, does not show that the tipster has knowledge of concealed criminal activity. The reasonable suspicion here at issue requires that a tip be reliable in its assertion of illegality, not just in its tendency to identify a determinate person. * * *

"Firearms are dangerous, and extraordinary dangers sometimes justify unusual precautions. Our decisions recognize the serious threat that armed criminals pose to public safety; *Terry*'s rule, which permits protective police searches on the basis of reasonable suspicion rather than demanding that officers meet the higher standard of probable cause, responds to this very concern. But an automatic firearm exception to our established reliability analysis [advanced by Florida and the United States as *amicus*] would rove too far. Such an exception would enable any person seeking to harass another to set in motion an intrusive, embarrassing police search of the targeted person simply by placing an anonymous call falsely reporting the target's unlawful carriage of a gun. Nor could one securely confine such an exception to allegations involving firearms. Several Courts of Appeals have held it per se foreseeable for people carrying significant amounts of illegal drugs to be carrying guns as well. If police officers may properly conduct Terry frisks on the basis of bare-boned tips about guns, it would be reasonable to maintain under the above-cited decisions that the police should similarly have discretion to frisk based on bare-boned tips about narcotics. * * *

"The facts of this case do not require us to speculate about the circumstances under which the danger alleged in an anonymous tip might be so great as to justify a search even without a showing of reliability. We do not say, for example, that a report of a person carrying a bomb need bear the indicia of reliability we demand for a report of a person carrying a firearm before the police can constitutionally conduct a frisk. Nor do we hold that public safety officials in quarters where the reasonable expectation of Fourth Amendment privacy is diminished, such as airports and schools, cannot conduct protective searches on the basis of information insufficient to justify searches elsewhere.

"Finally, the requirement that an anonymous tip bear standard indicia of reliability in order to justify a stop in no way diminishes a police officer's prerogative, in accord with *Terry*, to conduct a protective search of a person who has already been legitimately stopped. We speak in today's decision only of cases in which the officer's authority to make the initial stop is at issue. In that context, we hold that an anonymous tip lacking indicia of reliability of the kind contemplated in *Adams* and *White* does not justify a stop and frisk whenever and however it alleges the illegal possession of a firearm."

Justice KENNEDY, joined by The Chief Justice, concurring., added: "It seems appropriate to observe that a tip might be anonymous in some sense yet have certain other features, either supporting reliability or narrowing the likely class of informants, so that the tip does provide the lawful basis for some police action. One such feature, as the Court recognizes, is that the tip predicts future conduct of the alleged criminal. There may be others. For example, if an unnamed caller with a voice which sounds the same each time tells police on two successive nights about criminal activity which in fact occurs each night, a similar call on the third night ought not be treated automatically like the tip in the case now before us. In the instance supposed, there would be a plausible argument that experience cures some of the uncertainty surrounding the anonymity, justifying a proportionate police response. In today's case, however, the State provides us with no data about the reliability of anonymous tips. Nor do we know whether the dispatcher or arresting officer had any objective reason to believe that this tip had some particular indicia of reliability.

"If an informant places his anonymity at risk, a court can consider this factor in weighing the reliability of the tip. An instance where a tip might be considered anonymous but nevertheless sufficiently reliable to justify a proportionate police response may be when an unnamed person driving a car the police officer later describes stops for a moment and, face to face, informs the police that criminal activity is occurring. This too seems to be different from the tip in the present case.

"Instant caller identification is widely available to police, and, if anonymous tips are proving unreliable and distracting to police, squad cars can be sent within seconds to the location of the telephone used by the informant. Voice recording of telephone tips might, in appropriate cases, be used by police to locate the caller. It is unlawful to make false reports to the police, and the ability of the police to trace the identity of anonymous telephone informants may be a factor which lends reliability to what, years earlier, might have been considered unreliable anonymous tips."

9th ed., p. 324; in lieu of Note 7, add:

7. In ILLINOIS v. WARDLOW, 528 U.S. ___, 120 S.Ct. 673, 145 L.Ed.2d 570 (2000), a Chicago police officer in the last car of a 4–car caravan, which was converging on an area known for heavy narcotics trafficking in order to investigate drug transactions, saw defendant look in the direction of the officers and then run away; defendant was stopped and frisked and found to be carrying a handgun. The Court, per REHNQUIST, C.J., held "that the officer's stop did not violate the Fourth Amendment," reasoning: "An individual's presence in an area of expected criminal activity, standing alone, is not enough to support a reasonable, particularized suspicion that the person is committing a crime. But officers are not required to ignore the relevant characteristics of a location in determining whether the circumstances are sufficiently suspicious to warrant further investigation. Accordingly, we have previously noted the fact that the stop occurred in a 'high crime area' among the relevant contextual considerations in a *Terry* analysis.

"In this case, moreover, it was not merely respondent's presence in an area of heavy narcotics trafficking that aroused the officers' suspicion but his unprovoked flight upon noticing the police. Our cases have also recognized that nervous, evasive behavior is a pertinent factor in determining reasonable suspicion. Headlong flight–wherever it occurs–is the consummate act of evasion; it is not necessarily indicative of wrongdoing, but it is certainly suggestive of such." The Court emphasized in addition that while it had previously held that "refusal to cooperate, without more, does not furnish the minimal level of objective justification needed for a detention or seizure," "unprovoked flight is simply not a mere refusal to cooperate"; and that while it "is undoubtedly true" that "there are innocent reasons for flight from police," *Terry* "recognized that the officers could detain the individuals to resolve the ambiguity."

STEVENS, J., for the four Justices concurring in part and dissenting in part, first noted the majority had "wisely" not endorsed either the state's per se rule that flight at the sight of police is always grounds for a stop or the defendant's rule that such flight is never grounds for a stop, for the "inference we can reasonably draw about the motivation for a person's flight * * * will depend on a number of different circumstances. Factors such as the time of day, the number of people in the area, the character of the neighborhood, whether the officer was in uniform, the way the runner was dressed, the direction and speed of flight, and whether the person's behavior was otherwise unusual might be relevant in specific cases." (As for the State's claim "for a *per se* rule regarding "unprovoked flight upon seeing a clearly identifiable police officer," the four Justices responded that even this "described a category of activity too broad and varied to permit a *per se* reasonable inference regarding the motivation for the activity.") Noting that instead "the totality of the circumstances, as always, must dictate the result," the dissenters found the record as a whole failed to establish reasonable suspicion, considering that it did not show whether any vehicles in the caravan were marked, whether any other officers in the group were in uniform, where the intended destination of the officers was in relation to where defendant was seen, whether the caravan had passed before defendant ran, etc., and then concluded:

"The State, along with the majority of the Court, relies as well on the assumption that this flight occurred in a high crime area. Even if that assumption is accurate, it is insufficient because even in a high crime neighborhood unprovoked flight does not invariably lead to reasonable suspicion. On the contrary, because many factors providing innocent motivations for unprovoked flight are concentrated in high crime area, the character of the neighborhood arguably makes an inference of guilt less appropriate, rather than more so.[a] Like unprovoked flight itself, presence in a high crime neighborhood is a fact too generic and susceptible to innocent explanation to satisfy the reasonable suspicion inquiry."

Regarding the scope of the majority opinion: What kind of movement away from the police, short of what the majority calls "headlong flight" in *Wardow*, will qualify as "flight"? What police conduct would make the flight other than "unprovoked"? Does only flight "upon noticing the police" count, and if so what evidence is needed to establish that element? If the flight must coexist with presence in a "high crime area," what if anything needs to be shown about the nature of the crime problem in the area and where the area is vis-a-vis the suspect's location?

Considering the kinds of things the dissenters listed as shortcomings in the record, how would they have come out if the record had shown that the vehicles were marked, the officers were uniformed, the destination was nearby, and the caravan had not passed yet when defendant ran? In what way do the other "factors" listed by the dissenters (e.g., "time of day") manifest the likely presence or absence of an innocent motivation?

9th ed., p. 333; end of Note 1, add:

Is the quantum and reliability of information needed to support a frisk the same or less than that needed to support a stop? For example, what if the stop was made on a reliable informant's information the suspect possessed illegal gambling paraphernalia, and the officer had also received a report from an anonymous informant that this same person regularly carries

a. As the dissenters elsewhere stated: "Among some citizens, particularly minorities and those residing in high crime areas, there is also the possibility that the fleeing person is entirely innocent, but, with or without justification, believes that contact with the police can itself be dangerous, apart from any criminal activity associated with the officer's sudden presence. For such a person, unprovoked flight is neither 'aberrant' nor 'abnormal.' Moreover, these concerns and fears are known to the police officers themselves, and are validated by law enforcement investigations into their own practices. Accordingly the evidence supporting the reasonableness of these beliefs is too pervasive to be dismissed as random or rare, and too persuasive to be disparaged as inconclusive or insufficient."

a gun? Reconsider the final paragraph of Justice Ginsburg's opinion in *J. L.*, note 3 supra.

SECTION 9. CONSENT SEARCHES

9th ed., p. 359; after Note 4, add:

5. *Seizure vs. search.* "Up to now, [the third-party consent] principle has found expression only in the context of consent to the search of property–but there is no sound reason to restrict the principle rigidly to that milieu," as "the logic of third-party consent can be adapted to seizures in some instances." *United States v. Woodrum,* 202 F.3d 1 (1st Cir.2000) (relying on third-party consent in upholding a program whereby police may stop to check on the safety of drivers of those cabs bearing a decal indicating the owner is voluntarily participating in a program contemplating such stops, reasoning that "these decals symbolized both the owner's and the driver's consent to future stops," that "the driver's command of the taxi allows him to maintain control over the vehicle's speed and route of travel," and that "the driver has the authority to consent to a stop in his own right, and that the passenger, by entering the cab, assumes the risk that the driver may exercise his right to stop briefly along the way").

Chapter 8

POLICE INTERROGATION AND CONFESSIONS

SECTION 3. THE *MIRANDA* "REVOLUTION"

PROPHYLACTIC RULES, SUPERVISORY POWERS AND THE CONSTITUTIONALITY OF § 3501

9th ed., p. 506–509; delete discussion of *Leong* and lower court *Dickerson* cases and substitute the following:

DICKERSON v. UNITED STATES

___ U.S. ___, 120 S.Ct. 2326, ___ L.Ed.2d ___, (2000).

Chief Justice REHNQUIST delivered the opinion of the Court.

[In] the wake of [*Miranda*], Congress enacted 18 U.S.C. § 3501, which in essence laid down a rule that the admissibility of [a custodial suspect's] statements should turn only on whether or not they were voluntarily made. We hold that *Miranda*, being a constitutional decision of this Court, may not be in effect overruled by an Act of Congress, and we decline to overrule *Miranda* ourselves. We therefore hold that *Miranda* and its progeny in this Court govern the admissibility of statements made during custodial interrogation in both state and federal courts.

Petitioner Dickerson was indicted for bank robbery [and] conspiracy to commit bank robbery. [Before] trial, [he] moved to suppress a statement he had made at [an FBI] field office, on the grounds that he had not received "*Miranda* warnings" before being interrogated. The District Court granted his motion to suppress, and the Government took an interlocutory appeal to the United States Court of Appeals for the Fourth Circuit. That court [reversed.] It agreed [that] petitioner had not received *Miranda* warnings before making his statement. But it went on to hold that § 3501, which in effect makes the admissibility of statements such as Dickerson's turn solely on whether they were made voluntarily, was satisfied in this case. It then concluded that our decision in *Miranda* was not a constitutional holding, and that therefore Congress could by statute have the final say on the question of admissibility.

* * * Prior to *Miranda*, we evaluated the admissibility of a suspect's confession under a voluntariness test. [Over] time, our cases recognized two constitutional bases for the requirement that a confession be voluntary to be admitted into evidence: the Fifth Amendment right against self-incrimination and the Due Process Clause of the Fourteenth Amendment. See, *e.g.*, *Bram v. United States* (1897) (stating that the voluntariness test "is controlled by that portion of the Fifth Amendment ... commanding that no person 'shall be compelled in any criminal case to be a witness against himself' "); *Brown v. Mississippi* (1936) (reversing a criminal conviction under the Due Process Clause because it was based on a confession obtained by physical coercion).

While *Bram* was decided before *Brown* and its progeny, for the middle third of the 20th century our cases based the rule against admitting coerced confessions primarily, if not exclusively, on notions of due process. We applied the due process voluntariness test in "some 30 different cases decided during the era that intervened between *Brown* and *Escobedo v. Illinois*." Those cases refined the test into an inquiry that examines "whether a defendant's will was overborne" by the circumstances surrounding the giving of a confession. The due process test takes into consideration "the totality of all the surrounding circumstances—both the characteristics of the accused and the details of the interrogation." * * *

We have never abandoned this due process jurisprudence, and thus continue to exclude confessions that were obtained involuntarily. But our decisions in *Malloy* and *Miranda* changed the focus of much of the inquiry in determining the admissibility of suspects' incriminating statements. In *Malloy*, we held that the Fifth Amendment's Self–Incrimination Clause is incorporated in the Due Process Clause of the Fourteenth Amendment and thus applies to the States. We decided *Miranda* on the heels of *Malloy*.

In *Miranda*, we noted that the advent of modern custodial police interrogation brought with it an increased concern about confessions obtained by coercion. Because custodial police interrogation, by its very nature, isolates and pressures the individual, we stated that "even without employing brutality, the 'third degree' or [other] specific stratagems, ... custodial interrogation exacts a heavy toll on individual liberty and trades on the weakness of individuals." We concluded that the coercion inherent in custodial interrogation blurs the line between voluntary and involuntary statements, and thus heightens the risk that an individual will not be "accorded his privilege under the Fifth Amendment ... not to be compelled to incriminate himself." Accordingly, we laid down "concrete constitutional guidelines for law enforcement agencies and courts to follow."

Two years after *Miranda* was decided, Congress enacted § 3501. * * *

Given § 3501's express designation of voluntariness as the touchstone of admissibility, its omission of any warning requirement, and the instruction for trial courts to consider a nonexclusive list of factors relevant to the circumstances of a confession, we agree with the Court of Appeals that Congress intended by its enactment to overrule *Miranda*. Because of the obvious conflict between our decision in *Miranda* and § 3501, we must address whether Congress has constitutional authority to thus supersede *Miranda*. If Congress has such authority, § 3501's totality-of-the-circumstances approach must prevail over *Miranda*'s requirement of warnings; if not, that section must yield to *Miranda*'s more specific requirements.

The law in this area is clear. This Court has supervisory authority over the federal courts, and we may use that authority to prescribe rules of evidence and procedure that are binding in those tribunals. However, the power to judicially create and enforce nonconstitutional "rules of procedure and evidence for the federal courts exists only in the absence of a relevant Act of Congress." Congress retains the ultimate authority to modify or set aside any judicially created rules of evidence and procedure that are not required by the Constitution.

But Congress may not legislatively supersede our decisions interpreting and applying the Constitution. See, *e.g.*, *Boerne v. Flores*, 521 U.S. 507, 117 S. Ct. 2157, 138 L.Ed.2d 624 (1997). This case therefore turns on whether the *Miranda* Court announced a constitutional rule or merely exercised its supervisory authority to regulate evidence in the absence of congressional direction. [Relying] on the fact that we have created several exceptions to *Miranda*'s warnings requirement and that we have repeatedly referred to the *Miranda* warnings as "prophylactic," *Quarles*, and "not themselves rights protected by the Constitution," *Tucker*, the Court of Appeals concluded that the protections announced in *Miranda* are not constitutionally required.

We disagree * * *, although we concede that there is language in some of our opinions that supports the view taken by that court. But first and foremost of the factors on the other side—that *Miranda* is a constitutional decision—is that both *Miranda* and two of its companion cases applied the rule to proceedings in state courts—to wit, Arizona, California, and New York. Since that time, we have consistently applied *Miranda*'s rule to prosecutions arising in state courts. It is beyond dispute that we do not hold a supervisory power over the courts of the several States. With respect to proceedings in state courts, our "authority is limited to enforcing the commands of the United States Constitution."[1]

The *Miranda* opinion itself begins by stating that the Court granted certiorari "to explore some facets of the problems [of] applying the

1. Our conclusion regarding *Miranda*'s constitutional basis is further buttressed by the fact that we have allowed prisoners to bring alleged *Miranda* violations before the federal courts in habeas corpus proceedings. * * * Habeas corpus proceedings are available only for claims that a person "is in custody in violation of the Constitution or laws or treaties of the United States." 28 U.S.C. § 2254(a). Since the *Miranda* rule is clearly not based on federal laws or treaties, our decision allowing habeas review for *Miranda* claims obviously assumes that *Miranda* is of constitutional origin.

privilege against self-incrimination to in-custody interrogation, *and to give concrete constitutional guidelines for law enforcement agencies and courts to follow*." (emphasis added). In fact, the majority opinion is replete with statements indicating that the majority thought it was announcing a constitutional rule. Indeed, the Court's ultimate conclusion was that the unwarned confessions obtained in the four cases before the Court in *Miranda* "were obtained from the defendant under circumstances that did not meet constitutional standards for protection of the privilege."[5]

Additional support for our conclusion that *Miranda* is constitutionally based is found in the *Miranda* Court's invitation for legislative action to protect the constitutional right against coerced self-incrimination. [The] Court emphasized that it could not foresee "the potential alternatives for protecting the privilege which might be devised by Congress or the States," and it accordingly opined that the Constitution would not preclude legislative solutions that differed from the prescribed *Miranda* warnings but which were "at least as effective in apprising accused persons of their right of silence and in assuring a continuous opportunity to exercise it."[6]

The Court of Appeals also relied on the fact that we have, after our *Miranda* decision, made exceptions from its rule in cases such as *Quarles* and *Harris v. New York* [9th ed., p. 509]. But we have also broadened the application of the *Miranda* doctrine in cases such as *Doyle v. Ohio,* [9th ed., p. 822] and *Arizona v. Roberson* [9th ed., p. 548]. These decisions illustrate the principle—not that *Miranda* is not a constitutional rule—but that no constitutional rule is immutable. No court laying down a general rule can possibly foresee the various circumstances in which counsel will seek to apply it, and the sort of modifications represented by these cases are as much a normal part of constitutional law as the original decision.

The Court of Appeals also noted that in *Elstad*, we stated that " 'the *Miranda* exclusionary rule ... serves the Fifth Amendment and sweeps more broadly than the Fifth Amendment itself.' " Our decision in that case—refusing to apply the traditional "fruits" doctrine developed in Fourth Amendment cases—does not prove that *Miranda* is a nonconstitutional decision, but simply recognizes the fact that unreasonable

5. Many of our subsequent cases have also referred to *Miranda*'s constitutional underpinnings. See, *e.g.*, *Withrow v. Williams* [9th ed., p. 583] (" 'Prophylactic' though it may be, in protecting a defendant's Fifth Amendment privilege against self-incrimination, *Miranda* safeguards a 'fundamental trial right' "); *Illinois v. Perkins,* [9th ed., p. 528] (describing *Miranda*'s warning requirement as resting on "the Fifth Amendment privilege against self-incrimination"); * * * *Michigan v. Jackson* [9th ed., p. 565] ("The Fifth Amendment protection against compelled self-incrimination provides the right to counsel at custodial interrogations") * * *.

6. The Court of Appeals relied in part on our statement that the *Miranda* decision in no way "creates a 'constitutional straightjacket.' " However, a review of our opinion in *Miranda* clarifies that this disclaimer was intended to indicate that the Constitution does not require police to administer the particular *Miranda* warnings, not that the Constitution does not require a procedure that is effective in securing Fifth Amendment rights.

searches under the Fourth Amendment are different from unwarned interrogation under the Fifth Amendment.

As an alternative argument for sustaining the Court of Appeals' decision, the court-invited *amicus curiae*[7] contends that the section complies with the requirement that a legislative alternative to *Miranda* be equally as effective in preventing coerced confessions. We agree with the *amicus*' contention that there are more remedies available for abusive police conduct than there were at the time *Miranda* was decided. But we do not agree that these additional measures supplement § 3501's protections sufficiently to meet the constitutional minimum. *Miranda* requires procedures that will warn a suspect in custody of his right to remain silent and which will assure the suspect that the exercise of that right will be honored. As discussed above, § 3501 explicitly eschews a requirement of pre-interrogation warnings in favor of an approach that looks to the administration of such warnings as only one factor in determining the voluntariness of a suspect's confession. The additional remedies cited by *amicus* do not, in our view, render them, together with § 3501 an adequate substitute for the warnings required by *Miranda*.

The dissent argues that it is judicial overreaching for this Court to hold § 3501 unconstitutional unless we hold that the *Miranda* warnings are required by the Constitution, in the sense that nothing else will suffice to satisfy constitutional requirements. But we need not go farther than *Miranda* to decide this case. In *Miranda*, the Court noted that reliance on the traditional totality-of-the-circumstances test raised a risk of overlooking an involuntary custodial confession, a risk that the Court found unacceptably great when the confession is offered in the case in chief to prove guilt. The Court therefore concluded that something more than the totality test was necessary. Section 3501 reinstates the totality test as sufficient. [The statute] therefore cannot be sustained if *Miranda* is to remain the law.

Whether or not we would agree with *Miranda*'s reasoning and its resulting rule, were we addressing the issue in the first instance, the principles of *stare decisis* weigh heavily against overruling it now. * * * *Miranda* has become embedded in routine police practice to the point where the warnings have become part of our national culture. [While] we have overruled our precedents when subsequent cases have undermined their doctrinal underpinnings, we do not believe that this has happened to the *Miranda* decision. If anything, our subsequent cases have reduced the impact of the *Miranda* rule on legitimate law enforcement while reaffirming the decision's core ruling that unwarned statements may not be used as evidence in the prosecution's case in chief.

The disadvantage of the *Miranda* rule is that statements which may be by no means involuntary, made by a defendant who is aware of his "rights," may nonetheless be excluded and a guilty defendant go free as

7. Because no party to the underlying litigation argued in favor of § 3501's constitutionality in this Court, we invited Professor Paul Cassell to assist our deliberations by arguing in support of the judgment below.

a result. But experience suggests that the totality-of-the-circumstances test which § 3501 seeks to revive is more difficult than *Miranda* for law enforcement officers to conform to, and for courts to apply in a consistent manner. The requirement that *Miranda* warnings be given does not, of course, dispense with the voluntariness inquiry. But * * * "[c]ases in which a defendant can make a colorable argument that a self-incriminating statement was 'compelled' despite the fact that the law enforcement authorities adhered to the dictates of *Miranda* are rare."

In sum, we conclude that *Miranda* announced a constitutional rule that Congress may not supersede legislatively. Following the rule of *stare decisis*, we decline to overrule *Miranda* ourselves. * * *

Justice SCALIA, with whom Justice THOMAS joins, dissenting.

Those to whom judicial decisions are an unconnected series of judgments that produce either favored or disfavored results will doubtless greet today's decision as a paragon of moderation, since it declines to overrule *Miranda*. Those who understand the judicial process will appreciate that today's decision is not a reaffirmation of *Miranda*, but a radical revision of the most significant element of *Miranda* (as of all cases): the rationale that gives it a permanent place in our jurisprudence.

Marbury v. Madison held that an Act of Congress will not be enforced by the courts if what it prescribes violates the Constitution of the United States. That was the basis on which *Miranda* was decided. One will search today's opinion in vain, however, for a statement (surely simple enough to make) that what § 3501 prescribes—the use at trial of a voluntary confession, even when a *Miranda* warning or its equivalent has failed to be given—violates the Constitution. The reason the statement does not appear is not only (and perhaps not so much) that it would be absurd, inasmuch as § 3501 excludes from trial precisely what the Constitution excludes from trial, viz., compelled confessions; but also that Justices whose votes are needed to compose today's majority are on record as believing that a violation of *Miranda* is *not* a violation of the Constitution. And so, to justify today's agreed-upon result, the Court must adopt a significant *new*, if not entirely comprehensible, principle of constitutional law. As the Court chooses to describe that principle, statutes of Congress can be disregarded, not only when what they prescribe violates the Constitution, but when what they prescribe contradicts a decision of this Court that "announced a constitutional rule." As I shall discuss in some detail, the only thing that can possibly mean in the context of this case is that this Court has the power, not merely to apply the Constitution but to expand it, imposing what it regards as useful "prophylactic" restrictions upon Congress and the States. That is an immense and frightening antidemocratic power, and it does not exist.

It takes only a small step to bring today's opinion out of the realm of power-judging and into the mainstream of legal reasoning: The Court need only go beyond its carefully couched iterations that "*Miranda* is a constitutional decision," that "*Miranda* is constitutionally based," that *Miranda* has "constitutional underpinnings," and come out and say quite clearly: "We reaffirm today that custodial interrogation that is not preceded by *Miranda* warnings or their equivalent violates the Constitution of the United States." It cannot say that, because a majority of the Court does not believe it. The Court therefore acts in plain violation of the Constitution when it denies effect to this Act of Congress.

* * * The power we recognized in *Marbury* [will] permit us, indeed require us, to "disregard" § 3501, a duly enacted statute governing the admissibility of evidence in the federal courts, only if it "be in opposition to the Constitution"—here, assertedly, the dictates of the Fifth Amendment.

It was once possible to characterize the so-called *Miranda* rule as resting (however implausibly) upon the proposition that what the statute here before us permits—the admission at trial of un-*Mirandized* confessions—violates the Constitution. That is the fairest reading of the *Miranda* case itself. [Having] extended the privilege into the confines of the station house, the Court liberally sprinkled throughout its sprawling 60-page opinion suggestions that, because of the compulsion inherent in custodial interrogation, the privilege was violated by any statement thus obtained that did not conform to the rules set forth in *Miranda*, or some functional equivalent.

[The] dissenters, for their part, also understood *Miranda*'s holding to be based on the "premise [that] pressure on the suspect must be eliminated though it be only the subtle influence of the atmosphere and surroundings." (Harlan, J., dissenting). [And] at least one case decided shortly after *Miranda* explicitly confirmed the view. See *Orozco v. Texas* [9th ed., p. 516] ("The use of these admissions obtained in the absence of the required warnings was a flat violation of the Self-Incrimination Clause of the Fifth Amendment as construed in *Miranda*").

So understood, *Miranda* was objectionable for innumerable reasons, not least the fact that cases spanning more than 70 years had rejected its core premise that, absent the warnings and an effective waiver of the right to remain silent and of the (thitherto unknown) right to have an attorney present, a statement obtained pursuant to custodial interrogation was necessarily the product of compulsion. See *Crooker v. California*. * * * Moreover, history and precedent aside, the decision in *Miranda*, if read as an explication of what the Constitution *requires*, is preposterous. There is, for example, simply no basis in reason for concluding that a response to the very first question asked, by a suspect who already *knows* all of the rights described in the *Miranda* warning, is anything other than a volitional act. And even if one assumes that the elimination of compulsion absolutely requires informing even the most knowledgeable suspect of his right to remain silent, it cannot conceivably require the right to have *counsel* present. There is a world of difference, which the Court recognized under the traditional voluntariness test but ignored in *Miranda*, between compelling a suspect to incriminate himself and preventing him from foolishly doing so of his own accord. Only the latter (which is *not* required by the Constitution) could explain the

Court's inclusion of a right to counsel and the requirement that it, too, be knowingly and intelligently waived. Counsel's presence is not required to tell the suspect that he *need* not speak; the interrogators can do that. The only good reason for having counsel there is that he can be counted on to advise the suspect that he *should* not speak. * * *

Preventing foolish (rather than compelled) confessions is likewise the only conceivable basis for the rules (suggested in *Miranda*) that courts must exclude any confession elicited by questioning conducted, without interruption, after the suspect has indicated a desire to stand on his right to remain silent, or initiated by police after the suspect has expressed a desire to have counsel present. Nonthreatening attempts to persuade the suspect to reconsider that initial decision are not, without more, enough to render a change of heart the product of anything other than the suspect's free will. Thus, what is most remarkable about the *Miranda* decision—and what made it unacceptable as a matter of straightforward constitutional interpretation in the *Marbury* tradition—is its palpable hostility toward the act of confession *per se*, rather than toward what the Constitution abhors, *compelled* confession.

[For] these reasons, and others more than adequately developed in the *Miranda* dissents and in the subsequent works of the decision's many critics, any conclusion that a violation of the *Miranda* rules *necessarily* amounts to a violation of the privilege against compelled self-incrimination can claim no support in history, precedent, or common sense, and as a result would at least presumptively be worth reconsidering even at this late date. But that is unnecessary, since the Court has (thankfully) long since abandoned the notion that failure to comply with *Miranda*'s rules is itself a violation of the Constitution.

As the Court today acknowledges, since *Miranda* we have explicitly, and repeatedly, interpreted that decision as having announced, not the circumstances in which custodial interrogation runs afoul of the Fifth or Fourteenth Amendment, but rather only "prophylactic" rules that go beyond the right against compelled self-incrimination. Of course the seeds of this "prophylactic" interpretation of *Miranda* were present in the decision itself. [In] subsequent cases, the seeds have sprouted and borne fruit: The Court has squarely concluded that it is possible—indeed not uncommon—for the police to violate *Miranda* without also violating the Constitution.

Michigan v. Tucker, an opinion for the Court written by then-Justice Rehnquist, rejected the true-to-*Marbury*, failure-to-warn-as-constitutional-violation interpretation of *Miranda*. It held that exclusion of the "fruits" of a *Miranda* violation—the statement of a witness whose identity the defendant had revealed while in custody—was not required. The opinion explained that the question whether the "police conduct complained of directly infringed upon respondent's right against compulsory self-incrimination" was a "separate question" from "whether it instead violated only the prophylactic rules developed to protect that right." The "procedural safeguards" adopted in *Miranda*, the Court said, "were not themselves rights protected by the Constitution but were instead measures to insure that the right against compulsory self-incrimination was protected," and to "provide practical reinforcement for the right." [It] is clear from our cases, of course, that if the statement in *Tucker had* been obtained in violation of the Fifth Amendment, the statement and its fruits would have been excluded. See *Nix v. Williams* [9th ed., p. 797].

The next year, in *Oregon v. Hass* [9th ed., p. 813], the Court held that a defendant's statement taken in violation of *Miranda* that was nonetheless *voluntary* could be used at trial for impeachment purposes. This holding turned upon the recognition that violation of *Miranda* is not unconstitutional compulsion * * *.

Nearly a decade later, in *Quarles*, the Court relied upon the fact that "the prophylactic *Miranda* warnings [are] 'not themselves rights protected by the Constitution,'" (quoting *Tucker*), to create a "public safety" exception. [The Court] explicitly acknowledged that if the *Miranda* warnings were an imperative of the Fifth Amendment itself, such an exigency exception would be impossible, since the Fifth Amendment's bar on compelled self-incrimination is absolute, and its " 'strictures, unlike the Fourth's, are not removed by showing reasonableness.' "

[The] next year, the Court again declined to apply the "fruit of the poisonous tree" doctrine to a *Miranda* violation, this time allowing the admission of a suspect's properly warned statement even though it had been preceded (and, arguably, induced) by an earlier inculpatory statement taken in violation of *Miranda*, *Elstad*. "Errors [that] are made by law enforcement officers in administering the prophylactic *Miranda* procedures" [, the Court told us,] "should not breed the same irremediable consequences as police infringement of the Fifth Amendment itself."

In light of these cases, and our statements to the same effect in others, it is simply no longer possible for the Court to conclude, even if it wanted to, that a violation of *Miranda*'s rules is a violation of the Constitution. [What] makes a decision "constitutional" in the only sense relevant here—in the sense that renders it impervious to supersession by congressional legislation such as § 3501—is the determination that the Constitution *requires* the result that the decision announces and the statute ignores. By disregarding congressional action that concededly does not violate the Constitution, the Court flagrantly offends fundamental principles of separation of powers, and arrogates to itself prerogatives reserved to the representatives of the people.

The Court seeks to avoid this conclusion in two ways: First, by misdescribing these post-*Miranda* cases as mere dicta. [But it] is not a matter of *language*; it is a matter of *holdings*. The proposition that failure to comply with *Miranda*'s rules does not establish a constitutional violation was central to the *holdings* of *Tucker*, *Hass*, *Quarles*, and *Elstad*.

The second way the Court seeks to avoid the impact of these cases is simply to disclaim responsibility for reasoned decisionmaking. It says:

"These decisions illustrate the principle—not that *Miranda* is not a constitutional rule—but that no constitutional rule is immutable." * * *

[The] issue, however, is not whether court rules are "mutable"; they assuredly are. It is not whether, in the light of "various circumstances," they can be "modified"; they assuredly can. The issue is whether, *as mutated and modified*, they must *make sense*. The requirement that they do so is the only thing that prevents this Court from being some sort of nine-headed Caesar, giving thumbs-up or thumbs-down to whatever outcome, case by case, suits or offends its collective fancy. And if confessions procured in violation of *Miranda* are confessions "compelled" in violation of the Constitution, the post-*Miranda* decisions I have discussed do not make sense. The only reasoned basis for their outcome was that a violation of *Miranda* is *not* a violation of the Constitution. [To] say simply that "unreasonable searches under the Fourth Amendment are different from unwarned interrogation under the Fifth Amendment" is true but supremely unhelpful.

Finally, the Court asserts that *Miranda* must be a "constitutional decision" announcing a "constitutional rule," and thus immune to congressional modification, because we have since its inception applied it to the States. If this argument is meant as an invocation of *stare decisis*, it fails because, though it is true that our cases applying *Miranda* against the States must be reconsidered if *Miranda* is not required by the Constitution, it is likewise true that our cases (discussed above) based on the principle that *Miranda* is *not* required by the Constitution will have to be reconsidered if it *is*. So the *stare decisis* argument is a wash. [In] my view, our continued application of the *Miranda* code to the States despite our consistent statements that running afoul of its dictates does not necessarily—or even usually—result in an actual constitutional violation, represents not the source of *Miranda*'s salvation but rather evidence of its ultimate illegitimacy. See generally Joseph Grano, *Confessions, Truth, and the Law* 173–198 (1993); Joseph Grano, *Prophylactic Rules in Criminal Procedure: A Question of Article III Legitimacy*, 80 Nw. U. L. Rev. 100 (1985). * * *

There was available to the Court a means of reconciling the established proposition that a violation of *Miranda* does not itself offend the Fifth Amendment with the Court's assertion of a right to ignore the present statute. That means of reconciliation was argued strenuously by both petitioner and the United States, who were evidently more concerned than the Court is with maintaining the coherence of our jurisprudence. It is not mentioned in the Court's opinion because, I assume, a majority of the Justices intent on reversing believes that incoherence is the lesser evil. They may be right.

Petitioner and the United States contend that there is nothing at all exceptional, much less unconstitutional, about the Court's adopting prophylactic rules to buttress constitutional rights, and enforcing them against Congress and the States. Indeed, the United States argues that "prophylactic rules are now and have been for many years a feature of this Court's constitutional adjudication." That statement is not wholly inaccurate, if by "many years" one means since the mid–1960's. However, in their zeal to validate what is in my view a lawless practice, the United States and petitioner greatly overstate the frequency with which we have engaged in it. * * *

Petitioner and the United States are right on target [in] characterizing the Court's actions in a case decided within a few years of *Miranda*, *North Carolina v. Pearce* [9th ed., p. 1561]. There, the Court concluded that due process would be offended were a judge vindictively to resentence with added severity a defendant who had successfully appealed his original conviction. Rather than simply announce that vindictive sentencing violates the Due Process Clause, the Court went on to hold that "in order to assure the absence of such a [vindictive] motivation, [the] reasons for [imposing the increased sentence] must affirmatively appear" and must "be based upon objective information concerning identifiable conduct on the part of the defendant occurring after the time of the original sentencing proceeding." The Court later explicitly acknowledged *Pearce*'s prophylactic character, see *Michigan v. Payne* [9th eds., p. 1564]. It is true, therefore, that the case exhibits the same fundamental flaw as does *Miranda* when deprived (as it has been) of its original (implausible) pretension to announcement of what the Constitution itself required. That is, although the Due Process Clause may well prohibit punishment based on judicial vindictiveness, the Constitution by no means vests in the courts "any general power to prescribe particular devices 'in order to assure the absence of such a motivation' " (Black, J., dissenting). Justice Black surely had the right idea when he derided the Court's requirement as "pure legislation if there ever was legislation," although in truth *Pearce*'s rule pales as a legislative achievement when compared to the detailed code promulgated in *Miranda*.

The foregoing demonstrates that, petitioner's and the United States' suggestions to the contrary notwithstanding, what the Court did in *Miranda* (assuming, as later cases hold, that *Miranda* went beyond what the Constitution actually requires) is in fact extraordinary. That the Court has, on rare and recent occasion, repeated the mistake does not transform error into truth, but illustrates the potential for future mischief that the error entails. [The] power with which the Court would endow itself under a "prophylactic" justification for *Miranda* goes far beyond what it has permitted Congress to do under authority of [U.S. Const., Amdt. 14, § 5]. Whereas we have insisted that congressional action under § 5 of the Fourteenth Amendment must be "congruent" with, and "proportional" to, a *constitutional violation*, see *Boerne v. Flores*, the *Miranda* nontextual power to embellish confers authority to prescribe preventive measures against not only constitutionally prohibited compelled confessions, but also (as discussed earlier) foolhardy ones.

I applaud, therefore, the refusal of the Justices in the majority to enunciate this boundless doctrine of judicial empowerment as a means of rendering today's decision rational. In nonetheless joining the Court's judgment, however, they overlook two truisms: that actions speak louder than silence, and that (in judge-made law at least) logic will out. Since there is in fact no other principle that can reconcile today's judgment with the post-*Miranda* cases that the Court refuses to abandon, what today's decision will stand for, whether the Justices can bring themselves to say it or not, is the power of the Supreme Court to write a prophylactic, extraconstitutional Constitution, binding on Congress and the States.

Thus, while I agree with the Court that § 3501 cannot be upheld without also concluding that *Miranda* represents an illegitimate exercise of our authority to review state-court judgments, I do not share the Court's hesitation in reaching that conclusion. For while the Court is also correct that the doctrine of *stare decisis* demands some "special justification" for a departure from longstanding precedent—even precedent of the constitutional variety—that criterion is more than met here.

* * *

Neither am I persuaded by the argument for retaining *Miranda* that touts its supposed workability as compared with the totality-of-the-circumstances test it purported to replace. *Miranda*'s proponents cite *ad nauseam* the fact that the Court was called upon to make difficult and subtle distinctions in applying the "voluntariness" test in some 30–odd due process "coerced confessions" cases in the 30 years between *Brown* and *Miranda.* It is not immediately apparent, however, that the judicial burden has been eased by the "bright-line" rules adopted in *Miranda.* In fact, in the 34 years since *Miranda* was decided, this Court has been called upon to decide nearly *60* cases involving a host of *Miranda* issues * * *.

Moreover, it is not clear why the Court thinks that the "totality-of-the-circumstances test [is] more difficult than *Miranda* for law enforcement officers to conform to, and for courts to apply in a consistent manner." Indeed, I find myself persuaded by Justice O'Connor's rejection of this same argument in her opinion in *Withrow v. Williams* [9th ed., p. 583] (O'Conner, J., joined by Rehnquist, C.J., concurring in part and dissenting in part) * * *.

But even were I to agree that the old totality-of-the-circumstances test was more cumbersome, it is simply not true that *Miranda* has banished it from the law and replaced it with a new test. Under the current regime, which the Court today retains in its entirety, courts are frequently called upon to undertake *both* inquiries. That is [because] voluntariness remains the *constitutional* standard, and as such continues to govern the admissibility for impeachment purposes of statements taken in violation of *Miranda*, the admissibility of the "fruits" of such statements, and the admissibility of statements challenged as unconstitutionally obtained *despite* the interrogator's compliance with *Miranda*.

Finally, I am not convinced by petitioner's argument that *Miranda* should be preserved because the decision occupies a special place in the "public's consciousness." As far as I am aware, the public is not under the illusion that we are infallible. I see little harm in admitting that we made a mistake in taking away from the people the ability to decide for themselves what protections (beyond those required by the Constitution) are reasonably affordable in the criminal investigatory process. And I see much to be gained by reaffirming for the people the wonderful reality that they govern themselves—which means that "the powers not delegated to the United States by the Constitution" that the people adopted, "nor prohibited ... to the States" by that Constitution, "are reserved to the States respectively, or to the people," U.S. Const., Amdt. 10.

* * *

Today's judgment converts *Miranda* from a milestone of judicial overreaching into the very Cheops' Pyramid (or perhaps the Sphinx would be a better analogue) of judicial arrogance. In imposing its Court-made code upon the States, the original opinion at least *asserted* that it was demanded by the Constitution. Today's decision does not pretend that it is—and yet *still* asserts the right to impose it against the will of the people's representatives in Congress. Far from believing that *stare decisis* compels this result, I believe we cannot allow to remain on the books even a celebrated decision—*especially* a celebrated decision—that has come to stand for the proposition that the Supreme Court has power to impose extraconstitutional constraints upon Congress and the States. This is not the system that was established by the Framers, or that would be established by any sane supporter of government by the people.

I dissent from today's decision, and, until § 3501 is repealed, will continue to apply it in all cases where there has been a sustainable finding that the defendant's confession was voluntary.

Notes and Questions

1. *Original rationale.* According to the Chief Justice's opinion in *Dickerson*, the *Miranda* Court "noted that reliance on the traditional totality-of-the-circumstances test raised a risk of overlooking an involuntary custodial confession, a risk that the Court found unacceptably great." Was that the original rationale of *Miranda*?

2. *Foolish confessions.* Does *Miranda*, as Justice Scalia maintains in his *Dickerson* dissent, prevent suspects from foolishly deciding to talk to the police? Don't most custodial suspects waive their *Miranda* rights? Are not almost all decisions by suspects to talk to the police about their cases *before* meeting with a lawyer foolish decisions?

3. *Language in Dickerson.* A number of pre-*Dickerson* decisions, such as *Elstad*, seem to be based on the premise that *Miranda* is not a constitutional decision. Does it follow that such cases will (should) now be overruled? Or will defense lawyers be reminded by the Court, to quote *Dickerson*, that "no constitutional rule is immutable" and that "the sort of modifications" represented by the cases interpreting and applying *Miranda* narrowly "are as much a normal part of constitutional law as the original decision itself"? Will defense lawyers also be reminded, to quote *Dickerson* again, that cases

giving *Miranda* a begrudging reading "have reduced the impact of the *Miranda* rule on legitimate law enforcement while reaffirming the decision's core ruling that unwarned statements [as opposed to evidence brought to light as a result of these improperly obtained statements] may not be used as evidence in the prosecutor's case-in-chief [as opposed to its use on cross-examination if the defendant has the audacity to take the stand in his own defense]"? See Yale Kamisar, *Your Sort-of Right to Remain Silent*, National Law Journal, July 17, 2000, p. 18.

9th ed., p. 517; end of fn. a, add:

Compare *Mesa* with *State v. Finch*, Supp., immediately below.

9th ed., p. 538; end of Note (a), add:

As suggested in Note (a), in STATE v. FINCH, 975 P.2d 967 (Wash. 1999), the court quickly disposed of a *Miranda* issue growing out of a "hostage situation" by invoking the "public safety" exception. After shooting and killing two people (one of whom was a police officer), stating that he would shoot other officers, and indicating that he was suicidal, defendant engaged in a phone conversation with a SWAT team negotiator.

"Trying to plant a seed in [the defendant's] mind that maybe what he had done isn't as bad as it seemed," and "trying to offer him some hope in the light that he wouldn't take his life or somebody else's life," the negotiator suggested that perhaps the defendant had shot in self-defense. "Hell, it wasn't no self-defense," replied the defendant. "It was premeditated, man. I shot him."

Defendant argued this remark and other incriminating statements he made to the negotiator should have been suppressed for lack of *Miranda* warnings. But the court saw no need to decide whether defendant was being interrogated while in custody because "this case clearly falls within the public safety exception." Observed the court, per MADSEN, J.:

"Requiring the *Miranda* warning in the present case would have further upset Mr. Finch and eroded the potential for a peaceful resolution. The *Miranda* warnings are intended to 'warn' a suspect that the police have interests that are antagonistic to his, and that his statements can be used against him in court. This type of warning would erode the atmosphere of trust necessary to convince Mr. Finch to surrender peacefully."

Moreover, the *Miranda* warnings would have given defendant reason to discontinue communication with the negotiator, an activity that was probably preventing a more violent confrontation: "Establishing telephone contact keeps the individual's mind focused on the conversation at hand and not on committing another act of violence. Moreover, it was important to keep the defendant on the phone so the SWAT team would know exactly where he was when they entered to place him under arrest. Keeping a defendant on the line when the SWAT team enters distracts the defendant and makes injury less likely."

9th ed., p. 538; end of Note (b), add:

But consider PEOPLE v. OQUENDO, 685 N.Y.S.2d 437 (App.Div.N.Y., 1999). Responding to a radio report that a man meeting defendant's description had fired shots, an officer chased and caught defendant. When asked whether he had the gun, defendant replied that he had dropped it in a certain vicinity and that it was "only a BB gun." The officer retraced defendant's footsteps, but could not find the gun (The streets were covered with almost a foot of snow.) When taken to the police station, defendant agreed to tell the police where the gun was, but he repeatedly misled them. The defendant would tell the police where the gun was, the police would go out to search that spot in vain, and then return and resume questioning.

Some five hours after he had been taken to the station house, a detective told defendant that his co-defendant had told the police that the gun defendant had dropped was not a BB gun, but a 9 mm handgun. The police also told defendant that if someone found the gun and was injured, defendant would be responsible. At that point, defendant admitted he had misled the police as to the gun's location and told them where he had actually thrown the gun. Defendant then directed a detective to the proper location and the gun was recovered.

In holding that the *Quarles* exception to *Miranda* applied, a unanimous court, per ROSENBERGER, J., observed:

"While it is true that the interrogation in *Quarles* was briefer than in the instant case, and occurred on the spot rather than in the station house later on, these differences do not detract from the essential similarity of the public danger in both cases, namely a missing (possibly loaded) gun, which was left in a publicly accessible place but could not be found readily without the suspect's cooperation. Naturally, the snow-covered, three-block area over which defendant fled would take longer to search than a single supermarket, particularly when the defendant here misled the police as to the gun's true location * * *.

"The entire thrust of *Quarles* is that the police should have flexibility to respond to true emergency circumstances, whether the danger is momentary or ongoing * * *. That purpose would not be served by setting artificial limits as to the time and location of questions that are objectively necessary for the immediate public safety * * *."

9th ed., p. 546; end of Note 13, add:

On the connection between the exclusion of parents and the availability of juvenile's right to counsel, see Justice Stein's concurring opinion in *State v. Presha*, Supp., p. 48.

9th ed., p. 583; after Note 22 add new Note:

22a. *Confessions by juveniles*. In STATE v. PRESHA, 748 A.2d 1108 (2000), the Supreme Court of New Jersey addressed the admissibility of a confession by a juvenile defendant who has been taken into custody. The case grew out of the following facts: Defendant, at the time just two weeks shy of his seventeenth birthday, was brought to the prosecutor's office in the early hours of the morning. At about 4:20 a.m., defendant indicated that he understood his rights and then signed "a *Miranda* card" waiving them. His mother signed the same card as a witness. Defendant's mother was informed of her right to be present while her son was being questioned, but after discussing the matter with defendant they both decided she should leave the room during questioning. There were four "breaks" in the questioning. Sometime before 7:39 a.m., when defendant began making a taped confession, his mother asked to see him and also told one of the officers that she thought her son "should have a lawyer." The officer replied he did not think that was necessary because "we're just trying to get the truth." Defendant's mother did not see her son until after he had completed his taped statement.

Defendant was not tried in juvenile court. Rather, he was charged with, and convicted of, first-degree robbery and other crimes and sentenced to 20 years imprisonment.

The New Jersey Supreme Court, per VERNIERO, J. (who spoke for six of the seven state supreme court justices), held that defendant had effectively waived his *Miranda* rights and that his resulting confession was voluntary. Both in determining whether a valid waiver of rights had occurred and whether the resulting confession was voluntary, the absence of a parent or legal guardian from the interrogation area is "a highly significant fact," but "in the specific circumstances of this case, according enhanced weight to the absence of the parent from the interrogation, we conclude that the state has carried its burden":

"We emphasize that, because [he was nearly seventeen and] had been arrested on fifteen prior occasions, defendant was familiar with the criminal process at the time of his statement. Further, the police afforded defendant numerous breaks in the interrogation, time enough for him to evaluate his decision to proceed without a parent. He elected to continue, notwithstanding his mother's absence. Moreover, we view as especially important the fact that [defendant's mother] was present at the outset of the encounter with the police, before any questioning of her son. She had the opportunity to offer support to defendant, to witness the signing of the *Miranda* card, and she consented to her initial absence from the interrogation area.

"All of the facts—defendant's age and familiarity with the criminal process, his clear desire to be interviewed without a parent present, the presence of a parent at the outset of the questioning, and his fair treatment by police—compel us to conclude that defendant's will was not overborne by investigators, the critical factor in this inquiry. * * *

"We have referred to [defendant's mother] as being absent from the interrogation, as opposed to being deliberately excluded by the police, because the trial court found that, in concert with defendant, she voluntarily left the interrogation room at the start of the interview. * * * It is difficult for us to envision prosecutors successfully carrying their burdens in future cases in which there has been some deliberate exclusion of a juvenile's parent or legal guardian from the interrogation. However, because the proof in the present case is so compelling that defendant's will was not overborne and the police did not have the benefit of our direction at the time of the interrogation, we see no reason to disturb the judgments below. We are satisfied that on this record the police should be judged by the standards prevailing at the time the officers interrogated defendant, not by the stricter standards announced in this opinion. * * * [W]hen there has been a deliberate exclusion of a parent or legal guardian from the interrogation room and the police thereafter obtain the juvenile's confession, that confession almost invariably will be suppressed.

"* * * When the juvenile is under the age of fourteen, the adult's absence will render the young offender's statement inadmissible as a matter of law—unless the adult is truly unavailable, in which case, the voluntariness of the waiver should be determined by considering the totality of circumstances consistent with this opinion."

Concurring Justice STEIN criticized the majority for "not acknowledg[ing] the obvious connection between the exclusion of parents and the availability of a juvenile's right to counsel." He maintained that a parent and a lawyer hold "an equally 'critical position in our legal system' [quoting from *Fare v. Michael C.*, 9th ed. p. 546], a position that is indispensable if a juvenile in custody is to have a realistic opportunity to exercise the right to counsel. A juvenile's right to the assistance of counsel is hollow indeed unless a parent is present to assist the juvenile in retaining and paying for a lawyer. In that context, the deliberate exclusion of parents from a juvenile's interrogation room is the *de facto* equivalent of a denial of the right to counsel."

Compare *Presha* with *In re G.O. v. G.O.*, 727 N.E.2d 1003 (Ill. 2000), affirming the voluntariness of a confession by a 13–year-old offender who had been denied the right to confer with a parent before or during his interrogation. Moreover, the juvenile had had no previous contact or experience with the criminal justice system. G.O. was adjudicated a delinquent based on charges of first degree murder and aggravated battery.

The court, per Rathje, J., rejected the argument that a juvenile's confession should be suppressed whenever he was denied the opportunity to consult with a parent or other concerned adult, viewing this factor as simply "one of many" that courts should consider in determining whether a confession is voluntary. "However, we see no basis in the law to conclude that this single factor should be dispositive."

Dissenting Justice McMorrow argued that the majority "unreasonably assumes that a child of 13 is capable of making an intelligent waiver of his constitutional rights." He urged the court to "adopt a *per se* rule whereby no confession given by a juvenile under the age of 15 would be admitted into evidence unless the youth is permitted, before or during interrogation, to consult with a lawyer or other adult, preferably a family member, who is personally interested in the child's well-being," noting that other states, including Indiana, Iowa and Wisconsin had adopted similar *per se* rules.[a]

a. See generally Comment, *Testing the Validity of Confessions and Waivers of the Self-Incrimination Privilege in the Juvenile Courts*, 47 U. Kan. L. Rev. 1035 (1999).

SECTION 5. *MASSIAH* REVISITED; *MASSIAH* AND *MIRANDA* COMPARED AND CONTRASTED

A. The Revivification of *Massiah*

9th ed., p. 634; at end of the discussion of the "no-contact" rule in Note 5, add:

Vindicating the views of the American Bar Association and state ethics authorities who have long maintained that federal prosecutors should be held to the same standards as other lawyers, the Citizens Protection Act, 28 U.S.C. § 530B, went into effect on April 19, 1999. The Act requires federal prosecutors to comply with state laws and rules, as well as local federal court rules, that govern lawyer conduct in the states where the federal prosecutors work.

The Act went into effect over the strong objections of Sen. Orrin Hatch, who argued that it "would cripple the ability of the Department of Justice to enforce federal law and cede authority to regulate the conduct of federal criminal investigations and prosecutors to more than 50 state bar associations," 64 Crim.L.Rep. 319, 337–38 (Feb. 3, 1999). Moreover, at a March 24 hearing before the U.S. Senate Judiciary Committee's Subcommittee on Criminal Justice Oversight, current and former prosecutors warned that the ability of federal prosecutors to supervise multistate investigations would be seriously hindered by state ethics rules restricting lawyers' direct contacts with persons represented by counsel. However, other witnesses testified that federal government lawyers should be governed by the same rules of ethics that apply to lawyers generally and maintained that the Department of Justice (DOJ) had not substantiated its claim that it needed an exemption from these rules. See 65 Crim.L.Rep. 1, 19 (April 7, 1999).

The same day the Citizens' Protection Act went into effect, the DOJ issued an interim final regulation implementing the new statute. The interim rule, Ethical Standards for Attorneys for the Government, 28 CFR 77.1–77.5 (set forth in full in 65 Crim.L.Rep. 77, 110 (April 28, 1999)), requires DOJ attorneys and lawyers acting pursuant to DOJ authorization to comply only with state rules of ethical conduct, such as codes of professional responsibility—not with state evidentiary and procedural rules or substantive state law.

The DOJ's interim rule supersedes the much-criticized 1994 Justice regulation, 28 CFR 77.10(a), which purported to exempt federal government lawyers from state ethical rules prohibiting ex parte communications with persons represented by counsel if the communication occurred prior to the initiation of formal proceedings against the person. As indicated by the discussion in 9th ed. at 632–33, the 1994 regulation received a rocky reception in the federal courts.

UNITED STATES v. LOWERY, 166 F.3d 1119 (11th Cir. 1999) held, per CARNES, J., that even though the Citizens Protection Act requires federal prosecutors to comply with state or local rules of professional conduct, it does not follow that evidence obtained in violation of such rules has to be excluded:

"Assuming for present purposes that the [Florida Bar Rules of Professional Conduct are] violated when a prosecutor promises a witness some consideration regarding charges or sentencing in return for testimony, a state rule of professional conduct cannot provide an adequate basis for a federal court to suppress evidence that is otherwise admissible. * * * When it comes to the admissibility of evidence in federal court, the federal interest in enforcement of federal law, including federal evidentiary rules, is paramount.

"[Moreover,] the Southern District of Florida's adoption of [the state's] professional conduct rules does not affect our analysis or the result. [The] question is whether Congress' recent statutory directive * * * is aimed at admission of evidence in federal court. In other words, did Congress intend by the enactment to turn over to state supreme courts in every state—and state legislatures, too, assuming they can also enact codes of professional conduct for attorneys—the authority to decide that otherwise admissible evidence cannot be used in federal court? We think not.

" * * * If Congress wants to give state courts and legislatures veto power over the admission of evidence in federal court, it will have to tell us that in plain language using clear terms."

Chapter 10

GRAND JURY INVESTIGATIONS

SECTION 4. APPLICATION OF THE PRIVILEGE AGAINST SELF-INCRIMINATION

9th ed., p. 758; replace Note 7 with:

UNITED STATES v. HUBBELL

___ U.S. ___, 120 S.Ct. 2037, ___ L.Ed.2d ___ (2000).

Justice STEVENS delivered the opinion of the Court. The two questions presented concern the scope of a witness' protection against compelled self-incrimination: (1) whether the Fifth Amendment privilege protects a witness from being compelled to disclose the existence of incriminating documents that the Government is unable to describe with reasonable particularity; and (2) if the witness produces such documents pursuant to a grant of immunity, whether 18 U.S.C. § 6002 [9th ed., p. 729–30] prevents the Government from using them to prepare criminal charges against him.

This proceeding arises out of the second prosecution of respondent, Webster Hubbell, commenced by the Independent Counsel appointed in August 1994 to investigate possible violations of federal law relating to the Whitewater Development Corporation. The first prosecution was terminated pursuant to a plea bargain. In December 1994, respondent pleaded guilty to charges of mail fraud and tax evasion arising out of his billing practices as a member of an Arkansas law firm from 1989 to 1992, and was sentenced to 21 months in prison. In the plea agreement, respondent promised to provide the Independent Counsel with "full, complete, accurate, and truthful information" about matters relating to the Whitewater investigation.

The second prosecution resulted from the Independent Counsel's attempt to determine whether respondent had violated that promise. In October 1996, while respondent was incarcerated, the Independent Counsel served him with a subpoena duces tecum calling for the production of 11 categories of documents before a grand jury sitting in Little

Rock, Arkansas. See Appendix, infra.[a] On November 19, he appeared before the grand jury and invoked his Fifth Amendment privilege against self-incrimination. In response to questioning by the prosecutor, respondent initially refused "to state whether there are documents within my possession, custody, or control responsive to the Subpoena." Thereafter, the prosecutor produced an order, which had previously been obtained from the District Court pursuant to 18 U.S.C. § 6003(a), directing him to respond to the subpoena and granting him immunity "to the extent allowed by law." Respondent then produced 13,120 pages of documents and records and responded to a series of questions that established that those were all of the documents in his custody or control that were responsive to the commands in the subpoena, with the exception of a few documents he claimed were shielded by the attorney-client and attorney work-product privileges.

The contents of the documents produced by respondent provided the Independent Counsel with the information that led to this second prosecution. On April 30, 1998, a grand jury in the District of Columbia returned a 10–count indictment charging respondent with various tax-related crimes and mail and wire fraud. The District Court dismissed the indictment relying, in part, on the ground that the Independent Coun-

a. The Appendix to Justice Stevens' opinion set forth verbatim the "subpoena rider," which identified the 11 categories of documents in paragraphs (A)-(K). In essence, the 11 categories (each subject to a time frame limit of "January 1, 1993 to the present") were: (1) all documents "reflecting, referring, or relating to any direct or indirect sources of money or other things of value received by Webster Hubbell, his wife or children [collectively, the "Hubbell family"] * * *, including but not limited to the identity of employers or clients of legal or any other type of work"; (2) all documents "reflecting, referring, or related to" any "direct or indirect sources of money or other things of value" received by the Hubbell family, including "billing memoranda, draft statements, bills, final statements and/or bills for work performed or time billed"; (3) copies of all bank records of the Hubbell family, including "statements, registers, ledgers, canceled checks, deposit items and wire transfers"; (4) all documents reflecting, referring, or related to "time worked or billed by Webster Hubbell," including "original time sheets, books, notes, papers, and/or computer records"; (5) all documents reflecting "expenses incurred by and/or disbursements of money by Webster Hubbell for work performed or to be performed"; (6) all documents "reflecting, referring, or relating to Webster Hubbell's schedule of activities," including "all calendars, daytimers, time books, appointment books, diaries, records of reverse telephone toll charges, credit card calls, telephone message slips, logs, other telephone records, minutes databases, electronic mail messages, travel records, itineraries, tickets for transportation of any kind, payments, bills, expense backup documentation, schedules, and/or any other document or database that would disclose Webster Hubbell's activities"; (7) all documents "reflecting, referring, or relating to any retainer agreements or contracts for employment" of the Hubbell family; (8) all "tax returns, tax return information, including but not limited to all W–2s, form 1099s, schedules, draft returns, work papers, and backup documents filed, created or held by or on behalf of [the Hubbell family], and/or any business in which [the Hubbell family] holds or has held an interest"; (9) all documents "reflecting, referring, or relating to work performed or to be performed for the City of Los Angeles, the Los Angeles Department of Airports or any other Los Angeles municipal or governmental entity, Mary Leslie, and/or Alan Arkatov"; (10) all documents "reflecting, referring, or related to work performed by [the Hubbell family] on the recommendation, counsel, or other influence of Mary Leslie and/or Alan Arkatov"; and (11) all documents related to work performed for or on behalf of specified entities (e.g., Lippo Ltd.) and specified individuals (e.g., James Riady) "or any affiliate, subsidiary, or corporation owned or controlled by or related to the aforementioned entities or individuals."

sel's use of the subpoenaed documents violated § 6002 because all of the evidence he would offer against respondent at trial derived either directly or indirectly from the testimonial aspects of respondent's immunized act of producing those documents. Noting that the Independent Counsel had admitted that he was not investigating tax-related issues when he issued the subpoena, and that he had " 'learned about the unreported income and other crimes from studying the records' contents,' " the District Court characterized the subpoena as "the quintessential fishing expedition." * * *

The Court of Appeals vacated the judgment and remanded for further proceedings. The majority concluded that the District Court had incorrectly relied on the fact that the Independent Counsel did not have prior knowledge of the contents of the subpoenaed documents. The question the District Court should have addressed was the extent of the Government's independent knowledge of the documents' existence and authenticity, and of respondent's possession or control of them. It explained: "On remand, the district court should hold a hearing in which it seeks to establish the extent and detail of the [G]overnment's knowledge of Hubbell's financial affairs (or of the paperwork documenting it) on the day the subpoena issued. It is only then that the court will be in a position to assess the testimonial value of Hubbell's response to the subpoena. Should the Independent Counsel prove capable of demonstrating with reasonable particularity a prior awareness that the exhaustive litany of documents sought in the subpoena existed and were in Hubbell's possession, then the wide distance evidently traveled from the subpoena to the substantive allegations contained in the indictment would be based upon legitimate intermediate steps. To the extent that the information conveyed through Hubbell's compelled act of production provides the necessary linkage, however, the indictment deriving therefrom is tainted."

In the opinion of the dissenting judge, the majority failed to give full effect to the distinction between the contents of the documents and the limited testimonial significance of the act of producing them. In his view, as long as the prosecutor could make use of information contained in the documents or derived therefrom without any reference to the fact that respondent had produced them in response to a subpoena, there would be no improper use of the testimonial aspect of the immunized act of production. In other words, the constitutional privilege and the statute conferring use immunity would only shield the witness from the use of any information resulting from his subpoena response "beyond what the prosecutor would receive if the documents appeared in the grand jury room or in his office unsolicited and unmarked, like manna from heaven."

On remand, the Independent Counsel acknowledged that he could not satisfy the "reasonable particularity" standard prescribed by the Court of Appeals and entered into a conditional plea agreement with respondent. In essence, the agreement provides for the dismissal of the charges unless this Court's disposition of the case makes it reasonably likely that respondent's "act of production immunity" would not pose a significant bar to his prosecution. The case is not moot, however, because the agreement also provides for the entry of a guilty plea and a sentence that will not include incarceration if we should reverse and issue an opinion that is sufficiently favorable to the Government to satisfy that condition. Despite that agreement, we granted the Independent Counsel's petition for a writ of certiorari in order to determine the precise scope of a grant of immunity with respect to the production of documents in response to a subpoena. We now affirm.

It is useful to preface our analysis of the constitutional issue with a restatement of certain propositions that are not in dispute. The term "privilege against self-incrimination" is not an entirely accurate description of a person's constitutional protection against being "compelled in any criminal case to be a witness against himself." The word "witness" in the constitutional text limits the relevant category of compelled incriminating communications to those that are "testimonial" in character.[8] As Justice Holmes observed, there is a significant difference between the use of compulsion to extort communications from a defendant and compelling a person to engage in conduct that may be incriminating. Thus, even though the act may provide incriminating evidence, a criminal suspect may be compelled to put on a shirt, to provide a blood sample or handwriting exemplar, or to make a recording of his voice. The act of exhibiting such physical characteristics is not the same as a sworn communication by a witness that relates either express or implied assertions of fact or belief. * * *

More relevant to this case is the settled proposition that a person may be required to produce specific documents even though they contain incriminating assertions of fact or belief because the creation of those documents was not "compelled" within the meaning of the privilege. [*Fisher v. United States*]. * * * It is clear, therefore, that respondent Hubbell could not avoid compliance with the subpoena served on him merely because the demanded documents contained incriminating evidence, whether written by others or voluntarily prepared by himself. * * * On the other hand, we have also made it clear that the act of producing documents in response to a subpoena may have a compelled testimonial aspect. We have held that "the act of production" itself may implicitly communicate "statements of fact" [*Doe II*]. By "producing documents in compliance with a subpoena, the witness would admit that the papers existed, were in his possession or control, and were authentic." Moreover, as was true in this case, when the custodian of documents responds to a subpoena, he may be compelled to take the witness

8. "It is consistent with the history of and the policies underlying the Self-Incrimination Clause to hold that the privilege may be asserted only to resist compelled explicit or implicit disclosures of incriminating information. Historically, the privilege was intended to prevent the use of legal compulsion to extract from the accused a sworn communication of facts which would incriminate him. Such was the process of the ecclesiastical courts and the Star Chamber—the inquisitorial method of putting the accused upon his oath and compelling him to answer questions designed to uncover uncharged offenses, without evidence from another source. * * * " *Doe II*.

stand and answer questions designed to determine whether he has produced everything demanded by the subpoena. The answers to those questions, as well as the act of production itself, may certainly communicate information about the existence, custody, and authenticity of the documents. Whether the constitutional privilege protects the answers to such questions, or protects the act of production itself, is a question that is distinct from the question whether the unprotected contents of the documents themselves are incriminating.

Finally, the phrase "in any criminal case" in the text of the Fifth Amendment might have been read to limit its coverage to compelled testimony that is used against the defendant in the trial itself. It has, however, long been settled that its protection encompasses compelled statements that lead to the discovery of incriminating evidence even though the statements themselves are not incriminating and are not introduced into evidence. * * * Compelled testimony that communicates information that may "lead to incriminating evidence" is privileged even if the information itself is not inculpatory. * * * It is the Fifth Amendment's protection against the prosecutor's use of incriminating information derived directly or indirectly from the compelled testimony of the respondent that is of primary relevance in this case.

Acting pursuant to 18 U.S.C. § 6002, the District Court entered an order compelling respondent to produce "any and all documents" described in the grand jury subpoena and granting him "immunity to the extent allowed by law." In *Kastigar v. United States* [9th ed., p. 730], we upheld the constitutionality of § 6002 because the scope of the "use and derivative-use" immunity that it provides is coextensive with the scope of the constitutional privilege against self-incrimination. * * * We particularly emphasized the critical importance of protection against a future prosecution " 'based on knowledge and sources of information obtained from the compelled testimony.' " * * * [W]e held that the statute imposes an affirmative duty on the prosecution, not merely to show that its evidence is not tainted by the prior testimony, but "to prove that the evidence it proposes to use is derived from a legitimate source wholly independent of the compelled testimony." * * * The "compelled testimony" that is relevant in this case is not to be found in the contents of the documents produced in response to the subpoena. It is, rather, the testimony inherent in the act of producing those documents. The disagreement between the parties focuses entirely on the significance of that testimonial aspect.

The Government correctly emphasizes that the testimonial aspect of a response to a subpoena duces tecum does nothing more than establish the existence, authenticity, and custody of items that are produced. We assume that the Government is also entirely correct in its submission that it would not have to advert to respondent's act of production in order to prove the existence, authenticity, or custody of any documents that it might offer in evidence at a criminal trial; indeed, the Government disclaims any need to introduce any of the documents produced by respondent into evidence in order to prove the charges against him. It follows, according to the Government, that it has no intention of making improper "use" of respondent's compelled testimony. The question, however, is not whether the response to the subpoena may be introduced into evidence at his criminal trial. That would surely be a prohibited "use" of the immunized act of production. But the fact that the Government intends no such use of the act of production leaves open the separate question whether it has already made "derivative use" of the testimonial aspect of that act in obtaining the indictment against respondent and in preparing its case for trial. It clearly has.

It is apparent from the text of the subpoena itself that the prosecutor needed respondent's assistance both to identify potential sources of information and to produce those sources. See Appendix [fn. a supra]. Given the breadth of the description of the 11 categories of documents called for by the subpoena, the collection and production of the materials demanded was tantamount to answering a series of interrogatories asking a witness to disclose the existence and location of particular documents fitting certain broad descriptions. The assembly of literally hundreds of pages of material in response to a request for "any and all documents reflecting, referring, or relating to any direct or indirect sources of money or other things of value received by or provided to" an individual or members of his family during a 3-year period, is the functional equivalent of the preparation of an answer to either a detailed written interrogatory or a series of oral questions at a discovery deposition. Entirely apart from the contents of the 13,120 pages of materials that respondent produced in this case, it is undeniable that providing a catalog of existing documents fitting within any of the 11 broadly worded subpoena categories could provide a prosecutor with a "lead to incriminating evidence," or "a link in the chain of evidence needed to prosecute."

Indeed, the record makes it clear that that is what happened in this case. The documents were produced before a grand jury sitting in the Eastern District of Arkansas in aid of the Independent Counsel's attempt to determine whether respondent had violated a commitment in his first plea agreement. The use of those sources of information eventually led to the return of an indictment by a grand jury sitting in the District of Columbia for offenses that apparently are unrelated to that plea agreement. What the District Court characterized as a "fishing expedition" did produce a fish, but not the one that the Independent Counsel expected to hook. It is abundantly clear that the testimonial aspect of respondent's act of producing subpoenaed documents was the first step in a chain of evidence that led to this prosecution. The documents did not magically appear in the prosecutor's office like "manna from heaven." They arrived there only after respondent asserted his constitutional privilege, received a grant of immunity, and—under the compulsion of the District Court's order—took the mental and physical steps necessary to provide the prosecutor with an accurate inventory of the many sources of potentially incriminating evidence sought by the subpoena. It was only through respondent's truthful reply to the subpoena that the Government received the incriminating documents of which it made "substantial use . . . in the investigation that led to the indictment." Brief for United States 3.

For these reasons, we cannot accept the Government's submission that respondent's immunity did not preclude its derivative use of the produced documents because its "possession of the documents [was] the fruit only of a simple physical act—the act of producing the documents." Brief, at 29. It was unquestionably necessary for respondent to make extensive use of "the contents of his own mind" in identifying the hundreds of documents responsive to the requests in the subpoena. The assembly of those documents was like telling an inquisitor the combination to a wall safe, not like being forced to surrender the key to a strongbox. *Doe II*, at n. 9 [9th ed., p. 734]. The Government's anemic view of respondent's act of production as a mere physical act that is principally non-testimonial in character and can be entirely divorced from its "implicit" testimonial aspect so as to constitute a "legitimate, wholly independent source" (as required by *Kastigar*) for the documents produced simply fails to account for these realities.

In sum, we have no doubt that the constitutional privilege against self-incrimination protects the target of a grand jury investigation from being compelled to answer questions designed to elicit information about the existence of sources of potentially incriminating evidence. That constitutional privilege has the same application to the testimonial aspect of a response to a subpoena seeking discovery of those sources. Before the District Court, the Government arguably conceded that respondent's act of production in this case had a testimonial aspect that entitled him to respond to the subpoena by asserting his privilege against self-incrimination. * * * On appeal and again before this Court, however, the Government has argued that the communicative aspect of respondent's act of producing ordinary business records is insufficiently "testimonial" to support a claim of privilege because the existence and possession of such records by any businessman is a "foregone conclusion" under our decision in *Fisher v. United States*. This argument both misreads *Fisher* and ignores our subsequent decision in *Doe I*. * * * Whatever the scope of this "foregone conclusion" rationale, the facts of this case plainly fall outside of it. While in *Fisher* the Government already knew that the documents were in the attorneys' possession and could independently confirm their existence and authenticity through the accountants who created them, here the Government has not shown that it had any prior knowledge of either the existence or the whereabouts of the 13,120 pages of documents ultimately produced by respondent. The Government cannot cure this deficiency through the overbroad argument that a businessman such as respondent will always possess general business and tax records that fall within the broad categories described in this subpoena. The *Doe I* subpoenas also sought several broad categories of general business records, yet we upheld the District Court's finding that the act of producing those records would involve testimonial self-incrimination.

Given our conclusion that respondent's act of production had a testimonial aspect, at least with respect to the existence and location of the documents sought by the Government's subpoena, respondent could not be compelled to produce those documents without first receiving a grant of immunity under § 6003. As we construed § 6002 in *Kastigar*, such immunity is co-extensive with the constitutional privilege. *Kastigar* requires that respondent's motion to dismiss the indictment on immunity grounds be granted unless the Government proves that the evidence it used in obtaining the indictment and proposed to use at trial was derived from legitimate sources "wholly independent" of the testimonial aspect of respondent's immunized conduct in assembling and producing the documents described in the subpoena. The Government, however, does not claim that it could make such a showing. Rather, it contends that its prosecution of respondent must be considered proper unless someone—presumably respondent—shows that "there is some substantial relation between the compelled testimonial communications implicit in the act of production (as opposed to the act of production standing alone) and some aspect of the information used in the investigation or the evidence presented at trial." Brief for United States 9. We could not accept this submission without repudiating the basis for our conclusion in *Kastigar* that the statutory guarantee of use and derivative-use immunity is as broad as the constitutional privilege itself. This we are not prepared to do. Accordingly, the indictment against respondent must be dismissed. The judgment of the Court of Appeals is affirmed. * * *

Chief Justice REHNQUIST dissents and would reverse the judgment of the Court of Appeals in part, for the reasons given by Judge Williams in his dissenting opinion in that court, 167 F.3d 552, 597 (C.A.D.C.1999).

Justice THOMAS, with whom Justice SCALIA joins, concurring.

Our decision today involves the application of the act-of-production doctrine, which provides that persons compelled to turn over incriminating papers or other physical evidence pursuant to a subpoena duces tecum or a summons may invoke the Fifth Amendment privilege against self-incrimination as a bar to production only where the act of producing the evidence would contain "testimonial" features. I join the opinion of the Court because it properly applies this doctrine, but I write separately to note that this doctrine may be inconsistent with the original meaning of the Fifth Amendment's Self–Incrimination Clause. A substantial body of evidence suggests that the Fifth Amendment privilege protects against the compelled production not just of incriminating testimony, but of any incriminating evidence. In a future case, I would be willing to reconsider the scope and meaning of the Self–Incrimination Clause.

The Fifth Amendment provides that "[n]o person ... shall be compelled in any criminal case to be a witness against himself." The key word at issue in this case is "witness." The Court's opinion, relying on prior cases, essentially defines "witness" as a person who provides testimony, and thus restricts the Fifth Amendment's ban to only those communications "that are 'testimonial' in character." None of this Court's cases, however, has undertaken an analysis of the meaning of the term at the time of the founding. A review of that period reveals substantial support for the view that the term "witness" meant a person who gives or furnishes evidence, a broader meaning than that which our case law currently ascribes to the term. If this is so, a person who responds to a subpoena duces tecum would be just as much a "witness" as a person who responds to a subpoena ad testificandum.[1]

Dictionaries published around the time of the founding included definitions of the term "witness" as a person who gives or furnishes evidence. Legal dictionaries of that period defined "witness" as someone who "gives evidence in a cause." * * * Such a meaning of "witness" is consistent with, and may help explain, the history and framing of the Fifth Amendment. The 18th century common-law privilege against self-incrimination protected against the compelled production of incriminating physical evidence such as papers and documents. And this Court has noted that, for generations before the framing, "one cardinal rule of the court of chancery [wa]s never to decree a discovery which might tend to convict the party of a crime." *Boyd v. United States*. * * * Against this common-law backdrop, the privilege against self-incrimination was enshrined in the Virginia Declaration of Rights in 1776. * * * Following Virginia's lead, seven of the other original States included specific provisions in their Constitutions granting a right against compulsion "to give evidence" or "to furnish evidence." * * * And during ratification of the Federal Constitution, the four States that proposed bills of rights put forward draft proposals employing similar wording for a federal constitutional provision guaranteeing the right against compelled self-incrimination. Each of the proposals broadly sought to protect a citizen from "be[ing] compelled to give evidence against himself." * * * Similarly worded proposals to protect against compelling a person "to furnish evidence" against himself came from prominent voices outside the conventions. See Letter of Brutus, No. 2 (1788).

In response to such calls, James Madison penned the Fifth Amendment. In so doing, Madison substituted the phrase "to be a witness" for the proposed language "to give evidence" and "to furnish evidence." But it seems likely that Madison's phrasing was synonymous with that of the proposals. The definitions of the word "witness" and the background history of the privilege against self-incrimination, both discussed above, support this view. And this may explain why Madison's unique phrasing—phrasing that none of the proposals had suggested—apparently attracted no attention, much less opposition, in Congress, the state legislatures that ratified the Bill of Rights, or anywhere else. * * *

1. Even if the term "witness" in the Fifth Amendment referred to someone who provides testimony, as this Court's recent cases suggest without historical analysis, it may well be that at the time of the founding a person who turned over documents would be described as providing testimony. See Amey v. Long, 9 East. 472, 484, 103 Eng. Rep. 653, 658 (K.B.1808) (referring to documents requested by subpoenas duces tecum as "written ... testimony"). * * *

In addition, a broad definition of the term "witness"—one who gives evidence—is consistent with the same term (albeit in plural form) in the Sixth Amendment's Compulsory Process Clause. That Clause provides that "[i]n all criminal prosecutions, the accused shall enjoy the right ... to have compulsory process for obtaining witnesses in his favor." Soon after the adoption of the Bill of Rights, Chief Justice Marshall had occasion to interpret the Compulsory Process Clause while presiding over the treason trial of Aaron Burr. Burr moved for the issuance of a subpoena duces tecum to obtain from President Jefferson a letter that was said to incriminate Burr. The Government objected, arguing that compulsory process under the Sixth Amendment permits a defendant to secure a subpoena ad testificandum, but not a subpoena duces tecum. The Chief Justice dismissed the argument, holding that the right to compulsory process includes the right to secure papers—in addition to testimony—material to the defense. This Court has subsequently expressed agreement with this view of the Sixth Amendment. See *United States v. Nixon*, 418 U.S. 683, 711, 94 S.Ct. 3090, 41 L.Ed.2d 1039 (1974). Although none of our opinions has focused upon the precise language or history of the Compulsory Process Clause, a narrow definition of the term "witness" as a person who testifies seems incompatible with *Burr*'s holding. And if the term "witnesses" in the Compulsory Process Clause has an encompassing meaning, this provides reason to believe that the term "witness" in the Self–Incrimination Clause has the same broad meaning. Yet this Court's recent Fifth Amendment act-of-production cases implicitly rest upon an assumption that this term has different meanings in adjoining provisions of the Bill of Rights. * * *

This Court has not always taken the approach to the Fifth Amendment that we follow today. The first case interpreting the Self–Incrimination Clause—*Boyd v. United States*—was decided, though not explicitly, in accordance with the understanding that "witness" means one who gives evidence. In *Boyd*, this Court unanimously held that the Fifth Amendment protects a defendant against compelled production of books and papers. And the Court linked its interpretation of the Fifth Amendment to the common-law understanding of the self-incrimination privilege. But this Court's decision in *Fisher v. United States*, rejected this understanding, permitting the Government to force a person to furnish incriminating physical evidence and protecting only the "testimonial" aspects of that transfer. In so doing, *Fisher* not only failed to examine the historical backdrop to the Fifth Amendment, it also required—as illustrated by extended discussion in the opinions below in this case—a difficult parsing of the act of responding to a subpoena duces tecum. None of the parties in this case has asked us to depart from *Fisher*, but in light of the historical evidence that the Self–Incrimination Clause may have a broader reach than *Fisher* holds, I remain open to a reconsideration of that decision and its progeny in a proper case.

Chapter 11

THE SCOPE OF THE EXCLUSIONARY RULES

SECTION 1. "STANDING" TO OBJECT TO THE ADMISSION OF EVIDENCE

B. The Current Approach

9th ed., p. 780; beginning of opinion in *Minnesota v. Carter,* add:

The name of the author of the opinion of the Court, Chief Justice Rehnquist, was inadvertently omitted.

9th ed., p. 786; after *Minnesota v. Carter,* add:

Consider CRAIG BRADLEY, *The Fourth Amendment's Iron Triangle: Standing, Consent and Searchability*, Trial, Aug. 1999, p. 75:

"Who may be searched? Who may consent to a search? Who has standing to protest a search? These three, seemingly unrelated, questions frequently arise in criminal cases. But though these issues have always appeared to the Supreme Court to be unconnected, consideration of two recent cases, *Wyoming v. Houghton* [Supp., p. 18] and *Minnesota v. Carter*, has led me to the conclusion that these three questions hinge on exactly the same issue: *What is the subject's interest in or connection to the place to be searched?* Further, they should all have the same answer. That is, if a person has authority to consent to a search, he also has standing to protest it, and is searchable if found at the scene of the search, and vice versa. Recognition that the answer to these questions is the same means that once the Court has put one side of this equilateral triangle into position, the position of the other two sides has been resolved as well. Moreover, it may cause decision makers to think more carefully about finding no standing for passengers in a car, for example, if they realize that will lead to a reduction in authority of such passengers to consent to a search and their 'searchability' by virtue of their presence in that car.

"Consider first the issues of 'standing' and 'consent.' The standing doctrine holds that only a defendant who has a sufficient interest in a place that has been searched is entitled to move to exclude evidence found in that place from his trial. Thus, as the Court held in *Rakas v. Illinois*, a passenger in a car lacks standing to protest a search of that car since *he* has no 'legitimate expectation of privacy in the invaded place.'

"The doctrine of consent allows police to dispense with warrant and probable cause requirements in conducting a search if the person with control over the premises to be searched consents to the search. A person has authority to consent to a search if he has 'common authority over the premises.' That is, if he has 'joint access and control for most purposes.'

"Obviously, these two concepts are similar. A person with 'joint access and control' over certain premises is also more likely to have a 'legitimate expectation of privacy' than others. That is, he is more likely to be a person who has the authority to seek exclusion of evidence found in those premises. Indeed, the Court has recognized that an overnight guest has standing to protest the search of a house because he has 'a measure of control over the premises,' the same as the 'standing' test declared in *Rakas*. It follows that if a person has standing, he also has authority to consent to a search. If he lacks standing, he lacks authority to consent.

"This approach not only brings symmetry to Fourth Amendment law, it brings fairness. If the Supreme Court, at the government's urging, wants to limit standing, as it did in the recent case of *Minnesota v. Carter,* then it should accept that a person with insufficient interest in the property searched to have standing also lacks authority to consent to a search. Any narrowing of standing doctrine cuts into the ability of police to obtain consents. It would seem highly unfair for the government to be able to contend that a visitor to a home had authority to consent to a search, but then lacked standing to protest the fact that the search exceeded the bounds of the consent or was in some other way improper. * * *

"[Consider] *Carter* as a consent case. Suppose the police had come to the door, rather than peeping in the window, and asked consent to search. Under this approach, Carter, at the apartment for the purpose of bagging cocaine, would lack the authority to consent to the search on behalf of the resident. However, if Carter were an overnight guest, his own interest in the privacy of the premises would be enhanced, and it is reasonable to grant him the authority to consent.

"By the same token, had the police sought the consent of the passenger in *Rakas* to search the car, he would not have been empowered to give it. By contrast, as the six concurring and dissenting Justices in *Rakas* recognized, a passenger *does* have standing to protest the *stop* of a car because his right to proceed down the road unmolested by police is the same as the driver's. It follows that a passenger could (and should) be able to 'consent' to a stop, such as by flagging down a passing police car, should he desire the police to stop the car. If the police should smell marijuana and arrest the driver during such a stop, a court's holding that the passenger's consent was invalid and that the marijuana must be suppressed, would be unfair to the interests of law enforcement.

"One case, *Illinois v. Rodriguez* [9th ed., p. 352], may seem inconsistent with this analysis. *Rodriguez* held that if a person, such as a business visitor or a former resident, *reasonably appeared* to have authority to consent, the police may rely on that consent. But such a person would not have standing, as *Carter* has now made clear. Such a person would also not have actual authority to consent. Thus, *Rodriguez* should be seen, similarly to *United States v. Leon*, as a case where good faith reliance by police does not lead to evidentiary exclusion, despite a violation of the property owner's rights, rather than as any expansion of the *right* to consent. * * *

"Fourth Amendment law, which is designed to govern the behavior of police in the field, is ridiculously complicated. Even lawyers experienced in the criminal justice system are unlikely to have mastered its finer points and police certainly cannot. Supreme Court decisions, coming along once every five or ten years on a given issue, leave many questions undecided. Consequently, anything that makes decision simpler is desirable, unless simplicity is achieved at the expense of fairness. Does this approach unduly tip the balance of fairness to one side or the other? I don't think so, in part because, as noted, a gain on one issue will produce losses on the others. Since the issue of 'searchability' has not yet been developed by the Supreme Court, this triangle will help lower courts to resolve this issue consistently based on the more plentiful consent and standing cases that are already on the books.

"Thus, if *Carter* had held that business visitors have standing to protest searches of homes that they are visiting, as the dissent urged, then such visitors would have the right to consent to a search of that home and would be searchable if police came with a warrant. However, these latter two results do not seem correct. Most people would agree that the Fuller Brush man should *not* have authority to consent to a search of their house while they have stepped into the bathroom. Nor should the hapless salesman be searchable just because he's there when the police show up with a warrant. Thought of in these terms, the *Carter* holding seems clearly right.

"Even if courts are unwilling to rigidly answer these questions the same way, it is at least a useful double check as to a result on one issue, such as standing, to see how it comes out when authority to consent and searchability are considered. Thus, when the Court considers the issue of the social visitor after *Carter*, it would aid its analysis to consider whether such a person should have authority to consent and be searchable without individualized suspicion. If the answer to the latter two questions is 'No,' then this should at least raise doubts about whether the social visitor has enough connection to the home to have standing."

SECTION 2. THE "FRUIT OF THE POISONOUS TREE"

C. Is a Confession Obtained in Violation of *Miranda* a "Poisonous Tree"?

9th ed., p. 802; end of Note 4, add:

Is *Elstad* applicable even when: (a) The police deliberately decide to forego *Miranda* warnings until after an interrogation which results in a confession? (b) The first confession was obtained during extended custodial interrogation? (c) Less than 30 minutes elapsed between the end of the suspect's initial statement and the subsequent post-*Miranda* statement? In DAVIS v. UNITED STATES, 724 A.2d 1163 (D.C.App. 1998), a 2–1 majority per WAGNER, J., answered all three questions in the affirmative.

Davis, a murder suspect, was arrested and taken to the homicide office between 4:15 and 4:30 p.m. Two detectives (Collins and Sullivan) first spoke with Davis at about 5:30 p.m., informing that the was under arrest for the murder of Ben Holley. The detective then left the room for about 20 minutes to "prepare paperwork," but during that time they observed Davis through a video monitor. The detectives returned to the room around 6:00 p.m.

Detective Sullivan testified that he knew Davis had not been given his *Miranda* warning, but that he had made the decision not to read Davis his rights when he returned to the room. The detectives then told Davis that a co-defendant had implicated him in the murder of Holey (which was not true). At this point, Davis admitted his involvement in the murder. Shortly, thereafter, Davis asked Detective Sullivan to leave the room, apparently because Davis thought the detective was annoyed by his responses to the detective's questions.

After Detective Sullivan left the room (around 6:25 p.m.), Detective Collins questioned defendant further until 6:45 p.m. During this time, Davis described to the detective the weapon he had used to shoot Holley. At around 7:00 p.m., Detective Collins advised Davis of his *Miranda* rights. Davis then signed a waiver of rights form at 7:11 p.m. and gave the police a videotaped statement that essentially repeated the earlier incriminating statements. In upholding Davis's videotaped statement, the court, per Wagner, J., observed:

"Davis relies primarily on the Eight Circuit's opinion in *United States v. Carter*, 884 F.2d 368 (1989), [which] upheld the suppression of the defendant's post-*Miranda* confession where it came 'almost directly on the heels of the first [unwarned confession].' * * * Here, both detectives left Davis alone for a fifteen minute period after his initial statement before administering *Miranda* warnings, and his videotaped statement was made another eleven minutes thereafter. Thus, unlike *Carter*, some twenty-six minutes elapsed between the end of Davis' initial statement and the subsequent one. In *Elstad*, the time separation between the initial unwarned statement and the subsequent one given after *Miranda* warnings was approximately one hour. The *Elstad* holding did not turn on the time frame between the two confessions. Rather, *Elstad* seems to eschew rigid rules based upon such a factor. * * *

"[W]e are not persuaded by *Carter* to hold, particularly on the facts of this case, that what occurred here was one continuous interrogation requiring suppression of the statement obtained after *Miranda* warnings. Further, the Supreme Court has stated that in circumstances involving the admissibility of a properly warned confession which follows an unwarned, but clearly voluntary admission, a break between the two is not essential. * * *

"While the police officer's intentional decision to forego *Miranda* warnings may be a factor in the totality of the circumstances to be considered by the court in assessing the voluntariness of the confessions, it is not the sole factor. Voluntariness depends on the surrounding circumstances, including whether there were 'police tactics or methods offensive to due process that render the initial admission involuntary and undermine the suspect's will to invoke his rights once they are read to him.' *Elstad*. Here, the trial court considered the totality of the circumstances and applied *Elstad* properly to the facts as found from the evidence."[c]

Dissenting Judge RUIZ protested:

"Because of the central importance of *Miranda* warnings to the issue of voluntariness, the Court in *Elstad* took pains to show that the police officers in that case acted reasonably and did not purposely disregard their obligations nor the suspect's rights. First, the Court noted that one officer's failure to give *Miranda* warnings may have been the result of confusion as to whether the brief exchange qualified as 'custodial interrogation' * * *. Whatever the reasons for [the police officer's] *oversight*, the incident had none of the earmarks of coercion." (emphasis added).

"It is not possible to excuse or explain the police conduct in this case with similar niceties. At Davis' suppression hearing, Detective Sullivan testified that he had been the officer who obtained a warrant for Davis' arrest and that the warrant had been executed and Davis had been arrested at 4:00 p.m. on January 14, 1995. Thus, there is no question that the police here knew that Davis was in custody and that *Miranda* warnings were therefore required. Not only was the police officer in this case not confused about the need to give warnings—as the Court ventured may have been the case in *Elstad*—but Detective Sullivan also admitted, and gave no explanation for, having made a *conscious decision*, when active interrogation of Davis began almost two hours after the arrest, *not to give Miranda warnings*, as constitutionally mandated. *Miranda* warnings were not given to Davis until one hour into active police interrogation (three hours after arrest) and only *after* Davis had confessed to murder.

"Nor can we possibly derive confidence in the voluntariness of Davis' waiver of his rights—once they were tardily given—from the fact that, as in *Elstad*," [n]either the environment nor the manner of either 'interrogation' was coercive.' * * * By contrast, here, Davis was arrested, taken to the police station, and two hours later subjected to active police interrogation for

c. The court made plain that it did not "condone [the] deliberate failure of the police to inform a criminal suspect promptly of his rights under *Miranda*. In addition to the obvious impropriety of such conduct, it proceeds at some risk to the legitimate interests of the government and the citizens it serves. There is no guarantee that the suspect will provide the second confession once the warnings are given, and the failure to warn may, in some cases, be the factor which tips the scales in favor of exclusion of the confession."

at least forty-five minutes—hardly a 'brief stop.' During this time he was in an interrogation room handcuffed by one arm to a bolt in the floor—quite unlike being in the familiar surroundings of his own living room at home as in *Elstad*.

"Under these circumstances, the fact that the officers finally apprised Davis of his rights three hours after being taken into custody, after active interrogation had yielded a confession to murder, a mere ten or fifteen minutes before concluding the interrogation session by videotaping the confession is insufficient, under *Elstad*, to render the videotaped confession admissible. * * *

"This case is more like *Carter* than *Elstad*. As in *Carter*, Davis' videotaped confession was but the conclusion of a continuous interrogation. The number of minutes between unwarned and warned confessions is not, by itself, determinative. It is relevant in evaluating whether there was an opportunity to reconsider between the unwarned and the warned confessions sufficient to dissipate the taint of the unwarned confession. Here there was a ten-to-fifteen minute break during which Davis was left alone after he confessed the first time. This was merely the time it took the officers to set up the videotaping equipment. During that time, Davis continued to be in the same place, handcuffed to the floor, knowing that the officers were preparing for the final videotaping, which commenced some ten minutes later. The fact that Davis was alone during this brief period is negligible under the circumstances. Had *Miranda* warnings been given and then Davis had been left alone, it might be possible to consider this short interval as a period during which the interrogation stopped and Davis had some time to reflect and reconsider his statements in light of his rights. Instead, the officers here did not advise Davis of his rights until after they returned to begin to videotape his confession. * * *

"Suppression of the warned confession in *Elstad* would not have deterred police misconduct—significantly, the court found none—or even induced police to take greater care in providing prompt warnings. The situation before us, however, stands in stark contrast, for here the police purposely delayed advising Davis of his rights for a considerable period of time, not only after the police knew *Miranda* mandated that they be given, but even after they had engaged in active and persistent interrogation that had yielded a confession to murder."

SECTION 3. USE OF ILLEGALLY OBTAINED EVIDENCE FOR IMPEACHMENT PURPOSES

C. Use of Defendant's Prior Silence for Impeachment Purposes

9th ed., p. 825; after Notes and Questions following *Jenkins v. Anderson* and *Fletcher v. Weir*, add:

Distinguishing *Jenkins* and *Weir*, COMBS v. COYLE, 205 F.3d 269 (6th Cir. 2000), held, per MOORE, J., that the use of prearrest silence as *substantive* evidence of guilt violates the privilege against self-incrimination. (The federal courts of appeals are badly split on this issue.) The case arose as follows:

After shooting two people to death, defendant Combs was in turn shot by a police officer. At that point, a second officer (Ventre) arrived on the scene and found Combs sitting on the ground, holding a shotgun. Officer Ventre ordered Combs to drop his weapon and then pulled it away from him. As Combs was being placed into an ambulance, Officer Ventre asked him what had happened. Combs told the officer to "talk to my lawyer."

Combs was charged with two counts of murder. His defense was that he was too intoxicated from alcohol and drugs to form the requisite intent to kill or to have committed the killings with prior calculation and design. To support this theory, he presented the testimony of several witnesses who had seen him ingesting substantial quantities of drugs prior to the shootings. At the trial, Officer Ventre testified about Combs's "talk to my lawyer" statement. The trial judge then gave the jury a special instruction—it could consider Officer Ventre's testimony "as it relates to the purpose and prior calculations and design" of the defendant. Moreover, in closing argument, the prosecutor told the jury: "Talk to my lawyer. Does that sound like someone who's so intoxicated he does not know what is going on?"

Combs was convicted of murder and sentenced to death. The Sixth Circuit granted federal habeas relief, holding that the prosecution's use of Combs's "Talk to my lawyer" statement in its case in chief violated his right against self-incrimination:

"Although Combs's statement referred not to silence but to his right to an attorney, the admissibility of the statement is properly analyzed as a comment on prearrest silence. * * * Combs's statement is best understood as communicating a desire to remain silent outside the presence of an attorney. * * *

"*Jenkins* did not * * * address the question at issue in this case, namely whether the use of prearrest silence as substantive evidence of guilt violates the Fifth Amendment. [That] use of a defendant's prearrest silence as substantive evidence of guilt is significantly different than the use of prearrest silence to impeach a defendant's credibility on the stand is clear. In *Griffin v. California* [9th ed., p. 1449], the Supreme Court held that the Fifth Amendment 'forbids either comment by the prosecution on the accused's [refusal to testify at trial] or instructions by the court that such silence is evidence of guilt.' The Court reasoned that a contrary rule would allow the state to submit as substantive proof of the defendant's guilt his silence by not testifying.

"[The six federal courts of appeals] that have considered whether the government may comment on a defendant's prearrest silence in its case in chief care equally divided. [Today, we join the First, Seventh and Tenth Circuits] in holding that the use of a defendant's prearrest silence as substantive evidence of guilt violates [the] privilege against self-incrimination. Like those circuits, we believe 'that application of the privilege is not limited to persons in custody or charged with a crime; it may also be asserted by a suspect who is questioned during the investigation of a crime.'

"[Even] assuming that the Fifth Amendment is inapplicable to precustody contexts, the privilege would still be applicable to Combs, for we agree with the Ohio Supreme Court's finding that Combs was in custody at the time he made the 'talk to my lawyer' statement. [Under the circumstances, Officer Ventre having pointed his weapon at Combs several times and ordered him to drop his shotgun, a] reasonable person in Comb's situation could have believed that he was under arrest * * *.

"Having decided that the privilege against self-incrimination applies to a prearrest situation, [we conclude] that the use of prearrest silence as substantive evidence of guilt is an impermissible burden upon the exercise of that privilege. First, permitting the use of silence in the government's case in chief would substantially impair the policies behind the privilege [quoting at length from *Murphy v. Waterfront Commission*, 9th ed., pp. 716, 735].

"[If] prearrest silence may be used as substantive evidence of guilt regardless of whether or not the defendant testifies at trial, then the defendant is cast into the very trilemma outlined by the *Murphy* Court. Because in the case of substantive use a defendant cannot avoid the introduction of his past silence by refusing to testify, the defendant is under substantial pressure to waive the privilege against self-incrimination, either upon first contact with police or later at trial in order to explain the prior silence. Perhaps most importantly, use of a defendant's prearrest silence as substantive evidence of guilt substantially impairs the 'sense of fair play' underlying the privilege. Unlike in the case of impeachment use, the use of a defendant's prior silence as substantive evidence of guilt actually lessens the prosecution's burden of proving each element of the crime.

"We also conclude that the government's use of a defendant's prearrest silence in its case in chief is not a legitimate governmental practice. Unlike the use of silence for impeachment purposes, the use of silence as substantive evidence of guilt does not enhance the reliability of the criminal process. * * * [T]here are many reasons why a defendant may remain silent before arrest, such as a knowledge of his *Miranda* rights or a fear that his story may not be believed. The probative value of such silence is therefore minimal. Furthermore, the use of prearrest silence may even subvert the truthfinding process; because it pressures the defendant to explain himself or to a suffer a court-sanctioned inference of guilt, the likelihood of perjury is increased. In sum, permitting the use of a defendant's prearrest silence as substantive evidence of guilt would greatly undermine the policies behind the privilege against self-incrimination while adding virtually nothing to the reliability of the criminal process."

Part Three

THE COMMENCEMENT OF FORMAL PROCEEDINGS

Chapter 12

PRETRIAL RELEASE

SECTION 1. THE RIGHT TO BAIL; PRETRIAL RELEASE PROCEDURES

9th ed., p. 850; end of Note 8, add:

Douglas L. Colbert, *Thirty-Five Years After Gideon: The Illusory Right to Counsel at Bail Proceedings,* 1998 U.Ill.L.Rev. 1, 7, reports that "most states and localities deny indigent defendants counsel at the initial bail hearing. * * * [I]t is the exceptional jurisdiction which guarantees counsel when bail is set. Moreover, significant delay in assigning court-appointed counsel thereafter exacerbates the due process concerns and seriousness of states' denying counsel at the initial appearance."

Chapter 13

THE DECISION WHETHER TO PROSECUTE

SECTION 3. CHALLENGING THE PROSECUTOR'S DISCRETION

9th ed., p. 925; after Note 8, add:

9. Consider now a case somewhat like *Boyt*, except that the defendant *is* going to testify pursuant to the agreement, but the codefendant now claims that such a promise of leniency in exchange for testimony is itself proscribed by the criminal law. In *United States v. Singleton*, 144 F.3d 1343 (10th Cir.1998), a panel of the Tenth Circuit agreed with that contention, holding that testimony offered as a consequence of such an agreement should be suppressed because the government had violated the so-called "anti-gratuity statute," 18 U.S.C.A. § 201(c)(2), which makes it a criminal offense to give or offer "anything of value to any person, for or because of the testimony under oath or affirmation given or to be given by such person as a witness upon a trial." But upon rehearing en banc, 165 F.3d 1297 (10th Cir.1999), the court rejected that conclusion and affirmed the conviction obtained by use of testimony prompted by such an agreement. The court reasoned: (i) that a prosecutor who has entered into such an agreement "is the alter ego of the United States exercising its sovereign power of prosecution"; (ii) that the word "whoever," used in the statute to describe those to whom the statute applies, by its normal meaning "connotes a being" while the "United States is an inanimate entity, not a being"; (iii) that given the "longstanding" and "ingrained" practice of granting leniency in exchange for testimony, reading the statute as restricting that power would be "a diminution of sovereignty not countenanced in our jurisprudence"; and (iv) that, "had Congress intended that [the statute] overturn this ingrained aspect of American legal culture, it would have done so in clear, unmistakable, and unarguable language."[e]

e. The court added: "Our conclusion in no way permits an agent of the government to step beyond the limits of his or her office to make an offer to a witness other than one traditionally exercised by the sovereign. A prosecutor who offers something other than a concession normally granted by the government in exchange for testimony is no longer the alter ego of the sovereign and is divested of the protective mantle of the government. Thus, fears our decision would permit improper use or abuse of prosecutorial authority simply have no foundation."

Those fears were expressed by two concurring judges, who rejected the majority's approach and instead relied upon "long-established principles of statutory construction" for the proposition that "where specific statutes overlap with a general statute, the latter must give way, insofar as it would prohibit that which the narrow statutes would allow." This would mean, they explained, that "the general prohibition of § 201(c)(2)" *would* apply to prosecutors, subject to "specific exceptions" derived from other actions of Congress. Thus, they concluded: "Prosecutors may offer only those incentives that Congress has approved, and may bargain and execute agreements only within the narrow, specific procedures that Congress and the courts have articulated."

Chapter 17

THE LOCATION OF THE PROSECUTION

SECTION 2. APPLYING THE CRIME–COMMITTED FORMULA

9th ed., p. 1059; at the end of Note 4, add:

Consider also the Supreme Court's latest venue ruling:

UNITED STATES v. RODRIGUEZ–MORENO

526 U.S. 275, 119 S.Ct. 1239, 143 L.Ed.2d 388 (1999).

Justice THOMAS delivered the opinion of the Court.

This case presents the question whether venue in a prosecution for using or carrying a firearm "during and in relation to any crime of violence, in violation of 18 U.S.C. § 924(c)(1)", is proper in any district where the crime of violence was committed, even if the firearm was used or carried only in a single district. * * * During a drug transaction that took place in Houston, Texas, a New York drug dealer stole 30 kilograms of a Texas drug distributor's cocaine. The distributor hired respondent, Jacinto Rodriguez–Moreno, and others to find the dealer and to hold captive the middleman in the transaction, Ephrain Avendano, during the search. In pursuit of the dealer, the distributor and his henchmen drove from Texas to New Jersey with Avendano in tow. * * * They [then] moved to a house in New York and then to a house in Maryland, taking Avendano with them. Shortly after respondent and the others arrived at the Maryland house, the owner of the home passed around a .357 magnum revolver and respondent took possession of the pistol. As it became clear that efforts to find the New York drug dealer would not bear fruit, respondent told his employer that he thought they should kill the middleman and end their search for the dealer. He put the gun to the back of Avendano's neck but, at the urging of his cohorts, did not shoot. Avendano eventually escaped through the back door and ran to a neighboring house. The neighbors called the Maryland police, who arrested respondent along with the rest of the kidnappers. The police also seized the .357 magnum, on which they later found respondent's fingerprint.

Rodriguez–Moreno and his codefendants were tried jointly in the United States District Court for the District of New Jersey. Respondent was charged with, inter alia, conspiring to kidnap Avendano, kidnaping Avendano, and using and carrying a firearm in relation to the kidnaping of Avendano, in violation of 18 U.S.C. § 924(c)(1). At the conclusion of the Government's case, respondent moved to dismiss the § 924(c)(1) count for lack of venue. He argued that venue was proper only in Maryland, the only place where the Government had proved he had actually used a gun. The District Court denied the motion, and the jury found respondent guilty on the kidnaping counts and on the § 924(c)(1) charge as well. He was sentenced to 87 months' imprisonment on the kidnaping charges, and was given a mandatory consecutive term of 60 months' imprisonment for committing the § 924(c)(1) offense.

On a 2–to–1 vote, the Court of Appeals for the Third Circuit reversed respondent's § 924(c)(1) conviction. A majority of the Third Circuit panel applied what it called the "verb test" to § 924(c)(1), and determined that a violation of the statute is committed only in the district where a defendant "uses" or "carries" a firearm. Id., at 849. Accordingly, it concluded that venue for the § 924(c)(1) count was improper in New Jersey even though venue was proper there for the kidnaping of Avendano. * * *

As we confirmed just last Term, the " 'locus delicti [of the charged offense] must be determined from the nature of the crime alleged and the location of the act or acts constituting it.' " *United States v. Cabrales* * * *. In performing this inquiry, a court must initially identify the conduct constituting the offense (the nature of the crime) and then discern the location of the commission of the criminal acts. * * * At the time respondent committed the offense and was tried, 18 U.S.C. § 924(c)(1) provided:

> "Whoever, during and in relation to any crime of violence ... for which he may be prosecuted in a court of the United States, uses or carries a firearm, shall, in addition to the punishment provided for such crime of violence ... be sentenced to imprisonment for five years...."

The Third Circuit, as explained above, looked to the verbs of the statute to determine the nature of the substantive offense. But we have never before held, and decline to do so here, that verbs are the sole consideration in identifying the conduct that constitutes an offense. While the "verb test" certainly has value as an interpretative tool, it cannot be applied rigidly, to the exclusion of other relevant statutory language. The test unduly limits the inquiry into the nature of the offense and thereby creates a danger that certain conduct prohibited by statute will be missed.

In our view, the Third Circuit overlooked an essential conduct element of the § 924(c)(1) offense. Section 924(c)(1) prohibits using or carrying a firearm "during and in relation to any crime of violence ... for which [a defendant] may be prosecuted in a court of the United States." That the crime of violence element of the statute is embedded in a prepositional phrase and not expressed in verbs does not dissuade us from concluding that a defendant's violent acts are essential conduct elements. To prove the charged § 924(c)(1) violation in this case, the Government was required to show that respondent used a firearm, that he committed all the acts necessary to be subject to punishment for kidnaping (a crime of violence) in a court of the United States, and that he used the gun "during and in relation to" the kidnaping of Avendano. In sum, we interpret § 924(c)(1) to contain two distinct conduct elements—as is relevant to this case, the "using and carrying" of a gun and the commission of a kidnaping.

Respondent, however, argues that for venue purposes "the New Jersey kidnapping is completely irrelevant to the firearm crime, because respondent did not use or carry a gun during the New Jersey crime." In the words of one amicus, § 924(c)(1) is a "point-in-time" offense that only is committed in the place where the kidnaping and the use of a gun coincide. Brief for National Association of Criminal Defense Lawyers as Amicus Curiae 11. We disagree. Several Circuits have determined that kidnaping, as defined by 18 U.S.C. § 1201 (1994 ed. and Supp. III), is a unitary crime, and we agree with their conclusion. A kidnaping, once begun, does not end until the victim is free. It does not make sense, then, to speak of it in discrete geographic fragments. Section 924(c)(1) criminalized a defendant's use of a firearm "during and in relation to" a crime of violence; in doing so, Congress proscribed both the use of the firearm and the commission of acts that constitute a violent crime. It does not matter that respondent used the .357 magnum revolver, as the Government concedes, only in Maryland because he did so "during and in relation to" a kidnaping that was begun in Texas and continued in New York, New Jersey, and Maryland. In our view, § 924(c)(1) does not define a "point-in-time" offense when a firearm is used during and in relation to a continuing crime of violence. * * *

Justice SCALIA, with whom Justice STEVENS joins, dissenting.

* * * [Section 924(c)] prohibits the act of using or carrying a firearm "during" (and in relation to) a predicate offense. The provisions of the United States Code defining the particular predicate offenses already punish all of the defendant's alleged criminal conduct except his use or carriage of a gun; § 924(c)(1) itself criminalizes and punishes such use or carriage "during" the predicate crime, because that makes the crime more dangerous. This is a simple concept, and it is embodied in a straightforward text. To answer the question before us we need only ask where the defendant's alleged act of using a firearm during (and in relation to) a kidnaping occurred. Since it occurred only in Maryland, venue will lie only there. * * *

[T]he crime before us does not consist of "distinct" parts that can occur in different localities. Its two parts are bound inseparably together by the word "during." Where the gun is being used, the predicate act must be occurring as well, and vice versa. The Court quite simply reads this requirement out of the statute—as though there were no difference between a statute making it a crime to steal a cookie and eat it (which could be prosecuted either in New Jersey, where the cookie was stolen, or in Maryland, where it was eaten) and a statute making it a crime to eat a cookie while robbing a bakery (which could be prosecuted only where the ingestive theft occurred). * * * To disallow the New Jersey prosecution here, the Court suggests, is to convert § 924(c)(1) from a continuing offense to a "point-in-time" offense. That is simply not so. I in no way contend that the kidnaping, or, for that matter, the use of the gun, can occur only at one point in time. Each can extend over a protracted period, and in many places. But § 924(c)(1) is violated only so long as, and where, both continuing acts are being committed simultaneously. That is what the word "during" means. Thus, if the defendant here had used or carried the gun throughout the kidnaping, in Texas, New Jersey, New York, and Maryland, he could have been prosecuted in any of those States. As it was, however, he used a gun during a kidnaping only in Maryland.

The short of the matter is that this defendant, who has a constitutional right to be tried in the State and district where his alleged crime was "committed," U.S. Const., Art. III, § 2, cl. 3; Amdt. 6, has been prosecuted for using a gun during a kidnaping in a State and district where all agree he did not use a gun during a kidnaping. If to state this case is not to decide it, the law has departed further from the meaning of language than is appropriate for a government that is supposed to rule (and to be restrained) through the written word.

Chapter 18

THE SCOPE OF THE PROSECUTION: JOINDER AND SEVERANCE OF OFFENSES AND DEFENDANTS

SECTION 3. JOINDER AND SEVERANCE OF DEFENDANTS

9th ed., p. 1094; end of fn. a, add:

Nelson must be distinguished from *Lilly v. Virginia,* 527 U.S. 116, 119 S.Ct. 1887, 144 L.Ed.2d 117 (1999), where petitioner's accomplice in a 2–day crime spree, *not* joined for trial with petitioner, was called by the prosecution as a witness and invoked his privilege against self-incrimination, after which the court admitted his confession to police, blaming petitioner for the homicide occurring during the spree, as a declaration of an unavailable witness against penal interest. While the state court affirmed defendant's confession on the ground that the accomplice's confession fell within an exception to the hearsay rule, the Supreme Court, although divided as to the breadth of the applicable rule, concluded that "admission of the untested confession" in such circumstances "violated petitioner's Confrontation Clause rights."

Part Four

THE ADVERSARY SYSTEM AND THE DETERMINATION OF GUILT OR INNOCENCE

Chapter 20

THE ASSISTANCE OF COUNSEL

SECTION 1. WAIVER OF THE RIGHT TO COUNSEL; THE RIGHT TO PROCEED *PRO SE*

9th ed., p. 1130; after Note 2, add new Note:

2a. *Does the principle of self-representation apply to appeals as well?* In MARTINEZ v. COURT OF APPEAL OF CALIFORNIA, ___ U.S. ___, 120 S.Ct. 684, 145 L.Ed. 2d 597 (2000), defendant (who described himself as a self-taught paralegal with 25 years experience) was convicted of embezzlement after representing himself at trial. He sought to represent himself on appeal as well, but was rebuffed by the state appellate courts. The U.S. Supreme Court, per STEVENS, J., affirmed, holding without a dissent, that "neither the holding nor the reasoning in *Faretta* requires [a state] to recognize a constitutional right to self-representation on direct appeal from a criminal conviction":

"The *Farretta* majority based its conclusion on three inter-related arguments. First it examined historical evidence identifying a right of self-representation that had been protected by federal and state law since the beginning of our Nation. Second, it interpreted the structure of the Sixth Amendment, in the light of its English and colonial background. Third, it concluded that even though it 'is undeniable that in most criminal prosecutions defendants could better defend with counsel's guidance than by their own unskilled efforts,' a knowing and intelligent waiver 'must be honored out of "that respect for the individual which is the lifeblood of the law." '

Some of the Court's reasoning is applicable to appellate proceedings as well as to trials. There are, however, significant distinctions.

"The historical evidence relied upon by *Faretta* as identifying a right of self-representation is not always useful because it pertained to times when lawyers were scarce, often mistrusted, and not readily available to the average person accused of crime. For one who could not obtain a lawyer, self-representation was the only feasible alternative to asserting no defense at all. * * *

"It has since been recognized, however, that an indigent defendant in a criminal trial has a constitutional right to the assistance of appointed counsel. Thus, an individual's decision to represent himself is no longer compelled by the necessity of choosing self-representation over incompetent or nonexistent representation. * * * Therefore, while *Faretta* is correct in concluding that there is abundant support for the proposition that a right to self-representation has been recognized for centuries, the original reasons for protecting that right do not have the same force when the availability of competent counsel for every indigent defendant has displaced the need—although not always the desire—for self-representation. * * *

"We are not aware of any historical consensus establishing a right of self-representation on appeal. * * * Historical silence * * * has no probative force in the appellate context because there simply was no long-respected right of self-representation on appeal. In fact, the right of appeal itself is of relatively recent origin.

"Appeals as of right in federal courts were nonexistent for the first century of our Nation, and appellate review of any sort was 'rarely allowed.' [Thus,] unlike the inquiry in *Faretta*, the historical evidence does not provide any support for an affirmative constitutional right to appellate self-representation.

"The *Faretta* majority's reliance on the structure of the Sixth Amendment is also not relevant. The Sixth Amendment identifies the basic rights that the accused shall enjoy in 'all criminal prosecutions.' They are presented strictly as rights that are available in preparation for trial and at the trial itself. The Sixth Amendment does not include any right to appeal. [It] necessarily follows that the Amendment itself does not provide any basis for finding a right to self-representation on appeal. * * *

"Finally, the *Faretta* majority found that the right to self-representation at trial was grounded in part in a respect for individual autonomy. * * * In light of our conclusion that the Sixth Amendment does not apply to appellate proceedings, any individual right to self-representation on appeal based on autonomy principles must be grounded in the Due Process Clause. Under the practices that prevail in the Nation today, however, we are entirely unpersuaded that the risk of either disloyalty or suspicion of disloyalty is a sufficient concern to conclude that a constitutional right of self-representation is a necessary component of a fair appellate proceeding. * * *

"No one, including Martinez and the *Faretta* majority, attempts to argue that as a rule *pro se* representation is wise, desirable or efficient.[9] * * * Our

9. Some critics argue that the right to proceed *pro se* at trial in certain cases is akin to allowing the defendant to waive his right to a fair trial. * * *

experience has taught us that a 'pro se defense is usually a bad defense, particularly when compared to a defense provided by an experienced criminal defense attorney.'[10]

"As the *Faretta* opinion recognized, the right to self-representation is not absolute. [Even] at the trial level, therefore, the government's interest in ensuring the integrity and efficiency of the trial at times outweighs the defendant's interest in acting as his own lawyer.

"In the appellate context, the balance between the two competing interests surely tips in favor of the State. The status of the accused defendant, who retains a presumption of innocence throughout the trial process, changes dramatically when a jury returns a guilty verdict.

"[The] requirement of representation by trained counsel implies no disrespect for the individual inasmuch as it tends to benefit the appellant as well as the court. * * * Considering the change in position from defendant to appellant, the autonomy interests that survive a felony conviction are less compelling than those motivating the decision in *Faretta*. Yet the overriding state interest in the fair and efficient administration of justice remains as strong as at the trial level. Thus, the States are clearly within their discretion to conclude that the government's interests outweigh an invasion of the appellant's interest in self-representation.

" * * * Our holding * * * does not preclude the States from recognizing such a right under their own constitutions. Its impact on the law will be minimal, because a lay appellant's rights to participate in appellate proceedings have long been limited by the well-established conclusions that he has no right to be present during appellate proceedings. Meanwhile the rules governing appeals in California, and presumably those in other States as well, seem to protect the ability of indigent litigants to make *pro se* fillings. [In] requiring Martinez, under these circumstances, to accept against his will a state-appointed attorney, the California courts have not deprived him of a constitutional right."

Justice SCALIA concurred in the judgment, "not shar[ing] the apparent skepticism of today's opinion" regarding *Faretta*:

"I have no doubt that the Framers of our Constitution, who were suspicious enough of governmental power—including judicial power—that they insisted upon a citizen's right to be judged by an independent jury of private citizens, would not have found acceptable the compulsory assignment of counsel *by the Government* to plead a criminal defendant's case. * * * Our system of laws generally presumes that the criminal defendant, after being fully informed, knows his own best interests and does not need them dictated by the State. Any other approach is unworthy of a free people."

"Because Justice Scalia writes separately to underscore the continuing constitutional validity of *Faretta*," Justice BREYER, who joined the Court's

10. John F. Decker, The Sixth Amendment Right to Shoot Oneself in the Foot: An Assessment of the Guarantee of Self-Representation Twenty Years after *Faretta*, 6 Seton Hall Const. L. J. 483, 598 (1996).

opinion, wrote separately to "note that judges closer to the firing line have sometimes expressed dismay about the practical consequences" of *Faretta*. However, "without some strong factual basis for believing that *Faretta*'s holding has proved counterproductive in practice, we are not in a position to reconsider the constitutional assumptions that underlie that case."[a]

SECTION 3. THE RIGHT TO "EFFECTIVE" ASSISTANCE OF COUNSEL

9th ed., p. 1165; after Note 3, add new Note:

3a. *What constitutes representation that falls below an objective standard of reasonableness? (Terry) Williams v. Taylor* (set forth at Supp., p. 127) provides a recent example of counsel's performance that "fell short of professional standards." Williams' lawyers had, *inter alia*, failed: (a) to prepare for the death sentencing phrase of the proceeding until a week before the trial; (b) "to conduct an investigation that would have uncovered extensive records graphically describing Williams' nighmarish childhood, not because of any strategic calculation but because they incorrectly thought the state law barred access to such records"; (c) "to introduce available evidence that Williams was 'borderline mentally retarded' and did not advance beyond sixth grade in school"; and (d) "to seek prison records recording Williams' commendations for helping to crack a prison drug ring." Moreover, "the failure to introduce the comparatively voluminous amount of evidence [in] Williams' favor was not justified by a tactical decision to focus on Williams' voluntary confession."

9th ed., p. 1166; add to Note 6:

A study of the death penalty conducted by a team of lawyers and criminologists at Columbia University led by law professor James Liebman and released on June 12, 2000, *A Broken System: Error Rates in Capital Cases, 1973–1995*, revealed the following:

Of 5,760 death sentences imposed in the United States between 1973 and 1995, some 4, 578 (79%) were finally reviewed on "direct appeal" by a state court. Of these, 41% "were thrown out because of 'serious error,' *i.e.*, error that the reviewing court concluded has seriously undermined the reliability of the outcome or otherwise 'harmed' the defendant."

Nearly all of the remaining death sentences were then examined by state post-conviction courts. Of the death sentences that survived state direct and post-conviction review, 599 were finally reviewed in a first federal habeas corpus petition. Of these, 40% were overturned "due to serious error."

The "overall error-rate" for the entire 1973–1995 period, *i.e.*, the proportion of fully reviewed capital judgments overturned at one of the three stages due to serious error, was 68%.

a. Justice Kennedy, who joined the opinion of the Court, also wrote separately to observe that "[t]o resolve this case it is unnecessary to cast doubt upon the rationale of *Faretta*."

The most common error was "egregiously incompetent defense lawyering (accounting for 37% of the state post-conviction reversals)."

On retrial, when the errors are cured, "an astonishing 82% (247 out of 301) of the capital judgments that were reversed were replaced on retrial with a sentence *less* than death, or *no* sentence at all. In the latter regard, 7% (22/301) of the reversals for serious error resulted in a determination on retrial that the defendant was *not guilty* of the capital offense."

9th ed. p. 1170; end of Note 10:

In *(Terry) Williams v. Florida* (set forth in Supp. at p. 127), the Court rejected the view that *Lockhart v. Fretwell* "modified or in some way supplanted the rule set down in *Strickland*."

9th ed., p. 1170; after Note 10, add new Note:

11. *When does the right to counsel "attach" for purposes of ineffective counsel claims?* Consider UNITED STATES v. MOODY, 206 F.3d 609 (6th Cir. 2000), which arose as follows:

Moody participated in a conspiracy to deal cocaine. After the FBI executed 25 search warrants on targets of its investigation into this conspiracy, including Moody's home and business, Moody offered to cooperate, and did cooperate, with FBI agents in their continuing investigation of the conspiracy. During six meetings with the FBI, Moody, without the assistance of counsel, provided the agents with information about the role of others in the conspiracy and made a number of incriminating statements.

During these meetings, government attorneys offered Moody a deal—a maximum of five years imprisonment if he pled guilty and continued to cooperate. When Moody expressed a reservation about this, an Assistant U.S. Attorney suggested that he seek the advice of a lawyer. Moody did, but—without inquiring into the substance of Moody's interviews with the FBI or the nature of his admissions at these interviews—the attorney rejected the government's offer on Moody's behalf.

Moody was then indicted for conspiracy to distribute cocaine. His lawyer advised him to plead guilty because he could not overcome the incriminating statements he had made during his pre-indictment meetings with the authorities. Moody did plead guilty. Given the increased drug quantity now attributable to the conspiracy, the Sentencing Guidelines for his conviction were from 235–293 months of imprisonment. The district court granted the government's motion for downward departure and imposed a sentence of 120 months imprisonment. Moody filed a motion to vacate or correct his sentence, contending that he had been denied the effective assistance of counsel. The district court agreed, concluding that the plea negotiations, although pre-indictment, "were a 'critical stage' of the proceedings against him." The appropriate remedy, held the district court, was to resentence Moody in accordance with the original plea agreement.

On appeal, the government did not challenge the district court's finding that Moody had been denied the effective assistance of counsel. But it maintained that the Sixth Amendment right to counsel had not "attached" during Moody's pre-indictment negotiations with the government. The Sixth Circuit, per CLAY, J., reluctantly agreed:

"In *Kirby v. Illinois* [9th ed., p. 656], a plurality of the Supreme Court recognized that 'a person's Sixth and Fourteenth Amendment right to counsel attaches only at or after the time that adversary judicial proceedings have been initiated against him.' In *United States v. Gouveia* [9th ed., p. 76], the Court reaffirmed this bright line test, holding that 'the right to counsel does not attach until the initiation of adversary judicial proceedings' such as 'formal charge, preliminary hearing, indictment, information, or arraignment.' " The Court continued, '[i]t is only at that time that the government has committed itself to prosecute, and only then that the adverse positions of the government and defendant have solidified.' " * * *

"But for the delay of the prosecution in filing charges, Moody clearly would have been entitled to the effective assistance of counsel. Under the Supreme Court's and our Circuit's approach, he is not—even though the point at which the actions of Moody's counsel fell below an objective standard of reasonableness was no less a 'critical stage' of the proceedings against him. * * *

"We do not favor this bright line approach because it requires that we disregard the cold reality that faces a suspect in pre-indictment plea negotiations. There is no question in our minds that at formal plea negotiations, where a specific sentence is offered to an offender for a specific offense, the adverse positions of the government and the suspect have solidified. Indeed, it seems a triumph of the letter over the spirit of the law to hold that Moody had no right to counsel in his decision to accept or deny the offered plea bargain only because the government had not yet filed formal charges. We are faced with the ponderable realization that this is an occasion when justice must of necessity yield to the rule of law * * *."

Concurring Judge WISEMAN "emphasize[d] the pressures that the Federal Sentencing Guidelines have brought to bear on the criminal justice system and why such pressures make our rigid application of Supreme Court precedent a reluctant application." (See also the discussion in Supp. at p. 90) He maintained that defendants "need and should be entitled to counsel in order to navigate [the] troubled waters" of preindictment plea bargaining. He continued:

"The Sixth Amendment's underlying purpose is to protect defendants in critical stages of their prosecutions. Thus, the Sixth Amendment should guarantee the right to counsel during preindictment plea negotiations. Precedent, however, prevents me from endorsing this position which logic demands."

SECTION 5. THE ROLE OF APPOINTED COUNSEL

9th ed., p. 1201; delete Note 6 and add new Note:

6. *Is a state free to adopt other procedures than* Anders *for handling indigent criminal appeals?* Consider SMITH v. ROBBINS, ___ U.S. ___, 120 S.Ct. 746, 145 L.Ed.2d 756 (2000), which grew out of the following facts: Twelve years after *Anders*, in *People v. Wende*, 600 P.2d 1071 (Cal. 1979), California adopted a new procedure for dealing with potentially frivolous

appeals, under which, upon concluding that an appeal would be frivolous, counsel (a) "files a brief with the appellate court that summarizes the procedural and factual history of the case, with citations of the record"; (b) "attests that he has reviewed the record, explained the evaluation of the case to his client, provided the client with a copy of the brief and informed the client of his right to file a *pro se* supplemental brief"; and (c) "requests that the court independently examine the record for arguable issues." Upon receiving a "*Wende* brief," the appellate court must "conduct a review of the entire record." If, after doing so, the appellate court finds the appeal to be frivolous, it may affirm. However, if it finds an arguable issue (*i.e.*, nonfrivolous) issue, it orders briefing on that issue.

Respondent Robbins was convicted of second-degree murder and grand theft in a California court. Concluding that an appeal would be frivolous, Robbins's appointed counsel filed a brief with the state appellate court that complied with *Wende*, not *Anders*. Agreeing with counsel's assessment of the case, the state appellate court affirmed. Robbins sought federal habeas relief, claiming he had been denied effective assistance of appellate counsel because his lawyer's *Wende* brief had failed to comply with *Anders*. The federal district court granted relief, concluding there were at least two issues that, pursuant to *Anders*, counsel should have raised in his brief. The Ninth Circuit agreed with the district court on the *Anders* issue, viewing Anders, together with *Douglas v. California* [9th ed., p. 80], as "sett[ing] forth the exclusive procedure through which appointed counsel's performance can pass constitutional muster."

A 5–4 majority of the Supreme Court, per THOMAS, J., reversed. The *Anders* procedure, held the majority, "is merely one method of satisfying the requirements of the Constitution for indigent criminal appeals"; a state is free to adopt other procedures if these procedures "afford adequate and effective appellate review to indigent defendants" and a state's procedure provides such review "so long as it reasonably ensures [as does the *Wende* procedure] that an indigent's appeal will be resolved in a way that is related to the merit of that appeal":

"[T]he Ninth Circuit's view runs contrary to our established practice of permitting the States, within the broad bounds of the Constitution, to experiment with solutions to difficult questions of policy.

"In *McCoy*, we rejected a challenge to Wisconsin's variation on the *Anders* procedure. [That] procedure, by providing for one-sided briefing by counsel against his own client's best claims, probably made a court more likely to rule against the indigent than if the court had simply received an *Anders* brief.

"In *Pennsylvania v. Finley* [9th ed., p. 100], we explained that the *Anders* procedure is not 'an independent constitutional command,' but rather is just 'a prophylactic framework' that was established to vindicate the constitutional right to appellate counsel announced in *Douglas*. We did not say that our *Anders* procedure was the *only* prophylactic framework that could adequately vindicate this right; instead, by making clear that the Constitution itself does not compel the *Anders* procedure, we suggested otherwise.

"* * * [I]t is more in keeping with our status as a court, and particularly with our status as a court in a federal system, to avoid imposing a single solution on the States from the top down. We should, and do, evaluate state procedures one at a time, as they come before us, while leaving 'the more challenging task of crafting appropriate procedures [to] the laboratory of the States in the first instance.'

"* * * Accordingly, we hold that the *Anders* procedure is merely one method of satisfying the requirements of the Constitution for indigent criminal appeals. States may—and, we are confident, will—craft procedures that, in terms of policy, are superior to, or at least, as good as, that in *Anders*. The Constitution erects no barrier to their doing so.[7]

"* * * We think it clear that California's system does not violate the Fourteenth Amendment for it provides 'a criminal appellant pursuing a first appeal as of right [the] minimum safeguards necessary to make that appeal "adequate and effective,"' *Evitts v. Lacey* (quoting *Griffin v. Illinois* [9th ed., p. 78]).

"* * * We think the *Wende* procedure reasonably ensures that an indigent's appeal will be resolved in a way that is related to the merit of that appeal. Whatever the strengths or weaknesses as a matter of policy, we cannot say that it fails to afford indigents the adequate and effective appellate review that the Fourteenth Amendment requires. * * * Thus, there was no constitutional violation in this case simply because the *Wende* procedure was used.

"* * * [O]ur reversal does not necessarily mean that Robbins's claim that his appellate counsel rendered constitutionally ineffective assistance fails. For it may be, as Robbins argues, that his appeal was not frivolous and that he was thus entitled to a merits brief rather than to a *Wade* brief. * * *

"On remand, the proper standard for evaluating Robbins's claim that appellate counsel was ineffective in neglecting to file a merits brief is that enunciated in *Strickland*. * * * Respondent must first show that his counsel was objectively unreasonable in failing to find arguable issues to appeal—that is, that counsel unreasonably failed to discover nonfrivolous issues and to file a merits brief raising them. If Robbins succeeds in such a showing, he then has the burden of demonstrating prejudice. That is, he must show a reasonable probability that, but for his counsel's unreasonable failure to file a merits brief, he would have prevailed on his appeal.

"[The] applicability of *Strickland*'s actual-prejudice prong to Robbins's claim of ineffective counsel follows from *Penson v. Ohio*, 488 U.S. 75, 109 S. Ct. 346, 102 L. Ed. 2d 300 (1988), where we distinguished denial of counsel altogether on appeal, which warranted a presumption of prejudice, from mere ineffective assistance of counsel on appeal, which did not. * * * But where, as here, the defendant has received appellate counsel who has complied with a valid state procedure for determining whether the defendant's appeal is frivolous, and the State has not at any time left the

7. States have, in fact, already been doing this to some degree. See Martha C. Warner, *Anders* in the Fifty States: Some Appellants' Equal Protection is More Equal Than Others, 23 Fla. St. U. L. Rev. 625, 642–62 (1996).

defendant without counsel on appeal, there is no reason to assume that the defendant has been prejudiced."

Justice SOUTER, joined by Stevens, Ginsburg, and Breyer, JJ., dissented:

"A defendant's right to representation on appeal is limited by the prohibition against frivolous litigation, and I realize that when a lawyer's corresponding obligations are at odds with each other, there is no perfect place to draw the line between them. But because I believe the procedure adopted in *Wende* fails to assure representation by counsel with the adversarial character demanded by the Constitution, I respectfully dissent.

" * * * To guard against the possibility [that] counsel has not done the advocate's work of looking hard for potential issues, there must be some prod to find any reclusive merit in an ostensibly unpromising case and some process to assess the lawyer's efforts after the fact. A judicial process that renders constitutional error invisible is, after all, itself an affront to the Constitution.

"In *Anders*, we devised such a mechanism to ensure respect for an appellant's rights. A lawyer's request to withdraw on the ground that an appeal is frivolous 'must . . . be accompanied by a brief referring to anything in the record that might arguably support the appeal.' *Anders*. This simply means that counsel must do his partisan best, short of calling black white, to flag the points that come closest to being appealable; the lawyer's job is to state the issues that give the defendant his best chances to prevail, even if the best comes up short under the rule against trifling with the court. '[T]he court—not counsel—,' we continued, 'then proceeds, after a full examination of all the proceedings, to decide whether the case is wholly frivolous.'

"*Anders* thus contemplates two reviews of the record, each of a markedly different character. First comes review by the advocate, the defendant's interested representative. His job is to identify the best issues the partisan eye can spot. Then comes judicial review from a disinterested judge, who asks two questions: whether the lawyer really did function as a committed advocate, and whether he misjudged the legitimate appealability of any issue. In reviewing the advocate's work, the court is responsible for assuring that counsel has gone as far as advocacy will take him with the best issues undiscounted. We have repeatedly described the task of an appellate court in terms of this dual responsibility. * * *

"It is owing to the importance of assuring that an adversarial, not an inquisitorial, system is at work that I disagree with the Court's statement today that our cases approve of any state procedure that 'reasonably ensures that an indigent's appeal will be resolved in a way that is related to the merit of that appeal.' A purely inquisitorial system could satisfy that criterion, and so could one that appoints counsel only if the appellate court deems it useful. But we have rejected the former and have explicitly held the latter unconstitutional, see *Douglas*, the reason in each case being that the Constitution looks to the means as well as to the ends.[4] * * *

4. Of course, if appellate review is not constitutionally required, States may well be able to impose nonadversarial review on all appellants. They may not, however, reserve the adversary system for those able to afford counsel.

"We have not held the details of *Anders* to be exclusive, but it does make sense to read the case as exemplifying what substantial equality requires on behalf of indigent appellants entitled to an advocate's review and to reasonable certainty that arguable issues will be briefed on their merits. With *Anders* thus as a benchmark, California's *Wende* procedure fails to measure up. Its primary failing is in permitting counsel to refrain as a matter of course from mentioning possibly arguable issues in a no-merit brief; its second deficiency is a correlative of the first, in obliging an appellate court to search the record for arguable issues without benefit of an issue-spotting, no-merit brief to review.

"* * * *Anders* requires counsel to flag the best issues for the sake of keeping counsel on his toes and giving focus to judicial review of his judgment. *Wende* on the other hand requires no indication of conceivable issues and hence nothing specifically reviewable by a court bound to preserve the system's adversary character. *Wende* does no more to protect the indigent's right to advocacy than the no-merit letter condemned in *Anders*.

"On like reasoning, *Wende* is deficient in relying on a judge's nonpartisan review to assure that a defendant suffers no prejudice at the hands of a lawyer who has failed to document his best effort at partisan review. Exactly because our system assumes that a lawyer committed to a client is the most dependable guardian of the client's interest, we have consistently rejected procedures leaving the determination of frivolousness to the court in the first instance, see *Douglas*, or to the court following a conclusory declaration by counsel, see *Penson*. The defect in these procedures is their entire reliance on review by a detached magistrate who does not apply the partisan scrutiny in the first instance that defendants with paid lawyers get as a matter of course.

"It goes without saying, too, that *Wende*'s reliance on judges to start from scratch in seeking arguable issues adds substantially to the burden on the judicial shoulders. While I have no need to decide whether this drawback of the *Wende* scheme is of constitutional significance, it raises questions that certainly underscore the constitutional failing of relying on judicial scrutiny uninformed by counsel's partisan analysis. In an *amicus* brief filed in this case, 13 retired Justices of the Supreme Court or Courts of Appeal of California have pointed out the 'risk that the review of the cold record [under the *Wende* scheme] will be more perfunctory without the issue-spotting guidance, and associated record citations, of counsel.' The *amici* have candidly represented that '[w]hen a California appellate court receives a *Wende* brief, it assigns the case to a staff attorney who prepares a memorandum analyzing all possible legal issues in the case. Typically, the staff attorney then makes an oral presentation to the appellate panel....' When the responsibility of counsel is thrown onto the court, the court gives way to a staff attorney; it could not be clearer that *Wende* is seriously at odds with the respective obligations of counsel and the courts as contemplated by the Constitution.

"[The] assumption behind *Strickland*'s prejudice requirement is that the defendant had a lawyer who was representing him as his advocate at least at some level, whereas that premise cannot be assumed when a defendant receives the benefit of nothing more than a *Wende* brief. In a

Wende situation, nominal counsel is functioning merely as a friend of the court, helping the judge to grasp the structure of the record but not even purporting to highlight the record's nearest approach to supporting his client's hope to appeal. Counsel under *Wende* is doing less than the judge's law clerk (or staff attorney) might do, and he is doing nothing at all in the way of advocacy. When a lawyer abandons the role of advocate and adopts that of *amicus curiae*, he is no longer functioning as counsel or rendering assistance within the meaning of the Sixth Amendment. Since the apparently missing ingredient of the advocate's analysis goes to the very essence of the right to counsel, a lawyer who does nothing more than file a *Wende* brief is closer to being no counsel at all than to being subpar counsel under *Strickland*.

"This, I think, is the answer to any suggestion that a specific assessment of prejudice need be shown in order to get relief from *Wende*. A complete absence of counsel is a reversible violation of the constitutional right to representation, even when there is no question that at the end of the day the smartest lawyer in the world would have watched his client being led off to prison. We do not ask how the defendant would have fared if he had been given counsel, and we should not look to what sort of appeal might have ensued if an appellant's lawyer had flagged the points that came closest to appealable issues. Such a result is equally consistent with our cases holding a violation of due process to be complete when a defendant is denied a right to the appeal he is otherwise entitled to pursue.

"[The] *Wende* procedure does not assure even the most minimal assistance of counsel in an adversarial role. The Constitution demands such assurances, and I would hold Robbins entitled to an appeal that provides them."[a]

a. While he joined Justice Souter's dissent "without qualification," Stevens, J., joined by Ginsburg, J., also wrote a separate dissent.

Chapter 21
DISCOVERY AND DISCLOSURE

SECTION 5. THE PROSECUTION'S CONSTITUTIONAL DUTY TO DISCLOSE

9th ed., p. 1273; at the end of Note 3, add:

In STRICKLER v. GREENE, 527 U.S. 263, 119 S.Ct. 1936, 144 L.Ed.2d 286 (1999), the Court majority held that undisclosed impeaching eyewitness testimony as to circumstances of the abduction of the victim were favorable to the petitioner for the purposes of *Brady* (in contrast to the terrifying incident that the witness described in her testimony, her undisclosed original perception of the event was of "a trivial episode of college kids carrying on"), but the habeas petitioner could not show materiality under *Brady*. Speaking to the lack of materiality, SOUTER, J. (Joined by Kennedy, J.), dissenting in part, offered the following general comments on the materiality standard:

"Before I get to the analysis of prejudice I should say something about the standard for identifying it, and about the unfortunate phrasing of the shorthand version in which the standard is customarily couched. The Court speaks in terms of the familiar, and perhaps familiarly deceptive, formulation: whether there is a 'reasonable probability' of a different outcome if the evidence withheld had been disclosed. The Court rightly cautions that the standard intended by these words does not require defendants to show that a different outcome would have been more likely than not with the suppressed evidence, let alone that without the materials withheld the evidence would have been insufficient to support the result reached. * * * Instead, the Court restates the question (as I have done elsewhere) as whether ' "the favorable evidence could reasonably be taken to put the whole case in such a different light as to undermine confidence" ' in the outcome. See *Kyles v. Whitley*.

"Despite our repeated explanation of the shorthand formulation in these words, the continued use of the term 'probability' raises an unjustifiable risk of misleading courts into treating it as akin to the more demanding standard, 'more likely than not.' While any short phrases for what the cases are getting at will be 'inevitably imprecise,' *United States v. Agurs*, I think 'significant possibility' would do better at capturing the degree to which the undisclosed evidence would place the actual result in question, sufficient to warrant overturning a conviction or sentence. To see that this is so, we need to recall *Brady*'s evolution since the appearance of the rule as originally stated, that 'suppression by the prosecution of evidence favorable to an accused upon request violates due process where the evidence is material either to guilt or to punishment, irrespective of the good faith or bad faith of the prosecution.' *Brady v. Maryland*. *Brady* itself did not explain what it meant by 'material' (perhaps assuming the term would be given its usual meaning in the law of evidence, see *United States v. Bagley* (Marshall, J., dissenting)). We first essayed a partial definition in *United States v. Agurs*, supra, where we identified three situations arguably within the ambit of *Brady* and said that in the first, involving knowing use of perjured testimony, reversal was required if there was 'any reasonable likelihood' that the false testimony had affected the verdict. * * * We have treated 'reasonable likelihood' as synonymous with 'reasonable possibility' and thus have equated materiality in the perjured-testimony cases with a showing that suppression of the evidence was not harmless beyond a reasonable doubt. *Bagley*. * * * In *Agurs*, we thought a less demanding standard appropriate when the prosecution fails to turn over materials in the absence of a specific request. Although we refrained from attaching a label to that standard, we explained it as falling between the more-likely-than-not level and yet another criterion, whether the reviewing court's ' "conviction [was] sure that the error did not influence the jury, or had but very slight effect." ' *Kotteakos v. United States* [9th ed., p. 1492]. Finally, in *United States v. Bagley*, we embraced 'reasonable probability' as the appropriate standard to judge the materiality of information withheld by the prosecution whether or not the defense had asked first. *Bagley* took that phrase from *Strickland v. Washington*, where it had been used for the level of prejudice needed to make out a claim of constitutionally ineffective assistance of counsel. *Strickland* in turn cited two cases for its formulation, *Agurs* (which did not contain the expression 'reasonable probability') and *United States v. Valenzuela–Bernal* [9th ed., p. 1442] * * * (which held that sanctions against the Government for deportation of a potential defense witness were appropriate only if there was a 'reasonable likelihood' that the lost testimony 'could have affected the judgment of the trier of fact').

"The circuitous path by which the Court came to adopt 'reasonable probability' of a different result as the rule of *Brady* materiality suggests several things. First, while 'reasonable possibility' or 'reasonable likelihood,' the *Kotteakos* standard, and 'reasonable probability' express distinct levels of confidence concerning the hypothetical effects of errors on decisionmakers' reasoning, the differences among the standards are slight. Second, the gap between all three of those formulations and 'more likely than not' is greater than any differences among them. Third, because of that larger gap, it is misleading in *Brady* cases to use the term 'probability,' which is naturally read as the cognate of 'probably' and thus confused with 'more likely than not.' * * * We would be better off speaking of a 'significant possibility' of a different result to characterize the *Brady* materiality standard. Even then, given the soft edges of all these phrases, the touchstone of the enquiry must remain whether the evidentiary suppression 'undermines our confidence' that the factfinder would have reached the same result."

Chapter 22

COERCED, INDUCED AND NEGOTIATED GUILTY PLEAS; PROFESSIONAL RESPONSIBILITY

SECTION 1. SOME VIEWS ON NEGOTIATED PLEAS

9th ed., p. 1276; end of Note 5, add:

Compare *United States v. Rodriguez,* 162 F.3d 135 (1st Cir.1998), where the government indicted six defendants for engaging in the same conspiracy to distribute cocaine. Three of them pled guilty pursuant to a plea agreement that they would be held accountable only for the drugs each had personally handled, while the defendants who went to trial were convicted and held accountable for the entire 5,000 grams of cocaine distributed by the conspiracy. Thus, under the Sentencing Guidelines the guilty plea defendants received sentences of time served, 17 months and 60 months, respectively, while the other three defendants received sentences of 235 months, 260 months, and life imprisonment (the latter attributable to an additional charge of engaging in a continuing criminal enterprise). The defendants who received the 235 and 260 month sentences argued they were entitled to be resentenced because "this vast disparity on sentencing—a difference of more than 21 years * * *—* * * discriminates against those who exercise their right to a jury trial," but to no avail. The court acknowledged that this was an "enormous sentencing disparity," one that "would strike many as unfair," but then concluded that what had been done was "within the government's discretion" and "not in and of itself * * * an unconstitutional burden on one's right to go to trial."

SECTION 2. REJECTED, KEPT AND BROKEN BARGAINS; UNREALIZED EXPECTATIONS

9th ed., p. 1296; end of Note 3, add:

In a few jurisdictions the law forbids the prosecutor from engaging in plea bargaining under some circumstance and/or with respect to some offenses. If the prosecutor does so nonetheless and the defendant is thereafter convicted on his bargained guilty plea, may the defendant later challenge his conviction because of such illegality? The courts have been inclined to answer in the negative, sometimes on the ground that the defendant lacks standing to raise such an objection because the prohibition was not intended for the defendant's benefit, *People v. Webb*, 230 Cal.Rptr. 755 (Cal.App.1986), and sometimes on the notion that the defendant, having entered into the plea agreement and accepted its attendant benefits, is estopped from challenging the lawfulness of that agreement, *Woods v. State*, 958 P.2d 91 (Nev.1998).

9th ed., p. 1315; before Notes and Questions, add:

However, upon rehearing en banc, 172 F.3d 1153 (9th Cir.1999). that decision was reversed. The court, looking first at the district court's reasoning, concluded:

"Although Barron did not seek a new trial, the district court chose that option on the ground that Barron's plea agreement had forfeited an appeal on the basis of 'a favorable intervening change in the law,' so that the only way Barron's motion could be granted was by construing it as an attack on the plea agreement. In this analysis the district court was mistaken for three reasons. First, Barron was not appealing. Second, *Bailey* was not 'a favorable intervening change in the law'; it was a determination that at no time had the law forbidden use of a gun in the sense Barron had used a gun. Third, granting a new trial was not necessary to granting his motion. To grant his motion, the district court did not need to construct an argument against the plea agreement. The district court needed only to resentence.

"Barron's motion purely and simply asked the district court to vacate a conviction that was void as a matter of law. The motion did not attack the plea agreement in any way."

As for the panel's "package" concept, the court concluded that "the argument that plea bargains must be treated as a package logically applies only in cases in which a petitioner challenges the entire plea as unknowing or involuntary." The court added that the "drafter of the plea agreement could have anticipated the contingency that has arisen and included a provision protecting the government's interest in the event that Barron's conviction was vacated." Because the government had not done so, the appellate court concluded, the district court may only "vacate the judgment and resentence Barron on the two counts of conviction that still stand."

SECTION 3. PROFESSIONAL RESPONSIBILITY; ROLE OF PROSECUTOR AND DEFENSE COUNSEL

9th ed., p. 1318; after Note 3, add:

4. Reconsider *Moody*, Note 11 at Supp., p. 80, holding the Sixth Amendment right to counsel inapplicable at pre-indictment plea bargaining,

and Note 18, 9th ed., p. 1286, regarding such bargaining under the federal Sentencing Guidelines, which prompted Judge Wiseman, concurring in *Moody*, to observe:

"Under the Guidelines, both defendants and prosecutors benefit from engaging in such bargaining. Preindictment plea bargaining over charges and facts provides Assistant United States Attorneys ('AUSAs') enormous discretion because such bargaining is much less susceptible to review by supervisors or courts. Through such bargaining, AUSAs can more effectively determine the potential sentence for a defendant. By agreeing on the charges to be filed against the defendant, the prosecutors avoid having to draw both the court's and the probation officer's attention to facts relevant to other (potential) charges not pleaded to which might require higher sentencing levels under real offense sentencing. Defendants also favor preindictment plea negotiations for basically the same reasons—greater control over the eventual sentence .. For example, plea bargains (pre and postindictment) can stipulate both the quantity of a controlled substance for which the defendant will be held accountable and the 'relevant conduct' that the court may consider during sentencing. Both of these factors can play a major role in determining the eventual sentence of a defendant who, like Mr. Moody, is charged with conspiracy to distribute illegal drugs.

"The incentives to bargain over charges and facts only add to the already abundant pressure to bargain with prosecutors as soon as possible in drug conspiracy cases. In practical terms, drug conspiracy cases have become a race to the courthouse. When a conspiracy is exposed by an arrest or execution of search warrants, soon-to-be defendants know that the first one to 'belly up' and tell what he knows receives the best deal. The pressure is to bargain and bargain early, even if an indictment has not been filed.

"To the extent that preindictment plea bargaining undermines the intent of Congress as expressed in the Guidelines, it is not to be condoned. Regardless of its virtue, such bargaining does occur and will likely continue due to its advantages for both prosecutors and defendants. While preindictment plea bargaining continues, it remains a perilous encounter for defendants. Defendants, or—more formally—potential defendants, are faced with the loss of liberty and property. They are faced with a complicated procedural system and a more knowledgeable adversary. In short, these defendants need and should be entitled to counsel in order to navigate these troubled waters."

9th ed., p. 1327; following Note 5, add:

6. "Recently, a new dilemma has vexed some federal public defenders. To illustrate briefly, imagine that you are a federal public defender. You have a client charged with several bank robberies for which he faces a maximum of sixty years in prison. The Assistant U.S. Attorney has just offered your client a terrific plea agreement that would allow him to serve only eight years.

"The prosecutor insists that * * * she has given you every piece of 'material' evidence that reflects on your client's factual guilt or innocence. She has disclosed that several witnesses have identified your client as the bank robber, but nothing else. Your client wants to take the plea deal.

Lacking an effective defense, you want your client to sign the agreement as well.

"Looking over the agreement, you notice the following provision, which you have never seen before:

> The defendant understands that discovery may not have been completed in this case, and that there may be additional discovery to which he would have access if he elected to proceed to trial. The defendant agrees to waive his right to receive this additional discovery which may include, among other things, evidence tending to impeach the credibility of potential witnesses.

The prosecutor says that, as a result of this waiver, she has not examined the personnel files of key law enforcement witnesses in the case against your client. Nor has she disclosed to you any key witnesses' criminal and personal histories or any inconsistent statements that they may have made to prosecutors, all of which might impeach their credibility. You would receive this information if you went to trial. Then comes the tough choice: Do you urge your client to sign the plea agreement, taking the chance that significant impeaching evidence does not exist and that, if it did, it would not be crucial to developing your defense?" Note, 51 Stan.L.Rev. 567, 567–68 (1999). If the client does sign the agreement, should the courts "enforce" the waiver no matter what is later shown to be the nature of the information not disclosed?

SECTION 4. RECEIVING THE DEFENDANT'S PLEA; PLEA WITHDRAWAL

9th ed., p. 1338; before subsection D, add:

In *Mitchell v. United States*, 526 U.S. 314, 119 S.Ct. 1307, 143 L.Ed.2d 424 (1999). the Court later clarified that, at least in federal procedure, the waiver of rights which occurs upon entry of a guilty plea is a "waiver of a right to trial with its attendant privileges" and "not a waiver of the privileges which exist beyond the confines of the trial." That being the case, the Court in *Mitchell* concluded that the defendant's guilty plea did not amount to "a waiver of the privilege [against self-incrimination] at sentencing," which "would be a grave encroachment on the rights of defendants. * * * Were we to accept the Government's position, prosecutors could indict without specifying the quantity of drugs involved, obtain a guilty plea, and then put the defendant on the stand at sentencing to fill in the drug quantity. The result would be to enlist the defendant as an instrument in his or her own condemnation, undermining the long tradition and vital principle that criminal proceedings rely on accusations proved by the Government, not on inquisitions conducted to enhance its own prosecutorial power."

By recent amendment of Fed.R.Crim.P. 11(c), a federal judge must also inform the defendant "of the terms of any provision in a plea agreement waiving the right to appeal or to collaterally attack the sentence."

9th ed., p. 1338; following Note 1, add:

1a. In *Mitchell*, supra, the Court focused upon the self-incrimination aspects of inquiry of the defendant to establish the factual basis for a plea, and concluded: (a) because entry of a guilty plea is itself not a waiver of the privilege other than as an at-trial right lost by not standing trial, a defendant to whom a factual basis inquiry is made *could* decline to answer on Fifth Amendment grounds, but by doing so he "runs the risk the district court will find the factual basis inadequate"; (b) the guilty plea and statements made by the defendant in the plea colloquy, including the factual basis inquiry, "are later admissible against the defendant," for example, at sentencing; and (c) the fact the defendant has made incriminating statements at the factual basis inquiry does not itself constitute a waiver of the privilege at later proceedings such as sentencing. This is so, the Court explained, because that situation is unlike the case of a witness at a single proceeding (including a defendant at trial), who "may not testify voluntarily about a subject and then invoke the privilege against self-incrimination when questioned about the details," thereby "diminishing the integrity of the factual inquiry."

"There is no convincing reason why the narrow inquiry at the plea colloquy should entail such an extensive waiver of the privilege. Unlike the defendant taking the stand, * * * the defendant who pleads guilty puts nothing in dispute regarding the essentials of the offense. Rather, the defendant takes those matters out of dispute, often by making a joint statement with the prosecution or confirming the prosecution's version of the facts. Under these circumstances, there is little danger that the court will be misled by selective disclosure. In this respect a guilty plea is more like an offer to stipulate than a decision to take the stand. Here, petitioner's statement that she had done 'some of' the proffered conduct did not pose a threat to the integrity of factfinding proceedings, for the purpose of the District Court's inquiry was simply to ensure that petitioner understood the charges and that there was a factual basis for the Government's case."

Chapter 23
TRIAL BY JURY

SECTION 2. JURY SELECTION

9th ed., p. 1376; end of Note 8, add:

By recent amendment of Fed.R.Crim.P. 24(c), App. C, an alternate juror may replace a regular juror in a federal criminal trial even after the jury has retired to consider its verdict.

9th ed., p. 1378; at end of Note 4, add:

In *United States v. Martinez–Salazar*, 528 U.S. ___, 120 S.Ct. 774, 145 L.Ed.2d 792 (2000), where defendant exercised all of his peremptories but used one of them to excuse a juror the trial judge erroneously refused to excuse for cause, the defendant claimed he had consequently been denied the number of peremptory challenges he was entitled to have under Fed. R.Crim.P. 24(b), so that his conviction should be reversed. The Court declined to hold "that federal law, like the Oklahoma statute considered in *Ross*, should be read to require a defendant to use a peremptory challenge to strike a juror who should have been removed for cause, in order to preserve the claim that the for-cause ruling impaired the defendant's right to a fair trial," but did accept the "narrower contention" that Fed.R.Crim.P.24(b) "was not violated in this case" because it merely confers upon the defendant the choice "to stand on his objection to the erroneous denial of the challenge for cause or to use a peremptory challenge to effect an instantaneous cure of the error." (The Court in *Martinez-Salazar* went on to emphasize that the case before it was not one where "the trial court deliberately misapplied the law in order to force the defendant to use a peremptory challenge to correct the court's error," and that the trial court's ruling did not "result in the seating of any juror who should have been dismissed for cause.")

Chapter 24

"TRIAL BY NEWSPAPER"—AND TELEVISION

SECTION 3. CONDUCT OF THE TRIAL

B. THE BROADCASTING, PHOTOGRAPHING AND TELEVISING COURTROOM PROCEEDINGS

9th ed., p. 1409; following comments by Professor Pillsbury, add:

Consider, however, the complaint of PETER ARENELLA, *The Perils of TV Legal Punditry*, 1998 U.Chi.Legal F. 25, 39 (1998), that the constraints of television make the "aberrational high profile trial" the norm by which the public evaluates the legal system's legitimacy:

"For the most part, what is news to the media about our criminal justice system is what is out of the ordinary. It is not news that thousands of defendants plead guilty to serious felonies every day or that the acquittal rate for contested felonies is probably less than one percent nationally. Nor is the ordinary criminal trial newsworthy. By definition, the factors that make a case 'high-profile' are those unique and aberrational ingredients that distinguish it from the run-of-the-mill prosecution.

"Consider some of the elements that explain why a case elicits a strong visceral public reaction that transforms it into a high-profile trial at the local or national level: the notoriety of the defendant (John DeLorean, O.J. Simpson), the special vulnerability or status of the victims (the McMartins, Susan Smith, JonBenet Ramsey, Louise Woodward), the unusual or shocking nature of the crimes (Susan Smith, Lyle and Erik Menendez, Lorena Bobbitt, Jeffrey Dahmer, Ted Kaczynski, Timothy McVeigh and Terry Nichols), and the presence of 'hot button' social issues like child abuse, domestic violence, police brutality, and race relations.

"Television focuses on these high-profile cases because they provide compelling entertainment value while simultaneously rationalizing the viewing audience's curiosity because of the presence of some important social issue. While pundits may point out how exceptional each of these cases is, the point gets lost when television serves up high profile trials as its daily fare for coverage. Thus, the aberrational becomes the baseline by which the viewing public measures the system's legitimacy. This is a no-win situation for our criminal justice system because the same factors that make the case aberrational increase the probability that the case's outcome will not satisfy the majority's preferences. Very low acquittal rates are unlikely to mollify a public hungry for crime control that has O.J. Simpson and the Menendez brothers as its poster boys."

SECTION 4. PREVENTING PREJUDICIAL PUBLICITY

A. Restricting Public Statements

9th ed., p. 1420; after Note 4, add new Notes:

4a. *Does limiting defense attorneys' ability to make extrajudicial statements to the press promote the long-term interests of criminal defendants as a class?* Yes, maintains DAVID A. STRAUSS, *Why it's not Free Speech Versus Fair Trial*, 1998 U.Chi.Legal F. 109–10 (1998):

"A system in which it is thought that an important part of a defense lawyer's job is to be an out-of-court advocate is not a good system for criminal defendants. This is because out-of-court statements are very likely to involve a degree of personal vouching for the defendant by the defense lawyer. Many attorneys who would be willing, or even eager, to defend criminal suspects in court—who consider that to be an honorable aspect of their calling—will not be willing to make out-of-court statements that align their own reputations with their client's. They will represent criminal defendants only if it is understood that making such statements is not part of their job—that their responsibility is limited to being the defendant's advocate in the courtroom.

"So long as out-of-court advocacy is common, a lawyer who refuses to speak outside the courtroom will risk damaging her client's interests by appearing not to believe in the client fully. If out-of-court statements are allowed, an attorney's refusal to engage in an out-of-court public relations campaign may be taken to suggest a lack of enthusiasm for the client's case. Similarly, so long as out-of-court advocacy is considered a permissible and even desirable part of representing a criminal client, many defendants in high-profile cases will not want to hire an attorney who is unwilling to speak to the press—or who speaks carefully, in a way that shows that the attorney is not vouching for the defendant. This will not be true across the board * * *. But so long as talking to the press is a recognized and usual part of a criminal defense lawyer's job, many outstanding lawyers who are not criminal defense specialists may be unwilling to appear to lend their personal reputation and credibility (or that of members of that firm) to the client's cause."

4b. *"Substantial likelihood" vs. "reasonable likelihood."* The rule at issue in *Gentile* prohibited a lawyer from making extrajudicial statements to the press that she "knows or reasonably should know * * * will have a *substantial likelihood* of materially prejudicing an adjudicative proceeding."

(Emphasis added.) The local rule (Local Rule 57 of the U.S. District Court for the Eastern District of Virginia) at issue in *In re Morrissey*, 168 F.3d 134 (4th Cir. 1999) prohibited lawyers in criminal cases from disseminating information or opinion "if there is a *reasonable likelihood* that such dissemination would interfere with a fair trial or otherwise prejudice the due administration of justice." (Emphasis added). Is the "reasonable likelihood" standard less protective of freedom of speech then the "substantial likelihood" standard? Is the "reasonable likelihood" standard insufficiently narrowly tailored to withstand constitutional challenge? The Fourth Circuit, per Ervin J., answered both questions in the negative, rejecting the argument that *Gentile* had "silently overruled" *Hirschkop v. Snead*, 594 F.2d 356 (4th Cir. 1979), a case which had upheld a rule very similar to the rule at issue in *Morrissey*.

Chapter 25
THE CRIMINAL TRIAL

SECTION 3. THE DEFENDANT'S RIGHT TO REMAIN SILENT AND TO TESTIFY

9th ed., p. 1454; before Note 1, add:

0. In MITCHELL v. UNITED STATES, 526 U.S. 314, 119 S.Ct. 1307, 143 L.Ed.2d 424 (1999), also discussed at Supp. p. 78 and p. 103, the Court, 5–4, declined to adopt an exception to *Griffin* allowing the sentencing judge to draw an adverse inference from the defendant's silence at sentencing. In dissent, Justice SCALIA, joined by the Chief Justice and Justices O'Connor and Thomas, question the validity of *Griffin*, though not arguing for its reconsideration. (Justice Thomas, in a separate opinion, did suggest that "*Griffin* and its progeny * * * should be reexamined"). Justice Scalia noted:

"The majority muses that the no-adverse-inference rule has found 'wide acceptance in the legal culture' and has even become 'an essential feature of our legal tradition.' Although the latter assertion strikes me as hyperbolic, the former may be true—which is adequate reason not to overrule these cases, a course I in no way propose. It is not adequate reason, however, to extend these cases into areas where they do not yet apply, since neither logic nor history can be marshaled in defense of them. The illogic of the *Griffin* line is plain, for it runs exactly counter to normal evidentiary inferences: If I ask my son whether he saw a movie I had forbidden him to watch, and he remains silent, the import of his silence is clear. Indeed, we have on other occasions recognized the significance of silence, saying that ' "[f]ailure to contest an assertion ... is considered evidence of acquiescence ... if it would have been natural under the circumstances to object to the assertion in question." ' *Baxter v. Palmigiano* [inference allowed in state prison disciplinary proceeding].

"And as for history, *Griffin*'s pedigree is equally dubious. The question whether a factfinder may draw a logical inference from a criminal defendant's failure to offer formal testimony would not have arisen in 1791, because common-law evidentiary rules prevented a criminal defendant from testifying in his own behalf even if wanted to do so. That is not to say, however, that a criminal defendant was not allowed to speak in his own behalf, and a tradition of expecting the defendant to do so, and of drawing an adverse inference when he did not, strongly suggests that *Griffin* is out of sync with the historical understanding of the Fifth Amendment. Traditionally, defendants were expected to speak rather extensively at both the pretrial and trial stages of a criminal proceeding. The longstanding common-law principle, nemo tenetur seipsum prodere, was thought to ban only testimony forced by compulsory oath or physical torture, not voluntary, unsworn testimony. [Under the Marian Committal Statute, the justice of the peace was required to take the examination of the arrested person not under oath and to record his response]. * * * The justice of the peace testified at trial as to the content of the defendant's statement; if the defendant refused to speak, this would also have been reported to the jury. * * * At trial, defendants were expected to speak directly to the jury. Sir James Stephen described 17th- and 18th-century English trials as follows: '[T]he prisoner in cases of felony could not be defended by counsel, and had therefore to speak for himself. He was thus unable to say . . . that his mouth was closed. On the contrary his mouth was not only open, but the evidence given against him operated as so much indirect questioning, and if he omitted to answer the questions it suggested he was very likely to be convicted.' * * *

"Whatever the merits of prohibiting adverse inferences as a legislative policy, the text and history of the Fifth Amendment give no indication that there is a federal constitutional prohibition on the use of the defendant's silence as demeanor evidence. Our hardy forebearers, who thought of compulsion in terms of the rack and oaths forced by the power of law, would not have viewed the drawing of a commonsensical inference as equivalent pressure. And it is implausible that the Americans of 1791, who were subject to adverse inferences for failing to give unsworn testimony, would have viewed an adverse inference for failing to give sworn testimony as a violation of the Fifth Amendment. Nor can it reasonably be argued that the new statutes somehow created a 'revised' understanding of the Fifth Amendment that was incorporated into the Due Process Clause of the Fourteenth Amendment, since only nine States (and not the Federal Government) had enacted competency statutes when the Fourteenth Amendment was adopted, and three of them did not prohibit adverse inferences from failure to testify.

"The Court's decision in *Griffin*, however, did not even pretend to be rooted in a historical understanding of the Fifth Amendment. Rather, in a breathtaking act of sorcery it simply transformed legislative policy into constitutional command, quoting a passage from an earlier opinion describing the benevolent purposes of 18 U.S.C. § 3481, and then decreeing, with literally nothing to support it: 'If the words "Fifth Amendment" are substituted for "act" and for "statute," the spirit of the Self-Incrimination Clause is reflected.' Imagine what a constitution we would have if this mode of exegesis were generally applied—if, for example, without any evidence to prove the point, the Court could simply say of all federal procedural statutes, 'If the words "Fifth Amendment" are substituted for "act" and for "statute," the spirit of the Due Process Clause is reflected.' To my mind, *Griffin* was a wrong turn—which is not cause enough to overrule it, but is cause enough to resist its extension."

9th ed., p. 1454; after Note 6, add:

7. In PORTUONDO v. AGARD, 529 U.S. ___, 120 S.Ct. 1119, 146 L.Ed.2d 47 (2000), the prosecutor in closing argument, in questioning

defendant's credibility as a witness, pointed out that defendant, unlike the other witnesses, had been present throughout the trial and was thus able to hear what the others said before he testified. The defendant contended those comments "burdened his Sixth Amendment right to be present at trial and to be confronted with the witnesses against him, and his Fifth and Sixth Amendment rights to testify on his own behalf," and thus asked the Court to "extend to comments of the type the prosecutor made here the rationale of *Griffin.*" But the Court, per SCALIA, J., after finding no "historical support" for defendant's claim, found *Griffin* to be "a poor analogue * * * for several reasons": (1) "What we prohibited the prosecutor from urging the jury to do in *Griffin* was something *the jury is not permitted to do.* * * * By contrast, it *is* natural and irresistible for a jury, in evaluating the relative credibility of a defendant who testifies last, to have in mind and weigh in the balance the fact that he heard the testimonial of all those who preceded him." (2) "*Griffin* prohibited comments that suggest a defendant's silence is evidence of *guilt.* * * * The prosecutor's comments in this case, by contrast, concerned respondent's *credibility as a witness*, and were therefore in accord with the longstanding rule that when a defendant takes the stand, 'his credibility may be impeached and his testimony assailed like that of any other witness.' " As for the contention of GINSBURG and SOUTER, JJ., dissenting, "that the comments were impermissible here because they were made, not during cross-examination, but at summation, leaving the defense no opportunity to reply," the Court answered: "Our trial structure, which requires the defense to close before the prosecution, regularly forces the defense to predict what the prosecution will say."

SECTION 6. DELIBERATIONS AND VERDICT

9th ed., p. 1471; following Note 2, add:

3. In RICHARDSON v. UNITED STATES, 526 U.S. 813, 119 S.Ct. 1707, 143 L.Ed.2d 985 (1999), defendant was charged with violating a federal statute forbidding any person from "engag[ing] in a continuing criminal enterprise," defined as involving a violation of the drug statutes where "such violation is a part of a continuing series of violations." The government introduced evidence of more underlying drug offenses than the three assumed to be necessary to constitute a "series," and defendant was convicted following a jury instruction stating the jury had to agree that defendant had committed at least three such offenses but did not have to agree about which three. The Court, per BREYER, J., first noted:

"The question before us arises because a federal jury need not always decide unanimously which of several possible sets of underlying brute facts make up a particular element, say, which of several possible means the defendant used to commit an element of the crime. *Schad v. Arizona*. Where, for example, an element of robbery is force or the threat of force, some jurors might conclude that the defendant used a knife to create the threat; others might conclude he used a gun. But that disagreement—a disagreement about means—would not matter as long as all 12 jurors unanimously concluded that the Government had proved the necessary related element, namely that the defendant had threatened force.

"In this case, we must decide whether the statute's phrase 'series of violations' refers to one element, namely a 'series,' in respect to which the 'violations' constitute the underlying brute facts or means, or whether those words create several elements, namely the several 'violations,' in respect to *each* of which the jury must agree unanimously and separately. * * * If the statute creates a single element, a 'series,' in respect to which individual violations are but the means, then the jury need only agree that the defendant committed at least three of all the underlying crimes the Government has tried to prove. The jury need not agree about which three. On the other hand, if the statute makes each 'violation' a separate element, then the jury must agree unanimously about which three crimes the defendant committed."

In opting for the latter interpretation, the Court emphasized these considerations: (1) "To hold that each 'violation' here amounts to a separate element is consistent with a tradition of requiring jury unanimity where the issue is whether a defendant has engaged in conduct that violates the law." (2) The "statute's word 'violations' covers many different kinds of behavior of varying degrees of seriousness," which "increases the likelihood that treating violations simply as alternative means, by permitting a jury to avoid discussion of the specific factual details of each violation, will cover-up wide disagreement among the jurors about just what the defendant did, or did not, do." (3) Considering that the Court in *Schad* "indicated that the Constitution itself limits a State's power to define crimes in ways that would permit juries to convict while disagreeing about means, at least where that definition risks serious unfairness and lacks support in history or tradition," there is "no reason to believe that Congress intended to come close to, or to test, those constitutional limits when it wrote this statute." (4) This conclusion is supported by the analogy in "federal criminal law's treatment of recidivism,"where "one finds that commission of a prior crime will lead to an enhanced punishment only when a relevant factfinder, judge, or jury has found that the defendant committed that specific individual prior crime."

KENNEDY, J., for the three dissenters, concluded that there is "no reason to think Congress thought it necessary for the jury to agree on which particular predicate offenses made up the continuing series before an enhanced punishment may be imposed," and that "there is no due process problem with interpreting the continuing series requirement as a single element of the crime," as "the continuing series element advances the goals of the statute in a way that is neither unfair nor irrational." The majority's recidivism analogy, the dissenters concluded, is unsound because under the statute at issue "the mere proof of a series does not suffice to convict," for the government "must also prove action in concert with five or more persons, a leadership role for the defendant with respect to those persons, and substantial income or resources derived from the continuing series."

Chapter 27

SENTENCING

SECTION 2. CONTROLLING SENTENCING DISCRETION

A. Mandatory Minimum Sentences

9th ed., p. 1541; following Note 3, add:

Consider Michael Tonry & Kathleen Hatlestad, Sentencing Reform in Overcrowded Times–A Comparative Perspective 4 (1997) (arguing that in the United States, unlike other countries, because of successful attacks of political candidates as soft on crime since the 1980s, "[f]ew elected public officials dare oppose any 'toughness' proposal, whatever its unfairness, expense, or likely ineffectiveness"); Ronald F. Wright, *Three Strikes Legislation and Sentencing Commission Objectives,* 20 Law & Policy 429, 437 (1998) ("The fiscal costs of increased corrections, judicial, prosecutorial, and defense resources are rarely traced to particular statutes," and even when they are, "[b]y that time, most of the legislators who voted for the original punishment statute are long gone.").

B. Sentencing Guidelines

9th ed., p. 1539; Note 1, following "suit" in the first sentence, add:

, exploring, and in the case of Congress and at least seventeen states, adopting their own guidelines systems.

9th ed., p. 1539; Note 1, at end, add:

See also Richard S. Frase, *Sentencing Guidelines Are "Alive and Well" in the United States,* in Tonry & Hatlestad, supra (describing variations in state guidelines schemes).

SECTION 3. CONSTITUTIONAL LIMITS ON SENTENCING PROCEDURES

A. Information Considered in Setting the Sentence

9th ed., p. 1550; before B., add:

Consider MITCHELL v. UNITED STATES, 526 U.S. 314, 119 S.Ct. 1307, 143 L.Ed.2d 424 (1999). In *Mitchell,* the defendant pleaded guilty to several drug offenses, reserving the right to contest drug quantity at sentencing. At sentencing witnesses testified that over several months the defendant had sold a total of more than 5 kilograms of cocaine, an amount carrying a mandatory minimum sentence of 10 years. In explaining why he credited the testimony, the judge explained to the defendant: "I held it against you that you didn't come forward today and tell me that you really only did this a couple of times.... I'm taking the position that you should come forward and explain your side of this issue." Mitchell asserted in the Supreme Court that it was a violation of her Fifth Amendment privilege against self-incrimination for the trial judge to draw an adverse inference from her silence at sentencing. Justice KENNEDY's opinion for the Court agreed. "The concerns which mandate the rule [of *Griffin v. California*, 9th ed., p. 1449] against negative inferences at a criminal trial apply with equal force at sentencing." The majority distinguished the sentencing hearing from a civil proceeding, where the stakes are lower and adverse inferences from the invocation of the privilege are allowed. "Here, the inference ... may have resulted in decades of added imprisonment." Moreover, the government "often has a motive to demand a severe sentence, so the central purpose of the privilege–to protect a defendant from being the unwilling instrument of his or her own condemnation–remains of vital importance." The rule prohibiting an inference of guilt from a defendant's silence "has become an essential feature of our legal tradition," and a "vital instrument for teaching that the question in a criminal case is not whether the defendant committed the acts of which he is accused," but "whether the Government has carried its burden to prove its allegations while respecting the defendant's individual rights."

Justice SCALIA's dissenting opinion criticized the *Griffin* line of cases as illogical and lacking historical pedigree. "*Griffin* was a wrong turn–which is not cause enough to overrule it, but is cause enough to resist its extension." He argued that there is a "natural dichotomy between the guilt and the penalty phases" that the Court had recognized when it refused to extend to sentencing the trial rights to a jury, to confrontation, and to proof beyond a reasonable doubt.

The majority in *Mitchell* also declined to express a view on whether silence "bears upon the determination of lack of remorse, or upon acceptance of responsibility" for downward departure under the Guidelines. Justice Scalia in dissent argued that should the Court later decide that the " 'no inference' rule is indeed limited to 'determining the facts of the offense,' then we will have a system in which a state court can increase the sentence of a convicted drug possessor who refuses to say how many ounces he possessed–not because that suggests he possessed the large amount ...

but because his refusal to cooperate suggests he is unrepentant." "Ordinarily," he predicted, it will be "impossible to tell whether the sentencer has used the silence for either purpose or for neither." Alternatively, if the rule barring inferences from silence extends to a refusal to cooperate, the judge will be able to consider remote hearsay, but not "the most obvious piece of first-hand evidence standing in front of the judge."

C. Burden of Proof

9th ed., p. 1558; replacing Notes 3 & 4:

APPRENDI v. NEW JERSEY

___ U.S. ___, 120 S.Ct. 2348, ___ L.Ed.2d ___, (2000).

Justice STEVENS delivered the opinion of the Court.

[N. J. Stat. Ann. § 2C:44–3(e) (West Supp. 2000) (the "hate crime" statute) provides for an "extended term" of imprisonment if the trial judge finds, by a preponderance of the evidence, that "the defendant in committing the crime acted with a purpose to intimidate an individual or group of individuals because of race, color, gender, handicap, religion, sexual orientation or ethnicity." The extended term authorized for second-degree offenses is imprisonment for "between 10 and 20 years." Petitioner Apprendi fired shots into the home of an African–American family. When arrested, he stated that he did not want the occupants of the home in the neighborhood because of their race, a statement he later retracted. A state grand jury indicted him on 23 counts, none of which referred to the hate crime statute or alleged that Apprendi acted with a racially biased purpose. Apprendi agreed to plead guilty to two counts (Counts 3 and 18) of possession of a firearm for an unlawful purpose (classified by statute as a second degree offense punishable by imprisonment for "between five years and 10 years"), and another crime punishable by 3 to 5 years' imprisonment, in return for dismissal of the remaining counts. As part of the plea agreement, the State reserved the right to request the court to impose a higher "enhanced" sentence for Count 18 on the ground that offense was committed with a biased purpose, and Apprendi reserved the right to challenge the constitutionality of the hate crime sentence enhancement. After accepting the plea the trial judge held an evidentiary hearing on the issue of Apprendi's "purpose" for the shooting. Apprendi adduced evidence from a psychologist and from seven character witnesses who testified that he did not have a reputation for racial bias. He also took the stand himself, explaining that the incident was an unintended consequence of overindulgence in alcohol, denying that he was in any way biased against African–Americans, and denying that his statement to the police had been accurately described. The judge, however, found the police officer's testimony credible, and concluded that the evidence supported a finding "that the crime was motivated by racial bias." Having found by a preponderance of the evidence that Apprendi's actions were taken "with a purpose to intimidate," the judge sentenced him to 12 years on Count 18, to run concurrently with his other sentences.]

* * * The question presented is whether the Due Process Clause of the Fourteenth Amendment requires that a factual determination authorizing an increase in the maximum prison sentence for an offense from 10 to 20 years be made by a jury on the basis of proof beyond a reasonable doubt. * * *

* * * Our answer to [the question in this case] was foreshadowed by our opinion in *Jones v. United States*, 526 U.S. 227, 143 L.Ed.2d 311, 119 S.Ct. 1215 (1999), construing a federal statute[, we] noted that "under the Due Process Clause of the Fifth Amendment and the notice and jury trial guarantees of the Sixth Amendment, any fact (other than prior conviction) that increases the maximum penalty for a crime must be charged in an indictment, submitted to a jury, and proven beyond a reasonable doubt." The Fourteenth Amendment commands the same answer in this case involving a state statute.

* * * At stake in this case are constitutional protections of surpassing importance: the proscription of any deprivation of liberty without "due process of law," Amdt. 14, and the guarantee that "in all criminal prosecutions, the accused shall enjoy the right to a speedy and public trial, by an impartial jury," Amdt. 6.[3] * * * As we have, unanimously, explained, *United States v. Gaudin,* [9th ed., p. 1363], the historical foundation for our recognition of these principles extends down centuries into the common law. "To guard against a spirit of oppression and tyranny on the part of rulers," and "as the great bulwark of [our] civil and political liberties," 2 J. Story, Commentaries on the Constitution of the United States 540–541 (4th ed. 1873), trial by jury has been understood to require that "the truth of every accusation, whether preferred in the shape of indictment, information, or appeal, should afterwards be confirmed by the unanimous suffrage of twelve of [the defendant's] equals and neighbours...." 4 W. Blackstone, Commentaries on the Laws of England 343 (1769). * * * Equally well founded is the companion right to have the jury verdict based on proof beyond a reasonable doubt. * * *

Any possible distinction between an "element" of a felony offense and a "sentencing factor" was unknown to the practice of criminal indictment, trial by jury, and judgment by court * * * as it existed during the years surrounding our Nation's founding. As a general rule, criminal proceedings were submitted to a jury after being initiated by an indictment containing "all the facts and circumstances which constitute

3. Apprendi has not here asserted a constitutional claim based on the omission of any reference to sentence enhancement or racial bias in the indictment. He relies entirely on the fact that the "due process of law" that the Fourteenth Amendment requires the States to provide to persons accused of crime encompasses the right to a trial by jury * * * and the right to have every element of the offense proved beyond a reasonable doubt, * * * That Amendment has not, however, been construed to include the Fifth Amendment right to "presentment or indictment of a Grand Jury" that was implicated in our recent decision in *Almendarez-Torres v. United States* [9th ed., p. 1557]. We thus do not address the indictment question separately today.

the offence, ... stated with such certainty and precision, that the defendant ... may be enabled to determine the species of offence they constitute, in order that he may prepare his defence accordingly ... and that there may be no doubt as to the judgment which should be given, if the defendant be convicted." J. Archbold, Pleading and Evidence in Criminal Cases 44 (15th ed. 1862) (emphasis added). The defendant's ability to predict with certainty the judgment from the face of the felony indictment flowed from the invariable linkage of punishment with crime. * * *

Thus, with respect to the criminal law of felonious conduct, "the English trial judge of the later eighteenth century had very little explicit discretion in sentencing. The substantive criminal law tended to be sanction-specific; it prescribed a particular sentence for each offense. The judge was meant simply to impose that sentence (unless he thought in the circumstances that the sentence was so inappropriate that he should invoke the pardon process to commute it)." Langbein, The English Criminal Trial Jury on the Eve of the French Revolution, in The Trial Jury in England, France, Germany 1700–1900, pp. 36–37 (A. Schioppa ed. 1987). * * *

* * * Just as the circumstances of the crime and the intent of the defendant at the time of commission were often essential elements to be alleged in the indictment, so too were the circumstances mandating a particular punishment. "Where a statute annexes a higher degree of punishment to a common-law felony, if committed under particular circumstances, an indictment for the offence, in order to bring the defendant within that higher degree of punishment, must expressly charge it to have been committed under those circumstances, and must state the circumstances with certainty and precision. [2 M. Hale, Pleas of the Crown 170]." Archbold, Pleading and Evidence in Criminal Cases, at 51. If, then, "upon an indictment under the statute, the prosecutor prove the felony to have been committed, but fail in proving it to have been committed under the circumstances specified in the statute, the defendant shall be convicted of the common-law felony only." Id. at 188. * * *

We should be clear that nothing in this history suggests that it is impermissible for judges to exercise discretion—taking into consideration various factors relating both to offense and offender—in imposing a judgment within the range prescribed by statute. We have often noted that judges in this country have long exercised discretion of this nature in imposing sentence within statutory limits in the individual case.* * * As in *Williams v. New York* [9th ed., p. 1541], our periodic recognition of judges' broad discretion in sentencing—since the 19th-century shift in this country from statutes providing fixed-term sentences to those providing judges discretion within a permissible range, * * * has been regularly accompanied by the qualification that that discretion was bound by the range of sentencing options prescribed by the legislature. * * *

We do not suggest that trial practices cannot change in the course of centuries and still remain true to the principles that emerged from the Framers' fears "that the jury right could be lost not only by gross denial, but by erosion." * * * But practice must at least adhere to the basic principles undergirding the requirements of trying to a jury all facts necessary to constitute a statutory offense, and proving those facts beyond reasonable doubt. As we made clear in *Winship*, the "reasonable doubt" requirement "has a vital role in our criminal procedure for cogent reasons." Prosecution subjects the criminal defendant both to "the possibility that he may lose his liberty upon conviction and ... the certainty that he would be stigmatized by the conviction." We thus require this, among other, procedural protections in order to "provide concrete substance for the presumption of innocence," and to reduce the risk of imposing such deprivations erroneously. If a defendant faces punishment beyond that provided by statute when an offense is committed under certain circumstances but not others, it is obvious that both the loss of liberty and the stigma attaching to the offense are heightened; it necessarily follows that the defendant should not—at the moment the State is put to proof of those circumstances—be deprived of protections that have, until that point, unquestionably attached.

Since *Winship*, we have made clear beyond peradventure that *Winship*'s due process and associated jury protections extend, to some degree, "to determinations that [go] not to a defendant's guilt or innocence, but simply to the length of his sentence." *Almendarez-Torres*, [9th ed., p. 1557] (Scalia, J., dissenting). This was a primary lesson of *Mullaney v. Wilbur*, 421 U.S. 684, 44 L.Ed.2d 508, 95 S.Ct. 1881 (1975), in which we invalidated a Maine statute that presumed that a defendant who acted with an intent to kill possessed the "malice aforethought" necessary to constitute the State's murder offense (and therefore, was subject to that crime's associated punishment of life imprisonment). The statute placed the burden on the defendant of proving, in rebutting the statutory presumption, that he acted with a lesser degree of culpability, such as in the heat of passion, to win a reduction in the offense from murder to manslaughter (and thus a reduction of the maximum punishment of 20 years).

The State had posited in *Mullaney* that requiring a defendant to prove heat-of-passion intent to overcome a presumption of murderous intent did not implicate *Winship* protections because, upon conviction of either offense, the defendant would lose his liberty and face societal stigma just the same. Rejecting this argument, we acknowledged that criminal law "is concerned not only with guilt or innocence in the abstract, but also with the degree of criminal culpability" assessed. Because the "consequences" of a guilty verdict for murder and for manslaughter differed substantially, we dismissed the possibility that a State could circumvent the protections of *Winship* merely by "redefining the elements that constitute different crimes, characterizing them as factors that bear solely on the extent of punishment."[12]

* * * It was in *McMillan v. Pennsylvania,* [9th ed., p. 1549], that this Court, for the first time, coined the term "sentencing factor" to refer to a fact that was not found by a jury but that could affect the sentence imposed by the judge. * * * Articulating for the first time, and then applying, a multifactor set of criteria for determining whether the *Winship* protections applied to bar such a system, we concluded that the Pennsylvania statute did not run afoul of our previous admonitions against relieving the State of its burden of proving guilt, or tailoring the mere form of a criminal statute solely to avoid *Winship*'s strictures.

We did not, however, there budge from the position that (1) constitutional limits exist to States' authority to define away facts necessary to constitute a criminal offense, and (2) that a state scheme that keeps from the jury facts that "expose [defendants] to greater or additional punishment," may raise serious constitutional concern. * * * [13]

Finally, * * * *Almendarez-Torres* represents at best an exceptional departure from the historic practice that we have described. * * * Because Almendarez–Torres had admitted the three earlier convictions for aggravated felonies—all of which had been entered pursuant to proceedings with substantial procedural safeguards of their own—no question concerning the right to a jury trial or the standard of proof that would apply to a contested issue of fact was before the Court. Although our conclusion in that case was based in part on our application of the criteria we had invoked in *McMillan*, the specific question decided concerned the sufficiency of the indictment. More important,* * * our conclusion in *Almendarez-Torres* turned heavily upon the fact that the additional sentence to which the defendant was subject was "the prior commission of a serious crime."* * * Both the certainty that procedural

12. Contrary to the principal dissent's suggestion, *Patterson v. New York* [9th ed., p. 1550], posed no direct challenge to this aspect of *Mullaney*. In upholding a New York law allowing defendants to raise and prove extreme emotional distress as an affirmative defense to murder, *Patterson* made clear that the state law still required the State to prove every element of that State's offense of murder and its accompanying punishment. "No further facts are either presumed or inferred in order to constitute the crime." New York, unlike Maine, had not made malice aforethought, or any described mens rea, part of its statutory definition of second-degree murder; one could tell from the face of the statute that if one intended to cause the death of another person and did cause that death, one could be subject to sentence for a second-degree offense. Responding to the argument that our view could be seen "to permit state legislatures to reallocate burdens of proof by labeling as affirmative defenses at least some elements of the crimes now defined in their statutes," the Court made clear in the very next breath that there were "obviously constitutional limits beyond which the States may not go in this regard."

13. The principal dissent accuses us of today "overruling *McMillan*." We do not overrule *McMillan*. We limit its holding to cases that do not involve the imposition of a sentence more severe than the statutory maximum for the offense established by the jury's verdict—a limitation identified in the *McMillan* opinion itself. Conscious of the likelihood that legislative decisions may have been made in reliance on *McMillan*, we reserve for another day the question whether stare decisis considerations preclude reconsideration of its narrower holding.

safeguards attached to any "fact" of prior conviction, and the reality that Almendarez–Torres did not challenge the accuracy of that "fact" in his case, mitigated the due process and Sixth Amendment concerns otherwise implicated in allowing a judge to determine a "fact" increasing punishment beyond the maximum of the statutory range.

Even though it is arguable that *Almendarez-Torres* was incorrectly decided, and that a logical application of our reasoning today should apply if the recidivist issue were contested, Apprendi does not contest the decision's validity and we need not revisit it for purposes of our decision today to treat the case as a narrow exception to the general rule we recalled at the outset. Given its unique facts, it surely does not warrant rejection of the otherwise uniform course of decision during the entire history of our jurisprudence.

In sum, our reexamination of our cases in this area, and of the history upon which they rely, confirms the opinion that we expressed in *Jones*. Other than the fact of a prior conviction, any fact that increases the penalty for a crime beyond the prescribed statutory maximum must be submitted to a jury, and proved beyond a reasonable doubt. With that exception, we endorse the statement of the rule set forth in the concurring opinions in that case: "It is unconstitutional for a legislature to remove from the jury the assessment of facts that increase the prescribed range of penalties to which a criminal defendant is exposed. It is equally clear that such facts must be established by proof beyond a reasonable doubt."[16]

The New Jersey statutory scheme that Apprendi asks us to invalidate allows a jury to convict a defendant of a second-degree offense based on its finding beyond a reasonable doubt that he unlawfully possessed a prohibited weapon; after a subsequent and separate proceeding, it then allows a judge to impose punishment identical to that New Jersey

16. The principal dissent would reject the Court's rule as a "meaningless formalism," because it can conceive of hypothetical statutes that would comply with the rule and achieve the same result as the New Jersey statute. While a State could, hypothetically, undertake to revise its entire criminal code in the manner the dissent suggests,—extending all statutory maximum sentences to, for example, 50 years and giving judges guided discretion as to a few specially selected factors within that range—this possibility seems remote. Among other reasons, structural democratic constraints exist to discourage legislatures from enacting penal statutes that expose every defendant convicted of, for example, weapons possession, to a maximum sentence exceeding that which is, in the legislature's judgment, generally proportional to the crime. This is as it should be. Our rule ensures that a State is obliged "to make its choices concerning the substantive content of its criminal laws with full awareness of the consequence, unable to mask substantive policy choices" of exposing all who are convicted to the maximum sentence it provides. *Patterson v. New York,* 432 U.S. at 228–229, n. 13 (Powell, J., dissenting). So exposed, "the political check on potentially harsh legislative action is then more likely to operate." Ibid.

In all events, if such an extensive revision of the State's entire criminal code were enacted for the purpose the dissent suggests, or if New Jersey simply reversed the burden of the hate crime finding (effectively assuming a crime was performed with a purpose to intimidate and then requiring a defendant to prove that it was not), we would be required to question whether the revision was constitutional under this Court's prior decisions. See *Patterson,* 432 U.S. at 210; *Mullaney,* 421 U.S. at 698–702. * * *

provides for crimes of the first degree,* * * based upon the judge's finding, by a preponderance of the evidence, that the defendant's "purpose" for unlawfully possessing the weapon was "to intimidate" his victim on the basis of a particular characteristic the victim possessed. In light of the constitutional rule explained above, and all of the cases supporting it, this practice cannot stand.

* * * [T]his Court has previously considered and rejected the argument that the principles guiding our decision today render invalid state capital sentencing schemes regarding judges, after a jury verdict holding a defendant guilty of a capital crime, to find specific aggravating factors before imposing a sentence of death. *Walton v. Arizona*, 497 U.S. 639, 647–649 (1990); *id.*, at 709–714 (Stevens, J., dissenting). For reasons we have explained, the capital cases are not controlling:

> "Neither the cases cited, nor any other case, permits a judge to determine the existence of a factor which makes a crime a capital offense. What the cited cases hold is that, once a jury has found the defendant guilty of all the elements of an offense which carries as its maximum penalty the sentence of death, it may be left to the judge to decide whether that maximum penalty, rather than a lesser one, ought to be imposed... .The person who is charged with actions that expose him to the death penalty has an absolute entitlement to jury trial on all the elements of the charge." *Almendarez–Torres*, 523 U.S., at 257, n. 2 (Scalia, J., dissenting) (emphasis deleted). * * * [21]

* * * Accordingly, the judgment of the Supreme Court of New Jersey is reversed, and the case is remanded for further proceedings not inconsistent with this opinion.

[Justice SCALIA's concurring opinion is omitted.]

Justice THOMAS, with whom Justice SCALIA joins as to Parts I and II, concurring.

I join the opinion of the Court in full. I write separately to explain my view that the Constitution requires a broader rule than the Court adopts.

I

This case turns on the seemingly simple question of what constitutes a "crime." Under the Federal Constitution, "the accused" has the

21. The principal dissent, in addition, treats us to a lengthy disquisition on the benefits of determinate sentencing schemes, and the effect of today's decision on the federal Sentencing Guidelines. The Guidelines are, of course, not before the Court. We therefore express no view on the subject beyond what this Court has already held. See, e.g., *Edwards v. United States*, 523 U.S. 511, 515, 140 L. Ed. 2d 703, 118 S. Ct. 1475 (1998) (opinion of Breyer, J., for a unanimous court) (noting that "of course, petitioners' statutory and constitutional claims would make a difference if it were possible to argue, say, that the sentences imposed exceeded the maximum that the statutes permit for a cocaine-only conspiracy. That is because a maximum sentence set by statute trumps a higher sentence set forth in the Guidelines. [United States Sentencing Guidelines Manual] § 5G1.1.").

right (1) "to be informed of the nature and cause of the accusation" (that is, the basis on which he is accused of a crime), (2) to be "held to answer for a capital, or otherwise infamous crime" only on an indictment or presentment of a grand jury, and (3) to be tried by "an impartial jury of the State and district wherein the crime shall have been committed." Amdts. 5 and 6. See also Art. III, § 2, cl. 3. With the exception of the Grand Jury Clause, * * * the Court has held that these protections apply in state prosecutions * * *. Further, the Court has held that due process requires that the jury find beyond a reasonable doubt every fact necessary to constitute the crime. * * *

All of these constitutional protections turn on determining which facts constitute the "crime"—that is, which facts are the "elements" or "ingredients" of a crime. In order for an accusation of a crime (whether by indictment or some other form) to be proper under the common law, and thus proper under the codification of the common-law rights in the Fifth and Sixth Amendments, it must allege all elements of that crime; likewise, in order for a jury trial of a crime to be proper, all elements of the crime must be proved to the jury (and, under *Winship*, proved beyond a reasonable doubt).* * *

Thus, it is critical to know which facts are elements.* * * Courts have long had to consider which facts are elements in order to determine the sufficiency of an accusation (usually an indictment). The answer that courts have provided regarding the accusation tells us what an element is, and it is then a simple matter to apply that answer to whatever constitutional right may be at issue in a case—here, *Winship* and the right to trial by jury. A long line of essentially uniform authority addressing accusations, and stretching from the earliest reported cases after the founding until well into the 20th century, establishes that the original understanding of which facts are elements was even broader than the rule that the Court adopts today.

This authority establishes that a "crime" includes every fact that is by law a basis for imposing or increasing punishment (in contrast with a fact that mitigates punishment). Thus, if the legislature defines some core crime and then provides for increasing the punishment of that crime upon a finding of some aggravating fact—of whatever sort, including the fact of a prior conviction—the core crime and the aggravating fact together constitute an aggravated crime, just as much as grand larceny is an aggravated form of petit larceny. The aggravating fact is an element of the aggravated crime. Similarly, if the legislature, rather than creating grades of crimes, has provided for setting the punishment of a crime based on some fact—such as a fine that is proportional to the value of stolen goods—that fact is also an element. * * *

II

Cases from the founding to roughly the end of the Civil War establish the rule that I have described, applying it to all sorts of facts, including recidivism. As legislatures varied common-law crimes and created new crimes, American courts, particularly from the 1840's on, readily applied to these new laws the common-law understanding that a fact that is by law the basis for imposing or increasing punishment is an element.[2]

* * * Further evidence of the rule that a crime includes every fact that is by law a basis for imposing or increasing punishment comes from early cases addressing recidivism statutes. As Justice Scalia has explained, there was a tradition of treating recidivism as an element. See *Almendarez-Torres*, 523 U.S. at 256–257, 261 (dissenting opinion). * * *

* * *[T]his traditional understanding—that a "crime" includes every fact that is by law a basis for imposing or increasing punishment—continued well into the 20th century * * *. In fact, it is fair to say that *McMillan* began a revolution in the law regarding the definition of "crime." Today's decision, far from being a sharp break with the past, marks nothing more than a return to the status quo ante—the status quo that reflected the original meaning of the Fifth and Sixth Amendments.

III

The consequence of the above discussion for our decisions in *Almendarez Torres* and *McMillan* should be plain enough, but a few points merit special mention.

* * * [O]ne of the chief errors of *Almendarez-Torres*—an error to which I succumbed—was to attempt to discern whether a particular fact is traditionally (or typically) a basis for a sentencing court to increase an offender's sentence.* * * [I]t should be clear that this approach just defines away the real issue. What matters is the way by which a fact enters into the sentence. If a fact is by law the basis for imposing or increasing punishment—for establishing or increasing the prosecution's entitlement—it is an element. * * * One reason frequently offered for treating recidivism differently, a reason on which we relied in *Almendarez-Torres* * * * is a concern for prejudicing the jury by informing it of the prior conviction. But this concern, of which earlier courts were well aware, does not make the traditional understanding of what an element is any less applicable to the fact of a prior conviction. * * *[10]

2. It is strange that Justice O'Connor faults me for beginning my analysis with cases primarily from the 1840's, rather from the time of the founding. As the Court explains * * * and as she concedes, * * * the very idea of a sentencing enhancement was foreign to the common law of the time of the founding. Justice O'Connor therefore, and understandably, does not contend that any history from the founding supports her position. As far as I have been able to tell, the argument that a fact that was by law the basis for imposing or increasing punishment might not be an element did not seriously arise (at least not in reported cases) until the 1840's. As I explain below, from that time on—for at least a century—essentially all authority rejected that argument, and much of it did so in reliance upon the common law. I find this evidence more than sufficient.

10. In addition, it has been common practice to address this concern by permitting the defendant to stipulate to the prior conviction, in which case the charge of the prior conviction is not read to the jury, or, if the defendant decides not to stipulate, to bifurcate the trial, with the jury only considering the prior conviction after it has

* * * I think it clear that the common-law rule would cover the *McMillan* situation of a mandatory minimum sentence (in that case, for visible possession of a firearm during the commission of certain crimes). No doubt a defendant could, under such a scheme, find himself sentenced to the same term to which he could have been sentenced absent the mandatory minimum. * * * But it is equally true that his expected punishment has increased as a result of the narrowed range and that the prosecution is empowered, by invoking the mandatory minimum, to require the judge to impose a higher punishment than he might wish. * * * Thus, the fact triggering the mandatory minimum is part of "the punishment sought to be inflicted." * * * [11]

For the foregoing reasons, as well as those given in the Court's opinion, I agree that the New Jersey procedure at issue is unconstitutional.

Justice O'CONNOR, with Whom The CHIEF JUSTICE, Justice KENNEDY, and Justice BREYER join, dissenting.

* * * Today, in what will surely be remembered as a watershed change in constitutional law, the Court imposes as a constitutional rule the principle it first identified in *Jones*.

Our Court has long recognized that not every fact that bears on a defendant's punishment need be charged in an indictment, submitted to a jury, and proved by the government beyond a reasonable doubt. Rather, we have held that the "legislature's definition of the elements of the offense is usually dispositive." *McMillan* * * * . Although we have recognized that "there are obviously constitutional limits beyond which the States may not go in this regard," * * * and that "in certain limited circumstances *Winship*'s reasonable-doubt requirement applies to facts not formally identified as elements of the offense charged," * * * we have proceeded with caution before deciding that a certain fact must be treated as an offense element despite the legislature's choice not to characterize it as such. We have therefore declined to establish any bright-line rule for making such judgments and have instead approached each case individually, sifting through the considerations most relevant to determining whether the legislature has acted properly within its broad power to define crimes and their punishments or instead has sought to evade the constitutional requirements associated with the characterization of a fact as an offense element.* * *

In one bold stroke the Court today casts aside our traditional cautious approach and instead embraces a universal and seemingly bright-line rule limiting the power of Congress and state legislatures to define criminal offenses and the sentences that follow from convictions

reached a guilty verdict on the core crime. * * *

11. [It is] unnecessary to consider whether (and, if so, how) the rule regarding elements applies to the Sentencing Guidelines, given the unique status that they have under *Mistretta v. United States*, 488 U.S. 361, 102 L.Ed.2d 714, 109 S.Ct. 647 (1989). But it may be that this special status is irrelevant, because the Guidelines "have the force and effect of laws." 488 U.S. at 413 (Scalia, J., dissenting).

thereunder. * * * [T]he Court marshals virtually no authority to support its extraordinary rule. Indeed, it is remarkable that the Court cannot identify a single instance, in the over 200 years since the ratification of the Bill of Rights, that our Court has applied, as a constitutional requirement, the rule it announces today.

* * * None of the history contained in the Court's opinion requires the rule it ultimately adopts. The history cited by the Court can be divided into two categories: first, evidence that judges at common law had virtually no discretion in sentencing, and, second, statements from a 19th century criminal procedure treatise that the government must charge in an indictment and prove at trial the elements of a statutory offense for the defendant to be sentenced to the punishment attached to that statutory offense. The relevance of the first category of evidence can be easily dismissed. Indeed, the Court does not even claim that the historical evidence of nondiscretionary sentencing at common law supports its "increase in the maximum penalty" rule. Rather, almost as quickly as it recites that historical practice, the Court rejects it relevance to the constitutional question presented here due to the conflicting American practice of judges exercising sentencing discretion and our decisions recognizing the legitimacy of that American practice.

* * * Apparently, then, the historical practice on which the Court places so much reliance consists of only two quotations taken from an 1862 criminal procedure treatise. A closer examination of the two statements reveals that neither supports the Court's "increase in the maximum penalty" rule. Both of the excerpts pertain to circumstances in which a common-law felony had also been made a separate statutory offense carrying a greater penalty. Taken together, the statements from the Archbold treatise demonstrate nothing more than the unremarkable proposition that a defendant could receive the greater statutory punishment only if the indictment expressly charged and the prosecutor proved the facts that made up the statutory offense, as opposed to simply those facts that made up the common-law offense. In other words, for the defendant to receive the statutory punishment, the prosecutor had to charge in the indictment and prove at trial *the elements* of the statutory offense * * *. No Member of this Court questions the proposition that a State must charge in the indictment and prove at trial beyond a reasonable doubt the actual elements of the offense. This case, however, concerns the distinct questions of when a fact that bears on a defendant's punishment, but which the legislature has not classified as an element of the charged offense, must nevertheless be treated as an offense element. The excerpts drawn from the Archbold treatise do not speak to this question at all. The history on which the Court's opinion relies provides no support for its "increase in the maximum penalty" rule.

* * * The history cited by Justice Thomas does not require, as a matter of federal constitutional law, the application of the rule he advocates. * * * [His opinion fails] to discuss any historical practice, or to cite any decisions, predating (or contemporary with) the ratification of

the Bill of Rights. Rather, Justice Thomas divines the common-law understanding of the Fifth and Sixth Amendment rights by consulting decisions rendered by American courts well after the ratification of the Bill of Rights, ranging primarily from the 1840's to the 1890's. Whatever those decisions might reveal about the way American state courts resolved questions regarding the distinction between a crime and its punishment under general rules of criminal pleading or their own state constitutions, the decisions fail to demonstrate any settled understanding with respect to the definition of a crime under the relevant, preexisting common law. * * * The most relevant common-law principles in this area were that an indictment must charge the elements of the relevant offense and must do so with certainty.* * * Those principles, of course, say little about when a specific fact constitutes an element of the offense. * * *

That the Court's rule is unsupported by the history and case law it cites is reason enough to reject such a substantial departure from our settled jurisprudence. Significantly, the Court also fails to explain adequately why the Due Process Clauses of the fifth and Fourteenth Amendments and the jury trial guarantee of the Sixth Amendment require application of its rule. Upon closer examination, it is possible that the court's "increase in the maximum penalty" rule rests on a meaningless formalism that accords, at best, marginal protection for the constitutional rights that it seeks to effectuate.

* * * [T]he Court appears to hold that the Constitution requires that a fact be submitted to a jury and proved beyond a reasonable doubt only if that fact, as a formal matter, extends the range of punishment beyond the prescribed statutory maximum.* * * A State could, however, remove from the jury (and subject to a standard of proof below "beyond a reasonable doubt") the assessment of those facts that define narrower ranges of punishment, within the overall statutory range, to which the defendant may be sentenced. * * * Thus, apparently New Jersey could cure its sentencing scheme, and achieve virtually the same results, by drafting its weapons possession statute in the following manner: First, New Jersey could prescribe, in the weapons possession statute itself, a range of 5 to 20 years' imprisonment for one who commits that criminal offense. Second, New Jersey could provide that only those defendants convicted under the statute who are found by a judge, by a preponderance of the evidence, to have acted with a purpose to intimidate an individual on the basis of race may receive a sentence greater than 10 years' imprisonment.

The Court's proffered distinction of *Walton v. Arizona* [497 U.S. 639, 111 L.Ed.2d 511, 110 S.Ct. 3047 (1990)] suggests that it means to announce a rule of only this limited effect. The Court claims the Arizona capital sentencing scheme is consistent with the constitutional principle underlying today's decision because Arizona's first-degree murder statute itself authorizes both life imprisonment and the death penalty. * * * " 'Once a jury has found the defendant guilty of all the elements of an offense which carries as its maximum penalty the sentence of death, it may be left to the judge to decide whether that maximum penalty, rather than a lesser one, ought to be imposed.' " * * * Of course * * * an Arizona sentencing judge can impose the maximum penalty of death only if the judge first makes a statutorily required finding that at least one aggravating factor exists in the defendant's case. Thus, the Arizona first-degree murder statute authorizes a maximum penalty of death only in a formal sense. In real terms, however, the Arizona sentencing scheme removes from the jury the assessment of a fact that determines whether the defendant can receive that maximum punishment. The only difference, then, between the Arizona scheme and the New Jersey scheme we consider here—apart from the magnitude of punishment at stake—is that New Jersey has not prescribed the 20–year maximum penalty in the same statute that it defines the crime to be punished. It is difficult to understand, and the Court does not explain, why the Constitution would require a state legislature to follow such a meaningless and formalistic difference in drafting its criminal statutes.

Under another reading of the Court's decision, it may mean only that the Constitution requires that a fact be submitted to a jury and proved beyond a reasonable doubt if it, as a formal matter, *increases* the range of punishment *beyond that which could legally be imposed absent that fact* ... A State could, however, remove from the jury (and subject to a standard of proof below "beyond a reasonable doubt") the assessment of those facts that, as a formal matter, *decrease* the range of punishment *below that which could legally be imposed absent that fact.* Thus, consistent with our decision in *Patterson*, New Jersey could cure its sentencing scheme, and achieve virtually the same results, by drafting its weapons possession statute in the following manner: First, New Jersey could prescribe, in the weapons possession statute itself, a range of 5 to 20 years' imprisonment for one who commits that criminal offense. Second, New Jersey could provide that a defendant convicted under the statute whom a judge finds, by a preponderance of the evidence, *not* to have acted with a purpose to intimidate an individual on the basis of race may receive a sentence no greater than 10 years' imprisonment.

* * * If either of the above readings is all that the Court's decision means, "the Court's principle amounts to nothing more than chastising [the New Jersey Legislature] for failing to use the approved phrasing in expressing its intent as to how [unlawful weapons possession] should be punished." *Jones*, 526 U.S., at 257 (Kennedy, J., dissenting). If New Jersey can, consistent with the Constitution, make precisely the same differences in punishment turn on precisely the same facts, and can remove the assessment of those facts from the jury and subject them to a standard of proof below "beyond a reasonable doubt," it is impossible to say that the Fifth, Sixth, and Fourteenth Amendments require the Court's rule. For the same reason, the "structural democratic constraints" that might discourage a legislature from enacting either of the above hypothetical statutes would be no more significant than those that would discourage the enactment of New Jersey's present sentence-enhancement statute. See *ante*, at 24, n. 16 (majority opinion). In all

three cases, the legislature is able to calibrate punishment perfectly, and subject to a maximum penalty only those defendants whose cases satisfy the sentence-enhancement criterion.

Given the pure formalism of the above reasons of the Court's opinion, one suspects that the constitutional principle underlying its decision is more far reaching. The actual principle underlying the Court's decision may be that any fact (other than prior conviction) that has the effect, *in real terms*, of increasing the maximum punishment beyond an otherwise applicable range must be submitted to a jury and proved beyond a reasonable doubt. * * * The principle thus would apply not only to schemes like New Jersey's, under which a factual determination exposes the defendant to a sentence beyond the prescribed statutory maximum, but also to all determinate-sentencing schemes in which the length of a defendant's sentence within the statutory range turns on specific factual determinations (*e.g.*, the federal Sentencing Guidelines).

* * * I would reject any such principle. As explained above, it is inconsistent with our precedent and would require the Court to overrule, at a minimum, decisions like *Patterson* and *Walton*. More importantly, given our approval of—and the significant history in this country of—discretionary sentencing by judges, it is difficult to understand how the Fifth, Sixth, and Fourteenth Amendments could possibly require the Court's or Justice Thomas' rule. Finally, in light of the adoption of the Court's and Justice Thomas' rules in terms of sentencing schemes invalidated by today's decision will likely be severe.

* * * One important purpose of the Sixth Amendment's jury trial guarantee is to protect the criminal defendant against potentially arbitrary judges. It effectuates this promise by preserving, as a constitutional matter, certain fundamental decisions for a jury of one's peers, as opposed to a judge.* * * Clearly, the concerns animating the Sixth Amendment's jury trial guarantee, if they were to extend to the sentencing context at all, would apply with greater strength to a discretionary-sentencing scheme than to determinate sentencing. In the former scheme, the potential for mischief by an arbitrary judge is much greater, given that the judge's decision of where to set the defendant's sentence within the prescribed statutory range is left almost entirely to discretion. In contrast, under a determinate-sentencing system, the discretion the judge wields within the statutory range is tightly constrained. Accordingly, our approval of discretionary-sentencing schemes, in which a defendant is not entitled to have a jury make factual findings relevant to sentencing despite the effect those findings have on the severity of the defendant's sentence, demonstrates that the defendant should have no right to demand that a jury make the equivalent factual determinations under a determinate-sentencing scheme.

The Court appears to hold today, however, that a defendant is entitled to have a jury decide, by proof beyond a reasonable doubt, every fact relevant to the determination of sentence under a determinate-sentencing scheme. If this is an accurate description of the constitutional principle underlying the Court's opinion, its decision will have the effect of invalidating significant sentencing reform accomplished at the federal and state levels over the past three decades.* * *

* * * [I]t is ironic that the Court, in the name of constitutional rights meant to protect criminal defendants from the potentially arbitrary exercise of power by prosecutors and judges, appears to rest its decision on a principle that would render unconstitutional efforts by Congress and the state legislatures to place constraints on that very power in the sentencing context.

Finally, perhaps the most significant impact of the Court's decision will be a practical one—its unsettling effect on sentencing conducted under current federal and state determinate-sentencing schemes. As I have explained, the Court does not say whether these schemes are constitutional, but its reasoning strongly suggests that they are not. Thus, with respect to past sentences handed down by judges under determinate-sentencing schemes, the Court's decision threatens to unleash a flood of petitions by convicted defendants seeking to invalidate their sentences in whole or in part on the authority of the Court's decision today. Statistics compiled by the United States Sentencing Commission reveal that almost a half-million cases have been sentenced under the Sentencing Guidelines since 1989 * * * [and] federal criminal prosecutions represen[t] only about 0.4% of the total number of criminal prosecutions in federal and state courts. * * * Because many States, like New Jersey, have determinate-sentencing schemes, the number of individual sentences drawn into question by the Court's decision could be colossal. * * *

* * * I would evaluate New Jersey's sentence-enhancement statute by analyzing the factors we have examined in past cases.* * * First, the New Jersey statute does not shift the burden of proof on an essential ingredient of the offense by presuming that ingredient upon proof of other elements of the offense. * * * Second, the magnitude of the New Jersey sentence enhancement, as applied in petitioner's case, is constitutionally permissible. * * * The 10–year increase in the maximum penalty to which petitioner was exposed falls well within the range we have found permissible. See *Almendarez-Torres* (approving 18–year enhancement). Third, the New Jersey statute gives no impression of having been enacted to evade the constitutional requirements that attach when a State makes a fact an element of the charged offense. For example, New Jersey did not take what had previously been an element of the weapons possession offense and transform it into a sentencing factor. * * *

In sum, New Jersey "simply took one factor that has always been considered by sentencing courts to bear on punishment"—a defendant's motive for committing the criminal offense—"and dictated the precise weight to be given that factor" when the motive is to intimidate a person because of race. * * *

Justice BREYER, with whom Chief Justice REHNQUIST joins, dissenting.

* * * [The majority's] rule would seem to promote a procedural ideal—that of juries, not judges, determining the existence of those facts upon which increased punishment turns. But the real world of criminal justice cannot hope to meet any such ideal. It can function only with the help of procedural compromises, particularly in respect to sentencing. And those compromises, which are themselves necessary for the fair functioning of the criminal justice system, preclude implementation of the procedural model that today's decision reflects. At the very least, the impractical nature of the requirement that the majority now recognizes supports the proposition that the Constitution was not intended to embody it.

* * * [I]t is important for present purposes to understand why judges, rather than juries, traditionally have determined the presence or absence of such sentence-affecting facts in any given case. And it is important to realize that the reason is not a theoretical one, but a practical one. It does not reflect (Justice Scalia's opinion to the contrary notwithstanding) an ideal of procedural "fairness," * * * but rather an administrative need for procedural compromise. There are, to put it simply, far too many potentially relevant sentencing factors to permit submission of all (or even many) of them to a jury. As the Sentencing Guidelines state the matter,

> "[a] bank robber with (or without) a gun, which the robber kept hidden (or brandished), might have frightened (or merely warned), injured seriously (or less seriously), tied up (or simply pushed) a guard, a teller or a customer, at night (or at noon), for a bad (or arguably less bad) motive, in an effort to obtain money for other crimes (or for other purposes), in the company of a few (or many) other robbers, for the first (or fourth) time that day, while sober (or under the influence of drugs or alcohol), and so forth." Sentencing Guidelines, Part A, at 1.2.

The Guidelines note that "a sentencing system tailored to fit every conceivable wrinkle of each case can become unworkable and seriously compromise the certainty of punishment and its deterrent effect." Ibid. To ask a jury to consider all, or many, such matters would do the same.

At the same time, to require jury consideration of all such factors—say, during trial where the issue is guilt or innocence—could easily place the defendant in the awkward (and conceivably unfair) position of having to deny he committed the crime yet offer proof about how he committed it, e.g., "I did not sell drugs, but I sold no more than 500 grams." And while special postverdict sentencing juries could cure this problem, they have seemed (but for capital cases) not worth their administrative costs. * * *

Justice Thomas suggests, until fairly recent times many legislatures rarely focused upon sentencing factors. Rather, it appears they simply identified typical forms of antisocial conduct, defined basic "crimes," and attached a broad sentencing range to each definition—leaving judges free to decide how to sentence within those ranges in light of such factors as they found relevant. * * * But the Constitution does not freeze 19th-century sentencing practices into permanent law. And dissatisfaction with the traditional sentencing system (reflecting its tendency to treat similar cases differently) has led modern legislatures to write new laws that refer specifically to sentencing factors.* * *

With the possible exception of the last line of Justice Scalia's concurring opinion, the majority also makes no constitutional objection to a legislative delegation to a commission of the authority to create guidelines that determine how a judge is to exercise sentencing discretion.* * * But if the Constitution permits Guidelines, why does it not permit Congress similarly to guide the exercise of a judge's sentencing discretion? That is, if the Constitution permits a delegatee (the commission) to exercise sentencing-related rulemaking power, how can it deny the delegator (the legislature) what is, in effect, the same rulemaking power?

The majority appears to offer two responses. First, it argues for a limiting principle that would prevent a legislature with broad authority from transforming (jury-determined) facts that constitute elements of a crime into (judge-determined) sentencing factors, thereby removing procedural protections that the Constitution would otherwise require. * * * The majority's cure, however, is not aimed at the disease.

The same "transformational" problem exists under traditional sentencing law, where legislation, silent as to sentencing factors, grants the judge virtually unchecked discretion to sentence within a broad range. * * *

* * * [T]he solution to the problem lies, not in prohibiting legislatures from enacting sentencing factors, but in sentencing rules that determine punishments on the basis of properly defined relevant conduct, with sensitivity to the need for procedural protections where sentencing factors are determined by a judge (for example, use of a "reasonable doubt" standard), and invocation of the Due Process Clause where the history of the crime at issue, together with the nature of the facts to be proved, reveals unusual and serious procedural unfairness. Cf. *McMillan,* 477 U.S. at 88 (upholding statute in part because it "gives no impression of having been tailored to permit the [sentencing factor] to be a tail which wags the dog of the substantive offense").

Second, the majority, in support of its constitutional rule, emphasizes the concept of a statutory "maximum." * * * From a defendant's perspective, the legislature's decision to cap the possible range of punishment at a statutorily prescribed "maximum" would affect the actual sentence imposed no differently than a sentencing commission's (or a sentencing judge's) similar determination. Indeed, as a practical matter, a legislated mandatory "minimum" is far more important to an actual defendant. A judge and a commission, after all, are legally free to select any sentence below a statute's maximum, but they are not free to subvert a statutory minimum.

* * * [I am willing] to assume that the majority's rule would provide a degree of increased procedural protection in respect to those particular sentencing factors currently embodied in statutes. I nonetheless believe that any such increased protection provides little practical help and comes at too high a price. For one thing, by leaving mandatory minimum sentences untouched, the majority's rule simply encourages any legislature interested in asserting control over the sentencing process to do so by creating those minimums. That result would mean significantly less procedural fairness, not more. For another thing, this Court's case law, prior to *Jones* led legislatures to believe that they were permitted to increase a statutory maximum sentence on the basis of a sentencing factor.* * * And legislatures may well have relied upon that belief. * * * [T]he rationale that underlies the Court's rule suggests a principle—jury determination of all sentencing-related facts—that, unless restricted, threatens the workability of every criminal justice system (if applied to judges) or threatens efforts to make those systems more uniform, hence more fair (if applied to commissions). * * *

Part Five

APPEALS, POST-CONVICTION REVIEW

Chapter 28

APPEALS

SECTION 5. THE HARMLESS ERROR RULE

A. Non-Constitutional Errors

9th ed., p. 1596; at the end of Note 4, add:

5. *Burden of Proof.* In *O'Neal v. McAninch*, 513 U.S. 432, 115 S.Ct. 992, 130 L.Ed.2d 947 (1995), the Sixth Circuit, applying the *Kotteakos* harmless-error standard in a habeas context (see pt. E, 9th ed., p. 1659), held that the habeas petitioner must bear the "burden of establishing" by a preponderance of the evidence that the alleged trial error had a " 'substantial and injurious effect or influence in determining the jury's verdict.' " The Supreme Court majority disagreed. The Court initially noted: "As an initial matter, * * * we deliberately phrase the issue in this case in terms of a judge's grave doubt, instead of in terms of 'burden of proof.' The case before us does not involve a judge who shifts a 'burden' to help control the presentation of evidence at a trial, but rather involves judges who apply a legal standard (harmlessness) to a record that the presentation of evidence is no longer likely to affect. In such a case, we think it conceptually clearer for the judge to ask directly, 'Do I, the judge, think that the error substantially influenced the jury's decision?' than for the judge to try to put the same question in terms of proof burdens (e.g., 'Do I believe the party has borne its burden of showing . . .?'). As Chief Justice Traynor said:

> 'Whether or not counsel are helpful, it is still the responsibility of the . . . court, once it concludes there was an error, to determine whether the error affected the judgment. It must do so without benefit of such aids as presumptions or allocated burdens of proof

that expedite fact-finding at the trial.' R. Traynor, The Riddle of Harmless Error 26 (1970).

The case may sometimes arise, however, where the record is so evenly balanced that a conscientious judge is in grave doubt as to the harmlessness of an error. This is the narrow circumstance we address here."

Turning to that situation, the Court concluded that the Sixth Circuit erred in stating that the petitioner bears the burden of establishing prejudice: "As a practical matter, this statement apparently means that, if a judge is in grave doubt about the effect on the jury of this kind of error, the petitioner must lose. Thus, O'Neal might have lost in the Court of Appeals, not because the judges concluded that the error was harmless, but because the record of the trial left them in grave doubt about the effect of the error. * * * [But] [w]hen a federal judge in a habeas proceeding is in grave doubt about whether a trial error of federal law had 'substantial and injurious effect or influence in determining the jury's verdict,' that error is not harmless. And, the petitioner must win."

Chapter 29

POST-CONVICTION REVIEW: FEDERAL HABEAS CORPUS

SECTION 1. THE BASIC STRUCTURE OF FEDERAL HABEAS CORPUS RELIEF

9th ed., p. 1615; following note 5, add:

See also Slack v. McDaniel, ___ U.S. ___, 120 S.Ct. 1595, ___ L.Ed.2d ___ (2000) ("A habeas petition filed in the district court after an initial habeas petition was unadjudicated on its merits and dismissed for failure to exhaust state remedies is not a second or successive petition.").

9th ed., p. 1617; Note 5, 7th line down after "claim.", add:

See *O'Sullivan v. Boerckel*, 526 U.S. 838, 119 S.Ct. 1728, 144 L.Ed.2d 1 (1999) (exhaustion requires state prisoners to file petitions for discretionary review when that review is part of the ordinary appellate review procedure in the state).

SECTION 3. CLAIMS FORECLOSED BY PROCEDURAL DEFAULT

9th ed., p. 1633; end of note 1, before note 2, add:

(d) Concurring in *Edwards v. Carpenter*, ___ U.S. ___, 120 S.Ct. 1587, 146 L.Ed.2d 518 (2000), Justice Breyer questioned the complexity and fairness of the Court's procedural default doctrine, which, according to the majority, meant that a procedurally defaulted ineffective assistance claim can serve as cause to excuse the default of another habeas claim only if the petitioner can satisfy the "cause and prejudice" standard with respect to the default of the ineffective assistance claim itself. "The added complexity resulting from the Court's opinion is obvious. Consider a prisoner who wants to assert a federal constitutional claim (call it FCC). Suppose the State asserts as a claimed 'adequate and independent state ground' the prisoner's failure to raise the matter on his first state-court appeal. Suppose further that the prisoner replies by alleging that he had 'cause' for not raising the matter on appeal (call it C). After *Carrier*, if that alleged 'cause' (C) consists of the claim 'my attorney was constitutionally ineffective,' the prisoner must have exhausted C in the state courts first. And after today, if he did not follow state rules for presenting C to the state courts, he will have lost his basic claim, FCC, forever. But, I overstate. According to the opinion of the Court, he will not necessarily have lost FCC forever if he had 'cause' for not having followed those state rules (i.e., the rules for determining the existence of 'cause' for not having followed the state rules governing the basic claim, FCC) (call this 'cause' C*). The prisoner could therefore still obtain relief if he could demonstrate the merits of C*, C, and FCC. I concede that this system of rules has a certain logic, indeed an attractive power for those who like difficult puzzles. But I believe it must succumb to this question: Why should a prisoner, who may well be proceeding pro se, lose his basic claim because he runs afoul of state procedural rules governing the presentation to state courts of the 'cause' for his not having followed state procedural rules for the presentation of his basic federal claim? And, in particular, why should that special default rule apply when the 'cause' at issue is an 'ineffective-assistance-of-counsel' claim, but not when it is any of the many other 'causes' or circumstances that might excuse a failure to comply with state rules?"

9th ed., p. 1646; in lieu of Note 5, add:

5. *Factual default (failing to create a record in state court) after the 1996 amendments.* The AEDPA did replace the *Sykes* test in the context of factual defaults (see Note 5(a), 9th ed., pp. 1634–35), narrowing a petitioner's access to evidentiary hearings in federal court when facts had not been developed in state court. Section 2254(e)(2) now provides:

> If the applicant has failed to develop the factual basis of a claim in State court proceedings, the court shall not hold an evidentiary hearing on the claim unless the applicant shows that—
>
> (A) the claim relies on—
>
> (i) a new rule of constitutional law, made retroactive to cases on collateral review by the Supreme Court, that was previously unavailable; or
>
> (ii) a factual predicate that could not have been previously discovered through the exercise of due diligence; and
>
> (B) the facts underlying the claim would be sufficient to establish by clear and convincing evidence that but for constitutional error, no reasonable fact-finder would have found the applicant guilty of the underlying offense.

Writing for a unanimous Court, Justice KENNEDY construed this amendment in (MICHAEL) WILLIAMS v. TAYLOR, ___ U.S. ___, 120 S.Ct. 1479, 146 L.Ed.2d 435 (2000). He explained "As is evident from the similarity between the Court's phrasing in *Keeney* [9th ed., p. 1634], and the opening clause of § 2254(e)(2), Congress intended to preserve at least one aspect of *Keeney's* holding: prisoners who are at fault for the deficiency in the state-court record must satisfy a heightened standard to obtain an evidentiary hearing. To be sure, in requiring that prisoners who have not been diligent satisfy § 2254(e)(2)'s provisions rather than show cause and prejudice, and in eliminating a freestanding 'miscarriage of justice' exception, Congress raised the bar *Keeney* imposed on prisoners who were not diligent in state-court proceedings." However, a "fail[ure]" to develop the factual basis of a claim, the Court held, "is not established unless there is a lack of diligence, or some greater fault, attributable to the prisoner or the prisoner's counsel."

Diligence "depends upon whether the prisoner made a reasonable attempt, in light of the information available at the time, to investigate and pursue claims in state court" and "in the usual case," will require "that the prisoner, at a minimum, seek an evidentiary hearing in state court in the manner prescribed by state law." A petitioner who has "neglected his rights" through lack of diligence will be unable to secure an evidentiary hearing unless "efforts to discover the facts would have been in vain, see § 2254(e)(2)(A)(ii), and there is a convincing claim of innocence, see § 2254(e)(2)(B) * * *." "Though lack of diligence will not bar an evidentiary hearing if efforts to discover the facts would have been in vain, see § 2254(e)(2)(A)(ii), and there is a convincing claim of innocence, see § 2254(e)(2)(B), only a prisoner who has neglected his rights in state court need satisfy these conditions. The statute's later reference to diligence pertains to cases in which the facts could not have been discovered, whether there was diligence or not."

Applying the provision, Justice Kennedy concluded that Williams had not exercised the required diligence with respect to his claim that the prosecution failed to disclose a psychiatric report concerning the state's main witness. Williams' counsel in state habeas proceedings averred that he had not seen the report before filing the state habeas petition. Noting that Williams' postconviction counsel had notice of the report's existence and materiality prior to preparing the state petition, Justice Kennedy stated that Williams' counsel failed to make an adequate effort to find the report—"a diligent attorney would have done more." Because Williams conceded that he could not show by clear and convincing evidence that "no reasonable factfinder would have found petitioner guilty of capital murder but for the alleged constitutional error," § 2254(a)(2) barred an evidentiary hearing in federal court on this *Brady* claim.*

Evidentiary hearings were *not* barred on Williams' remaining claims of juror bias and prosecutorial misconduct. One of the jurors at his 1994 trial, who became the foreperson of the jury, had fifteen years earlier divorced one of the state's witnesses—the officer who had investigated the crime scene and interrogated the state's lead witness. Moreover, this juror was represented in the divorce by the attorney serving as William's prosecutor. None of this was disclosed at trial, and was discovered only after the investigator helping to prepare Williams' federal habeas petition interviewed two other trial jurors who referred in passing to the juror by her married name, leading the investigator to check the County's marriage records. Justice Kennedy concluded that Williams had made a reasonable effort to discover his claims, noting defense counsel should not be expected to "check public records containing personal information pertaining to each and every juror."

* If instead, Williams established that his trial counsel was the counsel not diligent in pursuing the report, how would Williams' effort to secure a hearing in federal court be analyzed under § 2254(e)(2)?

SECTION 4. REACHING THE MERITS: STANDARDS FOR REVIEWING STATE COURT DECISIONS

9th ed., p. 1659; after Note 4, add:

5. Consider the questions in notes 2 and 3 above in light of the Court's decision in *(Terry) Williams v. Taylor,* below.

(TERRY) WILLIAMS v. TAYLOR

___ U.S. ___, 120 S.Ct. 1495, 146 L.Ed.2d 389 (2000).

Justice STEVENS announced the judgment of the Court and delivered the opinion of the Court with respect to Parts I, III, and IV, and an opinion with respect to Parts II and V.*

The questions presented are whether Terry Williams' constitutional right to the effective assistance of counsel as defined in *Strickland v. Washington*, [9th ed., p. 1153], was violated, and whether the judgment of the Virginia Supreme Court refusing to set aside his death sentence "was contrary to, or involved an unreasonable application of, clearly established Federal law, as determined by the Supreme Court of the United States," within the meaning of 28 U.S.C. § 2254(d)(1) (1994 ed., Supp. III). We answer both questions affirmatively.

I

* * * In September 1986, Williams was convicted of robbery and capital murder.

At Williams' sentencing hearing, the prosecution proved that Williams had been convicted of armed robbery in 1976 and burglary and grand larceny in 1982. The prosecution also introduced the written confessions that Williams had made in April. The prosecution described two auto thefts and two separate violent assaults on elderly victims perpetrated after the Stone murder. * * * [, one of whom was] not expected to recover. Williams had also been convicted of arson for setting a fire in the jail while awaiting trial in this case. Two expert witnesses employed by the State testified that there was a "high probability" that Williams would pose a serious continuing threat to society.

The evidence offered by Williams' trial counsel at the sentencing hearing consisted of the testimony of Williams' mother [and] two neighbors, * * * described Williams as a "nice boy" and not a violent person[, and the taped statement of a psychiatrist, which] did little more than relate Williams' statement during an examination that in the course of one of his earlier robberies, he had removed the bullets from a gun so as not to injure anyone.

* * * Williams' counsel * * * asked the jury to give weight to the fact that he had "turned himself in, not on one crime but on four ...

* Justice Souter, Justice Ginsburg, and Justice Breyer join this opinion in its entirety. Justice O'Connor and Justice Kennedy join Parts I, III, and IV of this opinion.

that the [police otherwise] would not have solved." The weight of defense counsel's closing, however, was devoted to explaining that it was difficult to find a reason why the jury should spare Williams' life.[2]

The jury * * * unanimously fixed Williams' punishment at death. The trial judge * * * imposed the death sentence [and the] Virginia Supreme Court affirmed the conviction and sentence.

State Habeas Corpus Proceedings. In 1988 Williams filed for state collateral relief in the Danville Circuit Court [and] the Circuit Court (the same judge who had presided over Williams' trial and sentencing) held an evidentiary hearing on Williams' claim that trial counsel had been ineffective. * * * Judge Ingram found that Williams' conviction was valid, but that his trial attorneys had been ineffective during sentencing. * * *

The Virginia Supreme Court * * * disagreed with the trial judge's conclusion that Williams had suffered sufficient prejudice to warrant relief. * * * [The] Court accepted the factual determination that available evidence in mitigation had not been presented at the trial, but held that the trial judge had misapplied the law in two respects. First, relying on our decision in *Lockhart v. Fretwell* [p. 1169], the court held that it was wrong for the trial judge to rely " 'on mere outcome determination' " when assessing prejudice. Second, it construed the trial judge's opinion as having "adopted a per se approach" that would establish prejudice whenever any mitigating evidence was omitted.

The court * * * concluded that there was no reasonable possibility that the omitted evidence would have affected the jury's sentencing recommendation, and that Williams had failed to demonstrate that his sentencing proceeding was fundamentally unfair.

Federal Habeas Corpus Proceedings. Having exhausted his state remedies, Williams sought a federal writ of habeas corpus pursuant to 28 U.S.C. § 2254 (1994 ed. and Supp. III). * * * [T]he federal trial judge agreed with the Virginia trial judge: The death sentence was constitutionally infirm.

After noting that the Virginia Supreme Court had not addressed the question whether trial counsel's performance at the sentencing hearing fell below the range of competence demanded of lawyers in criminal cases, the judge began by addressing that issue in detail. He identified five categories of mitigating evidence that counsel had failed to introduce,[4] and he rejected the argument that counsel's failure to conduct an

2. In defense counsel's words: "I will admit too that it is very difficult to ask you to show mercy to a man who maybe has not shown much mercy himself. I doubt very seriously that he thought much about mercy when he was in Mr. Stone's bedroom that night with him. I doubt very seriously that he had mercy very highly on his mind when he was walking along West Green and the incident with Alberta Stroud. I doubt very seriously that he had mercy on his mind when he took two cars that didn't belong to him. Admittedly it is very difficult to get us and ask that you give this man mercy when he has shown so little of it himself. But I would ask that you would."

4. "(i) Counsel did not introduce evidence of the Petitioner's background.... (ii) Counsel did not introduce evidence that Petitioner was abused by his father. (iii)

adequate investigation had been a strategic decision to rely almost entirely on the fact that Williams had voluntarily confessed. * * *

Turning to the prejudice issue, the judge determined that there was " 'a reasonable probability that, but for counsel's unprofessional errors, the result of the proceeding would have been different.' He found that the Virginia Supreme Court had erroneously assumed that *Lockhart* had modified the *Strickland* standard for determining prejudice, and that it had made an important error of fact in discussing its finding of no prejudice.[5] Having introduced his analysis of Williams' claim with the standard of review applicable on habeas appeals provided by 28 U.S.C. § 2254(d)(1994 ed., Supp. III), the judge concluded that those errors established that the Virginia Supreme Court's decision "was contrary to, or involved an unreasonable application of, clearly established Federal law" within the meaning of § 2254(d)(1).

The Federal Court of Appeals reversed. * * * We granted certiorari, and now reverse.

II

* * *

* * * When federal judges exercise their federal-question jurisdiction under the "judicial Power" of Article III of the Constitution, it is "emphatically the province and duty" of those judges to "say what the law is." *Marbury v. Madison*, 5 U.S. 137, 1 Cranch 137, 177, 2 L. Ed. 60 (1803). At the core of this power is the federal courts' independent responsibility—independent from its coequal branches in the Federal Government, and independent from the separate authority of the several States—to interpret federal law. A construction of AEDPA that would require the federal courts to cede this authority to the courts of the States would be inconsistent with the practice that federal judges have traditionally followed in discharging their duties under Article III of the Constitution. If Congress had intended to require such an important change in the exercise of our jurisdiction, we believe it would have spoken with much greater clarity than is found in the text of AEDPA.

This basic premise informs our interpretation of both parts of § 2254(d)(1): first, the requirement that the determinations of state courts be tested only against "clearly established Federal law, as determined by the Supreme Court of the United States," and second, the

Counsel did not introduce testimony from correctional officers who were willing to testify that defendant would not pose a danger while incarcerated. Nor did counsel offer prison commendations awarded to Williams for his help in breaking up a prison drug ring and for returning a guard's wallet. (iv) Several character witnesses were not called to testify.... The testimony of Elliott, a respected CPA in the community, could have been quite important to the jury.... (v) Finally, counsel did not introduce evidence that Petitioner was borderline mentally retarded, though he was found competent to stand trial."

5. "Specifically, the * * * the Virginia Supreme Court ignored or overlooked the evidence of Williams' difficult childhood and abuse and his limited mental capacity. It is also unreasonable to characterize the additional evidence as coming from 'mostly relatives.' * * * Bruce Elliott, a respected professional in the community, and several correctional officers offered to testify on Williams behalf."

prohibition on the issuance of the writ unless the state court's decision is "contrary to, or involved an unreasonable application of," that clearly established law. We address each part in turn.

The "clearly established law" requirement. In *Teague v. Lane* [9th ed., p. 1648], we held that the petitioner was not entitled to federal habeas relief because he was relying on a rule of federal law that had not been announced until after his state conviction became final. The antiretroactivity rule recognized in *Teague*, which prohibits reliance on "new rules," is the functional equivalent of a statutory provision commanding exclusive reliance on "clearly established law." Because there is no reason to believe that Congress intended to require federal courts to ask both whether a rule sought on habeas is "new" under *Teague*—which remains the law—and also whether it is "clearly established" under AEDPA, it seems safe to assume that Congress had congruent concepts in mind. It is perfectly clear that AEDPA codifies *Teague* to the extent that *Teague* requires federal habeas courts to deny relief that is contingent upon a rule of law not clearly established at the time the state conviction became final.

Teague's core principles are therefore relevant to our construction of this requirement. Justice Harlan recognized the "inevitable difficulties" that come with "attempting 'to determine whether a particular decision has really announced a "new" rule at all or whether it has simply applied a well-established constitutional principle to govern a case which is closely analogous to those which have been previously considered in the prior case law.' " But *Teague* established some guidance for making this determination, explaining that a federal habeas court operates within the bounds of comity and finality if it applies a rule "dictated by precedent existing at the time the defendant's conviction became final." *Teague*, 489 U.S. at 301 (emphasis deleted). A rule that "breaks new ground or imposes a new obligation on the States or the Federal Government," ibid., falls outside this universe of federal law.

To this, AEDPA has added, immediately following the "clearly established law" requirement, a clause limiting the area of relevant law to that "determined by the Supreme Court of the United States." 28 U.S.C. § 2254(d)(1) (1994 ed., Supp. III). If this Court has not broken sufficient legal ground to establish an asked-for constitutional principle, the lower federal courts cannot themselves establish such a principle with clarity sufficient to satisfy the AEDPA bar. In this respect, we agree with the Seventh Circuit that this clause "extends the principle of *Teague* by limiting the source of doctrine on which a federal court may rely in addressing the application for a writ." *Lindh v. Murphy*, 96 F.3d 856, 869 (7th Cir.1996)[, rev'd on other grounds, 521 U.S. 320 (1997)]. * * *

A rule that fails to satisfy the foregoing criteria is barred by *Teague* from application on collateral review, and, similarly, is not available as a basis for relief in a habeas case to which AEDPA applies. * * *

The "contrary to, or an unreasonable application of," requirement. The message that Congress intended to convey by using the phrases, "contrary to" and "unreasonable application of" is not entirely clear. The prevailing view in the Circuits is that the former phrase requires de novo review of 'pure' questions of law and the latter requires some sort of "reasonability" review of so-called mixed questions of law and fact.

We are not persuaded that the phrases define two mutually exclusive categories of questions. * * *

The statutory text likewise does not obviously prescribe a specific, recognizable standard of review for dealing with either phrase. Significantly, it does not use any term, such as "*de novo*" or "plain error," that would easily identify a familiar standard of review. Rather, the text is fairly read simply as a command that a federal court not issue the habeas writ unless the state court was wrong as a matter of law or unreasonable in its application of law in a given case. The suggestion that a wrong state-court "decision"—a legal judgment rendered "after consideration of *facts, and* . . . *law*," Black's Law Dictionary 407 (6th ed. 1990) (emphasis added)—may no longer be redressed through habeas (because it is unreachable under the "unreasonable application" phrase) is based on a mistaken insistence that the § 2254(d)(1) phrases have not only independent, but mutually exclusive, meanings. Whether or not a federal court can issue the writ "under [the] 'unreasonable application' clause," the statute is clear that habeas may issue under § 2254(d)(1) if a state court "decision" is "contrary to . . . clearly established Federal law." We thus anticipate that there will be a variety of cases, like this one, in which both phrases may be implicated.

Even though we cannot conclude that the phrases establish "a body of rigid rules," they do express a "mood" that the federal judiciary must respect. *Universal Camera Corp. v. NLRB*, 340 U.S. 474, 487, 95 L.Ed. 456, 71 S.Ct. 456 (1951). In this respect, it seems clear that Congress intended federal judges to attend with the utmost care to state-court decisions, including all of the reasons supporting their decisions, before concluding that those proceedings were infected by constitutional error sufficiently serious to warrant the issuance of the writ. Likewise, the statute in a separate provision provides for the habeas remedy when a state-court decision "was based on an unreasonable determination of the facts *in light of the evidence presented in the State court proceeding*." 28 U.S.C. § 2254(d)(2) (1994 ed., Supp. III) (emphasis added). While this provision is not before us in this case, it provides relevant context for our interpretation of § 2254(d)(1); in this respect, it bolsters our conviction that federal habeas courts must make as the starting point of their analysis the state courts' determinations of fact, including that aspect of a "mixed question" that rests on a finding of fact. AEDPA plainly sought to ensure a level of "deference to the determinations of state courts," provided those determinations did not conflict with federal law or apply federal law in an unreasonable way. H. R. Conf. Rep. No. 104–518, p. 111 (1996). Congress wished to curb delays, to prevent "retrials" on federal habeas, and to give effect to state convictions to the extent possible under law. When federal courts are able to fulfill these goals within the bounds of the law, AEDPA instructs them to do so.

On the other hand, it is significant that the word "deference" does not appear in the text of the statute itself. Neither the legislative history, nor the statutory text, suggests any difference in the so-called "deference" depending on which of the two phrases is implicated. Whatever "deference" Congress had in mind with respect to both phrases, it surely is not a requirement that federal courts actually defer to a state-court application of the federal law that is, in the independent judgment of the federal court, in error. As Judge Easterbrook noted with respect to the phrase "contrary to": "Section 2254(d) requires us to give state courts' opinions a respectful reading, and to listen carefully to their conclusions, but when the state court addresses a legal question, it is the law 'as determined by the Supreme Court of the United States' that prevails." *Lindh*, 96 F.3d at 869.[14]

Our disagreement with Justice O'Connor about the precise meaning of the phrase "contrary to," and the word "unreasonable," is, of course, important, but should affect only a narrow category of cases. * * * [S]tate-court decisions that do not "conflict" with federal law will rarely be "unreasonable" under either her reading of the statute or ours. We all agree that state-court judgments must be upheld unless, after the closest examination of the state-court judgment, a federal court is firmly

14. The Court advances three reasons for adopting its alternative construction of the phrase "unreasonable application of." First, the use of the word "unreasonable" in the statute suggests that Congress was directly influenced by the "patently unreasonable" standard advocated by Justice THOMAS in his opinion in *Wright v. West* [9th ed., p. 1657]; second, the legislative history supports this view, and third, Congress must have intended to change the law more substantially than our reading 28 U.S.C. § 2254(d)(1) (1994 ed., Supp. III) permits.

None of these reasons is persuasive. First, even though, as the Court recognizes, the term "unreasonable" is "difficult to define," neither the statute itself nor the Court's explanation of it, suggests that AEDPA's "unreasonable application of" has the same meaning as Justice Thomas' " 'patently unreasonable' " standard mentioned in his dictum in *Wright*. To the extent the "broader debate" in *Wright* touched upon the Court's novel distinction today between what is "wrong" and what is "unreasonable," it was in the context of a discussion not about the standard of review habeas courts should use for law-application questions, but about whether a rule is "new" or "old" such that *Teague*'s retroactivity rule would bar habeas relief; Justice Thomas contended that *Teague* barred habeas "whenever the state courts have interpreted old precedents reasonably, not [as Justice O'Connor suggested] only when they have done so 'properly.' " *Teague*, of course, as Justice O'Connor correctly pointed out, "did not establish a standard of review at all"; rather than instructing a court how to review a claim, it simply asks, in absolute terms, whether a rule was clear at the time of a state-court decision. We thus do not think *Wright* "confirms" anything about the meaning of § 2254(d)(1), which is, as our division reflects, anything but "clear."

As for the other bases for Justice O'Connor's view, the only two specific citations to the legislative history upon which she relies, do no more than beg the question. One merely quotes the language of the statute without elaboration, and the other goes to slightly greater length in stating that state-court judgments must be upheld unless "unreasonable." Neither sheds any light on what the content of the hypothetical category of "decisions" that are wrong but nevertheless not "unreasonable." Finally, while we certainly agree with the Court that AEDPA wrought substantial changes in habeas law, there is an obvious fallacy in the assumption that because the statute changed pre-existing law in some respects, it must have rendered this specific change here.

convinced that a federal constitutional right has been violated. Our difference is as to the cases in which, at first-blush, a state-court judgment seems entirely reasonable, but thorough analysis by a federal court produces a firm conviction that that judgment is infected by constitutional error. In our view, such an erroneous judgment is "unreasonable" within the meaning of the act even though that conclusion was not immediately apparent.

In sum, the statute directs federal courts to attend to every state-court judgment with utmost care, but it does not require them to defer to the opinion of every reasonable state-court judge on the content of federal law. If, after carefully weighing all the reasons for accepting a state court's judgment, a federal court is convinced that a prisoner's custody—or, as in this case, his sentence of death—violates the Constitution, that independent judgment should prevail. Otherwise the federal "law as determined by the Supreme Court of the United States" might be applied by the federal courts one way in Virginia and another way in California. In light of the well-recognized interest in ensuring that federal courts interpret federal law in a uniform way,[15] we are convinced that Congress did not intend the statute to produce such a result.

III

In this case, Williams contends that he was denied his constitutionally guaranteed right to the effective assistance of counsel when his trial lawyers failed to investigate and to present substantial mitigating evidence to the sentencing jury. The threshold question under AEDPA is whether Williams seeks to apply a rule of law that was clearly established at the time his state-court conviction became final. * * *

It is past question that the rule set forth in *Strickland* qualifies as "clearly established Federal law, as determined by the Supreme Court of the United States." * * * This Court's precedent "dictated" that the Virginia Supreme Court apply the *Strickland* test at the time that court entertained Williams' ineffective-assistance claim. * * * Williams is therefore entitled to relief if the Virginia Supreme Court's decision rejecting his ineffective-assistance claim was either "contrary to, or involved an unreasonable application of," that established law. It was both.

IV

The Virginia Supreme Court erred in holding that our decision in *Lockhart* modified or in some way supplanted the rule set down in *Strickland*. It is true that while the *Strickland* test provides sufficient guidance for resolving virtually all ineffective-assistance-of-counsel claims, there are situations in which the overriding focus on fundamen-

15. Indeed, a contrary rule would be in substantial tension with the interest in uniformity served by Congress' modification in AEDPA of our previous *Teague* jurisprudence—now the law on habeas review must be "clearly established" by this Court alone. It would thus seem somewhat perverse to ascribe to Congress the entirely inconsistent policy of perpetuating disparate readings of our decisions under the guise of deference to anything within a conceivable spectrum of reasonableness.

tal fairness may affect the analysis. Thus, on the one hand, as *Strickland* itself explained, there are a few situations in which prejudice may be presumed. And, on the other hand, there are also situations in which it would be unjust to characterize the likelihood of a different outcome as legitimate "prejudice." Even if a defendant's false testimony might have persuaded the jury to acquit him, it is not fundamentally unfair to conclude that he was not prejudiced by counsel's interference with his intended perjury. *Nix v. Whiteside* [9th ed., p. 1171].

Similarly, in *Lockhart*, we concluded that, given the overriding interest in fundamental fairness, the likelihood of a different outcome attributable to an incorrect interpretation of the law should be regarded as a potential "windfall" to the defendant rather than the legitimate "prejudice" contemplated by our opinion in *Strickland*. The death sentence that Arkansas had imposed on Bobby Ray Fretwell was based on an aggravating circumstance (murder committed for pecuniary gain) that duplicated an element of the underlying felony (murder in the course of a robbery). Shortly before the trial, the United States Court of Appeals for the Eighth Circuit had held that such "double counting" was impermissible, but Fretwell's lawyer (presumably because he was unaware of [this] decision) failed to object to the use of the pecuniary gain aggravator. Before Fretwell's claim for federal habeas corpus relief reached this Court, the [Eighth Circuit] case was overruled. Accordingly, even though the Arkansas trial judge probably would have sustained a timely objection to the double counting, it had become clear that the State had a right to rely on the disputed aggravating circumstance. Because the ineffectiveness of Fretwell's counsel had not deprived him of any substantive or procedural right to which the law entitled him, we held that his claim did not satisfy the "prejudice" component of the *Strickland* test.

Cases such as *Nix* and *Lockhart* do not justify a departure from a straightforward application of *Strickland* when the ineffectiveness of counsel does deprive the defendant of a substantive or procedural right to which the law entitles him. In the instant case, it is undisputed that Williams had a right—indeed, a constitutionally protected right—to provide the jury with the mitigating evidence that his trial counsel either failed to discover or failed to offer.

Nevertheless, the Virginia Supreme Court read our decision in *Lockhart* to require a separate inquiry into fundamental fairness even when Williams is able to show that his lawyer was ineffective and that his ineffectiveness probably affected the outcome of the proceeding. It wrote:

> The prisoner argues there "is a 'reasonable probability' that at least one juror would have been moved to spare Petitioner's life had he heard" the mitigation evidence developed at the habeas hearing that was not presented at the trial. Summarizing, he contends there "is a 'reasonable probability' that had at least one juror heard any of this evidence—let alone all of this evidence—the outcome of this case

would have been different." We reject these contentions. The prisoner's discussion flies in the face of the Supreme Court's admonition in *Lockhart* that "an analysis focusing solely on mere outcome determination, without attention to whether the result of the proceeding was fundamentally unfair or unreliable, is defective."

Unlike the Virginia Supreme Court, the state trial judge omitted any reference to *Lockhart* and simply relied on our opinion in *Strickland* as stating the correct standard for judging ineffective-assistance claims. * * *

The trial judge analyzed the ineffective-assistance claim under the correct standard; the Virginia Supreme Court did not.

We are likewise persuaded that the Virginia trial judge correctly applied both components of that standard to Williams' ineffectiveness claim. [C]ounsel did not begin to prepare for that phase of the proceeding until a week before the trial[,] failed to conduct an investigation that would have uncovered extensive records graphically describing Williams' nightmarish childhood, * * * [,] failed to introduce available evidence that Williams was "borderline mentally retarded" and did not advance beyond sixth grade in school[,] failed to seek prison records recording Williams' commendations for helping to crack a prison drug ring and for returning a guard's missing wallet, or the testimony of prison officials who described Williams as among the inmates "least likely to act in a violent, dangerous or provocative way", [or the testimony of another witness] that Williams "seemed to thrive in a more regimented and structured environment," and that Williams was proud of the carpentry degree he earned while in prison.

Of course, not all of the additional evidence was favorable to Williams. The juvenile records revealed that he had been thrice committed to the juvenile system. * * * But as the Federal District Court correctly observed, the failure to introduce the comparatively voluminous amount of evidence that did speak in Williams' favor was not justified by a tactical decision to focus on Williams' voluntary confession. Whether or not those omissions were sufficiently prejudicial to have affected the outcome of sentencing, they clearly demonstrate that trial counsel did not fulfill their obligation to conduct a thorough investigation of the defendant's background. *See* 1 ABA Standards for Criminal Justice 4–4.1, commentary, pp. 4–55 (2d ed.1980).

We are also persuaded, unlike the Virginia Supreme Court, that counsel's unprofessional service prejudiced Williams within the meaning of *Strickland*. After hearing the additional evidence developed in the postconviction proceedings, the very judge who presided at Williams' trial and who once determined that the death penalty was "just" and "appropriate," concluded that there existed "a reasonable probability that the result of the sentencing phase would have been different" if the jury had heard that evidence. * * *

The Virginia Supreme Court's own analysis of prejudice reaching the contrary conclusion was thus unreasonable in at least two respects. First, as we have already explained, * * * it is evident to us that the court's decision turned on its erroneous view that a "mere" difference in outcome is not sufficient to establish constitutionally ineffective assistance of counsel. Its analysis in this respect was thus not only "contrary to," but also, inasmuch as the Virginia Supreme Court relied on the inapplicable exception recognized in *Lockhart*, an "unreasonable application of" the clear law as established by this Court.

Second, the State Supreme Court's prejudice determination was unreasonable insofar as it failed to evaluate the totality of the available mitigation evidence—both that adduced at trial, and the evidence adduced in the habeas proceeding—in reweighing it against the evidence in aggravation. See *Clemons v. Mississippi*, 494 U.S. 738, 751–752, 108 L.Ed.2d 725, 110 S.Ct. 1441 (1990). This error is apparent in its consideration of the additional mitigation evidence developed in the postconviction proceedings.

* * * [T]he state court failed even to mention the sole argument in mitigation that trial counsel did advance—Williams turned himself in, alerting police to a crime they otherwise would never have discovered, expressing remorse for his actions, and cooperating with the police after that. While this, coupled with the prison records and guard testimony, may not have overcome a finding of future dangerousness, the graphic description of Williams' childhood, filled with abuse and privation, or the reality that he was "borderline mentally retarded," might well have influenced the jury's appraisal of his moral culpability. See *Boyde v. California*, 494 U.S. 370, 387, 108 L.Ed.2d 316, 110 S.Ct. 1190 (1990). The circumstances recited in his several confessions are consistent with the view that in each case his violent behavior was a compulsive reaction rather than the product of cold-blooded premeditation. Mitigating evidence unrelated to dangerousness may alter the jury's selection of penalty, even if it does not undermine or rebut the prosecution's death-eligibility case. The Virginia Supreme Court did not entertain that possibility. It thus failed to accord appropriate weight to the body of mitigation evidence available to trial counsel.

V

* * * [T]he judgment of the Court of Appeals is reversed, and the case is remanded for further proceedings consistent with this opinion. It is so ordered.

Justice O'CONNOR delivered the opinion of the Court with respect to Part II (except as to the footnote), concurred in part, and concurred in the judgment.† * * *

† Justice Kennedy joins this opinion in its entirety. The Chief Justice and Justice Thomas join this opinion with respect to Part II. Justice Scalia joins this opinion with respect to Part II, except as to the footnote†, infra.

I

* * * If today's case were governed by the federal habeas statute prior to Congress' enactment of AEDPA in 1996, I would agree with Justice Stevens that Williams' petition for habeas relief must be granted if we, in our independent judgment, were to conclude that his Sixth Amendment right to effective assistance of counsel was violated.

II

A

Williams' case is not governed by the pre–1996 version of the habeas statute. Because he filed his petition in December 1997, Williams' case is governed by the statute as amended by AEDPA. * * *

Accordingly, for Williams to obtain federal habeas relief, he must first demonstrate that his case satisfies the condition set by § 2254(d)(1). That provision modifies the role of federal habeas courts in reviewing petitions filed by state prisoners.

Justice Stevens' opinion in Part II essentially contends that § 2254(d)(1) does not alter the previously settled rule of independent review. Indeed, the opinion concludes its statutory inquiry with the somewhat empty finding that § 2254(d)(1) does no more than express a " 'mood' that the federal judiciary must respect." For Justice Stevens, the congressionally enacted "mood" has two important qualities. First, "federal courts [must] attend to every state-court judgment with utmost care" by "carefully weighing all the reasons for accepting a state court's judgment." Second, if a federal court undertakes that careful review and yet remains convinced that a prisoner's custody violates the Constitution, "that independent judgment should prevail."

One need look no further than our decision in [*Miller v. Fenton*, 474 U.S. 104, 112, 88 L. Ed.2d 405, 106 S.Ct. 445 (1985)] to see that Justice Stevens' interpretation of § 2254(d)(1) gives the 1996 amendment no effect whatsoever. The command that federal courts should now use the "utmost care" by "carefully weighing" the reasons supporting a state court's judgment echoes our pre-AEDPA statement in *Miller* that federal habeas courts "should, of course, give great weight to the considered conclusions of a coequal state judiciary." Similarly, the requirement that the independent judgment of a federal court must in the end prevail essentially repeats the conclusion we reached in the very next sentence in *Miller* with respect to the specific issue presented there: "But, as we now reaffirm, the ultimate question whether, under the totality of the circumstances, the challenged confession was obtained in a manner compatible with the requirements of the Constitution *is a matter for independent federal determination*." (emphasis added).

That Justice Stevens would find the new § 2254(d)(1) to have no effect on the prior law of habeas corpus is remarkable given his apparent acknowledgment that Congress wished to bring change to the field. That acknowledgment is correct and significant to this case. It cannot be disputed that Congress viewed § 2254(d)(1) as an important means by which its goals for habeas reform would be achieved.

Justice Stevens arrives at his erroneous interpretation by means of one critical misstep. He fails to give independent meaning to both the "contrary to" and "unreasonable application" clauses of the statute. By reading § 2254(d)(1) as one general restriction on the power of the federal habeas court, Justice Stevens manages to avoid confronting the specific meaning of the statute's "unreasonable application" clause and its ramifications for the independent-review rule. It is, however, a cardinal principle of statutory construction that we must " 'give effect, if possible, to every clause and word of a statute.' " Section 2254(d)(1) defines two categories of cases in which a state prisoner may obtain federal habeas relief with respect to a claim adjudicated on the merits in state court. Under the statute, a federal court may grant a writ of habeas corpus if the relevant state-court decision was either (1) "contrary to ... clearly established Federal law, as determined by the Supreme Court of the United States," or (2) "involved an unreasonable application of ... clearly established Federal law, as determined by the Supreme Court of the United States."

The Court of Appeals for the Fourth Circuit properly accorded both the "contrary to" and "unreasonable application" clauses independent meaning. * * * The word "contrary" is commonly understood to mean "diametrically different," "opposite in character or nature," or "mutually opposed." Webster's Third New International Dictionary 495 (1976). The text of § 2254(d)(1) therefore suggests that the state court's decision must be substantially different from the relevant precedent of this Court. The Fourth Circuit's interpretation of the "contrary to" clause accurately reflects this textual meaning. A state-court decision will certainly be contrary to our clearly established precedent if the state court applies a rule that contradicts the governing law set forth in our cases. Take, for example, our decision in *Strickland.* If a state court were to reject a prisoner's claim of ineffective assistance of counsel on the grounds that the prisoner had not established by a preponderance of the evidence that the result of his criminal proceeding would have been different, that decision would be "diametrically different," "opposite in character or nature," and "mutually opposed" to our clearly established precedent because we held in *Strickland* that the prisoner need only demonstrate a "reasonable probability that ... the result of the proceeding would have been different." A state-court decision will also be contrary to this Court's clearly established precedent if the state court confronts a set of facts that are materially indistinguishable from a decision of this Court and nevertheless arrives at a result different from our precedent. Accordingly, in either of these two scenarios, a federal court will be unconstrained by § 2254(d)(1) because the state-court decision falls within that provision's "contrary to" clause.

On the other hand, a run-of-the-mill state-court decision applying the correct legal rule from our cases to the facts of a prisoner's case would not fit comfortably within § 2254(d)(1)'s "contrary to" clause.

Assume, for example, that a state-court decision on a prisoner's ineffective-assistance claim correctly identifies *Strickland* as the controlling legal authority and, applying that framework, rejects the prisoner's claim. Quite clearly, the state-court decision would be in accord with our decision in *Strickland* as to the legal prerequisites for establishing an ineffective-assistance claim, even assuming the federal court considering the prisoner's habeas application might reach a different result applying the *Strickland* framework itself. It is difficult, however, to describe such a run-of-the-mill state-court decision as "diametrically different" from, "opposite in character or nature" from, or "mutually opposed" to *Strickland*, our clearly established precedent. Although the state-court decision may be contrary to the federal court's conception of how *Strickland* ought to be applied in that particular case, the decision is not "mutually opposed" to *Strickland* itself.

Justice Stevens would instead construe § 2254(d)(1)'s "contrary to" clause to encompass such a routine state-court decision. That construction, however, saps the "unreasonable application" clause of any meaning. If a federal habeas court can, under the "contrary to" clause, issue the writ whenever it concludes that the state court's application of clearly established federal law was incorrect, the "unreasonable application" clause becomes a nullity. We must, however, if possible, give meaning to every clause of the statute. Justice Stevens not only makes no attempt to do so, but also construes the "contrary to" clause in a manner that ensures that the "unreasonable application" clause will have no independent meaning. We reject that expansive interpretation of the statute. Reading § 2254(d)(1)'s "contrary to" clause to permit a federal court to grant relief in cases where a state court's error is limited to the manner in which it *applies* Supreme Court precedent is suspect given the logical and natural fit of the neighboring "unreasonable application" clause to such cases.

The Fourth Circuit's interpretation of the "unreasonable application" clause of § 2254(d)(1) is generally correct. That court held in *Green v. French*, 143 F.3d 865 (4th Cir.1998) that a state-court decision can involve an "unreasonable application" of this Court's clearly established precedent in two ways. First, a state-court decision involves an unreasonable application of this Court's precedent if the state court identifies the correct governing legal rule from this Court's cases but unreasonably applies it to the facts of the particular state prisoner's case. Second, a state-court decision also involves an unreasonable application of this Court's precedent if the state court either unreasonably extends a legal principle from our precedent to a new context where it should not apply or unreasonably refuses to extend that principle to a new context where it should apply.

A state-court decision that correctly identifies the governing legal rule but applies it unreasonably to the facts of a particular prisoner's case certainly would qualify as a decision "involving an unreasonable application of . . . clearly established Federal law." Indeed, we used the almost identical phrase "application of law" to describe a state court's application of law to fact in the certiorari question we posed to the parties in *Wright.*†

The Fourth Circuit also held in *Green* that state-court decisions that unreasonably extend a legal principle from our precedent to a new context where it should not apply (or unreasonably refuse to extend a legal principle to a new context where it should apply) should be analyzed under § 2254(d)(1)'s "unreasonable application" clause. Although that holding may perhaps be correct, the classification does have some problems of precision. Just as it is sometimes difficult to distinguish a mixed question of law and fact from a question of fact, it will often be difficult to identify separately those state-court decisions that involve an unreasonable application of a legal principle (or an unreasonable failure to apply a legal principle) to a new context. Indeed, on the one hand, in some cases it will be hard to distinguish a decision involving an unreasonable extension of a legal principle from a decision involving an unreasonable application of law to facts. On the other hand, in many of the same cases it will also be difficult to distinguish a decision involving an unreasonable extension of a legal principle from a decision that "arrives at a conclusion opposite to that reached by this Court on a question of law." Today's case does not require us to decide how such "extension of legal principle" cases should be treated under § 2254(d)(1). For now it is sufficient to hold that when a state-court decision unreasonably applies the law of this Court to the facts of a prisoner's case, a federal court applying § 2254(d)(1) may conclude that the state-court decision falls within that provision's "unreasonable application" clause.

B

There remains the task of defining what exactly qualifies as an "unreasonable application" of law under § 2254(d)(1). The Fourth Circuit held in *Green* that a state-court decision involves an "unreasonable application of . . . clearly established Federal law" only if the state court has applied federal law "in a manner that reasonable jurists would all agree is unreasonable." The placement of this additional overlay on the "unreasonable application" clause was erroneous. * * * Stated simply, a federal habeas court making the "unreasonable application" inquiry should ask whether the state court's application of clearly established federal law was objectively unreasonable. The federal habeas court should not transform the inquiry into a subjective one by resting its determination instead on the simple fact that at least one of the Nation's jurists has applied the relevant federal law in the same manner the state court did in the habeas petitioner's case.

† The legislative history of § 2254(d)(1) also supports this interpretation. See, e.g., 142 Cong. Rec. 7799 (1996) (remarks of Sen. Specter) ("Under the bill deference will be owed to State courts' decisions on the application of Federal law to the facts. Unless it is unreasonable, a State court's decision applying the law to the facts will be upheld"); 141 Cong. Rec. 14666 (1995) (remarks of Sen. Hatch) ("We allow a Federal court to overturn a State court decision only if it is contrary to clearly established Federal law or if it involves an 'unreasonable application' of clearly established Federal law to the facts").

* * * The term "unreasonable" is no doubt difficult to define. That said, it is a common term in the legal world and, accordingly, federal judges are familiar with its meaning. For purposes of today's opinion, the most important point is that an unreasonable application of federal law is different from an incorrect application of federal law. Our opinions in *Wright*, for example, make that difference clear. * * * In § 2254(d)(1), Congress specifically used the word "unreasonable," and not a term like "erroneous" or "incorrect." Under § 2254(d)(1)'s "unreasonable application" clause, then, a federal habeas court may not issue the writ simply because that court concludes in its independent judgment that the relevant state-court decision applied clearly established federal law erroneously or incorrectly. Rather, that application must also be unreasonable.

Justice Stevens turns a blind eye to the debate in *Wright* because he finds no indication in § 2254(d)(1) itself that Congress was "directly influenced" by Justice Thomas' opinion in *Wright*. As Justice Stevens himself apparently recognizes, however, Congress need not mention a prior decision of this Court by name in a statute's text in order to adopt either a rule or a meaning given a certain term in that decision. In any event, whether Congress intended to codify the standard of review suggested by Justice Thomas in *Wright* is beside the point. *Wright* is important for the light it sheds on § 2254(d)(1)'s requirement that a federal habeas court inquire into the reasonableness of a state court's application of clearly established federal law. The separate opinions in *Wright* concerned the very issue addressed by § 2254(d)(1)'s "unreasonable application" clause—whether, in reviewing a state-court decision on a state prisoner's claims under federal law, a federal habeas court should ask whether the state-court decision was correct or simply whether it was reasonable. * * * The *Wright* opinions confirm what § 2254(d)(1)'s language already makes clear—that an unreasonable application of federal law is different from an incorrect or erroneous application of federal law.

Throughout this discussion the meaning of the phrase "clearly established Federal law, as determined by the Supreme Court of the United States" has been put to the side. That statutory phrase refers to the holdings, as opposed to the dicta, of this Court's decisions as of the time of the relevant state-court decision. In this respect, the "clearly established Federal law" phrase bears only a slight connection to our *Teague* jurisprudence. With one caveat, whatever would qualify as an old rule under our *Teague* jurisprudence will constitute "clearly established Federal law, as determined by the Supreme Court of the United States" under § 2254(d)(1). The one caveat, as the statutory language makes clear, is that § 2254(d)(1) restricts the source of clearly established law to this Court's jurisprudence.

In sum, § 2254(d)(1) places a new constraint on the power of a federal habeas court to grant a state prisoner's application for a writ of habeas corpus with respect to claims adjudicated on the merits in state court. Under § 2254(d)(1), the writ may issue only if one of the following two conditions is satisfied—the state-court adjudication resulted in a decision that (1) "was contrary to . . . clearly established Federal law, as determined by the Supreme Court of the United States," or (2) "involved an unreasonable application of . . . clearly established Federal law, as determined by the Supreme Court of the United States." Under the "contrary to" clause, a federal habeas court may grant the writ if the state court arrives at a conclusion opposite to that reached by this Court on a question of law or if the state court decides a case differently than this Court has on a set of materially indistinguishable facts. Under the "unreasonable application" clause, a federal habeas court may grant the writ if the state court identifies the correct governing legal principle from this Court's decisions but unreasonably applies that principle to the facts of the prisoner's case.

III

Although I disagree with Justice Stevens concerning the standard we must apply under § 2254(d)(1) in evaluating Terry Williams' claims on habeas, I agree with the Court that the Virginia Supreme Court's adjudication of Williams' claim of ineffective assistance of counsel resulted in a decision that was both contrary to and involved an unreasonable application of this Court's clearly established precedent. Specifically, I believe that the Court's discussion in Parts III and IV is correct and that it demonstrates the reasons that the Virginia Supreme Court's decision in Williams' case, even under the interpretation of § 2254(d)(1) I have set forth above, was both contrary to and involved an unreasonable application of our precedent. * * *

Accordingly, although I disagree with the interpretation of § 2254(d)(1) set forth in Part II of Justice Stevens' opinion, I join Parts I, III, and IV of the Court's opinion and concur in the judgment of reversal.

Chief Justice REHNQUIST, with whom Justice SCALIA and Justice THOMAS join, concurring in part and dissenting in part.

I agree with the Court's interpretation of 28 U.S.C. § 2254(d)(1) (1994 ed., Supp.III), see *ante* (opinion of O'Connor, J.), but disagree with its decision to grant habeas relief in this case. * * *

* * * Because the Virginia Supreme Court did not rely on Lockhart to make its decision, and, instead, appropriately relied on *Strickland*, that court's adjudication was not "contrary to" this Court's clearly established precedent. * * *

* * * [T]here was strong evidence that petitioner would continue to be a danger to society, both in and out of prison. It was not, therefore, unreasonable for the Virginia Supreme Court to decide that a jury would not have been swayed by evidence demonstrating that petitioner had a terrible childhood and a low IQ. The potential mitigating evidence that may have countered the finding that petitioner was a future danger was testimony that petitioner was not dangerous while in detention. But,

again, it is not unreasonable to assume that the jury would have viewed this mitigation as unconvincing upon hearing that petitioner set fire to his cell while awaiting trial for the murder at hand and has repeated visions of harming other inmates.

Accordingly, I would hold that habeas relief is barred by 28 U.S.C. § 2254(d) (1994 ed., Supp. III).

Appendix A

SELECTED PROVISIONS OF THE UNITED STATES CONSTITUTION

ARTICLE I

Section 9. * * *

[2] The privilege of the Writ of Habeas Corpus shall not be suspended, unless when in Cases of Rebellion or Invasion the public Safety may require it.

[3] No Bill of Attainder or ex post facto Law shall be passed.

ARTICLE III

Section 1. The judicial Power of the United States, shall be vested in one supreme Court, and in such inferior Courts as the Congress may from time to time ordain and establish. The Judges, both of the supreme and inferior Courts, shall hold their Offices during good Behaviour, and shall, at stated Times, receive for their Services a Compensation, which shall not be diminished during their Continuance in Office.

Section 2. [1] The judicial Power shall extend to all Cases, in Law and Equity, arising under this Constitution, the Laws of the United States, and Treaties made, or which shall be made, under their Authority;—to all Cases affecting Ambassadors, other public Ministers and Consuls;—to all Cases of admiralty and maritime Jurisdiction;—to Controversies to which the United States shall be a Party;—to Controversies between two or more States;—between a State and Citizens of another State;—between Citizens of different States;—between Citizens of the same State claiming Lands under the Grants of different States, and between a State, or the Citizens thereof, and foreign States, Citizens or Subjects.

[3] The trial of all Crimes, except in Cases of Impeachment, shall be by Jury; and such Trial shall be held in the State where the said Crimes shall have been committed; but when not committed within any State, the Trial shall be at such Place or Places as the Congress may by Law have directed.

Section 3. [1] Treason against the United States, shall consist only in levying War against them, or, in adhering to their Enemies, giving them Aid and Comfort. No Person shall be convicted of Treason unless on the Testimony of two Witnesses to the same overt Act, or on Confession in open Court.

[2] The Congress shall have Power to declare the Punishment of Treason, but no Attainder of Treason shall work Corruption of Blood, or Forfeiture except during the Life of the Person attainted.

Article IV

Section 2. [1] The Citizens of each State shall be entitled to all Privileges and Immunities of Citizens in the several States.

[2] A Person charged in any State with Treason, Felony, or other Crime, who shall flee from Justice, and be found in another State, shall on demand of the executive Authority of the State from which he fled, be delivered up, to be removed to the State having Jurisdiction of the Crime.

Article VI

[2] This Constitution, and the Laws of the United States which shall be made in Pursuance thereof; and all Treaties made, or which shall be made, under the Authority of the United States, shall be the supreme Law.

Amendment I [1791]

Congress shall make no law respecting an establishment of religion, or prohibiting the free exercise thereof; or abridging the freedom of speech, or of the press; or the right of the people peaceably to assemble, and to petition the Government for a redress of grievances.

Amendment II [1791]

A well regulated Militia, being necessary to the security of a free State, the right of the people to keep and bear Arms, shall not be infringed.

Amendment III [1791]

No Soldier shall, in time of peace be quartered in any house, without the consent of the Owner, nor in time of war, but in a manner to be prescribed by law.

Amendment IV [1791]

The right of the people to be secure in their persons, houses, papers, and effects, against unreasonable searches and seizures, shall not be violated, and no Warrants shall issue, but upon probable cause, supported by Oath or affirmation, and particularly describing the place to be searched, and the persons or things to be seized.

Amendment V [1791]

No person shall be held to answer for a capital, or otherwise infamous crime, unless on a presentment or indictment of a Grand Jury, except in cases arising in the land or naval forces, or in the Militia, when in actual service in time of War or public danger; nor shall any person be subject for the same offence to be twice put in jeopardy of life or limb; nor shall be compelled in any criminal case to be a witness against himself, nor be deprived of life, liberty, or property, without due process of law; nor shall private property be taken for public use, without just compensation.

Amendment VI [1791]

In all criminal prosecutions, the accused shall enjoy the right to a speedy and public trial, by an impartial jury of the State and district wherein the crime shall have been committed, which district shall have been previously ascertained by law, and to be informed of the nature and cause of the accusation; to be confronted with the witnesses against him; to have compulsory process for obtaining witnesses in his favor, and to have the Assistance of Counsel for his defence.

AMENDMENT VII [1791]

In Suits at common law, where the value in controversy shall exceed twenty dollars, the right of trial by jury shall be preserved, and no fact tried by jury, shall be otherwise re-examined in any Court of the United States, than according to the rules of the common law.

AMENDMENT VIII [1791]

Excessive bail shall not be required, nor excessive fines imposed, nor cruel and unusual punishments inflicted.

AMENDMENT IX [1791]

The enumeration in the Constitution, of certain rights, shall not be construed to deny or disparage others retained by the people.

AMENDMENT X [1791]

The powers not delegated to the United States by the Constitution, nor prohibited by it to the States, are reserved to the States respectively, or to the people.

AMENDMENT XIII [1865]

Section 1. Neither slavery nor involuntary servitude, except as a punishment for crime whereof the party shall have been duly convicted, shall exist within the United States, or any place subject to their jurisdiction.

Section 2. Congress shall have power to enforce this article by appropriate legislation.

AMENDMENT XIV [1868]

Section 1. All persons born or naturalized in the United States, and subject to the jurisdiction thereof, are citizens of the United States and of the State wherein they reside. No State shall make or enforce any law which shall abridge the privileges or immunities of citizens of the United States; nor shall any State deprive any person of life, liberty, or property, without due process of law; nor deny to any person within its jurisdiction the equal protection of the laws.

Section 5. The Congress shall have power to enforce, by appropriate legislation, the provisions of the article.

AMENDMENT XV [1870]

Section 1. The right of citizens of the United States to vote shall not be denied or abridged by the United States or by any State on account of race, color, or previous condition of servitude.

Section 2. The Congress shall have power to enforce this article by appropriate legislation.

Appendix B

SELECTED FEDERAL STATUTORY PROVISIONS

Analysis

WIRE AND ELECTRONIC COMMUNICATIONS INTERCEPTION AND INTERCEPTION OF ORAL COMMUNICATIONS

(18 U.S.C. §§ 2510–2511, 2515–2518, 2520–2521).

§ 2510. Definitions

As used in this chapter—

(1) "wire communication" means any aural transfer made in whole or in part through the use of facilities for the transmission of communications by the aid of wire, cable, or other like connection between the point of origin and the point of reception (including the use of such connection in a switching station) furnished or operated by any person engaged in providing or operating such facilities for the transmission of interstate or foreign communications or communications affecting interstate or foreign commerce and such term includes any electronic storage of such communication;

(2) "oral communication" means any oral communication uttered by a person exhibiting an expectation that such communication is not subject to interception under circumstances justifying such expectation, but such term does not include any electronic communication;

(3) "State" means any State of the United States, the District of Columbia, the Commonwealth of Puerto Rico, and any territory or possession of the United States;

(4) "intercept" means the aural or other acquisition of the contents of any wire, electronic, or oral communication through the use of any electronic, mechanical, or other device;

(5) "electronic, mechanical, or other device" means any device or apparatus which can be used to intercept a wire, oral, or electronic communication other than—

(a) any telephone or telegraph instrument, equipment or facility, or any component thereof, (i) furnished to the subscriber or user by a provider of wire or electronic communication service in the ordinary course of its business and being used by the subscriber or user in the ordinary course of its business or furnished by such subscriber or user for connection to the facilities of such service and used in the ordinary course of its business; or (ii) being used by a provider of wire or electronic communication service in the ordinary course of its business, or by an investigative or law enforcement officer in the ordinary course of his duties;

(b) a hearing aid or similar device being used to correct subnormal hearing to not better than normal;

(6) "person" means any employee, or agent of the United States or any State or political subdivision thereof, and any individual, partnership, association, joint stock company, trust, or corporation;

(7) "Investigative or law enforcement officer" means any officer of the United States or of a State or political subdivision thereof, who is empowered by law to conduct investigations of or to make arrests for offenses enumerated in this chapter, and any attorney authorized by law to prosecute or participate in the prosecution of such offenses;

(8) "contents", when used with respect to any wire, oral, or electronic communication, includes any information concerning the substance, purport, or meaning of that communication;

(9) "Judge of competent jurisdiction" means—

(a) a judge of a United States district court or a United States court of appeals; and

(b) a judge of any court of general criminal jurisdiction of a State who is authorized by a statute of that State to enter orders authorizing interceptions of wire, oral, or electronic communications;

(10) "communication common carrier" shall have the same meaning which is given the term "common carrier" by section 153(h) of title 47 of the United States Code;

(11) "aggrieved person" means a person who was a party to any intercepted wire, oral, or electronic communication or a person against whom the interception was directed;

(12) "electronic communication" means any transfer of signs, signals, writing, images, sounds, data, or intelligence of any nature transmitted in whole or in part by a wire, radio, electromagnetic, photoelectronic or photooptical system that affects interstate or foreign commerce, but does not include—

(A) any wire or oral communication;

(B) any communication made through a tone-only paging device;

(C) any communication from a tracking device (as defined in section 3117 of this title); or

(D) electronic funds transfer information stored by a financial institution in a communications system used for the electronic storage and transfer of funds;

(13) "user" means any person or entity who—

(A) uses an electronic communication service; and

(B) is duly authorized by the provider of such service to engage in such use;

(14) "electronic communications system" means any wire, radio, electromagnetic, photooptical or photoelectronic facilities for the transmission of electronic communications, and any computer facilities or related electronic equipment for the electronic storage of such communications;

(15) "electronic communication service" means any service which provides to users thereof the ability to send or receive wire or electronic communications;

(16) "readily accessible to the general public" means, with respect to a radio communication, that such communication is not—

(A) scrambled or encrypted;

(B) transmitted using modulation techniques whose essential parameters have been withheld from the public with the intention of preserving the privacy of such communication;

(C) carried on a subcarrier or other signal subsidiary to a radio transmission;

(D) transmitted over a communication system provided by a common carrier, unless the communication is a tone only paging system communication; or

(E) transmitted on frequencies allocated under part 25, subpart D, E, or F of part 74, or part 94 of the Rules of the Federal Communications Commission, unless, in the case of a communication transmitted on a frequency allocated under part 74 that is not exclusively allocated to broadcast auxiliary services, the communication is a two-way voice communication by radio;

(17) "electronic storage" means—

(A) any temporary, intermediate storage of a wire or electronic communication incidental to the electronic transmission thereof; and

(B) any storage of such communication by an electronic communication service for purposes of backup protection of such communication; and

(18) "aural transfer" means a transfer containing the human voice at any point between and including the point of origin and the point of reception.

§ 2511. Interception and disclosure of wire, oral, or electronic communications prohibited

(1) Except as otherwise specifically provided in this chapter any person who—

(a) intentionally intercepts, endeavors to intercept, or procures any other person to intercept or endeavor to intercept, any wire, oral, or electronic communication;

(b) intentionally uses, endeavors to use, or procures any other person to use or endeavor to use any electronic, mechanical, or other device to intercept any oral communication when—

(i) such device is affixed to, or otherwise transmits a signal through, a wire, cable, or other like connection used in wire communication; or

(ii) such device transmits communications by radio, or interferes with the transmission of such communication; or

(iii) such person knows, or has reason to know, that such device or any component thereof has been sent through the mail or transported in interstate or foreign commerce; or

(iv) such use or endeavor to use (A) takes place on the premises of any business or other commercial establishment the operations of which affect interstate or foreign commerce; or (B) obtains or is for the purpose of obtaining information relating to the operations of any business or other commercial establishment the operations of which affect interstate or foreign commerce; or

(v) such person acts in the District of Columbia, the Commonwealth of Puerto Rico, or any territory or possession of the United States;

(c) intentionally discloses, or endeavors to disclose, to any other person the contents of any wire, oral, or electronic communication, knowing or having reason to know that the information was obtained through the interception of a wire, oral, or electronic communication in violation of this subsection;

(d) intentionally uses, or endeavors to use, the contents of any wire, oral, or electronic communication, knowing or having reason to know that the information was obtained through the interception of a wire, oral, or electronic communication in violation of this subsection; or

(e)(i) intentionally discloses, or endeavors to disclose, to any other person the contents of any wire, oral, or electronic communication, intercepted by means authorized by sections 2511(2)(A)(ii), 2511(b)–(c), 2511(e), 2516, and 2518 of this subchapter, (ii) knowing or having reason to know that the information was obtained through the interception of such a communication in connection with a criminal investigation, (iii) having obtained or received the information in connection with a criminal investigation, and (iv) with intent to improperly obstruct, impede, or interfere with a duly authorized criminal investigation,

shall be punished as provided in subsection (4) or shall be subject to suit as provided in subsection (5).

(2)(a)(i) It shall not be unlawful under this chapter for an operator of a switchboard, or an officer, employee, or agent of a provider of wire or electronic communication service, whose facilities are used in the transmission of a wire or electronic communication, to intercept, disclose, or use that communication in the normal course of his employment while engaged in any activity which is a necessary incident to the rendition of his service or to the protection of the rights or property of the provider of that service, except that a provider of wire communication service to the public shall not utilize service observing or random monitoring except for mechanical or service quality control checks.

(ii) Notwithstanding any other law, providers of wire or electronic communication service, their officers, employees, and agents, landlords, custodians, or other persons, are authorized to provide information, facilities, or technical assistance to persons authorized by law to intercept wire, oral, or electronic communications or to conduct electronic surveillance, as defined in section 101 of the Foreign Intelligence Surveillance Act of 1978, if such provider, its officers, employees, or agents, landlord, custodian, or other specified person, has been provided with—

(A) a court order directing such assistance signed by the authorizing judge, or

(B) a certification in writing by a person specified in section 2518(7) of this title or the Attorney General of the United States that no warrant or court order is required by law, that all statutory requirements have been met, and that the specified assistance is required,

setting forth the period of time during which the provision of the information, facilities, or technical assistance is authorized and specifying the information, facilities, or technical assistance required. No provider of wire or electronic communication service, officer, employee, or agent thereof, or landlord, custodian, or other specified person shall disclose the existence of any interception or surveillance or the device used to accomplish the interception or surveillance with respect to which the person has been furnished a court order or certification under this chapter except as may otherwise be required by legal process and then only after prior notification to the Attorney General or to the principal prosecuting attorney of a State or any political subdivision of a State, as may be appropriate. Any such disclosure, shall render such person liable for the civil damages provided for in section 2520. No cause of action shall lie in any court against any provider of wire or electronic communication service, its officers, employees, or agents, landlord, custodian, or other specified person for providing information, facilities, or assistance in accordance with the terms of an order or certification under this subpar.

(b) It shall not be unlawful under this chapter for an officer, employee, or agent of the Federal Communications Commission, in the normal course of his employment and in discharge of the monitoring responsibilities exercised by the Commission in the enforcement of chapter 5 of title 47 of the United States Code, to intercept a wire or electronic communication, or oral communication transmitted by radio, or to disclose or use the information thereby obtained.

(c) It shall not be unlawful under this chapter for a person acting under color of law to intercept a wire, oral, or electronic communication, where such person is a party to the communication or one of the parties to the communication has given prior consent to such interception.

(d) It shall not be unlawful under this chapter for a person not acting under color of law to intercept a wire, oral, or electronic communication where such person is a party to the communication or where one of the parties to the communication has given prior consent to such interception unless such communication is intercepted for the purpose of committing any criminal or tortious act in violation of the Constitution or laws of the United States or of any State.

(e) Notwithstanding any other provision of this title or section 705 or 706 of the Communications Act of 1934, it shall not be unlawful for an officer, employee, or agent of the United States in the normal course of his official duty to conduct electronic surveillance, as defined in section 101 of the Foreign Intelligence Surveillance Act of 1978, as authorized by that Act.

(f) Nothing contained in this chapter or chapter 121, or section 705 of the Communications Act of 1934, shall be deemed to affect the acquisition by the United States Government of foreign intelligence information from international or foreign communications, or foreign intelligence activities conducted in accordance with otherwise applicable Federal law involving a foreign electronic communications system, utilizing a means other than electronic surveillance as defined in section 101 of the Foreign Intelligence Surveillance Act of 1978, and procedures in this chapter and the Foreign Intelligence Surveillance Act of 1978 shall be the exclusive means by which electronic surveillance, as defined in section 101 of such Act, and the interception of domestic wire and oral communications may be conducted.

(g) It shall not be unlawful under this chapter or chapter 121 of this title for any person—

(i) to intercept or access an electronic communication made through an electronic communication system that is configured so that such electronic communication is readily accessible to the general public;

(ii) to intercept any radio communication which is transmitted—

(I) by any station for the use of the general public, or that relates to ships, aircraft, vehicles, or persons in distress;

(II) by any governmental, law enforcement, civil defense, private land mobile, or public safety communications system, including police and fire, readily accessible to the general public;

(III) by a station operating on an authorized frequency within the bands allocated to the amateur, citizens band, or general mobile radio services; or

(IV) by any marine or aeronautical communications system;

(iii) to engage in any conduct which—

(I) is prohibited by section 633 of the Communications Act of 1934; or

(II) is excepted from the application of section 705(a) of the Communications Act of 1934 by section 705(b) of that Act;

(iv) to intercept any wire or electronic communication the transmission of which is causing harmful interference to any lawfully operating station or consumer electronic equipment, to the extent necessary to identify the source of such interference; or

(v) for other users of the same frequency to intercept any radio communication made through a system that utilizes frequencies monitored by individuals engaged in the provision or the use of such system, if such communication is not scrambled or encrypted.

(h) It shall not be unlawful under this chapter—

(i) to use a pen register or a trap and trace device (as those terms are defined for the purposes of chapter 206 (relating to pen registers and trap and trace devices) of this title); or

(ii) for a provider of electronic communication service to record the fact that a wire or electronic communication was initiated or completed in order to protect such provider, another provider furnishing service toward the completion of the wire or electronic communication, or a user of that service, from fraudulent, unlawful or abusive use of such service.

(3)(a) Except as provided in paragraph (b) of this subsection, a person or entity providing an electronic communication service to the public shall not intentionally divulge the contents of any communication (other than one to such person or entity, or an agent thereof) while in transmission on that service to any person or entity other than an addressee or intended recipient of such communication or an agent of such addressee or intended recipient.

(b) A person or entity providing electronic communication service to the public may divulge the contents of any such communication—

(i) as otherwise authorized in section 2511(2)(a) or 2517 of this title;

(ii) with the lawful consent of the originator or any addressee or intended recipient of such communication;

(iii) to a person employed or authorized, or whose facilities are used, to forward such communication to its destination; or

(iv) which were inadvertently obtained by the service provider and which appear to pertain to the commission of a crime, if such divulgence is made to a law enforcement agency.

(4)(a) Except as provided in paragraph (b) of this subsection or in subsection (5), whoever violates subsection (1) of this section shall be fined under this title or imprisoned not more than five years, or both.

(b) If the offense is a first offense under paragraph (a) of this subsection and is not for a tortious or illegal purpose or for purposes of direct or indirect commercial advantage or private commercial gain, and the wire or electronic communication with respect to which the offense under paragraph

(a) is a radio communication that is not scrambled or encrypted, or transmitted using modulation techniques the essential parameters of which have been withheld from the public with the intention of preserving the privacy of such communication, then—

(i) if the communication is not the radio portion of a cellular telephone communication, a cordless telephone communication that is transmitted between the cordless telephone handset and the base unit, a public land mobile radio service communication or a paging service communication, and the conduct is not that described in subsection (5), the offender shall be fined under this title or imprisoned not more than one year or both; and

(ii) if the communication is the radio portion of a cellular telephone communication, a cordless telephone communication that is transmitted between the cordless telephone handset and the base unit, a public land mobile radio service communication or a paging service communication, the offender shall be fined not more than $500.

(c) Conduct otherwise an offense under this subsection that consists of or relates to the interception of a satellite transmission that is not encrypted or scrambled and that is transmitted—

(i) to a broadcasting station for purposes of retransmission to the general public; or

(ii) as an audio subcarrier intended for redistribution to facilities open to the public, but not including data transmissions or telephone calls,

is not an offense under this subsection unless the conduct is for the purposes of direct or indirect commercial advantage or private financial gain.

(5)(a)(i) If the communication is—

(A) a private satellite video communication that is not scrambled or encrypted and the conduct in violation of this chapter is the private viewing of that communication and is not for a tortious or illegal purpose or for purposes of direct or indirect commercial advantage or private commercial gain; or

(B) a radio communication that is transmitted on frequencies allocated under subpart D of part 74 of the rules of the Federal Communications Commission that is not scrambled or encrypted and the conduct in violation of this chapter is not for a tortious or illegal purpose or for purposes of direct or indirect commercial advantage or private commercial gain,

then the person who engages in such conduct shall be subject to suit by the Federal Government in a court of competent jurisdiction.

(ii) In an action under this subsection—

(A) if the violation of this chapter is a first offense for the person under paragraph (a) of subsection (4) and such person has not been found liable in a civil action under section 2520 of this title, the Federal Government shall be entitled to appropriate injunctive relief; and

(B) if the violation of this chapter is a second or subsequent offense under paragraph (a) of subsection (4) or such person has been found liable in any prior civil action under section 2520, the person shall be subject to a mandatory $500 civil fine.

(b) The court may use any means within its authority to enforce an injunction issued under paragraph (ii)(A), and shall impose a civil fine of not less than $500 for each violation of such an injunction.

§ 2515. Prohibition of use as evidence of intercepted wire or oral communications

Whenever any wire or oral communication has been intercepted, no part of the contents of such communication and no evidence derived therefrom may be received in evidence in any trial, hearing, or other proceeding in or before any court, grand jury, department, officer, agency, regulatory body, legislative committee, or other authority of the United States, a State, or a political subdivision thereof if the disclosure of that information would be in violation of this chapter.

§ 2516. Authorization for interception of wire, oral, or electronic communications

(1) The Attorney General, Deputy Attorney General, Associate Attorney General, any Assistant Attorney General, any acting Assistant Attorney General, or any Deputy Assistant Attorney General or acting Deputy Assistant Attorney General in the Criminal Division specially designated by the Attorney General, may authorize an application to a Federal judge of competent jurisdiction for, and such judge may grant in conformity with section 2518 of this chapter an order authorizing or approving the interception of wire or oral communications by the Federal Bureau of Investigation, or a Federal agency having responsibility for the investigation of the offense as to which the application is made, when such interception may provide or has provided evidence of—

(a) any offense punishable by death or by imprisonment for more than one year under sections 2274 through 2277 of title 42 of the United States Code (relating to the enforcement of the Atomic Energy Act of 1954), section 2284 of title 42 of the United States Code (relating to sabotage of nuclear facilities or fuel), or under the following chapters of this title: chapter 37 (relating to espionage), chapter 90 (relating to protection of trade secrets), chapter 105 (relating to sabotage), chapter 115 (relating to treason), chapter 102 (relating to riots); chapter 65 (relating to malicious mischief), chapter 111 (relating to destruction of vessels), or chapter 81 (relating to piracy);

(b) a violation of section 186 or section 501(c) of title 29, United States Code (dealing with restrictions on payments and loans to labor organizations), or any offense which involves murder, kidnapping, robbery, or extortion, and which is punishable under this title;

(c) any offense which is punishable under the following sections of this title: section 201 (bribery of public officials and witnesses), section 224 (bribery in sporting contests), subsection (d), (e), (f), (g), (h), or (i) of section 844 (unlawful use of explosives), section 1084 (transmission of wagering information), section 751 (relating to escape), sections 1503, 1512, and 1513 (influencing or injuring an officer, juror, or witness generally), section 1510 (obstruction of criminal investigations), section 1511 (obstruction of State or local law enforcement), section 1751 (Presidential and Presidential staff assassination, kidnapping, and assault), section 1951 (interference with commerce by threats or violence), section 1952 (interstate and foreign travel or transportation in aid of racketeering enterprises), section 1952A (relating to use of interstate commerce facilities in the commission of murder for hire), section 1952B (relating to violent crimes in aid of racketeering activity), section 1954 (offer, acceptance, or solicitation to influence operations of employee benefit plan), section 1955 (prohibition of business enterprises of gambling), section 1956 (laundering of monetary instruments), section 1957 (relating to engaging in monetary transactions in property derived from specified unlawful activity), section 659 (theft from interstate shipment), section 664 (embezzlement from pension and welfare funds), section 1343 (fraud by wire, radio, or television), sections 2251 and 2252 (sexual exploitation of children), sections 2312, 2313, 2314, and 2315 (interstate transportation of stolen property), the second section 2320 (relating to trafficking in certain motor vehicles or motor vehicle parts), section 1203 (relating to hostage taking), section 1029 (relating to fraud and related activity in connection with access devices), section 3146 (relating to penalty for failure to appear), section 3521(b)(3)(relating to witness relocation and assistance), section 32 (relating to destruction of aircraft or aircraft facilities), section 38 (relating to aircraft parts fraud), section 1963 (violations with respect to racketeer influenced and corrupt organizations), section 115 (relating to threatening or retaliating against a Federal official), the section in chapter 65 (relating to destruction of an energy facility), and section 1341 (relating to mail fraud), section 351 (violations with respect to congressional, Cabinet, or Supreme Court assassinations, kidnapping, and assault), section 831 (relating to prohibited transactions involving nuclear materials), section 33 (relating to destruction of motor vehicles or motor vehicle facilities), section 175 (relating to biological weapons), or section 1992 (relating to wrecking trains);

(d) any offense involving counterfeiting punishable under section 471, 472, or 473 of this title;

(e) any offense involving fraud connected with a case under title 11 or the manufacture, importation, receiving, concealment, buying, selling, or otherwise dealing in narcotic drugs, marihuana, or other dangerous drugs, punishable under any law of the United States;

(f) any offense including extortionate credit transactions under sections 892, 893, or 894 of this title;

(g) a violation of section 5322 of title 31, United States Code (dealing with the reporting of currency transactions);

(h) any felony violation of sections 2511 and 2512 (relating to interception and disclosure of certain communications and to certain intercepting devices) of this title;

(i) any felony violation of chapter 71 (relating to obscenity) of this title;

(j) any violation of section 60123(b)(relating to destruction of a natural gas pipeline) or 46502 (relating to aircraft piracy) of title 49;

(k) any criminal violation of section 2778 of title 22 (relating to the Arms Export Control Act);

(*l*) the location of any fugitive from justice from an offense described in this section;

(m) any conspiracy to commit any of the foregoing offenses;

(n) any felony violation of sections 922 and 924 of title 18, United States Code (relating to firearms);

(*o*) a felony violation of section 1028 (relating to production of false identification documents), section 1542 (relating to false statements in passport applications), section 1546 (relating to fraud and misuse of visas, permits, and other documents) of this title or a violation of section 274, 277, or 278 of the Immigration and Nationality Act (relating to the smuggling of aliens); or

(p) any violation of section 5861 of the Internal Revenue Code of 1986 (relating to firearms).

(2) The principal prosecuting attorney of any State, or the principal prosecuting attorney of any political subdivision thereof, if such attorney is authorized by a statute of that State to make application to a State court judge of competent jurisdiction for an order authorizing or approving the interception of wire, oral, or electronic communications, may apply to such judge for, and such judge may grant in conformity with section 2518 of this chapter and with the applicable State statute an order authorizing, or approving the interception of wire, oral, or electronic communications by investigative or law enforcement officers having responsibility for the investigation of the offense as to which the application is made, when such interception may provide or has provided evidence of the commission of the offense of murder, kidnapping, gambling, robbery, bribery, extortion, or dealing in narcotic drugs, marihuana or other dangerous drugs, or other crime dangerous to life, limb, or property, and punishable by imprisonment for more than one year, designated in any applicable State statute authorizing such interception, or any conspiracy to commit any of the foregoing offenses.

(3) Any attorney for the Government (as such term is defined for the purposes of the Federal Rules of Criminal Procedure) may authorize an application to a Federal judge of competent jurisdiction for, and such judge may grant, in conformity with section 2518 of this title, an order authorizing or approving the interception of electronic communications by an investigative or law enforcement officer having responsibility for the investigation of the offense as to which the application is made, when such interception may provide or has provided evidence of any Federal felony.

§ 2517. Authorization for disclosure and use of intercepted wire, oral, or electronic communications

(1) Any investigative or law enforcement officer who, by any means authorized by this chapter, has obtained knowledge of the contents of any

wire, oral, or electronic communication, or evidence derived therefrom, may disclose such contents to another investigative or law enforcement officer to the extent that such disclosure is appropriate to the proper performance of the official duties of the officer making or receiving the disclosure.

(2) Any investigative or law enforcement officer who, by any means authorized by this chapter, has obtained knowledge of the contents of any wire, oral, or electronic communication or evidence derived therefrom may use such contents to the extent such use is appropriate to the proper performance of his official duties.

(3) Any person who has received, by any means authorized by this chapter, any information concerning a wire, oral, or electronic communication, or evidence derived therefrom intercepted in accordance with the provisions of this chapter may disclose the contents of that communication or such derivative evidence while giving testimony under oath or affirmation in any proceeding held under the authority of the United States or of any State or political subdivision thereof.

(4) No otherwise privileged wire, oral, or electronic communication intercepted in accordance with, or in violation of, the provisions of this chapter shall lose its privileged character.

(5) When an investigative or law enforcement officer, while engaged in intercepting wire, oral, or electronic communications in the manner authorized herein, intercepts wire, oral, or electronic communications relating to offenses other than those specified in the order of authorization or approval, the contents thereof, and evidence derived therefrom, may be disclosed or used as provided in subsections (1) and (2) of this section. Such contents and any evidence derived therefrom may be used under subsection (3) of this section when authorized or approved by a judge of competent jurisdiction where such judge finds on subsequent application that the contents were otherwise intercepted in accordance with the provisions of this chapter. Such application shall be made as soon as practicable.

§ 2518. Procedure for interception of wire, oral, or electronic communications

(1) Each application for an order authorizing or approving the interception of a wire, oral, or electronic communication under this chapter shall be made in writing upon oath or affirmation to a judge of competent jurisdiction and shall state the applicant's authority to make such application. Each application shall include the following information:

(a) the identity of the investigative or law enforcement officer making the application, and the officer authorizing the application;

(b) a full and complete statement of the facts and circumstances relied upon by the applicant, to justify his belief that an order should be issued, including (i) details as to the particular offense that has been, is being, is about to be committed, (ii) except as provided in subsection (11), a particular description of the nature and location of the facilities from which or the place where the communication is to be intercepted, (iii) a particular description of the type of communications sought to be intercepted, (iv) the identity of the person, if known, committing the offense and whose communications are to be intercepted;

(c) a full and complete statement as to whether or not other investigative procedures have been tried and failed or why they reasonably appear to be unlikely to succeed if tried or to be too dangerous;

(d) a statement of the period of time for which the interception is required to be maintained. If the nature of the investigation is such that the authorization for interception should not automatically terminate when the described type of communication has been first obtained, a particular description of facts establishing probable cause to believe that additional communications of the same type will occur thereafter;

(e) a full and complete statement of the facts concerning all previous applications known to the individual authorizing and making the application, made to any judge for authorization to intercept, or for approval of interceptions of, wire, oral, or electronic communications involving any of the same persons, facilities or places specified in the application, and the action taken by the judge on each such application; and

(f) where the application is for the extension of an order, a statement setting forth the results thus far obtained from the interception, or a reasonable explanation of the failure to obtain such results.

(2) The judge may require the applicant to furnish additional testimony or documentary evidence in support of the application.

(3) Upon such application the judge may enter an ex parte order, as requested or as modified, authorizing or approving interception of wire, oral, or electronic communications within the territorial jurisdiction of the court in which the judge is sitting (and outside that jurisdiction but within the United States in the case of a mobile interception device authorized by a Federal court within such jurisdiction), if the judge determines on the basis of the facts submitted by the applicant that—

(a) there is probable cause for belief that an individual is committing, has committed, or is about to commit a particular offense enumerated in section 2516 of this chapter;

(b) there is probable cause for belief that particular communications concerning that offense will be obtained through such interception;

(c) normal investigative procedures have been tried and have failed or reasonably appear to be unlikely to succeed if tried or to be too dangerous;

(d) except as provided in subsection (11), there is probable cause for belief that the facilities from which, or the place where, the wire, oral, or electronic communications are to be intercepted are being used, or are about to be used, in connection with the commission of such offense, or are leased to, listed in the name of, or commonly used by such person.

(4) Each order authorizing or approving the interception of any wire, oral, or electronic communication under this chapter shall specify—

(a) the identity of the person, if known, whose communications are to be intercepted;

(b) the nature and location of the communications facilities as to which, or the place where, authority to intercept is granted;

(c) a particular description of the type of communication sought to be intercepted, and a statement of the particular offense to which it relates;

(d) the identity of the agency authorized to intercept the communications, and of the person authorizing the application; and

(e) the period of time during which such interception is authorized, including a statement as to whether or not the interception shall automatically terminate when the described communication has been first obtained.

An order authorizing the interception of a wire, oral, or electronic communication under this chapter shall, upon request of the applicant, direct that a provider of wire or electronic communication service, landlord, custodian or other person shall furnish the applicant forthwith all information, facilities, and technical assistance necessary to accomplish the interception unobtrusively and with a minimum of interference with the services that such service provider, landlord, custodian, or person is according the person whose communications are to be intercepted. Any provider of wire or electronic communication service, landlord, custodian or other person furnishing such facilities or technical assistance shall be compensated therefor by the applicant for reasonable expenses incurred in providing such facilities or assistance. Pursuant to section 2522 of this chapter, an order may also be issued to enforce the assistance capability requirements under the Communication Assistance for Law Enforcement Act.

(5) No order entered under this section may authorize or approve the interception of any wire, oral, or electronic communication for any period longer than is necessary to achieve the objective of the authorization, nor in any event longer than thirty days. Such thirty-day period begins on the earlier of the day on which the investigative or law enforcement officer first begins to conduct an interception under the order or ten days after the order is entered. Extensions of an order may be granted, but only upon application for an extension made in accordance with subsection (1) of this section and the court making the findings required by subsection (3) of this section. The period of extension shall be no longer than the authorizing judge deems necessary to achieve the purposes for which it was granted and in no event for longer than thirty days. Every order and extension thereof shall contain a provision that the authorization to intercept shall be executed as soon as practicable, shall be conducted in such a way as to minimize the interception of communications not otherwise subject to interception under this chapter, and must terminate upon attainment of the authorized objective, or in any event in thirty days. In the event the intercepted communication is in a code or foreign language, and an expert in that foreign language or code is not reasonably available during the interception period, minimization may be accomplished as soon as practicable after such interception. An interception under this chapter may be conducted in whole or in part by Government personnel, or by an individual operating under a contract with the Government, acting under the supervision of an investigative or law enforcement officer authorized to conduct the interception.

(6) Whenever an order authorizing interception is entered pursuant to this chapter, the order may require reports to be made to the judge who issued the order showing what progress has been made toward achievement of the authorized objective and the need for continued interception. Such reports shall be made at such intervals as the judge may require.

(7) Notwithstanding any other provision of this chapter, any investigative or law enforcement officer, specially designated by the Attorney General, the Deputy Attorney General, the Associate Attorney General or by the principal prosecuting attorney of any State or subdivision thereof acting pursuant to a statute of that State, who reasonably determines that—

(a) an emergency situation exists that involves—

(i) immediate danger of death or serious physical injury to any person,

(ii) conspiratorial activities threatening the national security interest, or

(iii) conspiratorial activities characteristic of organized crime,

that requires a wire, oral, or electronic communication to be intercepted before an order authorizing such interception can, with due diligence, be obtained, and

(b) there are grounds upon which an order could be entered under this chapter to authorize such interception,

may intercept such wire, oral, or electronic communication if an application for an order approving the interception is made in accordance with this section within forty-eight hours after the interception has occurred, or begins to occur. In the absence of an order, such interception shall immediately terminate when the communication sought is obtained or when the application for the order is denied, whichever is earlier. In the event such application for approval is denied, or in any other case where the interception is terminated without an order having been issued, the contents of any wire, oral, or electronic communication intercepted shall be treated as having been obtained in violation of this chapter, and an inventory shall be served as provided for in subsection (d) of this section on the person named in the application.

(8)(a) The contents of any wire, oral, or electronic communication intercepted by any means authorized by this chapter shall, if possible, be recorded on tape or wire or other comparable device. The recording of the contents of any wire, oral or electronic communication under this subsection shall be done in such way as will protect the recording from editing or other alterations. Immediately upon the expiration of the period of the order, or extensions thereof, such recordings shall be made available to the judge issuing such order and sealed under his directions. Custody of the recordings shall be wherever the judge orders. They shall not be destroyed except upon an order of the issuing or denying judge and in any event shall be kept for ten years. Duplicate recordings may be made for use or disclosure pursuant to the provisions of subsections (1) and (2) of section 2517 of this chapter for investigations. The presence of the seal provided for by this subsection, or a satisfactory explanation for the absence thereof, shall be a prerequisite for the use or disclosure of the contents of any wire, oral, or electronic communication or evidence derived therefrom under subsection (3) of section 2517.

(b) Applications made and orders granted under this chapter shall be sealed by the judge. Custody of the applications and orders shall be wherever the judge directs. Such applications and orders shall be disclosed only upon a showing of good cause before a judge of competent jurisdiction and shall not be destroyed except on order of the issuing or denying judge, and in any event shall be kept for ten years.

(c) Any violation of the provisions of this subsection may be punished as contempt of the issuing or denying judge.

(d) Within a reasonable time but not later than ninety days after the filing of an application for an order of approval under section 2518(7)(b) which is denied or the termination of the period of an order or extensions thereof, the issuing or denying judge shall cause to be served, on the persons named in the order or the application, and such other parties to intercepted communications as the judge may determine in his discretion that is in the interest of justice, an inventory which shall include notice of—

(1) the fact of the entry of the order or the application;

(2) the date of the entry and the period of authorized, approved or disapproved interception, or the denial of the application; and

(3) the fact that during the period wire, oral or electronic communications were or were not intercepted.

The judge, upon the filing of a motion, may in his discretion make available to such person or his counsel for inspection such portions of the intercepted communications, applications and orders as the judge determines to be in the interest of justice. On an ex parte showing of good cause to a judge of competent jurisdiction the serving of the inventory required by this subsection may be postponed.

(9) The contents of any wire, oral, or electronic communication intercepted pursuant to this chapter or evidence derived therefrom shall not be received in evidence or otherwise disclosed in any trial, hearing, or other proceeding in a Federal or State court unless each party, not less than ten days before the trial, hearing, or proceeding, has been furnished with a copy of the court order, and accompanying application, under which the interception was authorized or approved. This ten-day period may be waived by the judge if he finds that it was not possible to furnish the party with the above information ten days before the trial, hearing, or proceeding and that the party will not be prejudiced by the delay in receiving such information.

(10)(a) Any aggrieved person in any trial, hearing, or proceeding in or before any court, department, officer, agency, regulatory body, or other authority of the United States, a State, or a political subdivision thereof, may move to suppress the contents of any wire or oral communication intercepted pursuant to this chapter, or evidence derived therefrom, on the grounds that—

(i) the communication was unlawfully intercepted;

(ii) the order of authorization or approval under which it was intercepted is insufficient on its face; or

(iii) the interception was not made in conformity with the order of authorization or approval.

Such motion shall be made before the trial, hearing, or proceeding unless there was no opportunity to make such motion or the person was not aware of the grounds of the motion. If the motion is granted, the contents of the intercepted wire or oral communication, or evidence derived therefrom, shall be treated as having been obtained in violation of this chapter. The judge, upon the filing of such motion by the aggrieved person, may in his discretion make available to the aggrieved person or his counsel for inspection such portions of the intercepted communication or evidence derived therefrom as the judge determines to be in the interests of justice.

(b) In addition to any other right to appeal, the United States shall have the right to appeal from an order granting a motion to suppress made under paragraph (a) of this subsection, or the denial of an application for an order of approval, if the United States attorney shall certify to the judge or other official granting such motion or denying such application that the appeal is not taken for purposes of delay. Such appeal shall be taken within thirty days after the date the order was entered and shall be diligently prosecuted.

(c) The remedies and sanctions described in this chapter with respect to the interception of electronic communications are the only judicial remedies and sanctions for nonconstitutional violations of this chapter involving such communications.

(11) The requirements of subsections (1)(b)(ii) and (3)(d) of this section relating to the specification of the facilities from which, or the place where, the communication is to be intercepted do not apply if—

(a) in the case of an application with respect to the interception of an oral communication—

(i) the application is by a Federal investigative or law enforcement officer and is approved by the Attorney General, the Deputy Attorney General, the Associate Attorney General, an Assistant Attorney General, or an acting Assistant Attorney General;

(ii) the application contains a full and complete statement as to why such specification is not practical and identifies the person committing the offense and whose communications are to be intercepted; and

(iii) the judge finds that such specification is not practical; and

(b) in the case of an application with respect to a wire or electronic communication—

(i) the application is by a Federal investigative or law enforcement officer and is approved by the Attorney General, the Deputy Attorney General, the Associate Attorney General, an Assistant Attorney General, or an acting Assistant Attorney General;

(ii) the application identifies the person believed to be committing the offense and whose communications are to be intercepted and the applicant makes a showing that there is probable cause to believe that the person's actions could have the effect of thwarting interception from a specified facility; and

(iii) the judge finds that such showing has been adequately made; and

(iv) the order authorizing or approving the interception is limited to interception only for such time as it is reasonable to presume that the person identified in the application is or was reasonably proximate to the instrument through which such communication will be or was transmitted.

(12) An interception of a communication under an order with respect to which the requirements of subsections (1)(b)(ii) and (3)(d) of this section do not apply by reason of subsection (11)(a) shall not begin until the place where the communication is to be intercepted is ascertained by the person implementing the interception order. A provider of wire or electronic communications service that has received an order as provided for in subsection (11)(b) may move the court to modify or quash the order on the ground that its assistance with respect to the interception cannot be performed in a timely or reasonable fashion. The court, upon notice to the government, shall decide such a motion expeditiously.

§ 2520. Recovery of civil damages authorized

(a) In general.—Except as provided in section 2511(2)(a)(ii), any person whose wire, oral, or electronic communication is intercepted, disclosed, or intentionally used in violation of this chapter may in a civil action recover from the person or entity which engaged in that violation such relief as may be appropriate.

(b) Relief.—In an action under this section, appropriate relief includes—

(1) such preliminary and other equitable or declaratory relief as may be appropriate;

(2) damages under subsection (c) and punitive damages in appropriate cases; and

(3) a reasonable attorney's fee and other litigation costs reasonably incurred.

(c) Computation of damages.—(1) In an action under this section, if the conduct in violation of this chapter is the private viewing of a private satellite video communication that is not scrambled or encrypted or if the communication is a radio communication that is transmitted on frequencies allocated under subpart D of part 74 of the rules of the Federal Communications Commission that is not scrambled or encrypted and the conduct is not for a tortious or illegal purpose or for purposes of direct or indirect commercial advantage or private commercial gain, then the court shall assess damages as follows:

(A) If the person who engaged in that conduct has not previously been enjoined under section 2511(5) and has not been found liable in a prior civil action under this section, the court shall assess the greater of the sum of actual damages suffered by the plaintiff, or statutory damages of not less than $50 and not more than $500.

(B) If, on one prior occasion, the person who engaged in that conduct has been enjoined under section 2511(5) or has been found liable in a civil action under this section, the court shall assess the greater of the sum of actual damages suffered by the plaintiff, or statutory damages of not less than $100 and not more than $1000.

(2) In any other action under this section, the court may assess as damages whichever is the greater of—

(A) the sum of the actual damages suffered by the plaintiff and any profits made by the violator as a result of the violation; or

(B) statutory damages of whichever is the greater of $100 a day for each day of violation or $10,000.

(d) Defense.—A good faith reliance on—

(1) a court warrant or order, a grand jury subpoena, a legislative authorization, or a statutory authorization;

(2) a request of an investigative or law enforcement officer under section 2518(7) of this title; or

(3) a good faith determination that section 2511(3) of this title permitted the conduct complained of;

is a complete defense against any civil or criminal action brought under this chapter or any other law.

(e) Limitation.—A civil action under this section may not be commenced later than two years after the date upon which the claimant first has a reasonable opportunity to discover the violation.

§ 2521. Injunction against illegal interception

Whenever it shall appear that any person is engaged or is about to engage in any act which constitutes or will constitute a felony violation of this chapter, the Attorney General may initiate a civil action in a district court of the United States to enjoin such violation. The court shall proceed as soon as practicable to the hearing and determination of such an action, and may, at any time before final determination, enter such a restraining order or prohibition, or take such other action, as is warranted to prevent a continuing and substantial injury to the United States or to any person or class of persons for whose protection the action is brought. A proceeding under this section is governed by the Federal Rules of Civil Procedure, except that, if an indictment has been returned against the respondent, discovery is governed by the Federal Rules of Criminal Procedure.

CRIMINAL JUSTICE ACT

(18 U.S.C. § 3006A).

§ 3006A. Adequate representation of defendants

(a) Choice of plan.—Each United States district court, with the approval of the judicial council of the circuit, shall place in operation throughout the district a plan for furnishing representation for any person financially unable to obtain adequate representation in accordance with this section. Representation under each plan shall include counsel and investigative, expert, and other services necessary for adequate representation. Each plan shall provide the following:

(1) Representation shall be provided for any financially eligible person who—

(A) is charged with a felony or a Class A misdemeanor;

(B) is a juvenile alleged to have committed an act of juvenile delinquency as defined in section 5031 of this title;

(C) is charged with a violation of probation;

(D) is under arrest, when such representation is required by law;

(E) is charged with a violation of supervised release or faces modification, reduction, or enlargement of a condition, or extension or revocation of a term of supervised release;

(F) is subject to a mental condition hearing under chapter 313 of this title;

(G) is in custody as a material witness;

(H) is entitled to appointment of counsel under the sixth amendment to the Constitution; or

(I) faces loss of liberty in a case, and Federal law requires the appointment of counsel; or

(J) is entitled to the appointment of counsel under section 4019 of this title.

(2) Whenever the United States magistrate or the court determines that the interests of justice so require, representation may be provided for any financially eligible person who—

(A) is charged with a Class B or C misdemeanor, or an infraction for which a sentence to confinement is authorized; or

(B) is seeking relief under section 2241, 2254, or 2255 of title 28.

(3) Private attorneys shall be appointed in a substantial proportion of the cases. Each plan may include, in addition to the provisions for private attorneys, either of the following or both:

(A) Attorneys furnished by a bar association or a legal aid agency.

(B) Attorneys furnished by a defender organization established in accordance with the provisions of subsection (g).

Prior to approving the plan for a district, the judicial council of the circuit shall supplement the plan with provisions for representation on appeal. The district court may modify the plan at any time with the approval of the judicial council of the circuit. It shall modify the plan when directed by the judicial council of the circuit. The district court shall notify the Administrative Office of the United States Courts of any modification of its plan.

(b) Appointment of counsel.—Counsel furnishing representation under the plan shall be selected from a panel of attorneys designated or approved by the court, or from a bar association, legal aid agency, or defender organization furnishing representation pursuant to the plan. In every case in which a person entitled to representation under a plan approved under subsection (a) appears without counsel, the United States magistrate or the court shall advise the person that he has the right to be represented by counsel and that counsel will be appointed to represent him if he is financially unable to obtain counsel. Unless the person waives representation by counsel, the United States magistrate or the court, if satisfied after appropriate inquiry that the person is financially unable to obtain counsel, shall appoint counsel to represent him. Such appointment may be made retroactive to include any representation furnished pursuant to the plan prior to appointment. The United States magistrate or the court shall appoint separate counsel for persons having interests that cannot properly be represented by the same counsel, or when other good cause is shown.

(c) Duration and substitution of appointments.—A person for whom counsel is appointed shall be represented at every stage of the proceedings from his initial appearance before the United States magistrate or the court through appeal, including ancillary matters appropriate to the proceedings. If at any time after the appointment of counsel the United States magistrate or the court finds that the person is financially able to obtain counsel or to make partial payment for the representation, it may terminate the appointment of counsel or authorize payment as provided in subsection (f), as the interests of justice may dictate. If at any stage of the proceedings, including an appeal, the United States magistrate or the court finds that the person is financially unable to pay counsel whom he had retained, it may appoint counsel as provided in subsection (b) and authorize payment as provided in subsection (d), as the interests of justice may dictate. The United States magistrate or the court may, in the interests of justice, substitute one appointed counsel for another at any stage of the proceedings.

(d) Payment for representation.—

(1) Hourly rate.—Any attorney appointed pursuant to this section or a bar association or legal aid agency or community defender organization which has provided the appointed attorney shall, at the conclusion of the representation or any segment thereof, be compensated at a rate not exceeding $60 per hour for time expended in court or before a United States magistrate and $40 per hour for time reasonably expended out of court, unless the Judicial Conference determines that a higher rate of not in excess of $75 per hour is justified for a circuit or for particular districts within a circuit, for time expended in court or before a United States magistrate and for time expended out of court. The Judicial Conference shall develop guidelines for determining the maximum hourly rates for each circuit in accordance with the preceding sentence, with variations by district, where appropriate, taking into account such factors as the minimum range of the prevailing hourly rates for qualified attorneys in the district in which the representation is provided and the recommendations of the judicial councils of the circuits. Not less than 3 years after the effective date of the Criminal Justice Act Revision of 1986, the Judicial Conference is authorized to raise the maximum hourly rates specified in this paragraph up to the aggregate of the overall average percentages of the adjustments in the rates of pay under the General Schedule made pursuant to section 5305 of title 5 on or after such effective date. After the rates are raised under the preceding sentence, such maximum hourly rates may be raised at intervals of not less than 1 year each, up to the aggregate of the overall average percentages of such adjustments made since the last raise was made under this paragraph. Attorneys shall be reimbursed for expenses reasonably incurred, including the costs of transcripts authorized by the United States magistrate or the court.

(2) Maximum amounts.—For representation of a defendant before the United States magistrate or the district court, or both, the compensation to be paid to an attorney or to a bar association or legal aid agency or community defender organization shall not exceed $3,500 for each attorney in a case in which one or more felonies are charged, and $1,000 for each attorney in a case in which only misdemeanors are charged. For representation of a defendant in an appellate court, the compensation to be paid to an attorney or to a bar association or legal aid agency or community defender organization shall not exceed $2,500 for each attorney in each court. For representation of an offender before the United States Parole Commission in a proceeding under section 4106A of this title, the compensation shall not exceed $750 for each attorney in each proceeding; for representation of an offender in an appeal from a determination of such Commission under such section, the compensation shall not exceed 2,500 for each attorney in each court. For any other representation required or authorized by this section, the compensation shall not exceed $750 for each attorney in each proceeding.

(3) Waiving maximum amounts.—Payment in excess of any maximum amount provided in paragraph (2) of this subsection may be made for extended or complex representation whenever the court in which the representation was rendered, or the United States magistrate if the representation was furnished exclusively before him,certifies that the amount of the excess payment is necessary to provide fair compensation and the payment is approved by the chief judge of the circuit. The chief judge of the circuit may delegate such approval authority to an active circuit judge.

(4) Disclosure of Fees.—

(A) In general.—Subject to subparagraphs (B) through (E), the amounts paid under this subsection for services in any case shall be made available to the public by the court upon the court's approval of the payment.

(B) Pre-trial or trial in progress.—If a trial is in pre-trial status or still in progress and after considering the defendant's interests as set forth in subparagraph (D), the court shall—

(i) redact any detailed information on the payment voucher provided by defense counsel to justify the expenses to the court; and

(ii) make public only the amounts approved for payment to defense counsel by dividing those amounts into the following categories:

(I) Arraignment and or plea.

(II) Bail and detention hearings.

(III) Motions.

(IV) Hearings.

(V) Interviews and conferences.

(VI) Obtaining and reviewing records.

(VII) Legal research and brief writing.

(VIII) Travel time.

(IX) Investigative work.

(X) Experts.

(XI) Trial and appeals.

(XII) Other.

(C) Trial completed.—

(i) In general.—If a request for payment is not submitted until after the completion of the trial and subject to consideration of the defendant's interests as set forth in subparagraph (D), the court shall make available to the public an unredacted copy of the expense voucher.

(ii) Protection of the rights of the defendant.—If the court determines that defendant's interests as set forth in subparagraph (D) require a limited disclosure, the court shall disclose amounts as provided in subparagraph (B).

(D) Considerations.—The interests referred to in subparagraphs (B) and (C) are—

(i) to protect any person's 5th amendment right against self-incrimination;

(ii) to protect the defendant's 6th amendment rights to effective assistance of counsel;

(iii) the defendant's attorney-client privilege;

(iv) the work product privilege of the defendant's counsel;

(v) the safety of any person; and

(vi) any other interest that justice may require, except that the amount of the fees shall not be considered a reason justifying any limited disclosure under section 3006A(d)(4) of title 18, United States Code.

(E) Notice.—The court shall provide reasonable notice of disclosure to the counsel of the defendant prior to the approval of the payments in order to allow the counsel to request redaction based on the considerations set forth in subparagraph (D). Upon completion of the trial, the court shall release unredacted copies of the vouchers provided by defense counsel to justify the expenses to the court. If there is an appeal, the court shall not release unredacted copies of the vouchers provided by defense counsel to justify the expenses to the court until such time as the appeals process is completed, unless the court determines that none of the defendant's interests set forth in subparagraph (D) will be compromised.

(F) Effective date.—The amendment made by paragraph (4) shall become effective 60 days after enactment of this Act, will apply only to cases filed on or after the effective date, and shall be in effect for no longer than 24 months after the effective date.

(5) Filing claims.—A separate claim for compensation and reimbursement shall be made to the district court for representation before the United States magistrate and the court, and to each appellate court before which the attorney provided representation to the person involved. Each claim shall be supported by a sworn written statement specifying the time expended, services rendered, and expenses incurred while the case was pending before the United States magistrate and the court, and the compensation and reimbursement applied for or received in the same case from any other source. The court shall fix the compensation and reimbursement to be paid to the attorney or to the bar association or legal aid agency or community defender organization which provided the appointed attorney. In cases where representation is furnished exclusively before a United States magistrate, the claim shall be submitted to him and he shall fix the compensation and reimbursement to be paid. In cases where representation is furnished other than before the United States magistrate, the district court, or an appellate court, claims shall be submitted to the district court which shall fix the compensation and reimbursement to be paid.

(6) New trials.—For purposes of compensation and other payments authorized by this section, an order by a court granting a new trial shall be deemed to initiate a new case.

(7) Proceedings before appellate courts.—If a person for whom counsel is appointed under this section appeals to an appellate court or petitions for a writ of certiorari, he may do so without prepayment of fees and costs or security therefor and without filing the affidavit required by section 1915(a) of title 28.

(e) Services other than counsel.—

(1) Upon request.—Counsel for a person who is financially unable to obtain investigative, expert, or other services necessary for an adequate representation may request them in an ex parte application. Upon finding, after appropriate inquiry in an ex parte proceeding, that the services are necessary and that the person is financially unable to obtain them, the court, or the United States magistrate if the services are required in connection with a matter over which he has jurisdiction, shall authorize counsel to obtain the services.

(2) Without prior request.—(A) Counsel appointed under this section may obtain, subject to later review, investigative, expert, and other services without prior authorization if necessary for adequate representation. Except as provided in subparagraph (B) of this paragraph, the total cost of services obtained without prior authorization may not exceed $300 and expenses reasonably incurred.

(B) The court, or the United States magistrate (if the services were rendered in a case disposed of entirely before the United States magistrate), may, in the interest of justice, and upon the finding that timely procurement of necessary services could not await prior authorization, approve payment for such services after they have been obtained, even if the cost of such services exceeds $300.

(3) Maximum amounts.—Compensation to be paid to a person for services rendered by him to a person under this subsection, or to be paid to an organization for services rendered by an employee thereof, shall not exceed $1,000, exclusive of reimbursement for expenses reasonably incurred, unless payment in excess of that limit is certified by the court, or by the United States magistrate if the services were rendered in connection with a case disposed of entirely before him, as necessary to provide fair compensation for services of an unusual character or duration, and the amount of the excess payment is approved by the chief judge of the circuit. The chief judge of the circuit may delegate such approval authority to an active circuit judge.

(4) Disclosure of fees.—The amounts paid under this subsection for services in any case shall be made available to the public.

(f) Receipt of other payments.—Whenever the United States magistrate or the court finds that funds are available for payment from or on behalf of a person furnished representation, it may authorize or direct that such funds be paid to the appointed attorney, to the bar association or legal aid agency or community defender organization which provided the appointed attorney, to any person or organization authorized pursuant to subsection (e) to render investigative, expert, or other services, or to the court for deposit in the Treasury as a reimbursement to the appropriation, current at the time of payment, to carry out the provisions of this section. Except as so authorized or directed, no such person or organization may request or accept any payment or promise of payment for representing a defendant.

(g) Defender organization.—

(1) Qualifications.—A district or a part of a district in which at least two hundred persons annually require the appointment of counsel may establish a defender organization as provided for either under subparagraphs (A) or (B) of paragraph (2) of this subsection or both. Two adjacent districts or parts of districts may aggregate the number of persons required to be represented to establish eligibility for a defender organization to serve both areas. In the event that adjacent districts or parts of districts are located in different circuits, the plan for furnishing representation shall be approved by the judicial council of each circuit.

(2) Types of defender organizations.—

(A) Federal Public Defender Organization.—A Federal Public Defender Organization shall consist of one or more full-time salaried attorneys. An organization for a district or part of a district or two adjacent districts or parts of districts shall be supervised by a Federal Public Defender appointed by the court of appeals of the circuit, without regard to the provisions of title 5 governing appointments in the competitive service, after considering recommendations from the district court or courts to be served. Nothing contained herein shall be deemed to authorize more than one Federal Public Defender within a single judicial district. The Federal Public Defender shall be appointed for a term of four years, unless sooner removed by the court of appeals of the circuit for incompetency, misconduct in office, or neglect of duty. Upon the expiration of his term, a Federal Public Defender may, by a majority vote of the judges of the court of appeals, continue to perform the duties of his office until his successor is appointed, or until one year after the expiration of such Defender's term, whichever is earlier. The compensation of the Federal Public Defender shall be fixed by the court of appeals of the circuit at a rate not to exceed the compensation received by the United States attorney for the district where representation is furnished or, if two districts or parts of districts are involved, the compensation of the higher paid United States attorney of the districts. The Federal Public Defender may appoint, without regard to the provisions of title 5 governing appointments in the competitive service, full-time attorneys in such number as may be approved by the court of appeals of the circuit and other personnel in such number as may be approved by the Director of the Administrative Office of the United States Courts. Compensation paid to such attorneys and other personnel of the organization shall be fixed by the Federal Public Defender at a rate not to exceed that paid to attorneys and other personnel of similar qualifications and experience in the Office of the United States attorney in the district where representation is furnished or, if two districts or parts of districts are involved, the higher compensation paid to persons of similar qualifications and experience in the districts. Neither the Federal Public Defender nor any attorney so appointed by him may engage in the private practice of law. Each organization shall submit to the Director of the Administrative Office of the United States Courts, at the time and in the form prescribed by him, reports of its activities and financial position and its proposed budget. The Director of the Administrative Office shall submit, in accordance with section 605 of title 28, a budget for each organization for each fiscal year and shall out of the appropriations therefor make payments to and on behalf of each organization. Payments under this subparagraph to an organization shall be in lieu of payments under subsection (d) or (e).

(B) Community Defender Organization.—A Community Defender Organization shall be a nonprofit defense counsel service established and administered by any group authorized by the plan to provide representation. The organization shall be eligible to furnish attorneys and receive payments under this section if its bylaws are set forth in the plan of the district or districts in which it will serve. Each organization shall submit to the Judicial Conference of the United States an annual report setting forth its activities and financial position and the anticipated caseload and expenses for the next fiscal year. Upon application an organization may, to the extent approved by the Judicial Conference of the United States:

(i) receive an initial grant for expenses necessary to establish the organization; and

(ii) in lieu of payments under subsection (d) or (e), receive periodic sustaining grants to provide representation and other expenses pursuant to this section. * * *

BAIL REFORM ACT OF 1984

(18 U.S.C. §§ 3141–3150).

§ 3141. Release and detention authority generally

(a) Pending Trial.—A judicial officer authorized to order the arrest of a person under section 3041 of this title before whom an arrested person is brought shall order that such person be released or detained, pending judicial proceedings, under this chapter.

(b) Pending sentence or appeal.—A judicial officer of a court of original jurisdiction over an offense, or a judicial officer of a Federal appellate court, shall order that, pending imposition or execution of sentence, or pending appeal of conviction or sentence, a person be released or detained under this chapter.

§ 3142. Release or detention of a defendant pending trial

(a) In general.—Upon the appearance before a judicial officer of a person charged with an offense, the judicial officer shall issue an order that, pending trial, the person be—

(1) released on his personal recognizance or upon execution of an unsecured appearance bond, under subsection (b) of this section;

(2) released on a condition or combination of conditions under subsection (c) of this section;

(3) temporarily detained to permit revocation of conditional release, deportation, or exclusion under subsection (d) of this section; or

(4) detained under subsection (e) of this section.

(b) Release on personal recognizance or unsecured appearance bond.—The judicial officer shall order the pretrial release of the person on personal recognizance, or upon execution of an unsecured appearance bond in an amount specified by the court, subject to the condition that the person not commit a Federal, State, or local crime during the period of release, unless the judicial officer determines that such release will not reasonably assure the appearance of the person as required or will endanger the safety of any other person or the community.

(c) Release on conditions.—(1) If the judicial officer determines that the release described in subsection (b) of this section will not reasonably assure the appearance of the person as required or will endanger the safety of any other person or the community, such judicial officer shall order the pretrial release of the person—

(A) subject to the condition that the person not commit a Federal, State, or local crime during the period of release; and

(B) subject to the least restrictive further condition, or combination of conditions, that such judicial officer determines will reasonably assure the appearance of the person as required and the safety of any other person and the community, which may include the condition that the person—

(i) remain in the custody of a designated person, who agrees to assume supervision and to report any violation of a release condition to the court, if the designated person is able reasonably to assure the judicial officer that the person will appear as required and will not pose a danger to the safety of any other person or the community;

(ii) maintain employment, or, if unemployed, actively seek employment;

(iii) maintain or commence an educational program;

(iv) abide by specified restrictions on personal associations, place of abode, or travel;

(v) avoid all contact with an alleged victim of the crime and with a potential witness who may testify concerning the offense;

(vi) report on a regular basis to a designated law enforcement agency, pretrial services agency, or other agency;

(vii) comply with a specified curfew;

(viii) refrain from possessing a firearm, destructive device, or other dangerous weapon;

(ix) refrain from excessive use of alcohol, or any use of a narcotic drug or other controlled substance, as defined in section 102 of the Controlled Substances Act (21 U.S.C. 802), without a prescription by a licensed medical practitioner;

(x) undergo available medical or psychiatric treatment, including treatment for drug or alcohol dependency, and remain in a specified institution if required for that purpose;

(xi) execute an agreement to forfeit upon failing to appear as required, such designated property, including money, as is reasonably necessary to assure the appearance of the person as required, and post with the court such indicia of ownership of the property or such percentage of the money as the judicial officer may specify;

(xii) execute a bail bond with solvent sureties in such amount as is reasonably necessary to assure the appearance of the person as required;

(xiii) return to custody for specified hours following release for employment, schooling, or other limited purposes; and

(xiv) satisfy any other condition that is reasonably necessary to assure the appearance of the person as required and to assure the safety of any other person and the community.

(2) The judicial officer may not impose a financial condition that results in the pretrial detention of the person.

(3) The judicial officer may at any time amend the order to impose additional or different conditions of release.

(d) Temporary detention to permit revocation of conditional release, deportation, or exclusion.—If the judicial officer determines that—

(1) the person—

(A) is, and was at the time the offense was committed, on—

(i) release pending trial for a felony under Federal, State, or local law;

(ii) release pending imposition or execution of sentence, appeal of sentence or conviction, or completion of sentence, for any offense under Federal, State, or local law; or

(iii) probation or parole for any offense under Federal, State, or local law; or

(B) is not a citizen of the United States or lawfully admitted for permanent residence, as defined in section 101(a)(20) of the Immigration and Nationality Act (8 U.S.C. 1101(a)(20)); and

(2) the person may flee or pose a danger to any other person or the community;

such judicial officer shall order the detention of the person, for a period of not more than ten days, excluding Saturdays, Sundays, and holidays, and direct the attorney for the Government to notify the appropriate court, probation or parole official, or State or local law enforcement official, or the appropriate official of the Immigration and Naturalization Service. If the official fails or declines to take the person into custody during that period, the person shall be treated in accordance with the other provisions of this section, notwithstanding the applicability of other provisions of law governing release pending trial or deportation or exclusion proceedings. If temporary detention is sought under paragraph (1)(B) of this subsection, the person has the burden of proving to the court such person's United States citizenship or lawful admission for permanent residence.

(e) Detention.—If, after a hearing pursuant to the provisions of subsection (f) of this section, the judicial officer finds that no condition or combination of conditions will reasonably assure the appearance of the person as required and the safety of any other person and the community, such judicial officer shall order the detention of the person before trial. In a case described in (f)(1) of this section, a rebuttable presumption arises that no condition or combination of conditions will reasonably assure the safety of any other person and the community if such judicial officer finds that—

(1) the person has been convicted of a Federal offense that is described in subsection (f)(1) of this section, or of a State or local offense that would have been an offense described in subsection (f)(1) of this section if a circumstance giving rise to Federal jurisdiction had existed;

(2) the offense described in paragraph (1) of this subsection was committed while the person was on release pending trial for a Federal, State, or local offense; and

(3) a period of not more than five years has elapsed since the date of conviction, or the release of the person from imprisonment, for the offense described in paragraph (1) of this subsection, whichever is later.

Subject to rebuttal by the person, it shall be presumed that no condition or combination of conditions will reasonably assure the appearance of the person as required and the safety of the community if the judicial officer finds that there is probable cause to believe that the person committed an offense for which a maximum term of imprisonment of ten years or more is prescribed in the Controlled Substances Act (21 U.S.C. 801 et seq.), the Controlled Substances Import and Export Act (21 U.S.C. 951 et seq.), section 1 of the Act of September 15, 1980 (21 U.S.C. 955a), or an offense under section 924(c), 956(a), or 2332(b) of title 18 of the United States Code.

(f) Detention hearing.—The judicial officer shall hold a hearing to determine whether any condition or combination of conditions set forth in subsection (c) of this section will reasonably assure the appearance of the person as required and the safety of any other person and the community in a case—

(1) upon motion of the attorney for the Government, that involves—

(A) a crime of violence;*

(B) an offense for which the maximum sentence is life imprisonment or death;

(C) an offense for which a maximum term of imprisonment of ten years or more is prescribed in the Controlled Substances Act (21 U.S.C. 801 et seq.), the Controlled Substances Import and Export Act (21 U.S.C. 951 et seq.), or section 1 of the Act of September 15, 1980 (21 U.S.C. 955a); or

(D) any felony if the person had been convicted of two or more prior offenses described in subparagraphs (A) through (C) of this paragraph, or two or more State or local offenses that would have been offenses described in subparagraphs (A) through (C) of this paragraph if a circumstance giving rise to Federal jurisdiction had existed or a combination of such offenses; or

(2) upon motion of the attorney for the Government or upon the judicial officer's own motion in a case, that involves—

(A) a serious risk that such person will flee;

(B) a serious risk that the person will obstruct or attempt to obstruct justice, or threaten, injure, or intimidate, or attempt to threaten, injure, or intimidate, a prospective witness or juror.

The hearing shall be held immediately upon the person's first appearance before the judicial officer unless that person, or the attorney for the Government, seeks a continuance. Except for good cause, a continuance on motion of the person may not exceed five days, and a continuance on motion of the attorney for the Government may not exceed three days. During a continuance, the person shall be detained, and the judicial officer, on motion of the attorney for the Government or sua sponte, may order that, while in custody, a person who appears to be a narcotics addict receive a medical examination to determine whether such person is an addict. At the hearing, the person has the right to be represented by counsel, and, if financially unable to obtain adequate representation, to have counsel appointed. The person shall be afforded an opportunity to testify, to present witnesses, to cross-examine witnesses who appear at the hearing, and to present information by proffer or otherwise. The rules concerning admissibility of evidence in criminal trials do not apply to the presentation and consideration of information at the hearing. The facts the judicial officer uses to support a finding pursuant to subsection (e) that no condition or combination of

* The phrase "crime of violence" is defined in 18 U.S.C. § 3156(a)(4) as meaning: "(A) an offense that has an element of the offense the use, attempted use, or threatened use of physical force against the person or property of another, or (B) any other offense that is a felony and that, by its nature, involves a substantial risk that physical force against the person or property of another may be used in the course of committing the offense."

conditions will reasonably assure the safety of any other person and the community shall be supported by clear and convincing evidence. The person may be detained pending completion of the hearing. The hearing may be reopened before or after a determination by the judicial officer, at any time before trial if the judicial officer finds that information exists that was not known to the movant at the time of the hearing and that has a material bearing on the issue of whether there are conditions of release that will reasonably assure the appearance of the person as required and the safety of any other person and the community.

(g) Factors to be considered.—The judicial officer shall, in determining whether there are conditions of release that will reasonably assure the appearance of the person as required and the safety of any other person and the community, take into account the available information concerning—

(1) the nature and circumstances of the offense charged, including whether the offense is a crime of violence or involves a narcotic drug;

(2) the weight of the evidence against the person;

(3) the history and characteristics of the person, including—

(A) the person's character, physical and mental condition, family ties, employment, financial resources, length of residence in the community, community ties, past conduct, history relating to drug or alcohol abuse, criminal history, and record concerning appearance at court proceedings; and

(B) whether, at the time of the current offense or arrest, the person was on probation, on parole, or on other release pending trial, sentencing, appeal, or completion of sentence for an offense under Federal, State, or local law; and

(4) the nature and seriousness of the danger to any person or the community that would be posed by the person's release. In considering the conditions of release described in subsection (c)(2)(K) or (c)(2)(L) [eds. note: intended references are to what is now subsection (c)(1)(B)(xi) or (c)(1)(B)(xii)], the judicial officer may upon his own motion, or shall upon the motion of the Government, conduct an inquiry into the source of the property to be designated for potential forfeiture or offered as collateral to secure a bond, and shall decline to accept the designation, or the use as collateral, of property that, because of its source, will not reasonably assure the appearance of the person as required.

(h) Contents of release order.—In a release order issued under subsection (b) or (c) of this section, the judicial officer shall—

(1) include a written statement that sets forth all the conditions to which the release is subject, in a manner sufficiently clear and specific to serve as a guide for the person's conduct; and

(2) advise the person of—

(A) the penalties for violating a condition of release, including the penalties for committing an offense while on pretrial release;

(B) the consequences of violating a condition of release, including the immediate issuance of a warrant for the person's arrest; and

(C) the provisions of sections 1503 of this title (relating to intimidation of witnesses, jurors, and officers of the court), 1510 (relating to obstruction of criminal investigations), 1512 (tampering with a witness, victim, or an informant), and 1513 (retaliating against a witness, victim, or an informant).

(i) Contents of detention order.—In a detention order issued under subsection (e) of this section, the judicial officer shall—

(1) include written findings of fact and a written statement of the reasons for the detention;

(2) direct that the person be committed to the custody of the Attorney General for confinement in a corrections facility separate, to the extent practicable, from persons awaiting or serving sentences or being held in custody pending appeal;

(3) direct that the person be afforded reasonable opportunity for private consultation with counsel; and

(4) direct that, on order of a court of the United States or on request of an attorney for the Government, the person in charge of the corrections facility in which the person is confined deliver the person to a United States marshal for the purpose of an appearance in connection with a court proceeding.

The judicial officer may, by subsequent order, permit the temporary release of the person, in the custody of a United States marshal or another appropriate person, to the extent that the judicial officer determines such release to be necessary for preparation of the person's defense or for another compelling reason.

(j) Presumption of innocence.—Nothing in this section shall be construed as modifying or limiting the presumption of innocence.

§ 3143. Release or detention of a defendant pending sentence or appeal

(a) Release or detention pending sentence.—(1) Except as provided in paragraph (2), the judicial officer shall order that a person who has been found guilty of an offense and who is awaiting imposition or execution of sentence, other than a person for whom the applicable guideline promulgated pursuant to 28 U.S.C. 994 does not recommend a term of imprisonment, be detained, unless the judicial officer finds by clear and convincing evidence that the person is not likely to flee or pose a danger to the safety of any other person or the community if released under section 3142(b) or (c). If the judicial officer makes such a finding, such judicial officer shall order the release of the person in accordance with section 3142(b) or (c).

(2) The judicial officer shall order that a person who has been found guilty of an offense in a case described in subparagraph (A), (B), or (C) of subsection (f)(1) of section 3142 and is awaiting imposition or execution of sentence be detained unless—

(A)(i) the judicial officer finds there is a substantial likelihood that a motion for acquittal or new trial will be granted; or

(ii) an attorney for the Government has recommended that no sentence of imprisonment be imposed on the person; and

(B) the judicial officer finds by clear and convincing evidence that the person is not likely to flee or pose a danger to any other person or the community.

(b) Release or detention pending appeal by the defendant.—(1) Except as provided in subparagraph (B)(iv) of this paragraph, the judicial officer shall order that a person who has been found guilty of an offense and sentenced to a term of imprisonment, and who has filed an appeal or a petition for a writ of certiorari, be detained, unless the judicial officer finds—

(A) by clear and convincing evidence that the person is not likely to flee or pose a danger to the safety of any other person or the community if released under section 3142(b) or (c) of this title; and

(B) that the appeal is not for the purpose of delay and raises a substantial question of law or fact likely to result in—

(i) reversal,

(ii) an order for a new trial,

(iii) a sentence that does not include a term of imprisonment, or

(iv) a reduced sentence to a term of imprisonment less than the total of the time already served plus the expected duration of the appeal process.

If the judicial officer makes such findings, such judicial officer shall order the release of the person in accordance with section 3142(b) or (c) of this title, except that in the circumstance described in subparagraph (B)(iv) of this paragraph, the judicial officer shall order the detention terminated at the expiration of the likely reduced sentence.

(2) The judicial officer shall order that a person who has been found guilty of an offense in a case described in subparagraph (A), (B), or (C) of subsection (f)(1) of section 3142 and sentenced to a term of imprisonment, and who has filed an appeal or a petition for a writ of certiorari, be detained.

(c) Release or detention pending appeal by the government.—The judicial officer shall treat a defendant in a case in which an appeal has been taken by the United States under section 3731 of this title, in accordance with section 3142 of this title, unless the defendant is otherwise subject to a release or detention order.

Except as provided in subsection (b) of this section, the judicial officer, in a case in which an appeal has been taken by the United States under section 3742, shall—

(1) if the person has been sentenced to a term of imprisonment, order that person detained; and

(2) in any other circumstance, release or detain the person under section 3142.

§ 3144. Release or detention of a material witness

If it appears from an affidavit filed by a party that the testimony of a person is material in a criminal proceeding, and if it is shown that it may become impracticable to secure the presence of the person by subpena, a judicial officer may order the arrest of the person and treat the person in accordance with the provisions of section 3142 of this title. No material witness may be detained because of inability to comply with any condition of release if the testimony of such witness can adequately be secured by deposition, and if further detention is not necessary to prevent a failure of justice. Release of a material witness may be delayed for a reasonable period of time until the deposition of the witness can be taken pursuant to the Federal Rules of Criminal Procedure.

§ 3145. Review and appeal of a release or detention order

(a) Review of a release order.—If a person is ordered released by a magistrate, or by a person other than a judge of a court having original jurisdiction over the offense and other than a Federal appellate court—

(1) the attorney for the Government may file, with the court having original jurisdiction over the offense, a motion for revocation of the order or amendment of the conditions of release; and

(2) the person may file, with the court having original jurisdiction over the offense, a motion for amendment of the conditions of release.

The motion shall be determined promptly.

(b) Review of a detention order.—If a person is ordered detained by a magistrate, or by a person other than a judge of a court having original jurisdiction over the offense and other than a Federal appellate court, the person may file, with the court having original jurisdiction over the offense, a motion for revocation or amendment of the order. The motion shall be determined promptly.

(c) Appeal from a release or detention order.—An appeal from a release or detention order, or from a decision denying revocation or amendment of such an order, is governed by the provisions of section 1291 of title 28 and section 3731 of this title. The appeal shall be determined promptly. A person subject to detention pursuant to section 3143(a)(2) or (b)(2), and who meets the conditions of release set forth in section 3143(a)(1) or (b)(1), may be ordered released, under appropriate conditions, by the judicial officer, if it is clearly shown that there are exceptional reasons why such person's detention would not be appropriate.

§ 3146. Penalty for failure to appear

(a) Offense.—Whoever, having been released under this chapter knowingly—

(1) fails to appear before a court as required by the conditions of his release; or

(2) fails to surrender for service of sentence pursuant to a court order; shall be punished as provided in subsection (b) of this section.

(b) Punishment.—(1) The punishment for an offense under this section is—

(A) if the person was released in connection with a charge of, or while awaiting sentence, surrender for service of sentence, or appeal or certiorari after conviction, for—

(i) an offense punishable by death, life imprisonment, or imprisonment for a term of 15 years or more, a fine under this title or imprisonment for not more than ten years, or both;

(ii) an offense punishable by imprisonment for a term of five years or more, a fine under this title or imprisonment for not more than five years, or both;

(iii) any other felony, a fine under this title or imprisonment for not more than two years, or both; or

(iv) a misdemeanor, a fine under this title or imprisonment for not more than one year, or both; and

(B) if the person was released for appearance as a material witness, a fine under this chapter or imprisonment for not more than one year, or both.

(2) A term of imprisonment imposed under this section shall be consecutive to the sentence of imprisonment for any other offense.

(c) Affirmative defense.—It is an affirmative defense to a prosecution under this section that uncontrollable circumstances prevented the person from appearing or surrendering, and that the person did not contribute to the creation of such circumstances in reckless disregard of the requirement that he appear or surrender, and that the person appeared or surrendered as soon as such circumstances ceased to exist.

(d) Declaration of forfeiture.—If a person fails to appear before a court as required, and the person executed an appearance bond pursuant to section 3142(b) of this title or is subject to the release condition set forth in clause (xi) or (xii) of section 3142(c)(1)(B) of this title, the judicial officer may, regardless of whether the person has been charged with an offense under this section, declare any property designated pursuant to that section to be forfeited to the United States.

§ 3147. Penalty for an offense committed while on release

A person convicted of an offense committed while released under this chapter shall be sentenced, in addition to the sentence prescribed for the offense to—

(1) a term of imprisonment of not less than two years and not more than ten years if the offense is a felony; or

(2) a term of imprisonment of not less than ninety days and not more than one year if the offense is a misdemeanor.

A term of imprisonment imposed under this section shall be consecutive to any other sentence of imprisonment.

§ 3148. Sanctions for violation of a release condition

(a) Available sanctions.—A person who has been released under section 3142 of this title, and who has violated a condition of his release, is subject to a revocation of release, an order of detention, and a prosecution for contempt of court.

(b) Revocation of release.—The attorney for the Government may initiate a proceeding for revocation of an order of release by filing a motion with the district court. A judicial officer may issue a warrant for the arrest of a person charged with violating a condition of release, and the person shall be brought before a judicial officer in the district in which such person's arrest was ordered for a proceeding in accordance with this section. To the extent practicable, a person charged with violating the condition of release that such person not commit a Federal, State, or local crime during the period of release shall be brought before the judicial officer who ordered the release and whose order is alleged to have been violated. The judicial officer shall enter an order of revocation and detention if, after a hearing, the judicial officer—

(1) finds that there is—

(A) probable cause to believe that the person has committed a Federal, State, or local crime while on release; or

(B) clear and convincing evidence that the person has violated any other condition of his release; and

(2) finds that—

(A) based on the factors set forth in section 3142(g) of this title, there is no condition or combination of conditions of release that will assure that the person will not flee or pose a danger to the safety of any other person or the community; or

(B) the person is unlikely to abide by any condition or combination of conditions of release.

If there is probable cause to believe that, while on release, the person committed a Federal, State, or local felony, a rebuttable presumption arises that no condition or combination of conditions will assure that the person will not pose a danger to the safety of any other person or the community. If the judicial officer finds that there are conditions of release that will assure that the person will not flee or pose a danger to the safety of any other person or the community, and that the person will abide by such conditions, the judicial officer shall treat the person in accordance with the provisions of section 3142 of this title and may amend the conditions of release accordingly.

(c) Prosecution for contempt.—The judge may commence a prosecution for contempt, pursuant to the provisions of section 401 of this title, if the person has violated a condition of release.

§ 3149. Surrender of an offender by a surety

A person charged with an offense, who is released upon the execution of an appearance bond with a surety, may be arrested by the surety, and if so arrested, shall be delivered promptly to a United States marshal and brought before a judicial officer. The judicial officer shall determine in accordance with the provisions of section 3148(b) whether to revoke the release of the person, and may absolve the surety of responsibility to pay all or part of the bond in accordance with the provisions of Rule 46 of the Federal Rules of Criminal Procedure. The person so committed shall be held in official detention until released pursuant to this chapter or another provision of law.

§ 3150. Applicability to a case removed from a State court

The provisions of this chapter apply to a criminal case removed to a Federal court from a State court.

SPEEDY TRIAL ACT OF 1974 (AS AMENDED)

(18 U.S.C. §§ 3161–3162, 3164).

§ 3161. Time limits and exclusions

(a) In any case involving a defendant charged with an offense, the appropriate judicial officer, at the earliest practicable time, shall, after consultation with the counsel for the defendant and the attorney for the Government, set the case for trial on a day certain, or list it for trial on a weekly or other short-term trial calendar at a place within the judicial district, so as to assure a speedy trial.

(b) Any information or indictment charging an individual with the commission of an offense shall be filed within thirty days from the date on which such individual was arrested or served with a summons in connection with such charges. If an individual has been charged with a felony in a district in which no grand jury has been in session during such thirty-day period, the period of time for filing of the indictment shall be extended an additional thirty days.

(c)(1) In any case in which a plea of not guilty is entered, the trial of a defendant charged in an information or indictment with the commission of an offense shall commence within seventy days from the filing date (and making public) of the information or indictment, or from the date the defendant has appeared before a judicial officer of the court in which such charge is pending, whichever date last occurs. If a defendant consents in writing to be tried before a magistrate on a complaint, the trial shall commence within seventy days from the date of such consent.

(2) Unless the defendant consents in writing to the contrary, the trial shall not commence less than thirty days from the date on which the defendant first appears through counsel or expressly waives counsel and elects to proceed pro se.

(d)(1) If any indictment or information is dismissed upon motion of the defendant, or any charge contained in a complaint filed against an individual is dismissed or otherwise dropped, and thereafter a complaint is filed against such defendant or individual charging him with the same offense or an offense based on the same conduct or arising from the same criminal episode, or an information or indictment is filed charging such defendant with the same offense or an offense based on the same conduct or arising from the same criminal episode, the provisions of subsections (b) and (c) of this section shall be applicable with respect to such subsequent complaint, indictment, or information, as the case may be.

(2) If the defendant is to be tried upon an indictment or information dismissed by a trial court and reinstated following an appeal, the trial shall commence within seventy days from the date the action occasioning the trial becomes final, except that the court retrying the case may extend the period for trial not to exceed one hundred and eighty days from the date the action occasioning the trial becomes final if the unavailability of witnesses or other factors resulting from the passage of time shall make trial within seventy days impractical. The periods of delay enumerated in section 3161(h) are excluded in computing the time limitations specified in this section. The sanctions of section 3162 apply to this subsection.

(e) If the defendant is to be tried again following a declaration by the trial judge of a mistrial or following an order of such judge for a new trial, the trial shall commence within seventy days from the date the action occasioning the retrial becomes final. If the defendant is to be tried again following an appeal or a collateral attack, the trial shall commence within seventy days from the date the action occasioning the retrial becomes final, except that the court retrying the case may extend the period for retrial not to exceed one hundred and eighty days from the date the action occasioning the retrial becomes final if unavailability of witnesses or other factors resulting from passage of time shall make trial within seventy days impractical. The periods of delay enumerated in section 3161(h) are excluded in computing the time limitations specified in this section. The sanctions of section 3162 apply to this subsection. * * *

(h) The following periods of delay shall be excluded in computing the time within which an information or an indictment must be filed, or in computing the time within which the trial of any such offense must commence:

(1) Any period of delay resulting from other proceedings concerning the defendant, including but not limited to—

(A) delay resulting from any proceeding, including any examinations, to determine the mental competency or physical capacity of the defendant;

(B) delay resulting from any proceeding, including any examination of the defendant, pursuant to section 2902 of title 28, United States Code;

(C) delay resulting from deferral of prosecution pursuant to section 2902 of title 28, United States Code;

(D) delay resulting from trial with respect to other charges against the defendant;

(E) delay resulting from any interlocutory appeal;

(F) delay resulting from any pretrial motion, from the filing of the motion through the conclusion of the hearing on, or other prompt disposition of, such motion;

(G) delay resulting from any proceeding relating to the transfer of a case or the removal of any defendant from another district under the Federal Rules of Criminal Procedure;

(H) delay resulting from transportation of any defendant from another district, or to and from places of examination or hospitalization, except that any time consumed in excess of ten days from the date an order of removal or an order directing such transportation, and the defendant's arrival at the destination shall be presumed to be unreasonable;

(I) delay resulting from consideration by the court of a proposed plea agreement to be entered into by the defendant and the attorney for the Government; and

(J) delay reasonably attributable to any period, not to exceed thirty days, during which any proceeding concerning the defendant is actually under advisement by the court.

(2) Any period of delay during which prosecution is deferred by the attorney for the Government pursuant to written agreement with the defendant, with the approval of the court, for the purpose of allowing the defendant to demonstrate his good conduct.

(3) (A) Any period of delay resulting from the absence or unavailability of the defendant or an essential witness.

(B) For purposes of subparagraph (A) of this paragraph, a defendant or an essential witness shall be considered absent when his whereabouts are unknown and, in addition, he is attempting to avoid apprehension or prosecution or his whereabouts cannot be determined by due diligence. For purposes of such subparagraph, a defendant or an essential witness shall be considered unavailable whenever his whereabouts are known but his presence for trial cannot be obtained by due diligence or he resists appearing at or being returned for trial.

(4) Any period of delay resulting from the fact that the defendant is mentally incompetent or physically unable to stand trial.

(5) Any period of delay resulting from the treatment of the defendant pursuant to section 2902 of title 28, United States Code.

(6) If the information or indictment is dismissed upon motion of the attorney for the Government and thereafter a charge is filed against the defendant for the same offense, or any offense required to be joined with that offense, any period of delay from the date the charge was dismissed to the date the time limitation would commence to run as to the subsequent charge had there been no previous charge.

(7) A reasonable period of delay when the defendant is joined for trial with a codefendant as to whom the time for trial has not run and no motion for severance has been granted.

(8)(A) Any period of delay resulting from a continuance granted by any judge on his own motion or at the request of the defendant or his counsel or at the request of the attorney for the Government, if the judge granted such continuance on the basis of his findings that the ends of justice served by taking such action outweigh the best interest of the public and the defendant in a speedy trial. No such period of delay resulting from a continuance granted by the court in accordance with this paragraph shall be excludable under this subsection unless the court sets forth, in the record of the case, either orally or in writing, its reasons for finding that the ends of justice served by the granting of such continuance outweigh the best interests of the public and the defendant in a speedy trial.

(B) The factors, among others, which a judge shall consider in determining whether to grant a continuance under subparagraph (A) of this paragraph in any case are as follows:

(i) Whether the failure to grant such a continuance in the proceeding would be likely to make a continuation of such proceeding impossible, or result in a miscarriage of justice.

(ii) Whether the case is so unusual or so complex, due to the number of defendants, the nature of the prosecution, or the existence of novel questions of fact or law, that it is unreasonable to expect adequate preparation for pretrial proceedings or for the trial itself within the time limits established by this section.

(iii) Whether, in a case in which arrest precedes indictment, delay in the filing of the indictment is caused because the arrest occurs at a time such that it is unreasonable to expect return and filing of the indictment within the period specified in section 3161(b), or because the facts upon which the grand jury must base its determination are unusual or complex.

(iv) Whether the failure to grant such a continuance in a case which, taken as a whole, is not so unusual or so complex as to fall within clause (ii), would deny the defendant reasonable time to obtain counsel, would unreasonably deny the defendant or the Government continuity of counsel, or would deny counsel for the defendant or the attorney for the Government the reasonable time necessary for effective preparation, taking into account the exercise of due diligence.

(C) No continuance under subparagraph (A) of this paragraph shall be granted because of general congestion of the court's calendar, or lack of diligent preparation or failure to obtain available witnesses on the part of the attorney for the Government.

(9) Any period of delay, not to exceed one year, ordered by a district court upon an application of a party and a finding by a preponderance of the evidence that an official request, as defined in section 3292 of this title, has been made for evidence of any such offense and that it reasonably appears, or reasonably appeared at the time the request was made, that such evidence is, or was, in such foreign country.

(i) If trial did not commence within the time limitation specified in section 3161 because the defendant had entered a plea of guilty or nolo contendere subsequently withdrawn to any or all charges in an indictment or information, the defendant shall be deemed indicted with respect to all charges therein contained within the meaning of section 3161, on the day the order permitting withdrawal of the plea becomes final.

(j)(1) If the attorney for the Government knows that a person charged with an offense is serving a term of imprisonment in any penal institution, he shall promptly—

(A) undertake to obtain the presence of the prisoner for trial; or

(B) cause a detainer to be filed with the person having custody of the prisoner and request him to so advise the prisoner and to advise the prisoner of his right to demand trial.

(2) If the person having custody of such prisoner receives a detainer, he shall promptly advise the prisoner of the charge and of the prisoner's right to demand trial. If at any time thereafter the prisoner informs the person having custody that he does demand trial, such person shall cause notice to that effect to be sent promptly to the attorney for the Government who caused the detainer to be filed.

(3) Upon receipt of such notice, the attorney for the Government shall promptly seek to obtain the presence of the prisoner for trial.

(4) When the person having custody of the prisoner receives from the attorney for the Government a properly supported request for temporary custody of such prisoner for trial, the prisoner shall be made available to that attorney for the Government (subject, in cases of interjurisdictional transfer, to any right of the prisoner to contest the legality of his delivery).

(k)(1) If the defendant is absent (as defined by subsection (h)(3)) on the day set for trial, and the defendant's subsequent appearance before the court on a bench warrant or other process or surrender to the court occurs more than 21 days after the day set for trial, the defendant shall be deemed to have first appeared before a judicial officer of the court in which the information or indictment is pending within the meaning of subsection (c) on the date of the defendant's subsequent appearance before the court.

(2) If the defendant is absent (as defined by subsection (h)(3)) on the day set for trial, and the defendant's subsequent appearance before the court on a bench warrant or other process or surrender to the court occurs not more than 21 days after the day set for trial, the time limit required by subsection (c), as extended by subsection (h), shall be further extended by 21 days.

§ 3162. Sanctions

(a)(1) If, in the case of any individual against whom a complaint is filed charging such individual with an offense, no indictment or information is filed within the time limit required by section 3161(b) as extended by section 3161(h) of this chapter, such charge against that individual contained in such complaint shall be dismissed or otherwise dropped. In determining whether to dismiss the case with or without prejudice, the court shall consider,among others, each of the following factors: the seriousness of the offense; the facts and circumstances of the case which led to the dismissal; and the impact of a reprosecution on the administration of this chapter and on the administration of justice.

(2) If a defendant is not brought to trial within the time limit required by section 3161(c) as extended by section 3161(h), the information or indictment shall be dismissed on motion of the defendant. The defendant

shall have the burden of proof of supporting such motion but the Government shall have the burden of going forward with the evidence in connection with any exclusion of time under subparagraph 3161(h)(3). In determining whether to dismiss the case with or without prejudice, the court shall consider, among others, each of the following factors: the seriousness of the offense; the facts and circumstances of the case which led to the dismissal; and the impact of a reprosecution on the administration of this chapter and on the administration of justice. Failure of the defendant to move for dismissal prior to trial or entry of a plea of guilty or nolo contendere shall constitute a waiver of the right to dismissal under this section.

(b) In any case in which counsel for the defendant or the attorney for the Government (1) knowingly allows the case to be set for trial without disclosing the fact that a necessary witness would be unavailable for trial; (2) files a motion solely for the purpose of delay which he knows is totally frivolous and without merit; (3) makes a statement for the purpose of obtaining a continuance which he knows to be false and which is material to the granting of a continuance; or (4) otherwise willfully fails to proceed to trial without justification consistent with section 3161 of this chapter, the court may punish any such counsel or attorney, as follows:

(A) in the case of an appointed defense counsel, by reducing the amount of compensation that otherwise would have been paid to such counsel pursuant to section 3006A of this title in an amount not to exceed 25 per centum thereof;

(B) in the case of a counsel retained in connection with the defense of a defendant, by imposing on such counsel a fine of not to exceed 25 per centum of the compensation to which he is entitled in connection with his defense of such defendant;

(C) by imposing on any attorney for the Government a fine of not to exceed $250;

(D) by denying any such counsel or attorney for the Government the right to practice before the court considering such case for a period of not to exceed ninety days; or

(E) by filing a report with an appropriate disciplinary committee.

The authority to punish provided for by this subsection shall be in addition to any other authority or power available to such court.

(c) The court shall follow procedures established in the Federal Rules of Criminal Procedure in punishing any counsel or attorney for the Government pursuant to this section.

§ 3164. Persons detained or designated as being of high risk

(a) The trial or other disposition of cases involving—

(1) a detained person who is being held in detention solely because he is awaiting trial, and

(2) a released person who is awaiting trial and has been designated by the attorney for the Government as being of high risk,

shall be accorded priority.

(b) The trial of any person described in subsection (a)(1) or (a)(2) of this section shall commence not later than ninety days following the beginning of such continuous detention or designation of high risk by the attorney for the Government. The periods of delay enumerated in section 3161(h) are excluded in computing the time limitation specified in this section.

(c) Failure to commence trial of a detainee as specified in subsection (b), through no fault of the accused or his counsel, or failure to commence trial of a designated releasee as specified in subsection (b), through no fault of the attorney for the Government, shall result in the automatic review by the court of the conditions of release. No detainee, as defined in subsection (a), shall be held in custody pending trial after the expiration of such ninety-day period required for the commencement of his trial. A designated releasee, as defined in subsection (a), who is found by the court to have intentionally delayed the trial of his case shall be subject to an order of the court modifying his nonfinancial conditions of release under this title to insure that he shall appear at trial as required.

LITIGATION CONCERNING SOURCES OF EVIDENCE

(18 U.S.C. § 3504).

§ 3504. Litigation concerning sources of evidence

(a) In any trial, hearing, or other proceeding in or before any court, grand jury, department, officer, agency, regulatory body, or other authority of the United States—

(1) upon a claim by a party aggrieved that evidence is inadmissible because it is the primary product of an unlawful act or because it was obtained by the exploitation of an unlawful act, the opponent of the claim shall affirm or deny the occurrence of the alleged unlawful act;

(2) disclosure of information for a determination if evidence is inadmissible because it is the primary product of an unlawful act occurring prior to June 19, 1968, or because it was obtained by the exploitation of an unlawful act occurring prior to June 19, 1968, shall not be required unless such information may be relevant to a pending claim of such inadmissibility; and

(3) no claim shall be considered that evidence of an event is inadmissible on the ground that such evidence was obtained by the exploitation of an unlawful act occurring prior to June 19, 1968, if such event occurred more than five years after such allegedly unlawful act.

(b) As used in this section "unlawful act" means any act the use of any electronic, mechanical, or other device (as defined in section 2510(5) of this title) in violation of the Constitution or laws of the United States or any regulation or standard promulgated pursuant thereto.

CRIMINAL APPEALS ACT OF 1970 (AS AMENDED)

(18 U.S.C. § 3731).

§ 3731. Appeal by United States

In a criminal case an appeal by the United States shall lie to a court of appeals from a decision, judgment, or order of a district court dismissing an indictment or information or granting a new trial after verdict or judgment, as to any one or more counts, except that no appeal shall lie where the double jeopardy clause of the United States Constitution prohibits further prosecution.

An appeal by the United States shall lie to a court of appeals from a decision or order of a district court suppressing or excluding evidence or requiring the return of seized property in a criminal proceeding, not made after the defendant has been put in jeopardy and before the verdict or finding on an indictment or information, if the United States attorney certifies to the district court that the appeal is not taken for purpose of delay and that the evidence is a substantial proof of a fact material in the proceeding.

An appeal by the United States shall lie to a court of appeals from a decision or order, entered by a district court of the United States, granting the release of a person charged with or convicted of an offense, or denying a motion for revocation of, or modification of the conditions of, a decision or order granting release.

The appeal in all such cases shall be taken within thirty days after the decision, judgment or order has been rendered and shall be diligently prosecuted.

The provisions of this section shall be liberally construed to effectuate its purposes.

JURY SELECTION AND SERVICE ACT OF 1968 (AS AMENDED)

(28 U.S.C. §§ 1861–1863, 1865–1867).

§ 1861. Declaration of policy

It is the policy of the United States that all litigants in Federal courts entitled to trial by jury shall have the right to grand and petit juries selected at random from a fair cross section of the community in the district or division wherein the court convenes. It is further the policy of the United States that all citizens shall have the opportunity to be considered for service on grand and petit juries in the district courts of the United States, and shall have an obligation to serve as jurors when summoned for that purpose.

§ 1862. Discrimination prohibited

No citizen shall be excluded from service as a grand or petit juror in the district courts of the United States or in the Court of International Trade on account of race, color, religion, sex, national origin, or economic status.

§ 1863. Plan for random jury selection

(a) Each United States district court shall devise and place into operation a written plan for random selection of grand and petit jurors that shall be designed to achieve the objectives of sections 1861 and 1862 of this title, and that shall otherwise comply with the provisions of this title. The plan shall be placed into operation after approval by a reviewing panel consisting of the members of the judicial council of the circuit and either the chief judge of the district whose plan is being reviewed or such other active district judge of that district as the chief judge of the district may designate. The panel shall examine the plan to ascertain that it complies with the provisions of this title. * * * The district court may modify a plan at any time and it shall modify the plan when so directed by the reviewing panel. * * *

(b) Among other things, such plan shall—

(1) either establish a jury commission, or authorize the clerk of the court, to manage the jury selection process. If the plan establishes a jury commission, the district court shall appoint one citizen to serve with the clerk of the court as the jury commission. * * * The citizen jury commissioner shall not belong to the same political party as the clerk serving with him. The clerk or the jury commission, as the case may be, shall act under the supervision and control of the chief judge of the district court or such other judge of the district court as the plan may provide. * * *

(2) specify whether the names of prospective jurors shall be selected from the voter registration lists or the lists of actual voters of the political subdivisions within the district or division. The plan shall prescribe some other source or sources of names in addition to voter lists where necessary to foster the policy and protect the rights secured by sections 1861 and 1862 of this title. * * *

(3) specify detailed procedures to be followed by the jury commission or clerk in selecting names from the sources specified in paragraph (2) of this subsection. These procedures shall be designed to ensure the random selection of a fair cross section of the persons residing in the community in the district or division wherein the court convenes. They shall ensure that names of persons residing in each of the counties, parishes, or similar political subdivisions within the judicial district or division are placed in a master jury wheel; and shall ensure that each county, parish, or similar political subdivision within the district or division is substantially proportionally represented in the master jury wheel for that judicial district, division, or combination of divisions. For the purposes of determining proportional representation in the master jury wheel, either the number of actual voters at the last general election in each county, parish, or similar political subdivision, or the number of registered voters if registration of voters is uniformly required throughout the district or division, may be used.

(4) provide for a master jury wheel (or a device similar in purpose and function) into which the names of those randomly selected shall be placed. The plan shall fix a minimum number of names to be placed initially in the master jury wheel, which shall be at least one-half of 1 per centum of the total number of persons on the lists used as a source

of names for the district or division; but if this number of names is believed to be cumbersome and unnecessary, the plan may fix a smaller number of names to be placed in the master wheel, but in no event less than one thousand. The chief judge of the district court, or such other district court judge as the plan may provide, may order additional names to be placed in the master jury wheel from time to time as necessary. The plan shall provide for periodic emptying and refilling of the master jury wheel at specified times, the interval for which shall not exceed four years.

(5) (A) except as provided in subparagraph (B), specify those groups of persons or occupational classes whose members shall, on individual request therefor, be excused from jury service. Such groups or classes shall be excused only if the district court finds, and the plan states, that jury service by such class or group would entail undue hardship or extreme inconvenience to the members thereof, and excuse of members thereof would not be inconsistent with sections 1861 and 1862 of this title.

(B) specify that volunteer safety personnel, upon individual request, shall be excused from jury service. For purposes of this subparagraph, the term "volunteer safety personnel" means individuals serving a public agency (as defined in section 1203(6) of title I of the Omnibus Crime Control and Safe Streets Act of 1968) in an official capacity, without compensation, as firefighters or members of a rescue squad or ambulance crew.

(6) specify that the following persons are barred from jury service on the ground that they are exempt: (A) members in active service in the Armed Forces of the United States; (B) members of the fire or police departments of any State, the District of Columbia, any territory or possession of the United States, or any subdivision of a State, the District of Columbia, or such territory or possession; (C) public officers in the executive, legislative, or judicial branches of the Government of the United States, or of any State, the District of Columbia, any territory or possession of the United States, or any subdivision of a State, the District of Columbia, or such territory or possession, who are actively engaged in the performance of official duties.

(7) fix the time when the names drawn from the qualified jury wheel shall be disclosed to parties and to the public. If the plan permits these names to be made public, it may nevertheless permit the chief judge of the district court, or such other district court judge as the plan may provide, to keep these names confidential in any case where the interests of justice so require.

(8) specify the procedures to be followed by the clerk or jury commission in assigning persons whose names have been drawn from the qualified jury wheel to grand and petit jury panels. * * *

§ 1865. Qualifications for jury service

(a) The chief judge of the district court, or such other district court judge as the plan may provide, on his initiative or upon recommendation of the clerk or jury commission, shall determine solely on the basis of information provided on the juror qualification form and other competent evidence whether a person is unqualified for, or exempt, or to be excused from jury service. The clerk shall enter such determination in the space provided on the juror qualification form and the alphabetical list of names drawn from the master jury wheel. If a person did not appear in response to a summons, such fact shall be noted on said list.

(b) In making such determination the chief judge of the district court, or such other district court judge as the plan may provide, shall deem any person qualified to serve on grand and petit juries in the district court unless he—

(1) is not a citizen of the United States eighteen years old who has resided for a period of one year within the judicial district;

(2) is unable to read, write, and understand the English language with a degree of proficiency sufficient to fill out satisfactorily the juror qualification form;

(3) is unable to speak the English language;

(4) is incapable, by reason of mental or physical infirmity, to render satisfactory jury service; or

(5) has a charge pending against him for the commission of, or has been convicted in a State or Federal court of record of, a crime punishable by imprisonment for more than one year and his civil rights have not been restored.

§ 1866. Selection and summoning of jury panels

* * *

(c) Except as provided in section 1865 of this title or in any jury selection plan provision adopted pursuant to paragraph (5) or (6) of section 1863(b) of this title, no person or class of persons shall be disqualified, excluded, excused, or exempt from service as jurors: *Provided*, That any person summoned for jury service may be (1) excused by the court, or by the clerk under supervision of the court if the court's jury selection plan so authorizes, upon a showing of undue hardship or extreme inconvenience, for such period as the court deems necessary, at the conclusion of which such person either shall be summoned again for jury service under subsections (b) and (c) of this section or, if the court's jury selection plan so provides, the name of such person shall be reinserted into the qualified jury wheel for selection pursuant to subsection (a) of this section, or (2) excluded by the court on the ground that such person may be unable to render impartial jury service or that his service as a juror would be likely to disrupt the proceedings, or (3) excluded upon peremptory challenge as provided by law, or (4) excluded pursuant to the procedure specified by law upon a challenge by any party for good cause shown, or (5) excluded upon determination by the court that his service as a juror would be likely to threaten the secrecy of the proceedings, or otherwise adversely affect the integrity of jury deliberations. No person shall be excluded under clause (5) of this subsection unless the judge, in open court, determines that such is warranted and that exclusion of the person will not be inconsistent with sections 1861 and 1862 of this title. The number of persons excluded under clause (5) of this subsection shall not exceed one per centum of the number of persons who return executed jury qualification forms during the period, specified in the plan, between two consecutive fillings of the master jury wheel. The names of persons excluded under clause (5) of this subsection, together with detailed explanations for the exclusions, shall be forwarded immediately to the judicial council of the circuit, which shall have the power to make any appropriate order, prospective or retroactive, to redress any misapplication of clause (5) of this subsection, but otherwise exclusions effectuated under such clause shall not be subject to challenge under the provisions of this title. Any person excluded from a particular jury under clause (2), (3), or (4) of this subsection shall be eligible to sit on another jury if the basis for his initial exclusion would not be relevant to his ability to serve on such other jury. * * *

§ 1867. Challenging compliance with selection procedures

(a) In criminal cases, before the voir dire examination begins, or within seven days after the defendant discovered or could have discovered, by the exercise of diligence, the grounds therefor, whichever is earlier, the defendant may move to dismiss the indictment or stay the proceedings against him on the ground of substantial failure to comply with the provisions of this title in selecting the grand or petit jury.

(b) In criminal cases, before the voir dire examination begins, or within seven days after the Attorney General of the United States discovered or could have discovered, by the exercise of diligence, the grounds therefor, whichever is earlier, the Attorney General may move to dismiss the indictment or stay the proceedings on the ground of substantial failure to comply with the provisions of this title in selecting the grand or petit jury. * * *

(d) Upon motion filed under subsection (a), (b), or (c) of this section, containing a sworn statement of facts which, if true, would constitute a substantial failure to comply with the provisions of this title, the moving party shall be entitled to present in support of such motion the testimony of the jury commission or clerk, if available, any relevant records and papers not public or otherwise available used by the jury commissioner or clerk, and any other relevant evidence. If the court determines that there has been a substantial failure to comply with the provisions of this title in selecting a grand jury, the court shall stay the proceedings pending the selection of a grand jury in conformity with this title or dismiss the indictment, whichever is appropriate. If the court determines that there has been a substantial failure to comply with the provisions of this title in selecting the petit jury, the court shall stay the proceedings pending the selection of a petit jury in conformity with this title.

(e) The procedures prescribed by this section shall be the exclusive means by which a person accused of a Federal crime, the Attorney General of the United States or a party in a civil case may challenge any jury on the ground that such jury was not selected in conformity with the provisions of this title. Nothing in this section shall preclude any person or the United States from pursuing any other remedy, civil or criminal, which may be available for the vindication or enforcement of any law prohibiting discrimination on account of race, color, religion, sex, national origin or economic status in the selection of persons for service on grand or petit juries. * * *

HABEAS CORPUS

(28 U.S.C. §§ 2241–2244, 2254–2255).

§ 2241. Power to grant writ

(a) Writs of habeas corpus may be granted by the Supreme Court, any justice thereof, the district courts and any circuit judge within their respective jurisdictions. The order of a circuit judge shall be entered in the records of the district court of the district wherein the restraint complained of is had.

(b) The Supreme Court, any justice thereof, and any circuit judge may decline to entertain an application for a writ of habeas corpus and may transfer the application for hearing and determination to the district court having jurisdiction to entertain it.

(c) The writ of habeas corpus shall not extend to a prisoner unless—

(1) He is in custody under or by color of the authority of the United States or is committed for trial before some court there of; or

(2) He is in custody for an act done or omitted in pursuance of an Act of Congress, or an order, process, judgment or decree of a court or judge of the United States; or

(3) He is in custody in violation of the Constitution or laws or treaties of the United States; or

(4) He, being a citizen of a foreign state and domiciled therein is in custody for an act done or omitted under any alleged right, title, authority, privilege, protection, or exemption claimed under the commission, order or sanction of any foreign state, or under color thereof, the validity and effect of which depend upon the law of nations; or

(5) It is necessary to bring him into court to testify or for trial.

(d) Where an application for a writ of habeas corpus is made by a person in custody under the judgment and sentence of a State court of a State which contains two or more Federal judicial districts, the application may be filed in the district court for the district wherein such person is in custody or in the district court for the district within which the State court was held which convicted and sentenced him and each of such district courts shall have concurrent jurisdiction to entertain the application. The district court for the district wherein such an application is filed in the exercise of its discretion and in furtherance of justice may transfer the application to the other district court for hearing and determination.

§ 2242. Application

Application for a writ of habeas corpus shall be in writing signed and verified by the person for whose relief it is intended or by someone acting in his behalf.

It shall allege the facts concerning the applicant's commitment or detention, the name of the person who has custody over him and by virtue of what claim or authority, if known.

It may be amended or supplemented as provided in the rules of procedure applicable to civil actions.

If addressed to the Supreme Court, a justice thereof or a circuit judge it shall state the reasons for not making application to the district court of the district in which the applicant is held.

§ 2243. Issuance of writ; return; hearing; decision

A court, justice or judge entertaining an application for a writ of habeas corpus shall forthwith award the writ or issue an order directing the respondent to show cause why the writ should not be granted, unless it appears from the application that the applicant or person detained is not entitled thereto.

The writ, or order to show cause shall be directed to the person having custody of the person detained. It shall be returned within three days unless for good cause additional time, not exceeding twenty days, is allowed.

The person to whom the writ or order is directed shall make a return certifying the true cause of the detention.

When the writ or order is returned a day shall be set for hearing, not more than five days after the return unless for good cause additional time is allowed.

Unless the application for the writ and the return present only issues of law the person to whom the writ is directed shall be required to produce at the hearing the body of the person detained.

The applicant or the person detained may, under oath, deny any of the facts set forth in the return or allege any other material facts.

The return and all suggestions made against it may be amended, by leave of court, before or after being filed.

The court shall summarily hear and determine the facts, and dispose of the matter as law and justice require.

§ 2244. Finality of determination

(a) No circuit or district judge shall be required to entertain an application for a writ of habeas corpus to inquire into the detention of a person pursuant to a judgment of a court of the United States if it appears that the legality of such detention has been determined by a judge or court of the United States on a prior application for a writ of habeas corpus, except as provided in section 2255.

(b)(1) A claim presented in a second or successive habeas corpus application under section 2254 that was presented in a prior application shall be dismissed.

(2) A claim presented in a second or successive habeas corpus application under section 2254 that was not presented in a prior application shall be dismissed unless—

(A) the applicant shows that the claim relies on a new rule of constitutional law, made retroactive to cases on collateral review by the Supreme Court, that was previously unavailable; or

(B)(i) the factual predicate for the claim could not have been discovered previously through the exercise of due diligence; and

(ii) the facts underlying the claim, if proven and viewed in light of the evidence as a whole, would be sufficient to establish by clear and convincing evidence that, but for constitutional error, no reasonable factfinder would have found the applicant guilty of the underlying offense.

(3)(A) Before a second or successive application permitted by this section is filed in the district court, the applicant shall move in the appropriate court of appeals for an order authorizing the district court to consider the application.

(B) A motion in the court of appeals for an order authorizing the district court to consider a second or successive application shall be determined by a three-judge panel of the court of appeals.

(C) The court of appeals may authorize the filing of a second or successive application only if it determines that the application makes a prima facie showing that the application satisfies the requirements of this subsection.

(D) The court of appeals shall grant or deny the authorization to file a second or successive application not later than 30 days after the filing of the motion.

(E) The grant or denial of an authorization by a court of appeals to file a second or successive application shall not be appealable and shall not be the subject of a petition for rehearing or for a writ of certiorari.

(4) A district court shall dismiss any claim presented in a second or successive application that the court of appeals has authorized to be filed unless the applicant shows that the claim satisfies the requirements of this section.

(c) In a habeas corpus proceeding brought in behalf of a person in custody pursuant to the judgment of a State court, a prior judgment of the Supreme Court of the United States on an appeal or review by a writ of certiorari at the instance of the prisoner of the decision of such State court, shall be conclusive as to all issues of fact or law with respect to an asserted denial of a Federal right which constitutes ground for discharge in a habeas corpus proceeding, actually adjudicated by the Supreme Court therein, unless the applicant for the writ of habeas corpus shall plead and the court shall find the existence of a material and controlling fact which did not appear in the record of the proceeding in the Supreme Court and the court shall further find that the applicant for the writ of habeas corpus could not have caused such fact to appear in such record by the exercise of reasonable diligence.

(d)(1) A 1-year period of limitation shall apply to an application for a writ of habeas corpus by a person in custody pursuant to the judgment of a State court. The limitation period shall run from the latest of—

(A) the date on which the judgment became final by the conclusion of direct review or the expiration of the time for seeking such review;

(B) the date on which the impediment to filing an application created by State action in violation of the Constitution or laws of the United States is removed, if the applicant was prevented from filing by such State action;

(C) the date on which the constitutional right asserted was initially recognized by the Supreme Court, if the right has been newly recognized by the Supreme Court and made retroactively applicable to cases on collateral review; or

(D) the date on which the factual predicate of the claim or claims presented could have been discovered through the exercise of due diligence.

(2) The time during which a properly filed application for State post-conviction or other collateral review with respect to the pertinent judgment or claim is pending shall not be counted toward any period of limitation under this subsection.

§ 2253. Appeal

(a) In a habeas corpus proceeding or a proceeding under section 2255 before a district judge, the final order shall be subject to review, on appeal, by the court of appeals for the circuit in which the proceeding is held.

(b) There shall be no right of appeal from a final order in a proceeding to test the validity of a warrant to remove to another district or place for commitment or trial a person charged with a criminal offense against the United States, or to test the validity of such person's detention pending removal proceedings.

(c)(1) Unless a circuit justice or judge issues a certificate of appealability, an appeal may not be taken to the court of appeals from—

(A) the final order in a habeas corpus proceeding in which the detention complained of arises out of process issued by a State court; or

(B) the final order in a proceeding under section 2255.

(2) A certificate of appealability may issue under paragraph (1) only if the applicant has made a substantial showing of the denial of a constitutional right.

(3) The certificate of appealability under paragraph (1) shall indicate which specific issue or issues satisfy the showing required by paragraph (2).

§ 2254. State custody; remedies in State courts

(a) The Supreme Court, a Justice thereof, a circuit judge, or a district court shall entertain an application for a writ of habeas corpus in behalf of a person in custody pursuant to the judgment of a State court only on the ground that he is in custody in violation of the Constitution or laws or treaties of the United States.

(b)(1) An application for a writ of habeas corpus on behalf of a person in custody pursuant to the judgment of a State court shall not be granted unless it appears that—

(A) the applicant has exhausted the remedies available in the courts of the State; or

(B)(i) there is an absence of available State corrective process; or

(ii) circumstances exist that render such process ineffective to protect the rights of the applicant.

(2) An application for a writ of habeas corpus may be denied on the merits, notwithstanding the failure of the applicant to exhaust the remedies available in the courts of the State.

(3) A State shall not be deemed to have waived the exhaustion requirement or be estopped from reliance upon the requirement unless the State, through counsel, expressly waives the requirement.

(c) An applicant shall not be deemed to have exhausted the remedies available in the courts of the State, within the meaning of this section, if he has the right under the law of the State to raise, by any available procedure, the question presented.

(d) An application for a writ of habeas corpus on behalf of a person in custody pursuant to the judgment of a State court shall not be granted with respect to any claim that was adjudicated on the merits in State court proceedings unless the adjudication of the claim—

(1) resulted in a decision that was contrary to, or involved an unreasonable application of, clearly established Federal law, as determined by the Supreme Court of the United States; or

(2) resulted in a decision that was based on an unreasonable determination of the facts in light of the evidence presented in the State court proceeding.

(e)(1) In a proceeding instituted by an application for a writ of habeas corpus by a person in custody pursuant to the judgment of a State court, a determination of a factual issue made by a State court shall be presumed to be correct. The applicant shall have the burden of rebutting the presumption of correctness by clear and convincing evidence.

(2) If the applicant has failed to develop the factual basis of a claim in State court proceedings, the court shall not hold an evidentiary hearing on the claim unless the applicant shows that—

(A) the claim relies on—

(i) a new rule of constitutional law, made retroactive to cases on collateral review by the Supreme Court, that was previously unavailable; or

(ii) a factual predicate that could not have been previously discovered through the exercise of due diligence; and

(B) the facts underlying the claim would be sufficient to establish by clear and convincing evidence that but for constitutional error, no reasonable factfinder would have found the applicant guilty of the underlying offense.

(f) If the applicant challenges the sufficiency of the evidence adduced in such State court proceeding to support the State court's determination of a factual issue made therein, the applicant, if able, shall produce that part of the record pertinent to a determination of the sufficiency of the evidence to support such determination. If the applicant, because of indigency or other reason is unable to produce such part of the record, then the State shall produce such part of the record and the Federal court shall direct the State to do so by order directed to an appropriate State official. If the State cannot provide such pertinent part of the record, then the court shall determine under the existing facts and circumstances what weight shall be given to the State court's factual determination.

(g) A copy of the official records of the State court, duly certified by the clerk of such court to be a true and correct copy of a finding, judicial opinion, or other reliable written indicia showing such a factual determination by the State court shall be admissible in the Federal court proceeding.

(h) Except as provided in section 408 of the Controlled Substances Act, in all proceedings brought under this section, and any subsequent proceedings on review, the court may appoint counsel for an applicant who is or becomes financially unable to afford counsel, except as provided by a rule promulgated by the Supreme Court pursuant to statutory authority. Appointment of counsel under this section shall be governed by section 3006A of title 18.

(i) The ineffectiveness or incompetence of counsel during Federal or State collateral post-conviction proceedings shall not be a ground for relief in a proceeding arising under section 2254.

§ 2255. Federal custody; remedies on motion attacking sentence

A prisoner in custody under sentence of a court established by Act of Congress claiming the right to be released upon the ground that the sentence was imposed in violation of the Constitution or laws of the United States, or that the court was without jurisdiction to impose such sentence, or that the sentence was in excess of the maximum authorized by law, or is otherwise subject to collateral attack, may move the court which imposed the sentence to vacate, set aside or correct the sentence.

Unless the motion and the files and records of the case conclusively show that the prisoner is entitled to no relief, the court shall cause notice thereof to be served upon the United States attorney, grant a prompt hearing thereon, determine the issues and make findings of fact and conclusions of law with respect thereto. If the court finds that the judgment was rendered without jurisdiction, or that the sentence imposed was not authorized by law or otherwise open to collateral attack, or that there has been such a denial or infringement of the constitutional rights of the prisoner as to render the judgment vulnerable to collateral attack, the court shall vacate and set the judgment aside and shall discharge the prisoner or resentence him or grant a new trial or correct the sentence as may appear appropriate.

A court may entertain and determine such motion without requiring the production of the prisoner at the hearing.

A 1–year period of limitation shall apply to a motion under this section. The limitation period shall run from the latest of—

(1) the date on which the judgment of conviction becomes final;

(2) the date on which the impediment to making a motion created by governmental action in violation of the Constitution or laws of the United

States is removed, if the movant was prevented from making a motion by such governmental action;

(3) the date on which the right asserted was initially recognized by the Supreme Court, if that right has been newly recognized by the Supreme Court and made retroactively applicable to cases on collateral review; or

(4) the date on which the facts supporting the claim or claims presented could have been discovered through the exercise of due diligence.

Except as provided in section 408 of the Controlled Substances Act, in all proceedings brought under this section, and any subsequent proceedings on review, the court may appoint counsel, except as provided by a rule promulgated by the Supreme Court pursuant to statutory authority. Appointment of counsel under this section shall be governed by section 3006A of title 18.

A second or successive motion must be certified as provided in section 2244 by a panel of the appropriate court of appeals to contain—

(1) newly discovered evidence that, if proven and viewed in light of the evidence as a whole, would be sufficient to establish by clear and convincing evidence that no reasonable factfinder would have found the movant guilty of the offense; or

(2) a new rule of constitutional law, made retroactive to cases on collateral review by the Supreme Court, that was previously unavailable.

An appeal may be taken to the court of appeals from the order entered on the motion as from a final judgment on application for a writ of habeas corpus.

An application for a writ of habeas corpus in behalf of a prisoner who is authorized to apply for relief by motion pursuant to this section, shall not be entertained if it appears that the applicant has failed to apply for relief, by motion, to the court which sentenced him, or that such court has denied him relief, unless it also appears that the remedy by motion is inadequate or ineffective to test the legality of his detention.

§ 2261. Prisoners in State custody subject to capital sentence; appointment of counsel; requirement of rule of court or statute; procedures for appointment

(a) This chapter shall apply to cases arising under section 2254 brought by prisoners in State custody who are subject to a capital sentence. It shall apply only if the provisions of subsections (b) and (c) are satisfied.

(b) This chapter is applicable if a State establishes by statute, rule of its court of last resort, or by another agency authorized by State law, a mechanism for the appointment, compensation, and payment of reasonable litigation expenses of competent counsel in State post-conviction proceedings brought by indigent prisoners whose capital convictions and sentences have been upheld on direct appeal to the court of last resort in the State or have otherwise become final for State law purposes. The rule of court or statute must provide standards of competency for the appointment of such counsel.

(c) Any mechanism for the appointment, compensation, and reimbursement of counsel as provided in subsection (b) must offer counsel to all State prisoners under capital sentence and must provide for the entry of an order by a court of record—

(1) appointing one or more counsels to represent the prisoner upon a finding that the prisoner is indigent and accepted the offer or is unable competently to decide whether to accept or reject the offer;

(2) finding, after a hearing if necessary, that the prisoner rejected the offer of counsel and made the decision with an understanding of its legal consequences; or

(3) denying the appointment of counsel upon a finding that the prisoner is not indigent.

(d) No counsel appointed pursuant to subsections (b) and (c) to represent a State prisoner under capital sentence shall have previously represented the prisoner at trial or on direct appeal in the case for which the appointment is made unless the prisoner and counsel expressly request continued representation.

(e) The ineffectiveness or incompetence of counsel during State or Federal post-conviction proceedings in a capital case shall not be a ground for relief in a proceeding arising under section 2254. This limitation shall not preclude the appointment of different counsel, on the court's own motion or at the request of the prisoner, at any phase of State or Federal post-conviction proceedings on the basis of the ineffectiveness or incompetence of counsel in such proceedings.

§ 2262. Mandatory stay of execution; duration; limits on stays of execution; successive petitions

(a) Upon the entry in the appropriate State court of record of an order under section 2261(c), a warrant or order setting an execution date for a State prisoner shall be stayed upon application to any court that would have jurisdiction over any proceedings filed under section 2254. The application shall recite that the State has invoked the post-conviction review procedures of this chapter and that the scheduled execution is subject to stay.

(b) A stay of execution granted pursuant to subsection (a) shall expire if—

(1) a State prisoner fails to file a habeas corpus application under section 2254 within the time required in section 2263;

(2) before a court of competent jurisdiction, in the presence of counsel, unless the prisoner has competently and knowingly waived such counsel, and after having been advised of the consequences, a State prisoner under capital sentence waives the right to pursue habeas corpus review under section 2254; or

(3) a State prisoner files a habeas corpus petition under section 2254 within the time required by section 2263 and fails to make a substantial showing of the denial of a Federal right or is denied relief in the district court or at any subsequent stage of review.

(c) If one of the conditions in subsection (b) has occurred, no Federal court thereafter shall have the authority to enter a stay of execution in the case, unless the court of appeals approves the filing of a second or successive application under section 2244(b).

§ 2263. Filing of habeas corpus application; time requirements; tolling rules

(a) Any application under this chapter for habeas corpus relief under section 2254 must be filed in the appropriate district court not later than 180 days after final State court affirmance of the conviction and sentence on direct review or the expiration of the time for seeking such review.

(b) The time requirements established by subsection (a) shall be tolled—

(1) from the date that a petition for certiorari is filed in the Supreme Court until the date of final disposition of the petition if a State prisoner files the petition to secure review by the Supreme Court of the affirmance of a capital sentence on direct review by the court of last resort of the State or other final State court decision on direct review;

(2) from the date on which the first petition for post-conviction review or other collateral relief is filed until the final State court disposition of such petition; and

(3) during an additional period not to exceed 30 days, if—

(A) a motion for an extension of time is filed in the Federal district court that would have jurisdiction over the case upon the filing of a habeas corpus application under section 2254; and

(B) a showing of good cause is made for the failure to file the habeas corpus application within the time period established by this section.

§ 2264. Scope of Federal review; district court adjudications

(a) Whenever a State prisoner under capital sentence files a petition for habeas corpus relief to which this chapter applies, the district court shall only consider a claim or claims that have been raised and decided on the merits in the State courts, unless the failure to raise the claim properly is—

(1) the result of State action in violation of the Constitution or laws of the United States;

(2) the result of the Supreme Court's recognition of a new Federal right that is made retroactively applicable; or

(3) based on a factual predicate that could not have been discovered through the exercise of due diligence in time to present the claim for State or Federal post-conviction review.

(b) Following review subject to subsections (a), (d), and (e) of section 2254, the court shall rule on the claims properly before it.

§ 2265. Application to State unitary review procedure

(a) For purposes of this section, a 'unitary review' procedure means a State procedure that authorizes a person under sentence of death to raise, in the course of direct review of the judgment, such claims as could be raised on collateral attack. This chapter shall apply, as provided in this section, in relation to a State unitary review procedure if the State establishes by rule of its court of last resort or by statute a mechanism for the appointment, compensation, and payment of reasonable litigation expenses of competent counsel in the unitary review proceedings, including expenses relating to the litigation of collateral claims in the proceedings. The rule of court or statute must provide standards of competency for the appointment of such counsel.

(b) To qualify under this section, a unitary review procedure must include an offer of counsel following trial for the purpose of representation on unitary review, and entry of an order, as provided in section 2261(c), concerning appointment of counsel or waiver or denial of appointment of counsel for that purpose. No counsel appointed to represent the prisoner in the unitary review proceedings shall have previously represented the prisoner at trial in the case for which the appointment is made unless the prisoner and counsel expressly request continued representation.

(c) Sections 2262, 2263, 2264, and 2266 shall apply in relation to cases involving a sentence of death from any State having a unitary review procedure that qualifies under this section. References to State 'post-conviction review' and 'direct review' in such sections shall be understood as referring to unitary review under the State procedure. The reference in section 2262(a) to 'an order under section 2261(c)' shall be understood as referring to the post-trial order under subsection (b) concerning representation in the unitary review proceedings, but if a transcript of the trial proceedings is unavailable at the time of the filing of such an order in the appropriate State court, then the start of the 180–day limitation period under section 2263 shall be deferred until a transcript is made available to the prisoner or counsel of the prisoner.

§ 2266. Limitation periods for determining applications and motions

(a) The adjudication of any application under section 2254 that is subject to this chapter, and the adjudication of any motion under section 2255 by a person under sentence of death, shall be given priority by the district court and by the court of appeals over all noncapital matters.

(b)(1)(A) A district court shall render a final determination and enter a final judgment on any application for a writ of habeas corpus brought under this chapter in a capital case not later than 180 days after the date on which the application is filed.

(B) A district court shall afford the parties at least 120 days in which to complete all actions, including the preparation of all pleadings and briefs, and if necessary, a hearing, prior to the submission of the case for decision.

(C)(i) A district court may delay for not more than one additional 30–day period beyond the period specified in subparagraph (A), the rendering of a determination of an application for a writ of habeas corpus if the court issues a written order making a finding, and stating the reasons for the finding, that the ends of justice that would be served by allowing the delay outweigh the best interests of the public and the applicant in a speedy disposition of the application.

(ii) The factors, among others, that a court shall consider in determining whether a delay in the disposition of an application is warranted are as follows:

(I) Whether the failure to allow the delay would be likely to result in a miscarriage of justice.

(II) Whether the case is so unusual or so complex, due to the number of defendants, the nature of the prosecution, or the existence of novel questions of fact or law, that it is unreasonable to expect adequate briefing within the time limitations established by subparagraph (A).

(III) Whether the failure to allow a delay in a case that, taken as a whole, is not so unusual or so complex as described in subclause (II), but would otherwise deny the applicant reasonable time to obtain counsel, would unreasonably deny the applicant or the government continuity of counsel, or would deny counsel for the applicant or the government the reasonable time necessary for effective preparation, taking into account the exercise of due diligence.

(iii) No delay in disposition shall be permissible because of general congestion of the court's calendar.

(iv) The court shall transmit a copy of any order issued under clause (i) to the Director of the Administrative Office of the United States Courts for inclusion in the report under paragraph (5).

(2) The time limitations under paragraph (1) shall apply to—

(A) an initial application for a writ of habeas corpus;

(B) any second or successive application for a writ of habeas corpus; and

(C) any redetermination of an application for a writ of habeas corpus following a remand by the court of appeals or the Supreme Court for further proceedings, in which case the limitation period shall run from the date the remand is ordered.

(3)(A) The time limitations under this section shall not be construed to entitle an applicant to a stay of execution, to which the applicant would otherwise not be entitled, for the purpose of litigating any application or appeal.

(B) No amendment to an application for a writ of habeas corpus under this chapter shall be permitted after the filing of the answer to the application, except on the grounds specified in section 2244(b).

(4)(A) The failure of a court to meet or comply with a time limitation under this section shall not be a ground for granting relief from a judgment of conviction or sentence.

(B) The State may enforce a time limitation under this section by petitioning for a writ of mandamus to the court of appeals. The court of appeals shall act on the petition for a writ of mandamus not later than 30 days after the filing of the petition.

(5)(A) The Administrative Office of the United States Courts shall submit to Congress an annual report on the compliance by the district courts with the time limitations under this section.

(B) The report described in subparagraph (A) shall include copies of the orders submitted by the district courts under paragraph (1)(B)(iv).

(c)(1)(A) A court of appeals shall hear and render a final determination of any appeal of an order granting or denying, in whole or in part, an application brought under this chapter in a capital case not later than 120 days after the date on which the reply brief is filed, or if no reply brief is filed, not later than 120 days after the date on which the answering brief is filed.

(B)(i) A court of appeals shall decide whether to grant a petition for rehearing or other request for rehearing en banc not later than 30 days after the date on which the petition for rehearing is filed unless a responsive pleading is required, in which case the court shall decide whether to grant the petition not later than 30 days after the date on which the responsive pleading is filed.

(ii) If a petition for rehearing or rehearing en banc is granted, the court of appeals shall hear and render a final determination of the appeal not later than 120 days after the date on which the order granting rehearing or rehearing en banc is entered.

(2) The time limitations under paragraph (1) shall apply to—

(A) an initial application for a writ of habeas corpus;

(B) any second or successive application for a writ of habeas corpus; and

(C) any redetermination of an application for a writ of habeas corpus or related appeal following a remand by the court of appeals en banc or the Supreme Court for further proceedings, in which case the limitation period shall run from the date the remand is ordered.

(3) The time limitations under this section shall not be construed to entitle an applicant to a stay of execution, to which the applicant would otherwise not be entitled, for the purpose of litigating any application or appeal.

(4)(A) The failure of a court to meet or comply with a time limitation under this section shall not be a ground for granting relief from a judgment of conviction or sentence.

(B) The State may enforce a time limitation under this section by applying for a writ of mandamus to the Supreme Court.

(5) The Administrative Office of the United States Courts shall submit to Congress an annual report on the compliance by the courts of appeals with the time limitations under this section.[a]

a. The enacting legislation states that new sections 2261–2266 "shall apply to cases pending on or after the date of enactment of this Act."

PRIVACY PROTECTION ACT OF 1980

(42 U.S.C. §§ 2000aa–2000aa–12).

§ 2000aa. Searches and seizures by government officers and employees in connection with investigation or prosecution of criminal offenses

(a) Notwithstanding any other law, it shall be unlawful for a government officer or employee, in connection with the investigation or prosecution of a criminal offense, to search for or seize any work product materials possessed by a person reasonably believed to have a purpose to disseminate to the public a newspaper, book, broadcast, or other similar form of public communication, in or affecting interstate or foreign commerce; but this provision shall not impair or affect the ability of any government officer or employee, pursuant to otherwise applicable law, to search for or seize such materials, if—

(1) there is probable cause to believe that the person possessing such materials has committed or is committing the criminal offense to which the materials relate: *Provided, however*, That a government officer or employee may not search for or seize such materials under the provisions of this paragraph if the offense to which the materials relate consists of the receipt, possession, communication, or withholding of such materials or the information contained therein (but such a search or seizure may be conducted under the provisions of this paragraph if the offense consists of the receipt, possession, or communication of information relating to the national defense, classified information, or restricted data under the provisions of section 793, 794, 797, or 798 of Title 18, or section 2274, 2275 or 2277 of this title, or section 783 of Title 50, or if the offense involves the production, possession, receipt, mailing, sale, distribution, shipment, or transportation of child pornography, the sexual exploitation of children, or the sale or purchase of children under section 2251, 2251A, 2252, or 2252A of Title 18); or

(2) there is reason to believe that the immediate seizure of such materials is necessary to prevent the death of, or serious bodily injury to, a human being.

(b) Notwithstanding any other law, it shall be unlawful for a government officer or employee, in connection with the investigation or prosecution of a criminal offense, to search for or seize documentary materials, other than work product materials, possessed by a person in connection with a purpose to disseminate to the public a newspaper, book, broadcast, or other similar form of public communication, in or affecting interstate or foreign commerce; but this provision shall not impair or affect the ability of any government officer or employee, pursuant to otherwise applicable law, to search for or seize such materials, if—

(1) there is probable cause to believe that the person possessing such materials has committed or is committing the criminal offense to which the materials relate: *Provided, however*, That a government officer or employee may not search for or seize such materials under the provisions of this paragraph if the offense to which the materials relate consists of the receipt, possession, communication, or withholding of such materials or the information contained therein (but such a search

or seizure may be conducted under the provisions of this paragraph if the offense consists of the receipt, possession, or communication of information relating to the national defense, classified information, or restricted data under the provisions of section 793, 794, 797, or 798 of Title 18, or section 2274, 2275 or 2277 of this title, or section 783 of Title 50, or if the offense involves the production, possession, receipt, mailing, sale, distribution, shipment, or transportation of child pornography, the sexual exploitation of children, or the sale or purchase of children under section 2251, 2251A, 2252, or 2252A of Title 18);

(2) there is reason to believe that the immediate seizure of such materials is necessary to prevent the death of, or serious bodily injury to, a human being;

(3) there is reason to believe that the giving of notice pursuant to a subpena duces tecum would result in the destruction, alteration, or concealment of such materials; or

(4) such materials have not been produced in response to a court order directing compliance with a subpena duces tecum, and—

(A) all appellate remedies have been exhausted; or

(B) there is reason to believe that the delay in an investigation or trial occasioned by further proceedings relating to the subpena would threaten the interests of justice.

(c) In the event a search warrant is sought pursuant to paragraph (4)(B) of subsection (b) of this section, the person possessing the materials shall be afforded adequate opportunity to submit an affidavit setting forth the basis for any contention that the materials sought are not subject to seizure.

§ 2000aa–5. Border and customs searches

This chapter shall not impair or affect the ability of a government officer or employee, pursuant to otherwise applicable law, to conduct searches and seizures at the borders of, or at international points of, entry into the United States in order to enforce the customs laws of the United States.

§ 2000aa–6. Civil actions by aggrieved persons

(a) A person aggrieved by a search for or seizure of materials in violation of this chapter shall have a civil cause of action for damages for such search or seizure—

(1) against the United States, against a State which has waived its sovereign immunity under the Constitution to a claim for damages resulting from a violation of this chapter, or against any other governmental unit, all of which shall be liable for violations of this chapter by their officers or employees while acting within the scope or under color of their office or employment; and

(2) against an officer or employee of a State who has violated this chapter while acting within the scope or under color of his office or employment, if such State has not waived its sovereign immunity as provided in paragraph (1).

(b) It shall be a complete defense to a civil action brought under paragraph (2) of subsection (a) of this section that the officer or employee had a reasonable good faith belief in the lawfulness of his conduct.

(c) The United States, a State, or any other governmental unit liable for violations of this chapter under subsection (a)(1) of this section, may not assert as a defense to a claim arising under this chapter the immunity of the officer or employee whose violation is complained of or his reasonable good faith belief in the lawfulness of his conduct, except that such a defense may be asserted if the violation complained of is that of a judicial officer.

(d) The remedy provided by subsection (a)(1) of this section against the United States, a State, or any other governmental unit is exclusive of any other civil action or proceeding for conduct constituting a violation of this chapter, against the officer or employee whose violation gave rise to the claim, or against the estate of such officer or employee.

(e) Evidence otherwise admissible in a proceeding shall not be excluded on the basis of a violation of this chapter.

(f) A person having a cause of action under this section shall be entitled to recover actual damages but not less than liquidated damages of $1,000, and such reasonable attorneys' fees and other litigation costs reasonably incurred as the court, in its discretion, may award: *Provided, however*, That the United States, a State, or any other governmental unit shall not be liable for interest prior to judgment.

(g) The Attorney General may settle a claim for damages brought against the United States under this section, and shall promulgate regulations to provide for the commencement of an administrative inquiry following a determination of a violation of this chapter by an officer or employee of the United States and for the imposition of administrative sanctions against such officer or employee, if warranted.

(h) The district courts shall have original jurisdiction of all civil actions arising under this section.

§ 2000aa–7. Definitions

(a) "Documentary materials", as used in this chapter, means materials upon which information is recorded, and includes, but is not limited to, written or printed materials, photographs, motion picture films, negatives, video tapes, audio tapes, and other mechanically, magnetically or electronically recorded cards, tapes, or discs, but does not include contraband or the fruits of a crime or things otherwise criminally possessed, or property designed or intended for use, or which is or has been used as, the means of committing a criminal offense.

(b) "Work product materials", as used in this chapter, means materials, other than contraband or the fruits of a crime or things otherwise criminally possessed, or property designed or intended for use, or which is or has been used, as the means of committing a criminal offense, and—

(1) in anticipation of communicating such materials to the public, are prepared, produced, authored, or created, whether by the person in possession of the materials or by any other person;

(2) are possessed for the purposes of communicating such materials to the public; and

(3) include mental impressions, conclusions, opinions, or theories of the person who prepared, produced, authored, or created such material.

(c) "Any other governmental unit", as used in this chapter, includes the District of Columbia, the Commonwealth of Puerto Rico, any territory or possession of the United States, and any local government, unit of local government, or any unit of State government.

§ 2000aa–11. Guidelines for federal officers and employees

(a) The Attorney General shall * * * issue guidelines for the procedures to be employed by any Federal officer or employee, in connection with the investigation or prosecution of an offense, to obtain documentary materials in the private possession of a person when the person is not reasonably believed to be a suspect in such offense or related by blood or marriage to such a suspect, and when the materials sought are not contraband or the fruits or instrumentalities of an offense. * * *

§ 2000aa–12. Binding nature of guidelines; disciplinary actions for violations; legal proceedings for non-compliance prohibited

Guidelines issued by the Attorney General under this subchapter shall have the full force and effect of Department of Justice regulations and any violation of these guidelines shall make the employee or officer involved subject to appropriate administrative disciplinary action. However, an issue relating to the compliance, or the failure to comply, with guidelines issued pursuant to this subchapter may not be litigated, and a court may not entertain such an issue as the basis for the suppression or exclusion of evidence.

[EDITOR'S NOTE: These guidelines appear in 28 C.F.R. Pt. 59. The procedural provisions are set out below.]

§ 59.4 Procedures

(a) *Provisions governing the use of search warrants generally.*

(1) A search warrant should not be used to obtain documentary materials believed to be in the private possession of a disinterested third party unless it appears that the use of a subpoena, summons, request, or other less intrusive alternative means of obtaining the materials would substantially jeopardize the availability or usefulness of the materials sought, and the application for the warrant has been authorized as provided in paragraph (a)(2) of this section.

(2) No federal officer or employee shall apply for a warrant to search for and seize documentary materials believed to be in the private possession of a disinterested third party unless the application for the warrant has been authorized by an attorney for the government. Provided, however, that in an emergency situation in which the immediacy of the need to seize the materials does not permit an opportunity to secure the authorization of an attorney for the government, the application may be authorized by a

supervisory law enforcement officer in the applicant's department or agency, if the appropriate United States Attorney (or where the case is not being handled by a United States Attorney's Office, the appropriate supervisory official of the Department of Justice) is notified of the authorization and the basis for justifying such authorization under this part within 24 hours of the authorization.

(b) *Provisions governing the use of search warrants which may intrude upon professional, confidential relationships.*

(1) A search warrant should not be used to obtain documentary materials believed to be in the private possession of a disinterested third party physician, lawyer, or clergyman, under circumstances in which the materials sought, or other materials likely to be reviewed during the execution of the warrant, contain confidential information on patients, clients, or parishioners which was furnished or developed for the purposes of professional counseling or treatment, unless—

(i) It appears that the use of a subpoena, summons, request or other less intrusive alternative means of obtaining the materials would substantially jeopardize the availability or usefulness of the materials sought;

(ii) Access to the documentary materials appears to be of substantial importance to the investigation or prosecution for which they are sought; and

(iii) The application for the warrant has been approved as provided in paragraph (b)(2) of this section.

(2) No federal officer or employee shall apply for a warrant to search for and seize documentary materials believed to be in the private possession of a disinterested third party physician, lawyer, or clergyman under the circumstances described in paragraph (b)(1) of this section, unless, upon the recommendation of the United States Attorney (or where a case is not being handled by a United States Attorney's Office, upon the recommendation of the appropriate supervisory official of the Department of Justice), an appropriate Deputy Assistant Attorney General has authorized the application for the warrant. Provided, however, that in an emergency situation in which the immediacy of the need to seize the materials does not permit an opportunity to secure the authorization of a Deputy Assistant Attorney General, the application may be authorized by the United States Attorney (or where the case is not being handled by a United States Attorney's Office, by the appropriate supervisory official of the Department of Justice) if an appropriate Deputy Assistant Attorney General is notified of the authorization and the basis for justifying such authorization under this part within 72 hours of the authorization.

(3) Whenever possible, a request for authorization by an appropriate Deputy Assistant Attorney General of a search warrant application pursuant to paragraph (b)(2) of this section shall be made in writing and shall include:

(i) The application for the warrant; and

(ii) A brief description of the facts and circumstances advanced as the basis for recommending authorization of the application under this part.

If a request for authorization of the application is made orally or if, in an emergency situation, the application is authorized by the United States Attorney or a supervisory official of the Department of Justice as provided in paragraph (b)(2) of this section, a written record of the request including the materials specified in paragraphs (b)(3)(i) and (ii) of this section shall be transmitted to an appropriate Deputy Assistant Attorney General within 7 days. The Deputy Assistant Attorneys General shall keep a record of the disposition of all requests for authorizations of search warrant applications made under paragraph (b) of this section.

(4) A search warrant authorized under paragraph (b)(2) of this section shall be executed in such a manner as to minimize, to the greatest extent practicable, scrutiny of confidential materials.

(5) Although it is impossible to define the full range of additional doctor-like therapeutic relationships which involve the furnishing or development of private information, the United States Attorney (or where a case is not being handled by a United States Attorney's Office, the appropriate supervisory official of the Department of Justice) should determine whether a search for documentary materials held by other disinterested third party professionals involved in such relationships (e.g. psychologists or psychiatric social workers or nurses) would implicate the special privacy concerns which are addressed in paragraph (b) of this section. If the United States Attorney (or other supervisory official of the Department of Justice) determines that such a search would require review of extremely confidential information furnished or developed for the purposes of professional counseling or treatment, the provisions of this subsection should be applied. Otherwise, at a minimum, the requirements of paragraph (a) of this section must be met.

(c) *Considerations bearing on choice of methods.*

In determining whether, as an alternative to the use of a search warrant, the use of a subpoena or other less intrusive means of obtaining documentary materials would substantially jeopardize the availability or usefulness of the materials sought, the following factors, among others, should be considered:

(1) Whether it appears that the use of a subpoena or other alternative which gives advance notice of the government's interest in obtaining the materials would be likely to result in the destruction, alteration, concealment, or transfer of the materials sought; considerations, among others, bearing on this issue may include:

(i) Whether a suspect has access to the materials sought;

(ii) Whether there is a close relationship of friendship, loyalty, or sympathy between the possessor of the materials and a suspect;

(iii) Whether the possessor of the materials is under the domination or control of a suspect;

(iv) Whether the possessor of the materials has an interest in preventing the disclosure of the materials to the government;

(v) Whether the possessor's willingness to comply with a subpoena or request by the government would be likely to subject him to intimidation or threats of reprisal;

(vi) Whether the possessor of the materials has previously acted to obstruct a criminal investigation or judicial proceeding or refused to comply with or acted in defiance of court orders; or

(vii) Whether the possessor has expressed an intent to destroy, conceal, alter, or transfer the materials;

(2) The immediacy of the government's need to obtain the materials; considerations, among others, bearing on this issue may include:

(i) Whether the immediate seizure of the materials is necessary to prevent injury to persons or property;

(ii) Whether the prompt seizure of the materials is necessary to preserve their evidentiary value;

(iii) Whether delay in obtaining the materials would significantly jeopardize an ongoing investigation or prosecution; or

(iv) Whether a legally enforceable form of process, other than a search warrant, is reasonably available as a means of obtaining the materials.

The fact that the disinterested third party possessing the materials may have grounds to challenge a subpoena or other legal process is not in itself a legitimate basis for the use of a search warrant.

Appendix C

FEDERAL RULES OF CRIMINAL PROCEDURE FOR THE UNITED STATES DISTRICT COURTS

I. SCOPE, PURPOSE, AND CONSTRUCTION

Rule 1. Scope

These rules govern the procedure in all criminal proceedings in the courts of the United States, as provided in Rule 54(a); and, whenever specifically provided in one of the rules, to preliminary, supplementary, and special proceedings before United States magistrate judges and at proceedings before state and local judicial officers.

Rule 2. Purpose and Construction

These rules are intended to provide for the just determination of every criminal proceeding. They shall be construed to secure simplicity in procedure, fairness in administration and the elimination of unjustifiable expense and delay.

II. PRELIMINARY PROCEEDINGS

Rule 3. The Complaint

The complaint is a written statement of the essential facts constituting the offense charged. It shall be made upon oath before a magistrate judge.

Rule 4. Arrest Warrant or Summons upon Complaint

(a) Issuance. If it appears from the complaint, or from an affidavit or affidavits filed with the complaint, that there is probable cause to believe that an offense has been committed and that the defendant has committed it, a warrant for the arrest of the defendant shall issue to any officer authorized by law to execute it. Upon the request of the attorney for the government a summons instead of a warrant shall issue. More than one warrant or summons may issue on the same complaint. If a defendant fails to appear in response to the summons, a warrant shall issue.

(b) Probable Cause. The finding of probable cause may be based upon hearsay evidence in whole or in part.

(c) Form.

(1) Warrant. The warrant shall be signed by the magistrate judge and shall contain the name of the defendant or, if the defendant's name is unknown, any name or description by which the defendant can be identified with reasonable certainty. It shall describe the offense charged in the complaint. It shall command that the defendant be arrested and brought before the nearest available magistrate judge.

(2) Summons. The summons shall be in the same form as the warrant except that it shall summon the defendant to appear before a magistrate at a stated time and place.

(d) Execution or Service; and Return.

(1) By Whom. The warrant shall be executed by a marshal or by some other officer authorized by law. The summons may be served by any person authorized to serve a summons in a civil action.

(2) Territorial Limits. The warrant may be executed or the summons may be served at any place within the jurisdiction of the United States.

(3) Manner. The warrant shall be executed by the arrest of the defendant. The officer need not have the warrant at the time of the arrest but upon request shall show the warrant to the defendant as soon as possible. If the officer does not have the warrant at the time of the arrest, the officer shall then inform the defendant of the offense charged and of the fact that a warrant has been issued. The summons shall be served upon a defendant by delivering a copy to the defendant personally, or by leaving it at the defendant's dwelling house or usual place of abode with some person of suitable age and discretion then residing therein and by mailing a copy of the summons to the defendant's last known address.

(4) Return. The officer executing a warrant shall make return thereof to the magistrate judge or other officer before whom the defendant is brought pursuant to Rule 5. At the request of the attorney for the government any unexecuted warrant shall be returned to and canceled by the magistrate judge by whom it was issued. On or before the return day the person to whom a summons was delivered for service shall make return thereof to the magistrate judge before whom the summons is returnable. At the request of the attorney for the government made at any time while the complaint is pending, a warrant returned unexecuted and not canceled or a summons returned unserved or a duplicate thereof may be delivered by the magistrate judge to the marshal or other authorized person for execution or service.

Rule 5. Initial Appearance Before the Magistrate Judge

(a) In General. Except as otherwise provided in this rule, an officer making an arrest under a warrant issued upon a complaint or any person making an arrest without a warrant shall take the arrested person without unnecessary delay before the nearest available federal magistrate judge or, if a federal magistrate judge is not reasonably available, before a state or local judicial officer authorized by 18 U.S.C. § 3041. If a person arrested without a warrant is brought before a magistrate judge, a complaint, satisfying the probable cause requirements of Rule 4(a), shall be promptly filed. When a person, arrested with or without a warrant or given a summons, appears initially before the magistrate judge, the magistrate judge shall proceed in accordance with the applicable subdivisions of this rule. An officer making an arrest under a warrant issued upon a complaint charging solely a violation of 18 U.S.C. § 1073 need not comply with this rule if the person arrested is transferred without unnecessary delay to the custody of appropriate state or local authorities in the district of arrest and an attorney for the government moves promptly, in the district in which the warrant was issued, to dismiss the complaint.

(b) Misdemeanors and Other Petty Offenses. If the charge against the defendant is a misdemeanor or other petty offense triable by a United States magistrate judge under 18 U.S.C. § 3401, the United States magistrate judge shall proceed in accordance with Rule 58.

(c) Offenses Not Triable by the United States Magistrate Judge. If the charge against the defendant is not triable by the United States magistrate judge, the defendant shall not be called upon to plead. The magistrate judge shall inform the defendant of the complaint against the defendant and of any affidavit filed therewith, of the defendant's right to retain counsel or to request the assignment of counsel if the defendant is unable to obtain counsel, and of the general circumstances under which the defendant may secure pretrial release. The magistrate judge shall inform the defendant that the defendant is not required to make a statement and that any statement made by the defendant may be used against the defendant. The magistrate judge shall also inform the defendant of the right to a preliminary examination. The magistrate judge shall allow the defendant reasonable time and opportunity to consult counsel and shall detain or conditionally release the defendant as provided by statute or in these rules.

A defendant is entitled to a preliminary examination, unless waived, when charged with any offense, other than a petty offense, which is to be tried by a judge of the district court. If the defendant waives preliminary examination, the magistrate judge shall forthwith hold the defendant to answer in the district court. If the defendant does not waive the preliminary examination, the magistrate judge shall schedule a preliminary examination. Such examination shall be held within a reasonable time but in any event not later than 10 days following the initial appearance if the defendant is in custody and no later than 20 days if the defendant is not in custody, provided, however, that the preliminary examination shall not be held if the defendant is indicted or if an information against the defendant is filed in district court before the date set for the preliminary examination. With the consent of the defendant and upon a showing of good cause, taking into account the public interest in the prompt disposition of criminal cases, time limits specified in this subdivision may be extended one or more times by a federal magistrate judge. In the absence of such consent by the defendant, time limits may be extended by a judge of the United States only upon a showing that extraordinary circumstances exist and that delay is indispensable to the interests of justice.

Rule 5.1. Preliminary Examination

(a) Probable Cause Finding. If from the evidence it appears that there is probable cause to believe that an offense has been committed and that the defendant committed it, the federal magistrate judge shall forthwith hold the defendant to answer in district court. The finding of probable cause may be based upon hearsay evidence in whole or in part. The defendant may cross-examine adverse witnesses and may introduce evidence. Objections to evidence on the ground that it was acquired by unlawful means are not properly made at the preliminary examination. Motions to suppress must be made to the trial court as provided in Rule 12.

(b) Discharge of Defendant. If from the evidence it appears that there is no probable cause to believe that an offense has been committed or that the defendant committed it, the federal magistrate judge shall dismiss the complaint and discharge the defendant. The discharge of the defendant shall not preclude the government from instituting a subsequent prosecution for the same offense.

(c) Records. After concluding the proceeding the federal magistrate judge shall transmit forthwith to the clerk of the district court all papers in the proceeding. The magistrate judge shall promptly make or cause to be made a record or summary of such proceeding.

(1) On timely application to a federal magistrate judge, the attorney for a defendant in a criminal case may be given the opportunity to have the recording of the hearing on preliminary examination made available to that attorney in connection with any further hearing or preparation for trial. The court may, by local rule, appoint the place for and define the conditions under which such opportunity may be afforded counsel.

(2) On application of a defendant addressed to the court or any judge thereof, an order may issue that the federal magistrate judge make available a copy of the transcript, or of a portion thereof, to defense counsel. Such order shall provide for prepayment of costs of such transcript by the defendant unless the defendant makes a sufficient affidavit that the defendant is unable to pay or to give security therefor, in which case the expense shall be paid by the Director of the Administrative Office of the United States Courts from available appropriated funds. Counsel for the government may move also that a copy of the transcript, in whole or in part, be made available to it, for good cause shown, and an order may be entered granting such motion in whole or in part, on appropriate terms, except that the government need not prepay costs nor furnish security therefor.

(d) Production of Statements.

(1) In General. Rule 26.2(a)-(d) and (f) applies at any hearing under this rule, unless the court, for good cause shown, rules otherwise in a particular case.

(2) Sanctions for Failure to Produce Statement. If a party elects not to comply with an order under Rule 26.2(a) to deliver a statement to the moving party, the court may not consider the testimony of a witness whose statement is withheld.

III. INDICTMENT AND INFORMATION

Rule 6. The Grand Jury

(a) Summoning Grand Juries.

(1) Generally. The court shall order one or more grand juries to be summoned at such time as the public interest requires. The grand jury shall consist of not less than 16 nor more than 23 members. The court shall direct that a sufficient number of legally qualified persons be summoned to meet this requirement.

(2) Alternate Jurors. The court may direct that alternate jurors may be designated at the time a grand jury is selected. Alternate jurors in the order in which they were designated may thereafter be impanelled as provided in subdivision (g) of this rule. Alternate jurors shall be drawn in the same manner and shall have the same qualifications as the regular jurors, and if impanelled shall be subject to the same challenges, shall take the same oath and shall have the same functions, powers, facilities and privileges as the regular jurors.

(b) Objections to Grand Jury and to Grand Jurors.

(1) Challenges. The attorney for the government or a defendant who has been held to answer in the district court may challenge the array of jurors on the ground that the grand jury was not selected, drawn or summoned in accordance with law, and may challenge an individual juror on the ground that the juror is not legally qualified. Challenges shall be made before the administration of the oath to the jurors and shall be tried by the court.

(2) Motion to Dismiss. A motion to dismiss the indictment may be based on objections to the array or on the lack of legal qualification of an individual juror, if not previously determined upon challenge. It shall be made in the manner prescribed in 28 U.S.C. § 1867(e) and shall be granted under the conditions prescribed in that statute. An indictment shall not be dismissed on the ground that one or more members of the grand jury were not legally qualified if it appears from the record kept pursuant to subdivision (c) of this rule that 12 or more jurors, after deducting the number not legally qualified, concurred in finding the indictment.

(c) Foreperson and Deputy Foreperson. The court shall appoint one of the jurors to be foreperson and another to be deputy foreperson. The foreperson shall have power to administer oaths and affirmations and shall sign all indictments. The foreperson or another juror designated by the foreperson shall keep record of the number of jurors concurring in the finding of every indictment and shall file the record with the clerk of the court, but the record shall not be made public except on order of the court. During the absence of the foreperson, the deputy foreperson shall act as foreperson.

(d) Who May Be Present.

(1) While Grand Jury is in Session. Attorneys for the government, the witness under examination, interpreters when needed and, for the purpose of taking the evidence, a stenographer or operator of a recording device may be present while the grand jury is in session.

(2) During Deliberations and Voting. No person other than the jurors, and any interpreter necessary to assist a juror who is hearing or speech impaired, may be present while the grand jury is deliberating or voting.

(e) Recording and Disclosure of Proceedings.

(1) Recording of Proceedings. All proceedings, except when the grand jury is deliberating or voting, shall be recorded stenographically or by an electronic recording device. An unintentional failure of any recording to reproduce all or any portion of a proceeding shall not affect the validity of the prosecution. The recording or reporter's notes or any transcript prepared therefrom shall remain in the custody or control of the attorney for the government unless otherwise ordered by the court in a particular case.

(2) General Rule of Secrecy. A grand juror, an interpreter, a stenographer, an operator of a recording device, a typist who transcribes recorded testimony, an attorney for the government, or any person to whom disclosure is made under paragraph (3)(A)(ii) of this subdivision shall not disclose matters occurring before the grand jury, except as otherwise provided for in these rules. No obligation of secrecy may be imposed on any person except in accordance with this rule. A knowing violation of Rule 6 may be punished as a contempt of court.

(3) Exceptions.

(A) Disclosure otherwise prohibited by this rule of matters occurring before the grand jury, other than its deliberations and the vote of any grand juror, may be made to—

(i) an attorney for the government for use in the performance of such attorney's duty; and

(ii) such government personnel (including personnel of a state or subdivision of a state) as are deemed necessary by an attorney for the government to assist an attorney for the government in the performance of such attorney's duty to enforce federal criminal law.

(B) Any person to whom matters are disclosed under subparagraph (A)(ii) of this paragraph shall not utilize that grand jury material for any purpose other than assisting the attorney for the government in the performance of such attorney's duty to enforce federal criminal law. An attorney for the government shall promptly provide the district court, before which was impaneled the grand jury whose material has been so disclosed, with the names of the persons to whom such disclosure has been made, and shall certify that the attorney has advised such persons of their obligation of secrecy under this rule.

(C) Disclosure otherwise prohibited by this rule of matters occurring before the grand jury may also be made—

(i) when so directed by a court preliminarily to or in connection with a judicial proceeding;

(ii) when permitted by a court at the request of the defendant, upon a showing that grounds may exist for a motion to dismiss the indictment because of matters occurring before the grand jury;

(iii) when the disclosure is made by an attorney for the government to another federal grand jury; or

(iv) when permitted by a court at the request of an attorney for the government, upon a showing that such matters may disclose a violation of state criminal law, to an appropriate official of a state or subdivision of a state for the purpose of enforcing such law.

If the court orders disclosure of matters occurring before the grand jury, the disclosure shall be made in such manner, at such time, and under such conditions as the court may direct.

(D) A petition for disclosure pursuant to subdivision (e)(3)(C)(i) shall be filed in the district where the grand jury convened. Unless the hearing is ex parte, which it may be when the petitioner is the government, the petitioner shall serve written notice of the petition upon (i) the attorney for the government, (ii) the parties to the judicial proceeding if disclosure is sought in connection with such a proceeding, and (iii) such other persons as the court may direct. The court shall afford those persons a reasonable opportunity to appear and be heard.

(E) If the judicial proceeding giving rise to the petition is in a federal district court in another district, the court shall transfer the matter to that court unless it can reasonably obtain sufficient knowledge of the proceeding to determine whether disclosure is proper. The court shall order transmitted to the court to which the matter is transferred the material sought to be disclosed, if feasible, and a written evaluation of the need for continued grand jury secrecy. The court to which the matter is transferred shall afford the aforementioned persons a reasonable opportunity to appear and be heard.

(4) Sealed Indictments. The federal magistrate judge to whom an indictment is returned may direct that the indictment be kept secret until the defendant is in custody or has been released pending trial. Thereupon the clerk shall seal the indictment and no person shall disclose the return of the indictment except when necessary for the issuance and execution of a warrant or summons.

(5) Closed Hearing. Subject to any right to an open hearing in contempt proceedings, the court shall order a hearing on matters affecting a grand jury proceeding to be closed to the extent necessary to prevent disclosure of matters occurring before a grand jury.

(6) Sealed Records. Records, orders and subpoenas relating to grand jury proceedings shall be kept under seal to the extent and for such time as is necessary to prevent disclosure of matters occurring before a grand jury.

(f) Finding and Return of Indictment. A grand jury may indict only upon the concurrence of 12 or more jurors. The indictment shall be returned by the grand jury, or through the foreperson or deputy foreperson on its behalf, to a federal magistrate judge in open court. If a complaint or information is pending against the defendant and 12 jurors do not vote to indict, the foreperson shall so report to a federal magistrate judge in writing as soon as possible.

(g) Discharge and Excuse. A grand jury shall serve until discharged by the court, but no grand jury may serve more than 18 months unless the court extends the service of the grand jury for a period of six months or less upon a determination that such extension is in the public interest. At any time for cause shown the court may excuse a juror either temporarily or permanently, and in the latter event the court may impanel another person in place of the juror excused.

Rule 7. The Indictment and the Information

(a) Use of Indictment or Information. An offense which may be punished by death shall be prosecuted by indictment. An offense which may be punished by imprisonment for a term exceeding one year or at hard labor shall be prosecuted by indictment or, if indictment is waived, it may be prosecuted by information. Any other offense may be prosecuted by indictment or by information. An information may be filed without leave of court.

(b) Waiver of Indictment. An offense which may be punished by imprisonment for a term exceeding one year or at hard labor may be prosecuted by information if the defendant, after having been advised of the nature of the charge and of the rights of the defendant, waives in open court prosecution by indictment.

(c) Nature and Contents.

(1) In General. The indictment or the information shall be a plain, concise and definite written statement of the essential facts constituting the offense charged. It shall be signed by the attorney for the government. It need not contain a formal commencement, a formal conclusion or any other matter not necessary to such statement. Allegations made in one count may be incorporated by reference in another count. It may be alleged in a single count that the means by which the defendant committed the offense are unknown or that the defendant committed it by one or more specified means. The indictment or information shall state for each count the official or customary citation of the statute, rule, regulation or other provision of law which the defendant is alleged therein to have violated.

(2) Criminal Forfeiture. No judgment of forfeiture may be entered in a criminal proceeding unless the indictment or the information shall allege the extent of the interest or property subject to forfeiture.

(3) Harmless Error. Error in the citation or its omission shall not be ground for dismissal of the indictment or information or for reversal of a conviction if the error or omission did not mislead the defendant to the defendant's prejudice.

(d) Surplusage. The court on motion of the defendant may strike surplusage from the indictment or information.

(e) Amendment of Information. The court may permit an information to be amended at any time before verdict or finding if no additional or different offense is charged and if substantial rights of the defendant are not prejudiced.

(f) Bill of Particulars. The court may direct the filing of a bill of particulars. A motion for a bill of particulars may be made before arraignment or within ten days after arraignment or at such later time as the court may permit. A bill of particulars may be amended at any time subject to such conditions as justice requires.

Rule 8. Joinder of Offenses and of Defendants

(a) Joinder of Offenses. Two or more offenses may be charged in the same indictment or information in a separate count for each offense if the offenses charged, whether felonies or misdemeanors or both, are of the same or similar character or are based on the same act or transaction or on two or more acts or transactions connected together or constituting parts of a common scheme or plan.

(b) Joinder of Defendants. Two or more defendants may be charged in the same indictment or information if they are alleged to have participated in the same act or transaction or in the same series of acts or transactions constituting an offense or offenses. Such defendants may be charged in one or more counts together or separately and all of the defendants need not be charged in each count.

Rule 9. Warrant or Summons Upon Indictment or Information

(a) Issuance. Upon the request of the attorney for the government the court shall issue a warrant for each defendant named in an information supported by a showing of probable cause under oath as is required by Rule 4(a), or in an indictment. Upon the request of the attorney for the government a summons instead of a warrant shall issue. If no request is made, the court may issue either a warrant or a summons in its discretion. More than one warrant or summons may issue for the same defendant. The clerk shall deliver the warrant or summons to the marshal or other person authorized by law to execute or serve it. If a defendant fails to appear in response to the summons, a warrant shall issue. When a defendant arrested with a warrant or given a summons appears initially before a magistrate judge, the magistrate judge shall proceed in accordance with the applicable subdivisions of Rule 5.

(b) Form.

(1) Warrant. The form of the warrant shall be as provided in Rule 4(c)(1) except that it shall be signed by the clerk, it shall describe the offense charged in the indictment or information and it shall command that the defendant be arrested and brought before the nearest available magistrate judge. The amount of bail may be fixed by the court and endorsed on the warrant.

(2) Summons. The summons shall be in the same form as the warrant except that it shall summon the defendant to appear before a magistrate judge at a stated time and place.

(c) Execution or Service; and Return.

(1) Execution or Service. The warrant shall be executed or the summons served as provided in Rule 4(d)(1), (2) and (3). A summons to a corporation shall be served by delivering a copy to an officer or to a managing or general agent or to any other agent authorized by appointment or by law to receive service of process and, if the agent is one authorized by statute to receive service and the statute so requires, by also mailing a copy to the corporation's last known address within the district or at its principal place of business elsewhere in the United States. The officer executing the warrant shall bring the arrested person without unnecessary delay before the nearest available federal magistrate judge or, in the event that a federal magistrate judge is not reasonably available, before a state or local judicial officer authorized by 18 U.S.C. § 3041.

(2) Return. The officer executing a warrant shall make return thereof to the magistrate judge or other officer before whom the defendant is brought. At the request of the attorney for the government any unexecuted warrant shall be returned and cancelled. On or before the return day the person to whom a summons was delivered for service shall make return thereof. At the request of the attorney for the government made at any time while the indictment or information is pending, a warrant returned unexecuted and not cancelled or a summons returned unserved or a duplicate thereof may be delivered by the clerk to the marshal or other authorized person for execution or service.

[(d) Remand to United States Magistrate for Trial of Minor Offenses] (Abrogated Apr. 28, 1982, eff. Aug. 1, 1982).

IV. ARRAIGNMENT AND PREPARATION FOR TRIAL

Rule 10. Arraignment

Arraignment shall be conducted in open court and shall consist of reading the indictment or information to the defendant or stating to the defendant the substance of the charge and calling on the defendant to plead thereto. The defendant shall be given a copy of the indictment or information before being called upon to plead.

Rule 11. Pleas

(a) Alternatives.

(1) In General. A defendant may plead guilty, not guilty, or nolo contendere. If a defendant refuses to plead, or if a defendant organization, as defined in 18 U.S.C. §§ 18, fails to appear, the court shall enter a plea of not guilty.

(2) Conditional Pleas. With the approval of the court and the consent of the government, a defendant may enter a conditional plea of guilty or nolo contendere, reserving in writing the right, on appeal from the judgment, to review of the adverse determination of any specified pretrial motion. A defendant who prevails on appeal shall be allowed to withdraw the plea.

(b) Nolo Contendere. A defendant may plead nolo contendere only with the consent of the court. Such a plea shall be accepted by the court only after due consideration of the views of the parties and the interest of the public in the effective administration of justice.

(c) Advice to Defendant. Before accepting a plea of guilty or nolo contendere, the court must address the defendant personally in open court and inform the defendant of, and determine that the defendant understands, the following:

(1) the nature of the charge to which the plea is offered, the mandatory minimum penalty provided by law, if any, and the maximum possible penalty provided by law, including the effect of any special

parole or supervised release term, the fact that the court is required to consider any applicable sentencing guidelines but many depart from those guidelines under some circumstances, and, when applicable, that the court may also order the defendant to make restitution to any victim of the offense; and

(2) if the defendant is not represented by an attorney, that the defendant has the right to be represented by an attorney at every stage of the proceeding and, if necessary, one will be appointed to represent the defendant; and

(3) that the defendant has the right to plead not guilty or to persist in that plea if it has already been made, the right to be tried by a jury and at that trial the right to the assistance of counsel, the right to confront and cross-examine adverse witnesses, and the right against compelled self-incrimination; and

(4) that if a plea of guilty or nolo contendere is accepted by the court there will not be a further trial of any kind, so that by pleading guilty or nolo contendere the defendant waives the right to a trial; and

(5) if the court intends to question the defendant under oath, on the record, and in the presence of counsel about the offense to which the defendant has pleaded, that the defendant's answers may later be used against the defendant in a prosecution for perjury or false statement; and

(6) the terms of any provision in a plea agreement waiving the right to appeal or to collaterally attack the sentence.

(d) Insuring That the Plea is Voluntary. The court shall not accept a plea of guilty or nolo contendere without first, by addressing the defendant personally in open court, determining that the plea is voluntary and not the result of force or threats or of promises apart from a plea agreement. The court shall also inquire as to whether the defendant's willingness to plead guilty or nolo contendere results from prior discussions between the attorney for the government and the defendant or the defendant's attorney.

(e) Plea Agreement Procedure.

(1) In General. The attorney for the government and the attorney for the defendant—or the defendant when acting pro se—may agree that, upon the defendant's entering a plea of guilty or nolo contendere to a charged offense, or to a lesser or related offense, the attorney for the government will:

(A) move to dismiss other charges; or

(B) recommend, or agree not to oppose the defendant's request for a particular sentence or sentencing range, or that a particular provision of the Sentencing Guidelines, or policy statement, or sentencing factor is or is not applicable to the case. Any such recommendation or request is not binding on the court; or

(C) agree that a specific sentence or sentencing range is the appropriate disposition of the case, or that a particular provision of the Sentencing Guidelines, or policy statement, or sentencing factor is or is not applicable to the case. Such a plea agreement is binding on the court once it is accepted by the court.

The court shall not participate in any discussions between the parties concerning any such plea agreement.

(2) Notice of Such Agreement. If a plea agreement has been reached by the parties, the court shall, on the record, require the disclosure of the agreement in open court or, on a showing of good cause, in camera, at the time the plea is offered. If the agreement is of the type specified in subdivision (e)(1)(A) or (C), the court may accept or reject the agreement, or may defer its decision as to the acceptance or rejection until there has been an opportunity to consider the presentence report. If the agreement is of the type specified in subdivision (e)(1)(B), the court shall advise the defendant that if the court does not accept the recommendation or request the defendant nevertheless has no right to withdraw the plea.

(3) Acceptance of a Plea Agreement. If the court accepts the plea agreement, the court shall inform the defendant that it will embody in the judgment and sentence the disposition provided for in the plea agreement.

(4) Rejection of a Plea Agreement. If the court rejects the plea agreement, the court shall, on the record, inform the parties of this fact, advise the defendant personally in open court or, on a showing of good cause, in camera, that the court is not bound by the plea agreement, afford the defendant the opportunity to then withdraw the plea, and advise the defendant that if the defendant persists in a guilty plea or plea of nolo contendere the disposition of the case may be less favorable to the defendant than that contemplated by the plea agreement.

(5) Time of Plea Agreement Procedure. Except for good cause shown, notification to the court of the existence of a plea agreement shall be given at the arraignment or at such other time, prior to trial, as may be fixed by the court.

(6) Inadmissibility of Pleas, Plea Discussions, and Related Statements. Except as otherwise provided in this paragraph, evidence of the following is not, in any civil or criminal proceeding, admissible against the defendant who made the plea or was a participant in the plea discussions:

(A) a plea of guilty which was later withdrawn;

(B) a plea of nolo contendere;

(C) any statement made in the course of any proceedings under this rule regarding either of the foregoing pleas; or

(D) any statement made in the course of plea discussions with an attorney for the government which do not result in a plea of guilty or which result in a plea of guilty later withdrawn.

However, such a statement is admissible (i) in any proceeding wherein another statement made in the course of the same plea or plea discussions has been introduced and the statement ought in fairness be considered contemporaneously with it, or (ii) in a criminal proceeding for perjury or false statement if the statement was made by the defendant under oath, on the record, and in the presence of counsel.

(f) Determining Accuracy of Plea. Notwithstanding the acceptance of a plea of guilty, the court should not enter a judgment upon such plea without making such inquiry as shall satisfy it that there is a factual basis for the plea.

(1) By Whom. The warrant shall be executed by a marshal or by some other officer authorized by law. The summons may be served by any person authorized to serve a summons in a civil action.

(g) Record of Proceedings. A verbatim record of the proceedings at which the defendant enters a plea shall be made and, if there is a plea of guilty or nolo contendere, the record shall include, without limitation, the court's advice to the defendant, the inquiry into the voluntariness of the plea including any plea agreement, and the inquiry into the accuracy of a guilty plea.

(h) Harmless Error. Any variance from the procedures required by this rule which does not affect substantial rights shall be disregarded.

Rule 12. Pleadings and Motions Before Trial; Defenses and Objections

(a) Pleadings and Motions. Pleadings in criminal proceedings shall be the indictment and the information, and the pleas of not guilty, guilty and nolo contendere. All other pleas, and demurrers and motions to quash are abolished, and defenses and objections raised before trial which heretofore could have been raised by one or more of them shall be raised only by motion to dismiss or to grant appropriate relief, as provided in these rules.

(b) Pretrial Motions. Any defense, objection, or request which is capable of determination without the trial of the general issue may be raised before trial by motion. Motions may be written or oral at the discretion of the judge. The following must be raised prior to trial:

(1) Defenses and objections based on defects in the institution of the prosecution; or

(2) Defenses and objections based on defects in the indictment or information (other than that it fails to show jurisdiction in the court or to charge an offense which objections shall be noticed by the court at any time during the pendency of the proceedings); or

(3) Motions to suppress evidence; or

(4) Requests for discovery under Rule 16; or

(5) Requests for a severance of charges or defendants under Rule 14.

(c) Motion Date. Unless otherwise provided by local rule, the court may, at the time of the arraignment or as soon thereafter as practicable, set a time for the making of pretrial motions or requests and, if required, a later date of hearing.

(d) Notice by the Government of the Intention to Use Evidence.

(1) At the Discretion of the Government. At the arraignment or as soon thereafter as is practicable, the government may give notice to the defendant of its intention to use specified evidence at trial in order to afford the defendant an opportunity to raise objections to such evidence prior to trial under subdivision (b)(3) of this rule.

(2) At the Request of the Defendant. At the arraignment or as soon thereafter as is practicable the defendant may, in order to afford an opportunity to move to suppress evidence under subdivision (b)(3) of this rule, request notice of the government's intention to use (in its evidence in chief at trial) any evidence which the defendant may be entitled to discover under Rule 16 subject to any relevant limitations prescribed in Rule 16.

(e) Ruling on Motion. A motion made before trial shall be determined before trial unless the court, for good cause, orders that it be deferred for determination at the trial of the general issue or until after verdict, but no such determination shall be deferred if a party's right to appeal is adversely affected. Where factual issues are involved in determining a motion, the court shall state its essential findings on the record.

(f) Effect of Failure To Raise Defenses or Objections. Failure by a party to raise defenses or objections or to make requests which must be made prior to trial, at the time set by the court pursuant to subdivision (c), or prior to any extension thereof made by the court, shall constitute waiver thereof, but the court for cause shown may grant relief from the waiver.

(g) Records. A verbatim record shall be made of all proceedings at the hearing, including such findings of fact and conclusions of law as are made orally.

(h) Effect of Determination. If the court grants a motion based on a defect in the institution of the prosecution or in the indictment or information, it may also order that the defendant be continued in custody or that bail be continued for a specified time pending the filing of a new indictment or information. Nothing in this rule shall be deemed to affect the provisions of any Act of Congress relating to periods of limitations.

(i) Production of Statements at Suppression Hearing. Rule 26.2 applies at a hearing on a motion to suppress evidence under subdivision (b)(3) of this rule. For purposes of this subdivision, a law enforcement officer is deemed a government witness.

Rule 12.1. Notice of Alibi

(a) Notice by Defendant. Upon written demand of the attorney for the government stating the time, date, and place at which the alleged offense was committed, the defendant shall serve within ten days, or at such different time as the court may direct, upon the attorney for the government a written notice of the defendant's intention to offer a defense of alibi. Such notice by the defendant shall state the specific place or places at which the defendant claims to have been at the time of the alleged offense and the names and addresses of the witnesses upon whom the defendant intends to rely to establish such alibi.

(b) Disclosure of Information and Witness. Within ten days thereafter, but in no event less than ten days before trial, unless the court otherwise directs, the attorney for the government shall serve upon the defendant or the defendant's attorney a written notice stating the names and addresses of the witnesses upon whom the government intends to rely to establish the defendant's presence at the scene of the alleged offense and any other witnesses to be relied on to rebut testimony of any of the defendant's alibi witnesses.

(c) Continuing Duty to Disclose. If prior to or during trial, a party learns of an additional witness whose identity, if known, should have been included in the information furnished under subdivision (a) or (b), the party shall promptly notify the other party or the other party's attorney of the existence and identity of such additional witness.

(d) Failure to Comply. Upon the failure of either party to comply with the requirements of this rule, the court may exclude the testimony of any undisclosed witness offered by such party as to the defendant's absence from or presence at, the scene of the alleged offense. This rule shall not limit the right of the defendant to testify.

(e) Exceptions. For good cause shown, the court may grant an exception to any of the requirements of subdivisions (a) through (d) of this rule.

(f) Inadmissibility of Withdrawn Alibi. Evidence of an intention to rely upon an alibi defense, later withdrawn, or of statements made in connection with such intention, is not, in any civil or criminal proceeding, admissible against the person who gave notice of the intention.

Rule 12.2. Notice of Insanity Defense or Expert Testimony of Defendant's Mental Condition

(a) Defense of Insanity. If a defendant intends to rely upon the defense of insanity at the time of the alleged offense, the defendant shall, within the time provided for the filing of pretrial motions or at such later time as the court may direct, notify the attorney for the government in writing of such intention and file a copy of such notice with the clerk. If there is a failure to comply with the requirements of this subdivision, insanity may not be raised as a defense. The court may for cause shown allow late filing of the notice or grant additional time to the parties to prepare for trial or make such other order as may be appropriate.

(b) Expert Testimony of Defendant's Mental Condition. If a defendant intends to introduce expert testimony relating to a mental disease or defect or any other mental condition of the defendant bearing upon the issue of guilt, the defendant shall, within the time provided for the filing of pretrial motions or at such later time as the court may direct, notify the attorney for the government in writing of such intention and file a copy of such notice with the clerk. The court may for cause shown allow late filing of the notice or grant additional time to the parties to prepare for trial or make such other order as may be appropriate.

(c) Mental Examination of Defendant. In an appropriate case the court may, upon motion of the attorney for the government, order the defendant to submit to an examination pursuant to 18 U.S.C. 4241 or 4242. No statement made by the defendant in the course of any examination provided for by this rule, whether the examination be with or without the consent of the defendant, no testimony by the expert based upon such statement, and no other fruits of the statement shall be admitted in evidence against the defendant in any criminal proceeding except on an issue respecting mental condition on which the defendant has introduced testimony.

(d) Failure To Comply. If there is a failure to give notice when required by subdivision (b) of this rule or to submit to an examination when ordered under subdivision (c) of this rule, the court may exclude the testimony of any expert witness offered by the defendant on the issue of the defendant's guilt.

(e) Inadmissibility of Withdrawn Intention. Evidence of an intention as to which notice was given under subdivision (a) or (b), later withdrawn, is not, in any civil or criminal proceeding, admissible against the person who gave notice of the intention.

Rule 12.3. Notice of Defense Based Upon Public Authority

(a) Notice by Defendant; Government Response; Disclosure of Witnesses.

(1) Defendant's Notice and Government's Response. A defendant intending to claim a defense of actual or believed exercise of public authority on behalf of a law enforcement or Federal intelligence agency at the time of the alleged offense shall, within the time provided for the filing of pretrial motions or at such later time as the court may direct, serve upon the attorney for the Government a written notice of such intention and file a copy of such notice with the clerk. Such notice shall identify the law enforcement or Federal intelligence agency and any member of such agency on behalf of which and the period of time in which the defendant claims the actual or believed exercise of public authority occurred. If the notice identifies a Federal intelligence agency, the copy filed with the clerk shall be under seal. Within ten days after receiving the defendant's notice, but in no event less than twenty days before the trial, the attorney for the Government shall serve upon the defendant or the defendant's attorney a written response which shall admit or deny that the defendant exercised the public authority identified in the defendant's notice.

(2) Disclosure of Witnesses. At the time that the Government serves its response to the notice or thereafter, but in no event less than twenty days before the trial, the attorney for the Government may serve upon the defendant or the defendant's attorney a written demand for the names and addresses of the witnesses, if any, upon whom the defendant intends to rely in establishing the defense identified in the notice. Within seven days after receiving the Government's demand, the defendant shall serve upon the attorney for the Government a written statement of the names and addresses of any such witnesses. Within seven days after receiving the defendant's written statement, the attorney for the Government shall serve upon the defendant or the defendant's attorney a written statement of the names and addresses of the witnesses, if any, upon whom the Government intends to rely in opposing the defense identified in the notice.

(3) Additional Time. If good cause is shown, the court may allow a party additional time to comply with any obligation imposed by this rule.

(b) Continuing Duty to Disclose. If, prior to or during trial, a party learns of any additional witness whose identity, if known, should have been included in the written statement furnished under subdivision (a)(2) of this rule, that party shall promptly notify in writing the other party or the other party's attorney of the name and address of any such witness.

(c) Failure to Comply. If a party fails to comply with the requirements of this rule, the court may exclude the testimony of any undisclosed witness offered in support of or in opposition to the defense, or enter such other order as it deems just under the circumstances. This rule shall not limit the right of the defendant to testify.

(d) Protective Procedures Unaffected. This rule shall be in addition to and shall not supersede the authority of the court to issue appropriate protective orders, or the authority of the court to order that any pleading be filed under seal.

(e) Inadmissibility of Withdrawn Defense Based Upon Public Authority. Evidence of an intention as to which notice was given under subdivision (a), later withdrawn, is not, in any civil or criminal proceeding, admissible against the person who gave notice of the intention.

Rule 13. Trial Together of Indictments or Informations

The court may order two or more indictments or informations or both to be tried together if the offenses, and the defendants if there is more than one, could have been joined in a single indictment or information. The procedure shall be the same as if the prosecution were under such single indictment or information.

Rule 14. Relief from Prejudicial Joinder

If it appears that a defendant or the government is prejudiced by a joinder of offenses or of defendants in an indictment or information or by such joinder for trial together, the court may order an election or separate trials of counts, grant a severance of defendants or provide whatever other relief justice requires. In ruling on a motion by a defendant for severance the court may order the attorney for the government to deliver to the court for inspection *in camera* any statements or confessions made by the defendants which the government intends to introduce in evidence at the trial.

Rule 15. Depositions

(a) When Taken. Whenever due to exceptional circumstances of the case it is in the interest of justice that the testimony of a prospective witness of a party be taken and preserved for use at trial, the court may upon motion of such party and notice to the parties order that testimony of such witness be taken by deposition and that any designated book, paper, document, record, recording, or other material not privileged, be produced at the same time and place. If a witness is detained pursuant to section 3144 of title 18, United States Code, the court on written motion of the witness and upon notice to the parties may direct that the witness' deposition be taken. After the deposition has been subscribed the court may discharge the witness.

(b) Notice of Taking. The party at whose instance a deposition is to be taken shall give to every party reasonable written notice of the time and place for taking the deposition. The notice shall state the name and address of each person to be examined. On motion of a party upon whom the notice is served, the court for cause shown may extend or shorten the time or change the place for taking the deposition. The officer having custody of a defendant shall be notified of the time and place set for the examination and shall, unless the defendant waives in writing the right to be present, produce the defendant at the examination and keep the defendant in the presence of the witness during the examination, unless, after being warned by the court that disruptive conduct will cause the defendant's removal from the place of the taking of the deposition, the defendant persists in conduct which is such as to justify exclusion from that place. A defendant not in custody shall have the right to be present at the examination upon request subject to such terms as may be fixed by the court, but a failure, absent good cause shown, to appear after notice and tender of expenses in accordance with subdivision (c) of this rule shall constitute a waiver of that right and of any objection to the taking and use of the deposition based upon that right.

(c) Payment of Expenses. Whenever a deposition is taken at the instance of the government, or whenever a deposition is taken at the instance of a defendant who is unable to bear the expenses of the taking of the deposition, the court may direct that the expense of travel and subsistence of the defendant and the defendant's attorney for attendance at the examination and the cost of the transcript of the deposition shall be paid by the government.

(d) How Taken. Subject to such additional conditions as the court shall provide, a deposition shall be taken and filed in the manner provided in civil actions except as otherwise provided in these rules, provided that (1) in no event shall a deposition be taken of a party defendant without that defendant's consent, and (2) the scope and manner of examination and cross-examination shall be such as would be allowed in the trial itself. The government shall make available to the defendant or the defendant's counsel for examination and use at the taking of the deposition any statement of the witness being deposed which is in the possession of the government and to which the defendant would be entitled at the trial.

(e) Use. At the trial or upon any hearing, a part or all of a deposition, so far as otherwise admissible under the rules of evidence, may be used as substantive evidence if the witness is unavailable, as unavailability is defined in Rule 804(a) of the Federal Rules of Evidence, or the witness gives testimony at the trial or hearing inconsistent with that witness' deposition. Any deposition may also be used by any party for the purpose of contradicting or impeaching the testimony of the deponent as a witness. If only a part of a deposition is offered in evidence by a party, an adverse party may require the offering of all of it which is relevant to the part offered and any party may offer other parts.

(f) Objections to Deposition Testimony. Objections to deposition testimony or evidence or parts thereof and the grounds for the objection shall be stated at the time of the taking of the deposition.

(g) Deposition by Agreement Not Precluded. Nothing in this rule shall preclude the taking of a deposition, orally or upon written questions, or the use of a deposition, by agreement of the parties with the consent of the court.

Rule 16. Discovery and Inspection

(a) Governmental Disclosure of Evidence.

(1) Information Subject to Disclosure.

(A) Statement of Defendant. Upon request of a defendant the government must disclose to the defendant and make available for inspection, copying, or photographing: any relevant written or recorded statements made by the defendant, or copies thereof, within the possession, custody, or control of the government, the existence of which is known, or by the exercise of due diligence may become known, to the attorney for the government; that portion of any written record containing the substance of any relevant oral statement made by the defendant whether before or after arrest in response to interrogation by any person then known to the defendant to be a government agent; and recorded testimony of the defendant before a grand jury which relates to the offense charged. The government must also disclose to the defendant the substance of any other relevant oral statement made by the defendant whether before or after arrest in response to interrogation by any person then known by the defendant to be a government agent if the government intends to use that statement at trial. Upon request of a defendant which is an organization such as a corporation, partnership, association or labor union, the government must disclose to the defendant any of the foregoing statements made by a person who the government contends (1) was, at the time of making the statement, so situated as a director, officer, employee, or agent as to have been able legally to bind the defendant in respect to the subject of the statement, or (2) was, at the time of the offense, personally involved in the alleged conduct constituting the offense and so situated as a director, officer, employee, or agent as to have been able legally to bind the defendant in respect to that alleged conduct in which the person was involved.

(B) Defendant's Prior Record. Upon request of the defendant, the government shall furnish to the defendant such copy of the defendant's prior criminal record, if any, as is within the possession, custody, or control of the government, the existence of which is known, or by the exercise of due diligence may become known, to the attorney for the government.

(C) Documents and Tangible Objects. Upon request of the defendant the government shall permit the defendant to inspect and copy or photograph books, papers, documents, photographs, tangible objects, buildings or places, or copies or portions thereof, which are within the possession, custody or control of the government, and which are material to the preparation of the defendant's defense or are intended for use by the government as evidence in chief at the trial, or were obtained from or belong to the defendant.

(D) Reports of Examinations and Tests. Upon request of a defendant the government shall permit the defendant to inspect and copy or photograph any results or reports of physical or mental examinations, and of scientific tests or experiments, or copies thereof, which are within the possession, custody, or control of the government, the existence of which is known, or by the exercise of due diligence may become known, to the attorney for the government, and which are material to the preparation of the defense or are intended for use by the government as evidence in chief at the trial.

(E) Expert Witnesses. At the defendant's request, the government shall disclose to the defendant a written summary of testimony that the government intends to use under Rules 702, 703, or 705 of the Federal Rules of Evidence during its case-in-chief at trial. If the government requests discovery under subdivision (b)(1)(C)(ii) of this rule and the defendant complies, the government shall, at the defendant's request, disclose to the defendant a written summary of testimony the government intends to use under Rules 702, 703, or 705 as evidence at trial on the issue of the defendant's mental condition. The summary provided under this subdivision shall describe the witnesses' opinions, the bases and the reasons for those opinions, and the witnesses' qualifications.

(2) Information Not Subject to Disclosure. Except as provided in paragraphs (A), (B), (D), and (E) of subdivision (a)(1), this rule does not authorize the discovery or inspection of reports, memoranda, or other internal government documents made by the attorney for the government or any other government agent investigating or prosecuting the case. Nor does the rule authorize the discovery or inspection of statements made by government witnesses or prospective government witnesses except as provided in 18 U.S.C. § 3500.

(3) Grand Jury Transcripts. Except as provided in Rules 6, 12(i) and 26.2, and subdivision (a)(1)(A) of this rule, these rules do not relate to discovery or inspection of recorded proceedings of a grand jury.

[(4) Failure to Call Witness.] (Deleted Dec. 12, 1975)

(b) The Defendant's Disclosure of Evidence.

(1) Information Subject to Disclosure.

(A) Documents and Tangible Objects. If the defendant requests disclosure under subdivision (a)(1)(C) or (D) of this rule, upon compliance with such request by the government, the defendant, on request of the government, shall permit the government to inspect and copy or photograph books, papers, documents, photographs, tangible objects, or copies or portions thereof, which are within the possession, custody, or control of the defendant and which the defendant intends to introduce as evidence in chief at the trial.

(B) Reports of Examinations and Tests. If the defendant requests disclosure under subdivision (a)(1)(C) or (D) of this rule, upon compliance with such request by the government, the defendant, on request of the government, shall permit the government to inspect and copy or photograph any results or reports of physical or mental examinations and of scientific tests or experiments made in connection with the particular case, or copies thereof, within the possession or control of the defendant, which the defendant intends to introduce as evidence in chief at the trial or which were prepared by a witness whom the defendant intends to call at the trial when the results or reports relate to that witness' testimony.

(C) Expert Witnesses. Under the following circumstances, the defendant shall, at the government's request, disclose to the government a written summary of testimony that the defendant intends to use under Rules 702, 703, or 705 of the Federal Rules of Evidence as evidence at trial: (i) if the defendant requests disclosure under subdivision (a)(1)(E) of this rule and the government complies, or (ii) if the defendant has given notice under Rule 12.2(b) of an intent to present expert testimony on the defendant's mental condition. This summary shall describe the witnesses' opinions, the bases and reasons for those opinions, and the witnesses' qualifications.

(2) Information Not Subject To Disclosure. Except as to scientific or medical reports, this subdivision does not authorize the discovery or inspection of reports, memoranda, or other internal defense documents made by the defendant, or the defendant's attorneys or agents in connection with the investigation or defense of the case, or of statements made by the defendant, or by government or defense witnesses, or by prospective government or defense witnesses, to the defendant, the defendant's agents or attorneys.

[(3) Failure to Call Witness.] (Deleted Dec. 12, 1975)

(c) Continuing Duty to Disclose. If, prior to or during trial, a party discovers additional evidence or material previously requested or ordered, which is subject to discovery or inspection under this rule, such party shall promptly notify the other party or that other party's attorney or the court of the existence of the additional evidence or material.

(d) Regulation of Discovery.

(1) Protective and Modifying Orders. Upon a sufficient showing the court may at any time order that the discovery or inspection be denied, restricted, or deferred, or make such other order as is appropriate. Upon motion by a party, the court may permit the party to make such showing, in whole or in part, in the form of a written statement to be inspected by the judge alone. If the court enters an order granting relief following such an ex parte showing, the entire text of the party's statement shall be sealed and preserved in the records of the court to be made available to the appellate court in the event of an appeal.

(2) Failure To Comply With a Request. If at any time during the course of the proceedings it is brought to the attention of the court that a party has failed to comply with this rule, the court may order such party to permit the discovery or inspection, grant a continuance, or prohibit the party from introducing evidence not disclosed, or it may enter such other order as it deems just under the circumstances. The court may specify the time, place and manner of making the discovery and inspection and may prescribe such terms and conditions as are just.

(e) Alibi Witnesses. Discovery of alibi witnesses is governed by Rule 12.1.

Rule 17. Subpoena

(a) For Attendance of Witnesses; Form; Issuance. A subpoena shall be issued by the clerk under the seal of the court. It shall state the name of the court and the title, if any, of the proceeding, and shall command each person to whom it is directed to attend and give testimony at the time and place specified therein. The clerk shall issue a subpoena, signed and sealed but otherwise in blank to a party requesting it, who shall fill in the blanks before it is served. A subpoena shall be issued by a United States magistrate judge in a proceeding before that magistrate judge, but it need not be under the seal of the court.

(b) Defendants Unable to Pay. The court shall order at any time that a subpoena be issued for service on a named witness upon an *ex parte* application of a defendant upon a satisfactory showing that the defendant is financially unable to pay the fees of the witness and that the presence of the witness is necessary to an adequate defense. If the court orders the subpoena to be issued the costs incurred by the process and the fees of the witness so subpoenaed shall be paid in the same manner in which similar costs and fees are paid in case of a witness subpoenaed in behalf of the government.

(c) For Production of Documentary Evidence and of Objects. A subpoena may also command the person to whom it is directed to produce the books, papers, documents or other objects designated therein. The court on motion made promptly may quash or modify the subpoena if compliance would be unreasonable or oppressive. The court may direct that books, papers, documents or objects designated in the subpoena be produced before the court at a time prior to the trial or prior to the time when they are to be offered in evidence and may upon their production permit the books, papers, documents or objects or portions thereof to be inspected by the parties and their attorneys.

(d) Service. A subpoena may be served by the marshal, by a deputy marshal or by any other person who is not a party and who is not less than 18 years of age. Service of a subpoena shall be made by delivering a copy thereof to the person named and by tendering to that person the fee for 1 day's attendance and the mileage allowed by law. Fees and mileage need not be tendered to the witness upon service of a subpoena issued in behalf of the United States or an officer or agency thereof.

(e) Place of Service.

(1) In United States. A subpoena requiring the attendance of a witness at a hearing or trial may be served at any place within the United States.

(2) Abroad. A subpoena directed to a witness in a foreign country shall issue under the circumstances and in the manner and be served as provided in Title 28, U.S.C., § 1783.

(f) For Taking Deposition; Place of Examination.

(1) Issuance. An order to take a deposition authorizes the issuance by the clerk of the court for the district in which the deposition is to be taken of subpoenas for the persons named or described therein.

(2) Place. The witness whose deposition is to be taken may be required by subpoena to attend at any place designated by the trial court, taking into account the convenience of the witness and the parties.

(g) Contempt. Failure by any person without adequate excuse to obey a subpoena served upon that person may be deemed a contempt of the court from which the subpoena issued or of the court for the district in which it issued if it was issued by a United States magistrate judge.

(h) Information Not Subject to Subpoena. Statements made by witnesses or prospective witnesses may not be subpoenaed from the government or the defendant under this rule, but shall be subject to production only in accordance with the provisions of Rule 26.2.

Rule 17.1. Pretrial Conference

At any time after the filing of the indictment or information the court upon motion of any party or upon its own motion may order one or more conferences to consider such matters as will promote a fair and expeditious trial. At the conclusion of a conference the court shall prepare and file a memorandum of the matters agreed upon. No admissions made by the defendant or the defendant's attorney at the conference shall be used against the defendant unless the admissions are reduced to writing and signed by the defendant and the defendant's attorney. This rule shall not be invoked in the case of a defendant who is not represented by counsel.

V. VENUE

Rule 18. Place of Prosecution and Trial

Except as otherwise permitted by statute or by these rules, the prosecution shall be had in a district in which the offense was committed. The court shall fix the place of trial within the district with due regard to the convenience of the defendant and the witnesses and the prompt administration of justice.

Rule 19. Rescinded Feb. 28, 1966, eff. July 1, 1966

Rule 20. Transfer From the District for Plea and Sentence

(a) Indictment or Information Pending. A defendant arrested, held, or present in a district other than that in which an indictment or information is pending against that defendant may state in writing a wish to plead guilty or nolo contendere, to waive trial in the district in which the indictment or information is pending, and to consent to disposition of the case in the district in which that defendant was arrested, held, or present, subject to the approval of the United States attorney for each district. Upon receipt of the defendant's statement and of the written approval of the United States attorneys, the clerk of the court in which the indictment or information is pending shall transmit the papers in the proceeding or certified copies thereof to the clerk of the court for the district in which the defendant is arrested, held, or present, and the prosecution shall continue in that district.

(b) Indictment or Information Not Pending. A defendant arrested, held, or present, in a district other than the district in which a complaint is pending against that defendant may state in writing a wish to plead guilty or nolo contendere, to waive venue and trial in the district in which the warrant was issued, and to consent to disposition of the case in the district in which that defendant was arrested, held, or present, subject to the approval of the United States attorney for each district. Upon filing the written waiver of venue in the district in which the defendant is present, the prosecution may proceed as if venue were in such district.

(c) Effect of Not Guilty Plea. If after the proceeding has been transferred pursuant to subdivision (a) or (b) of this rule the defendant pleads not guilty, the clerk shall return the papers to the court in which the prosecution was commenced, and the proceeding shall be restored to the docket of that court. The defendant's statement that the defendant wishes to plead guilty or nolo contendere shall not be used against that defendant.

(d) Juveniles. A juvenile (as defined in 18 U.S.C. § 5031) who is arrested, held, or present in a district other than that in which the juvenile is alleged to have committed an act in violation of a law of the United States not punishable by death or life imprisonment may, after having been advised by counsel and with the approval of the court and the United States attorney for each district, consent to be proceeded against as a juvenile delinquent in the district in which the juvenile is arrested, held, or present. The consent shall be given in writing before the court but only after the court has apprised the juvenile of the juvenile's rights, including the right to be returned to the district in which the juvenile is alleged to have committed the act, and of the consequences of such consent.

Rule 21. Transfer From the District for Trial

(a) For Prejudice in the District. The court upon motion of the defendant shall transfer the proceeding as to that defendant to another district whether or not such district is specified in the defendant's motion if the court is satisfied that there exists in the district where the prosecution is pending so great a prejudice against the defendant that the defendant cannot obtain a fair and impartial trial at any place fixed by law for holding court in that district.

(b) Transfer in Other Cases. For the convenience of parties and witnesses, and in the interest of justice, the court upon motion of the defendant may transfer the proceeding as to that defendant or any one or more of the counts thereof to another district.

(c) Proceedings on Transfer. When a transfer is ordered the clerk shall transmit to the clerk of the court to which the proceeding is transferred all papers in the proceeding or duplicates thereof and any bail taken, and the prosecution shall continue in that district.

Rule 22. Time of Motion to Transfer

A motion to transfer under these rules may be made at or before arraignment or at such other time as the court or these rules may prescribe.

VI. TRIAL

Rule 23. Trial by Jury or by the Court

(a) Trial by Jury. Cases required to be tried by jury shall be so tried unless the defendant waives a jury trial in writing with the approval of the court and the consent of the government.

(b) Jury of Less Than Twelve. Juries shall be of 12 but at any time before verdict the parties may stipulate in writing with the approval of the court that the jury shall consist of any number less than 12 or that a valid verdict may be returned by a jury of less than 12 should the court find it necessary to excuse one or more jurors for any just cause after trial commences. Even absent such stipulation, if the court finds it necessary to excuse a juror for just cause after the jury has retired to consider its verdict, in the discretion of the court a valid verdict may be returned by the remaining 11 jurors.

(c) Trial Without a Jury. In a case tried without a jury the court shall make a general finding and shall in addition, on request made before the general finding, find the facts specially. Such findings may be oral. If an opinion or memorandum of decision is filed, it will be sufficient if the findings of fact appear therein.

Rule 24. Trial Jurors

(a) Examination. The court may permit the defendant or the defendant's attorney and the attorney for the government to conduct the examination of prospective jurors or may itself conduct the examination. In the latter event the court shall permit the defendant or the defendant's attorney and the attorney for the government to supplement the examination by such further inquiry as it deems proper or shall itself submit to the prospective jurors such additional questions by the parties or their attorneys as it deems proper.

(b) Peremptory Challenges. If the offense charged is punishable by death, each side is entitled to 20 peremptory challenges. If the offense charged is punishable by imprisonment for more than one year, the government is entitled to 6 peremptory challenges and the defendant or defendants jointly to 10 peremptory challenges. If the offense charged is punishable by imprisonment for not more than one year or by fine or both, each side is entitled to 3 peremptory challenges. If there is more than one defendant, the court may allow the defendants additional peremptory challenges and permit them to be exercised separately or jointly.

(c) Alternate Jurors.

(1) In General. The court may empanel no more than 6 jurors, in addition to the regular jury, to sit as alternate jurors. An alternate juror, in the order called, shall replace a juror who becomes or is found to be unable or disqualified to perform juror duties. Alternate jurors shall (i) be drawn in the same manner, (ii) have the same qualifications, (iii) be subject to the same examination and challenges, and (iv) take the same oath as regular jurors. An alternate juror has the same functions, powers, facilities and privileges as a regular juror.

(2) Peremptory Challenges. In addition to challenges otherwise provided by law, each side is entitled to 1 additional peremptory challenge if 1 or 2 alternate jurors are empaneled, 2 additional peremptory challenges if 3 or 4 alternate jurors are empaneled, and 3 additional peremptory challenges if 5 or 6 alternate jurors are empaneled. The additional peremptory challenges may be used to remove an alternate juror only, and the other peremptory challenges allowed by these rules may not be used to remove an alternate juror.

(3) Retention of Alternate Jurors. When the jury retires to consider the verdict, the court in its discretion may retain the alternate jurors during deliberations. If the court decides to retain the alternate jurors, it shall ensure that they do not discuss the case with any other person unless and until they replace a regular juror during deliberations. If an alternate replaces a juror after deliberations have begun, the court shall instruct the jury to begin its deliberations anew.

Rule 25. Judge; Disability

(a) During Trial. If by reason of death, sickness or other disability the judge before whom a jury trial has commenced is unable to proceed with the trial, any other judge regularly sitting in or assigned to the court, upon certifying familiarity with the record of the trial, may proceed with and finish the trial.

(b) After Verdict or Finding of Guilt. If by reason of absence, death, sickness or other disability the judge before whom the defendant has been tried is unable to perform the duties to be performed by the court after a verdict or finding of guilt, any other judge regularly sitting in or assigned to the court may perform those duties; but if that judge is satisfied that a judge who did not preside at the trial cannot perform those duties or that it is appropriate for any other reason, that judge may grant a new trial.

Rule 26. Taking of Testimony

In all trials the testimony of witnesses shall be taken orally in open court, unless otherwise provided by an Act of Congress or by these rules, the Federal Rules of Evidence, or other rules adopted by the Supreme Court.

Rule 26.1. Determination of Foreign Law

A party who intends to raise an issue concerning the law of a foreign country shall give reasonable written notice. The court, in determining foreign law, may consider any relevant material or source, including testimony, whether or not submitted by a party or admissible under the Federal Rules of Evidence. The court's determination shall be treated as a ruling on a question of law.

Rule 26.2. Production of Witness Statements

(a) Motion for Production. After a witness other than the defendant has testified on direct examination, the court, on motion of a party who did not call the witness, shall order the attorney for the government or the defendant and the defendant's attorney, as the case may be, to produce, for the examination and use of the moving party, any statement of the witness that is in their possession and that relates to the subject matter concerning which the witness has testified.

(b) Production of Entire Statement. If the entire contents of the statement relate to the subject matter concerning which the witness has testified, the court shall order that the statement be delivered to the moving party.

(c) Production of Excised Statement. If the other party claims that the statement contains privileged information or matter that does not relate to the subject matter concerning which the witness has testified, the court shall order that it be delivered to the court in camera. Upon inspection, the court shall excise the portions of the statement that are privileged or that do not relate to the subject matter concerning which the witness has testified, and shall order that the statement, with such material excised, be delivered to the moving party. Any portion of the statement that is withheld from the defendant over the defendant's objection must be preserved by the attorney for the government, and, if the defendant appeals a conviction, shall be made available to the appellate court for the purpose of determining the correctness of the decision to excise the portion of the statement.

(d) Recess for Examination of Statement. Upon delivery of the statement to the moving party, the court, upon application of that party, may recess the proceedings so that counsel may examine the statement and prepare to use it in the proceedings.

(e) Sanction for Failure to Produce Statement. If the other party elects not to comply with an order to deliver a statement to the moving party, the court shall order that the testimony of the witness be stricken from the record and that the trial proceed, or, if it is the attorney for the government who elects not to comply, shall declare a mistrial if required by the interest of justice.

(f) Definition. As used in this rule, a "statement" of a witness means:

(1) a written statement made by the witness that is signed or otherwise adopted or approved by the witness;

(2) a substantially verbatim recital of an oral statement made by the witness that is recorded contemporaneously with the making of the oral statement and that is contained in a stenographic, mechanical, electrical, or other recording or a transcription thereof; or

(3) a statement, however taken or recorded, or a transcription thereof, made by the witness to a grand jury.

(g) Scope of Rule. This rule applies at a suppression hearing conducted under Rule 12, at trial under this rule, and to the extent specified:

(1) in Rule 32(c)(2) at sentencing;

(2) in Rule 32.1(c) at a hearing to revoke or modify probation or supervised release;

(3) in Rule 46(i) at a detention hearing;

(4) in Rule 8 of the Rules Governing Proceedings under 28 U.S.C. § 2255; and

(5) in Rule 5.1 at a preliminary examination.

Rule 26.3. Mistrial

Before ordering a mistrial, the court shall provide an opportunity for the government and for each defendant to comment on the propriety of the order, including whether each party consents or objects to a mistrial, and to suggest any alternatives.

Rule 27. Proof of Official Record

An official record or an entry therein or the lack of such a record or entry may be proved in the same manner as in civil actions.

Rule 28. Interpreters

The court may appoint an interpreter of its own selection and may fix the reasonable compensation of such interpreter. Such compensation shall be paid out of funds provided by law or by the government, as the court may direct.

Rule 29. Motion for Judgment of Acquittal

(a) Motion Before Submission to Jury. Motions for directed verdict are abolished and motions for judgment of acquittal shall be used in their place. The court on motion of a defendant or of its own motion shall order the entry of judgment of acquittal of one or more offenses charged in the indictment or information after the evidence on either side is closed if the evidence is insufficient to sustain a conviction of such offense or offenses. If a defendant's motion for judgment of acquittal at the close of the evidence offered by the government is not granted, the defendant may offer evidence without having reserved the right.

(b) Reservation of Decision on Motion. The court may reserve decision on a motion for judgment of acquittal, proceed with the trial (where the motion is made before the close of all the evidence), submit the case to the jury and decide the motion either before the jury returns a verdict or after it returns a verdict of guilty or is discharged without having returned a verdict. If the court reserves decision, it must decide the motion on the basis of the evidence at the time the ruling was reserved.

(c) Motion After Discharge of Jury. If the jury returns a verdict of guilty or is discharged without having returned a verdict, a motion for judgment of acquittal may be made or renewed within 7 days after the jury is discharged or within such further time as the court may fix during the 7–day period. If a verdict of guilty is returned the court may on such motion set aside the verdict and enter judgment of acquittal. If no verdict is returned the court may enter judgment of acquittal. It shall not be necessary to the making of such a motion that a similar motion has been made prior to the submission of the case to the jury.

(d) Same: Conditional Ruling on Grant of Motion. If a motion for judgment of acquittal after verdict of guilty under this Rule is granted, the court shall also determine whether any motion for a new trial should be granted if the judgment of acquittal is thereafter vacated or reversed, specifying the grounds for such determination. If the motion for a new trial is granted conditionally, the order thereon does not affect the finality of the judgment. If the motion for a new trial has been granted conditionally and the judgment is reversed on appeal, the new trial shall proceed unless the appellate court has otherwise ordered. If such motion has been denied conditionally, the appellee on appeal may assert error in that denial, and if the judgment is reversed on appeal, subsequent proceedings shall be in accordance with the order of the appellate court.

Rule 29.1. Closing Argument

After the closing of evidence the prosecution shall open the argument. The defense shall be permitted to reply. The prosecution shall then be permitted to reply in rebuttal.

Rule 30. Instructions

At the close of the evidence or at such earlier time during the trial as the court reasonably directs, any party may file written requests that the court instruct the jury on the law as set forth in the requests. At the same time copies of such requests shall be furnished to all parties. The court shall inform counsel of its proposed action upon the requests prior to their arguments to the jury. The court may instruct the jury before or after the arguments are completed or at both times. No party may assign as error any portion of the charge or omission therefrom unless that party objects thereto before the jury retires to consider its verdict, stating distinctly the matter to which that party objects and the grounds of the objection. Opportunity shall be given to make the objection out of the hearing of the jury and, on request of any party, out of the presence of the jury.

Rule 31. Verdict

(a) Return. The verdict shall be unanimous. It shall be returned by the jury to the judge in open court.

(b) Several Defendants. If there are two or more defendants, the jury at any time during its deliberations may return a verdict or verdicts with respect to a defendant or defendants as to whom it has agreed; if the jury cannot agree with respect to all, the defendant or defendants as to whom it does not agree may be tried again.

(c) Conviction of Less Offense. The defendant may be found guilty of an offense necessarily included in the offense charged or of an attempt to commit either the offense charged or an offense necessarily included therein if the attempt is an offense.

(d) Poll of Jury. After a verdict is returned but before the jury is discharged, the court shall, on a party's request, or may on its own motion, poll the jurors individually. If the poll reveals a lack of unanimity, the court may direct the jury to deliberate further or may declare a mistrial and discharge the jury.

(e) Criminal Forfeiture. If the indictment or the information alleges that an interest or property is subject to criminal forfeiture, a special verdict shall be returned as to the extent of the interest or property subject to forfeiture, if any.

VII. JUDGMENT

Rule 32. Sentence and Judgment

(a) In General; Time for Sentencing. When a presentence investigation and report are made under subdivision (b)(1), sentence should be imposed without unnecessary delay following completion of the process prescribed by subdivision (b)(6). The time limits prescribed in subdivision (b)(6) may be either shortened or lengthened for good cause.

(b) Presentence Investigation and Report.

(1) When Made. The probation officer must make a presentence investigation and submit a report to the court before the sentence is imposed, unless:

(A) the court finds that the information in the record enables it to exercise its sentencing authority meaningfully under 18 U.S.C. § 3553; and

(B) the court explains this finding on the record.

Notwithstanding the preceding sentence, a presentence investigation and report, or other report containing information sufficient for the court to enter an order of restitution, as the court may direct, shall be required in any case in which restitution is required to be ordered.

(2) Presence of Counsel. On request, the defendant's counsel is entitled to notice and a reasonable opportunity to attend any interview of the defendant by a probation officer in the course of a presentence investigation.

(3) Nondisclosure. The report must not be submitted to the court or its contents disclosed to anyone unless the defendant has consented in writing, has pleaded guilty or nolo contendere, or has been found guilty.

(4) Contents of the Presentence Report. The presentence report must contain—

(A) information about the defendant's history and characteristics, including any prior criminal record, financial condition, and any circumstances that, because they affect the defendant's behavior, may be helpful in imposing sentence or in correctional treatment;

(B) the classification of the offense and of the defendant under the categories established by the Sentencing Commission under 28 U.S.C. § 994(a), as the probation officer believes to be applicable to the defendant's case; the kinds of sentence and the sentencing range suggested for such a category of offense committed by such a category of defendant as set forth in the guidelines issued by the Sentencing Commission under 28 U.S.C. § 994(a)(1); and the probation officer's explanation of any factors that may suggest a different sentence—within or without the applicable guideline—that would be more appropriate, given all the circumstances;

(C) a reference to any pertinent policy statement issued by the Sentencing Commission under 28 U.S.C. § 994(a)(2);

(D) verified information, stated in a nonargumentative style, containing an assessment of the financial, social, psychological, and medical impact on any individual against whom the offense has been committed;

(E) in appropriate cases, information about the nature and extent of nonprison programs and resources available for the defendant;

(F) in appropriate cases, information sufficient for the court to enter an order of restitution;

(G) any report and recommendation resulting from a study ordered by the court under 18 U.S.C. § 3552(b); and

(H) any other information required by the court.

(5) Exclusions. The presentence report must exclude:

(A) any diagnostic opinions that, if disclosed, might seriously disrupt a program of rehabilitation;

(B) sources of information obtained upon a promise of confidentiality; or

(C) any other information that, if disclosed, might result in harm, physical or otherwise, to the defendant or other persons.

(6) Disclosure and Objections.

(A) Not less than 35 days before the sentencing hearing—unless the defendant waives this minimum period—the probation officer must furnish the presentence report to the defendant, the defendant's counsel, and the attorney for the Government. The court may, by local rule or in individual cases, direct that the probation officer not disclose the probation officer's recommendation, if any, on the sentence.

(B) Within 14 days after receiving the presentence report, the parties shall communicate in writing to the probation officer, and to each other, any objections to any material information, sentencing classifications, sentencing guideline ranges, and policy statements contained in or omitted from the presentence report. After receiving objections, the probation officer may meet with the defendant, the defendant's counsel, and the attorney for the Government to discuss those objections. The probation officer may also conduct a further investigation and revise the presentence report as appropriate.

(C) Not later than 7 days before the sentencing hearing, the probation officer must submit the presentence report to the court, together with an addendum setting forth any unresolved objections, the grounds for those objections, and the probation officer's comments on the objections. At the same time, the probation officer must furnish the revisions of the presentence report and the addendum to the defendant, the defendant's counsel, and the attorney for the Government.

(D) Except for any unresolved objection under subdivision (b)(6)(B), the court may, at the hearing, accept the presentence report as its findings of fact. For good cause shown, the court may allow a new objection to be raised at any time before imposing sentence.

(c) Sentence.

(1) Sentencing Hearing. At the sentencing hearing, the court must afford counsel for the defendant and for the Government an opportunity to comment on the probation officer's determinations and on other matters relating to the appropriate sentence, and must rule on any unresolved objections to the presentence report. The court may, in its discretion, permit the parties to introduce testimony or other evidence on the objections. For each matter controverted, the court must make either a finding on the allegation or a determination that no finding is necessary because the controverted matter will not be taken into account in, or will not affect, sentencing. A written record of these findings and determinations must be appended to any copy of the presentence report made available to the Bureau of Prisons.

(2) Production of Statements at Sentencing Hearing. Rule 26.2(a)–(d) and (f) applies at a sentencing hearing under this rule. If a party elects not to comply with an order under Rule 26.2(a) to deliver a statement to the movant, the court may not consider the affidavit or testimony of the witness whose statement is withheld.

(3) Imposition of Sentence. Before imposing sentence, the court must:

(A) verify that the defendant and defendant's counsel have read and discussed the presentence report made available under subdivision (b)(6)(A). If the court has received information excluded from the presentence report under subdivision (b)(5) the court—in lieu of making that information available—must summarize it in writing, if the information will be relied on in determining sentence. The court must also give the defendant and the defendant's counsel a reasonable opportunity to comment on that information;

(B) afford defendant's counsel an opportunity to speak on behalf of the defendant;

(C) address the defendant personally and determine whether the defendant wishes to make a statement and to present any information in mitigation of the sentence;

(D) afford the attorney for the Government an opportunity equivalent to that of the defendant's counsel to speak to the court; and

(E) if sentence is to be imposed for a crime of violence or sexual abuse, address the victim personally if the victim is present at the sentencing hearing and determine if the victim wishes to make a statement or present any information in relation to the sentence.

(4) In Camera Proceedings. The court's summary of information under subdivision (c)(3)(A) may be in camera. Upon joint motion by the defendant and by the attorney for the Government, the court may hear in camera the statements—made under subdivision (c)(3)(B), (C), (D), and (E)—by the defendant, the defendant's counsel, the victim, or the attorney for the Government.

(5) Notification of Right to Appeal. After imposing sentence in a case which has gone to trial on a plea of not guilty, the court must advise the defendant of the right to appeal. After imposing sentence in any case, the court must advise the defendant of any right to appeal the sentence, and of the right of a person who is unable to pay the cost of an appeal to apply for leave to appeal in forma pauperis. If the defendant so requests, the clerk of the court must immediately prepare and file a notice of appeal on behalf of the defendant.

(d) Judgment.

(1) In General. A judgment of conviction must set forth the plea, the verdict or findings, the adjudication, and the sentence. If the defendant is found not guilty or for any other reason is entitled to be discharged, judgment must be entered accordingly. The judgment must be signed by the judge and entered by the clerk.

(2) Criminal Forfeiture. If a verdict contains a finding that property is subject to a criminal forfeiture, or if a defendant enters a guilty plea subjecting property to such forfeiture, the court may enter a preliminary order of forfeiture after providing notice to the defendant and a reasonable opportunity to be heard on the timing and form of the order. The order of forfeiture shall authorize the Attorney General to seize the property subject to forfeiture, to conduct any discovery that the court considers proper to help identify, locate, or dispose of the property, and to begin proceedings consistent with any statutory requirements pertaining to ancillary hearings and the rights of third parties. At sentencing, a final order of forfeiture shall be made part of the sentence and included in the judgment. The court may include in the final order such conditions as may be reasonably necessary to preserve the value of the property pending any appeal.

(e) Plea Withdrawal. If a motion to withdraw a plea of guilty or nolo contendere is made before sentence is imposed, the court may permit the plea to be withdrawn if the defendant shows any fair and just reason. At any later time, a plea may be set aside only on direct appeal or by motion under 28 U.S.C. § 2255.

(f) Definitions. For purposes of this rule—

(1) "victim" means any individual against whom an offense has been committed for which a sentence is to be imposed, but the right of allocution under subdivision (c)(3)(E) may be exercised instead by—

(A) a parent or legal guardian if the victim is below the age of eighteen years or incompetent; or

(B) one or more family members or relatives designated by the court if the victim is deceased or incapacitated;

if such person or persons are present at the sentencing hearing, regardless of whether the victim is present; and

(2) "crime of violence or sexual abuse" means a crime that involved the use or attempted or threatened use of physical force against the person or property of another, or a crime under chapter 109A of title 18, United States Code.

Rule 32.1. Revocation or Modification of Probation or Supervised Release

(a) Revocation of Probation or Supervised Release.

(1) Preliminary Hearing. Whenever a person is held in custody on the ground that the person has violated a condition of probation or supervised release, the person shall be afforded a prompt hearing before any judge, or a United States magistrate who has been given authority pursuant to 28 U.S.C. § 636 to conduct such hearings, in order to determine whether there is probable cause to hold the person for a revocation hearing. The person shall be given

(A) notice of the preliminary hearing and its purpose and of the alleged violation;

(B) an opportunity to appear at the hearing and present evidence in the person's own behalf;

(C) upon request, the opportunity to question witnesses against the person unless, for good cause, the federal magistrate decides that justice does not require the appearance of the witness; and

(D) notice of the person's right to be represented by counsel.

The proceedings shall be recorded stenographically or by an electronic recording device. If probable cause is found to exist, the person shall be held for a revocation hearing. The person may be released pursuant to Rule 46(c) pending the revocation hearing. If probable cause is not found to exist, the proceeding shall be dismissed.

(2) Revocation Hearing. The revocation hearing, unless waived by the person, shall be held within a reasonable time in the district of jurisdiction. The person shall be given

(A) written notice of the alleged violation;

(B) disclosure of the evidence against the person;

(C) an opportunity to appear and to present evidence in the person's own behalf;

(D) the opportunity to question adverse witnesses; and

(E) notice of the person's right to be represented by counsel.

(b) Modification of Probation or Supervised Release. A hearing and assistance of counsel are required before the terms or conditions of probation or supervised release can be modified, unless the relief to be granted to the person on probation or supervised release upon the person's request or the court's own motion is favorable to the person, and the attorney for the government, after having been given notice of the proposed relief and a reasonable opportunity to object, has not objected. An extension of the term of probation or supervised release is not favorable to the person for the purposes of this rule.

(c) Production of Statements.

(1) In General. Rule 26.2(a)–(d) and (f) applies at any hearing under this rule.

(2) Sanctions for Failure to Produce Statement. If a party elects not to comply with an order under Rule 26.2(a) to deliver a statement to the moving party, the court may not consider the testimony of a witness whose statement is withheld.

Rule 33. New Trial

On a defendant's motion, the court may grant a new trial to that defendant if the interests of justice so require. If trial was by the court without a jury, the court may—on defendant's motion for new trial—vacate the judgment, take additional testimony, and direct the entry of a new judgment. A motion for new trial based on newly discovered evidence may be made only within three years after the verdict or finding of guilty. But if an appeal is pending, the court may grant the motion only on remand of the case. A motion for a new trial based on any other grounds may be made only within 7 days after the verdict or finding of guilty or within such further time as the court may fix during the 7–day period.

Rule 34. Arrest of Judgment

The court on motion of a defendant shall arrest judgment if the indictment or information does not charge an offense or if the court was without jurisdiction of the offense charged. The motion in arrest of judgment shall be made within 7 days after verdict or finding of guilty, or after plea of guilty or *nolo contendere,* or within such further time as the court may fix during the 7–day period.

Rule 35. Correction of Sentence

(a) Correction of a Sentence on Remand. The court shall correct a sentence that is determined on appeal under 18 U.S.C. 3742 to have been imposed in violation of law, to have been imposed as a result of an incorrect application of the sentencing guidelines, or to be unreasonable, upon remand of the case to the court—

(1) for imposition of a sentence in accord with the findings of the court of appeals; or

(2) for further sentencing proceedings if, after such proceedings, the court determines that the original sentence was incorrect.

(b) Reduction of Sentence for Substantial Assistance. If the Government so moves within one year after the sentence is imposed, the court may reduce a sentence to reflect a defendant's subsequent substantial assistance in investigating or prosecuting another person, in accordance with the guidelines and policy statements issued by the Sentencing Commission under 28 U.S.C. § 994. The court may consider a government motion to reduce a sentence made one year or more after the sentence is imposed if the defendant's substantial assistance involves information or evidence not known by the defendant until one year or more after sentence is imposed. In evaluating whether substantial assistance has been rendered, the court may consider the defendant's pre-sentence assistance. In applying this subdivision, the court may reduce the sentence to a level below that established by statute as a minimum sentence.

(c) Correction of Sentence by Sentencing Court. The court, acting within 7 days after the imposition of sentence, may correct a sentence that was imposed as a result of arithmetical, technical, or other clear error.

Rule 36. Clerical Mistakes

Clerical mistakes in judgments, orders or other parts of the record and errors in the record arising from oversight or omission may be corrected by the court at any time and after such notice, if any, as the court orders.

[VIII. APPEAL] (Abrogated Dec. 4, 1967, eff. July 1, 1968)

[Rule 37. Taking Appeal; and Petition for Writ of Certiorari.] (Abrogated Dec. 4, 1967, Eff. July 1, 1968)

Rule 38. Stay of Execution

(a) Death. A sentence of death shall be stayed if an appeal is taken from the conviction or sentence.

(b) Imprisonment. A sentence of imprisonment shall be stayed if an appeal is taken from the conviction or sentence and the defendant is released pending disposition of appeal pursuant to Rule 9(b) of the Federal Rules of Appellate Procedure. If not stayed, the court may recommend to the Attorney General that the defendant be retained at, or transferred to, a place of confinement near the place of trial or the place where an appeal is to be heard, for a period reasonably necessary to permit the defendant to assist in the preparation of an appeal to the court of appeals.

(c) Fine. A sentence to pay a fine or a fine and costs, if an appeal is taken, may be stayed by the district court or by the court of appeals upon such terms as the court deems proper. The court may require the defendant pending appeal to deposit the whole or any part of the fine and costs in the registry of the district court, or to give bond for the payment thereof, or to submit to an examination of assets, and it may make any appropriate order to restrain the defendant from dissipating such defendant's assets.

(d) Probation. A sentence of probation may be stayed if an appeal from the conviction or sentence is taken. If the sentence is stayed, the court shall fix the terms of the stay.

(e) Criminal Forfeiture, Notice to Victims, and Restitution. A sanction imposed as part of the sentence pursuant to 18 U.S.C. 3554, 3555, or 3556 may, if an appeal of the conviction or sentence is taken, be stayed by the district court or by the court of appeals upon such terms as the court finds appropriate. The court may issue such orders as may be reasonably necessary to ensure compliance with the sanction upon disposition of the appeal, including the entering of a restraining order or an injunction or requiring a deposit in whole or in part of the monetary amount involved into the registry of the district court or execution of a performance bond.

(f) Disabilities. A civil or employment disability arising under a Federal statute by reason of the defendant's conviction or sentence, may, if an appeal is taken, be stayed by the district court or by the court of appeals upon such terms as the court finds appropriate. The court may enter a restraining order or an injunction, or take any other action that may be reasonably necessary to protect the interest represented by the disability pending disposition of the appeal.

[Rule 39. Supervision of Appeal.] (Abrogated Dec. 4, 1967, Eff. July 1, 1968)

IX. SUPPLEMENTARY AND SPECIAL PROCEEDINGS

Rule 40. Commitment to Another District

(a) Appearance Before Federal Magistrate Judge. If a person is arrested in a district other than that in which the offense is alleged to have been committed, that person shall be taken without unnecessary delay before the nearest available federal magistrate judge, in accordance with the provisions of Rule 5. Preliminary proceedings concerning the defendant shall be conducted in accordance with Rules 5 and 5.1, except that if no preliminary examination is held because an indictment has been returned or an information filed or because the defendant elects to have the preliminary examination conducted in the district in which the prosecution is pending, the person shall be held to answer upon a finding that such person is the person named in the indictment, information or warrant. If held to answer, the defendant shall be held to answer in the district court in which the prosecution is pending—provided that a warrant is issued in that district if the arrest was made without a warrant—upon production of the warrant or a certified copy thereof. The warrant or certified copy may be produced by facsimile transmission.

(b) Statement by Federal Magistrate Judge. In addition to the statements required by Rule 5, the federal magistrate judge shall inform the defendant of the provisions of Rule 20.

(c) Papers. If a defendant is held or discharged, the papers in the proceeding and any bail taken shall be transmitted to the clerk of the district court in which the prosecution is pending.

(d) Arrest of Probationer or Supervised Releasee. If a person is arrested for a violation of probation or supervised release in a district other than the district having jurisdiction, such person must be taken without unnecessary delay before the nearest available federal magistrate judge. The person may be released under Rule 46(c). The federal magistrate judge shall:

(1) Proceed under Rule 32.1 if jurisdiction over the person is transferred to that district;

(2) Hold a prompt preliminary hearing if the alleged violation occurred in that district, and either (i) hold the person to answer in the district court of the district having jurisdiction or (ii) dismiss the proceedings and so notify that court; or

(3) Otherwise order the person held to answer in the district court of the district having jurisdiction upon production of certified copies of the judgment, the warrant, and the application for the warrant, and upon a finding that the person before the magistrate judge is the person named in the warrant.

(e) Arrest for Failure to Appear. If a person is arrested on a warrant in a district other than that in which the warrant was issued, and the warrant was issued because of the failure of the person named therein to appear as required pursuant to a subpoena or the terms of that person's release, the person arrested must be taken without unnecessary delay before the nearest available federal magistrate judge. Upon production of the warrant or a certified copy thereof and upon a finding that the person before the magistrate judge is the person named in the warrant, the federal magistrate judge shall hold the person to answer in the district in which the warrant was issued.

(f) Release or Detention. If a person was previously detained or conditionally released, pursuant to chapter 207 of title 18, United States Code, in another district where a warrant, information, or indictment issued, the federal magistrate judge shall take into account the decision previously made and the reasons set forth therefor, if any, but will not be bound by that decision. If the federal magistrate judge amends the release or detention decision or alters the conditions of release, the magistrate judge shall set forth the reasons therefore [1] in writing.

Rule 41. Search and Seizure

(a) Authority to Issue Warrant. Upon the request of a federal law enforcement officer or an attorney for the government, a search warrant authorized by this rule may be issued (1) by a federal magistrate judge, or a state court of record within the federal district, for a search of property or for a person within the district, (2) by a federal magistrate judge for a search of property or for a person either within or outside the district if the property or person is within the district when the warrant is sought but might move outside the district before the warrant is executed.

(b) Property or Persons Which May Be Seized With a Warrant. A warrant may be issued under this rule to search for and seize any (1) property that constitutes evidence of the commission of a criminal offense; or (2) contraband, the fruits of crime, or things otherwise criminally pos-

1. So in original.

sessed; or (3) property designed or intended for use or which is or has been used as the means of committing a criminal offense; or (4) person for whose arrest there is probable cause, or who is unlawfully restrained.

(c) Issuance and Contents.

(1) Warrant Upon Affidavit. A warrant other than a warrant upon oral testimony under paragraph (2) of this subdivision shall issue only on an affidavit or affidavits sworn to before the federal magistrate judge or state judge and establishing the grounds for issuing the warrant. If the federal magistrate judge or state judge is satisfied that grounds for the application exist or that there is probable cause to believe that they exist, that magistrate judge or state judge shall issue a warrant identifying the property or person to be seized and naming or describing the person or place to be searched. The finding of probable cause may be based upon hearsay evidence in whole or in part. Before ruling on a request for a warrant the federal magistrate judge or state judge may require the affiant to appear personally and may examine under oath the affiant and any witnesses the affiant may produce, provided that such proceeding shall be taken down by a court reporter or recording equipment and made part of the affidavit. The warrant shall be directed to a civil officer of the United States authorized to enforce or assist in enforcing any law thereof or to a person so authorized by the President of the United States. It shall command the officer to search, within a specified period of time not to exceed 10 days, the person or place named for the property or person specified. The warrant shall be served in the daytime, unless the issuing authority, by appropriate provision in the warrant, and for reasonable cause shown, authorizes its execution at times other than daytime. It shall designate a federal magistrate judge to whom it shall be returned.

(2) Warrant Upon Oral Testimony.

(A) General Rule. If the circumstances make it reasonable to dispense, in whole or in part, with a written affidavit, a Federal magistrate judge may issue a warrant based upon sworn testimony communicated by telephone or other appropriate means, including facsimile transmission.

(B) Application. The person who is requesting the warrant shall prepare a document to be known as a duplicate original warrant and shall read such duplicate original warrant, verbatim, to the Federal magistrate judge. The Federal magistrate judge shall enter, verbatim, what is so read to such magistrate judge on a document to be known as the original warrant. The Federal magistrate judge may direct that the warrant be modified.

(C) Issuance. If the Federal magistrate judge is satisfied that the circumstances are such as to make it reasonable to dispense with a written affidavit and that grounds for the application exist or that there is probable cause to believe that they exist, the Federal magistrate judge shall order the issuance of a warrant by directing the person requesting the warrant to sign the Federal magistrate judge's name on the duplicate original warrant. The Federal magistrate judge shall immediately sign the original warrant and enter on the face of the original warrant the exact time when the warrant was ordered to be issued. The finding of probable cause for a warrant upon oral testimony may be based on the same kind of evidence as is sufficient for a warrant upon affidavit.

(D) Recording and Certification of Testimony. When a caller informs the Federal magistrate judge that the purpose of the call is to request a warrant, the Federal magistrate judge shall immediately place under oath each person whose testimony forms a basis of the application and each person applying for that warrant. If a voice recording device is available, the Federal magistrate judge shall record by means of such device all of the call after the caller informs the Federal magistrate judge that the purpose of the call is to request a warrant. Otherwise a stenographic or longhand verbatim record shall be made. If a voice recording device is used or a stenographic record made, the Federal magistrate judge shall have the record transcribed, shall certify the accuracy of the transcription, and shall file a copy of the original record and the transcription with the court. If a longhand verbatim record is made, the Federal magistrate judge shall file a signed copy with the court.

(E) Contents. The contents of a warrant upon oral testimony shall be the same as the contents of a warrant upon affidavit.

(F) Additional Rule for Execution. The person who executes the warrant shall enter the exact time of execution on the face of the duplicate original warrant.

(G) Motion to Suppress Precluded. Absent a finding of bad faith, evidence obtained pursuant to a warrant issued under this paragraph is not subject to a motion to suppress on the ground that the circumstances were not such as to make it reasonable to dispense with a written affidavit.

(d) Execution and Return with Inventory. The officer taking property under the warrant shall give to the person from whom or from whose premises the property was taken a copy of the warrant and a receipt for the property taken or shall leave the copy and receipt at the place from which the property was taken. The return shall be made promptly and shall be accompanied by a written inventory of any property taken. The inventory shall be made in the presence of the applicant for the warrant and the person from whose possession or premises the property was taken, if they are present, or in the presence of at least one credible person other than the applicant for the warrant or the person from whose possession or premises the property was taken, and shall be verified by the officer. The federal magistrate judge shall upon request deliver a copy of the inventory to the person from whom or from whose premises the property was taken and to the applicant for the warrant.

(e) Motion for Return of Property. A person aggrieved by an unlawful search and seizure or by the deprivation of property may move the district court for the district in which the property was seized for the return of the property on the ground that such person is entitled to lawful possession of the property. The court shall receive evidence on any issue of fact necessary to the decision of the motion. If the motion is granted, the property shall be returned to the movant, although reasonable conditions may be imposed to protect access and use of the property in subsequent proceedings. If a motion for return of property is made or comes on for hearing in the district of trial after an indictment or information is filed, it shall be treated also as a motion to suppress under Rule 12.

(f) Motion to Suppress. A motion to suppress evidence may be made in the court of the district of trial as provided in Rule 12.

(g) Return of Papers to Clerk. The federal magistrate judge before whom the warrant is returned shall attach to the warrant a copy of the return, inventory and all other papers in connection therewith and shall file them with the clerk of the district court for the district in which the property was seized.

(h) Scope and Definition. This rule does not modify any act, inconsistent with it, regulating search, seizure and the issuance and execution of search warrants in circumstances for which special provision is made. The term "property" is used in this rule to include documents, books, papers and any other tangible objects. The term "daytime" is used in this rule to mean the hours from 6:00 a.m. to 10:00 p.m. according to local time. The phrase "federal law enforcement officer" is used in this rule to mean any government agent, other than an attorney for the government as defined in Rule 54(c), who is engaged in the enforcement of the criminal laws and is within any category of officers authorized by the Attorney General to request the issuance of a search warrant.

Rule 42. Criminal Contempt

(a) Summary Disposition. A criminal contempt may be punished summarily if the judge certifies that the judge saw or heard the conduct constituting the contempt and that it was committed in the actual presence of the court. The order of contempt shall recite the facts and shall be signed by the judge and entered of record.

(b) Disposition Upon Notice and Hearing. A criminal contempt except as provided in subdivision (a) of this rule shall be prosecuted on notice. The notice shall state the time and place of hearing, allowing a reasonable time for the preparation of the defense, and shall state the essential facts constituting the criminal contempt charged and describe it as such. The notice shall be given orally by the judge in open court in the presence of the defendant or, on application of the United States attorney or of an attorney appointed by the court for that purpose, by an order to show cause or an order of arrest. The defendant is entitled to a trial by jury in any case in which an act of Congress so provides. The defendant is entitled to admission to bail as provided in these rules. If the contempt charged involves disrespect to or criticism of a judge, that judge is disqualified from presiding at the trial or hearing except with the defendant's consent. Upon a verdict or finding of guilt the court shall enter an order fixing the punishment.

X. GENERAL PROVISIONS

Rule 43. Presence of the Defendant

(a) Presence Required. The defendant shall be present at the arraignment, at the time of the plea, at every stage of the trial including the impaneling of the jury and the return of the verdict, and at the imposition of sentence, except as otherwise provided by this rule.

(b) Continued Presence Not Required. The further progress of the trial to and including the return of the verdict, and the imposition of sentence, will not be prevented and the defendant will be considered to have waived the right to be present whenever a defendant, initially present at trial, or having pleaded guilty or nolo contendere,

(1) is voluntarily absent after the trial has commenced (whether or not the defendant has been informed by the court of the obligation to remain during the trial),

(2) in a noncapital case, is voluntarily absent at the imposition of sentence, or

(3) after being warned by the court that disruptive conduct will cause the removal of the defendant from the courtroom, persists in conduct which is such as to justify exclusion from the courtroom.

(c) Presence Not Required. A defendant need not be present:

(1) when represented by counsel and the defendant is an organization, as defined in 18 U.S.C. s 18;

(2) when the offense is punishable by fine or by imprisonment for not more than one year or both, and the court, with the written consent of the defendant, permits arraignment, plea, trial, and imposition of sentence in the defendant's absence;

(3) when the proceeding involves only a conference or hearing upon a question of law; or

(4) when the proceeding involves a reduction or correction of sentence under Rule 35(b) or (c) or 18 U.S.C. § 3582(c).

Rule 44. Right to and Assignment of Counsel

(a) Right to Assigned Counsel. Every defendant who is unable to obtain counsel shall be entitled to have counsel assigned to represent that defendant at every stage of the proceedings from initial appearance before the federal magistrate judge or the court through appeal, unless that defendant waives such appointment.

(b) Assignment Procedure. The procedures for implementing the right set out in subdivision (a) shall be those provided by law and by local rules of court established pursuant thereto.

(c) Joint Representation. Whenever two or more defendants have been jointly charged pursuant to Rule 8(b) or have been joined for trial pursuant to Rule 13, and are represented by the same retained or assigned counsel or by retained or assigned counsel who are associated in the practice of law, the court shall promptly inquire with respect to such joint representation and shall personally advise each defendant of the right to the effective assistance of counsel, including separate representation. Unless it appears that there is good cause to believe no conflict of interest is likely to arise, the court shall take such measures as may be appropriate to protect each defendant's right to counsel.

Rule 45. Time

(a) Computation. In computing any period of time the day of the act or event from which the designated period of time begins to run shall not be included. The last day of the period so computed shall be included, unless it is a Saturday, a Sunday, or a legal holiday, or, when the act to be done is the filing of some paper in court, a day on which weather or other conditions have made the office of the clerk of the district court inaccessible, in which event the period runs until the end of the next day which is not one of the aforementioned days. When a period of time prescribed or allowed is less than 11 days, intermediate Saturdays, Sundays and legal holidays shall be excluded in the computation. As used in these rules, "legal holiday" includes New Year's Day, Birthday of Martin Luther King, Jr., Washington's Birthday, Memorial Day, Independence Day, Labor Day, Columbus Day, Veterans Day, Thanksgiving Day, Christmas Day, and any other day appointed as a holiday by the President or the Congress of the United States, or by the state in which the district court is held.

(b) Enlargement. When an act is required or allowed to be done at or within a specified time, the court for cause shown may at any time in its discretion (1) with or without motion or notice, order the period enlarged if request therefor is made before the expiration of the period originally prescribed or as extended by a previous order or (2) upon motion made after the expiration of the specified period permit the act to be done if the failure to act was the result of excusable neglect; but the court may not extend the time for taking any action under Rules 29, 33, 34 and 35, except to the extent and under the conditions stated in them.

[(c) Unaffected by Expiration of Term.] (Rescinded Feb. 28, 1966, eff. July 1, 1966.)

(d) For Motions; Affidavits. A written motion, other than one which may be heard *ex parte,* and notice of the hearing thereof shall be served not later than 5 days before the time specified for the hearing unless a different period is fixed by rule or order of the court. For cause shown such an order may be made on *ex parte* application. When a motion is supported by affidavit, the affidavit shall be served with the motion; and opposing affidavits may be served not less than 1 day before the hearing unless the court permits them to be served at a later time.

(e) Additional Time After Service by Mail. Whenever a party has the right or is required to do an act within a prescribed period after the service of a notice or other paper upon that party and the notice or other paper is served by mail, 3 days shall be added to the prescribed period.

Rule 46. Release From Custody

(a) Release Prior to Trial. Eligibility for release prior to trial shall be in accordance with 18 U.S.C. §§ 3142 and 3144.

(b) Release During Trial. A person released before trial shall continue on release during trial under the same terms and conditions as were previously imposed unless the court determines that other terms and conditions or termination of release are necessary to assure such person's presence during the trial or to assure that such person's conduct will not obstruct the orderly and expeditious progress of the trial.

(c) Pending Sentence and Notice of Appeal. Eligibility for release pending sentence or pending notice of appeal or expiration of the time allowed for filing notice of appeal, shall be in accordance with 18 U.S.C. § 3143. The burden of establishing that the defendant will not flee or pose a danger to any other person or to the community rests with the defendant.

(d) Justification of Sureties. Every surety, except a corporate surety which is approved as provided by law, shall justify by affidavit and may be required to describe in the affidavit the property by which the surety proposes to justify and the encumbrances thereon, the number and amount of other bonds and undertakings for bail entered into by the surety and remaining undischarged and all the other liabilities of the surety. No bond shall be approved unless the surety thereon appears to be qualified.

(e) Forfeiture.

(1) Declaration. If there is a breach of condition of a bond, the district court shall declare a forfeiture of the bail.

(2) Setting Aside. The court may direct that a forfeiture be set aside in whole or in part, upon such conditions as the court may impose, if a person released upon execution of an appearance bond with a surety is subsequently surrendered by the surety into custody or if it otherwise appears that justice does not require the forfeiture.

(3) Enforcement. When a forfeiture has not been set aside, the court shall on motion enter a judgment of default and execution may issue thereon. By entering into a bond the obligors submit to the jurisdiction of the district court and irrevocably appoint the clerk of the court as their agent upon whom any papers affecting their liability may be served. Their liability may be enforced on motion without the necessity of an independent action. The motion and such notice of the motion as the court prescribes may be served on the clerk of the court, who shall forthwith mail copies to the obligors to their last known addresses.

(4) Remission. After entry of such judgment, the court may remit it in whole or in part under the conditions applying to the setting aside of forfeiture in paragraph (2) of this subdivision.

(f) Exoneration. When the condition of the bond has been satisfied or the forfeiture thereof has been set aside or remitted, the court shall exonerate the obligors and release any bail. A surety may be exonerated by a deposit of cash in the amount of the bond or by a timely surrender of the defendant into custody.

(g) Supervision of Detention Pending Trial. The court shall exercise supervision over the detention of defendants and witnesses within the district pending trial for the purpose of eliminating all unnecessary detention. The attorney for the government shall make a biweekly report to the court listing each defendant and witness who has been held in custody pending indictment, arraignment or trial for a period in excess of ten days. As to each witness so listed the attorney for the government shall make a statement of the reasons why such witness should not be released with or without the taking of a deposition pursuant to Rule 15(a). As to each defendant so listed the attorney for the government shall make a statement of the reasons why the defendant is still held in custody.

(h) Forfeiture of Property. Nothing in this rule or in chapter 207 of title 18, United States Code, shall prevent the court from disposing of any charge by entering an order directing forfeiture of property pursuant to 18 U.S.C. 3142(c)(1)(B)(xi) if the value of the property is an amount that would be an appropriate sentence after conviction of the offense charged and if such forfeiture is authorized by statute or regulation.

(i) Production of Statements.

(1) In General. Rule 26.2(a)–(d) and (f) applies at a detention hearing held under 18 U.S.C. § 3144, unless the court, for good cause shown, rules otherwise in a particular case.

(2) Sanctions for Failure to Produce Statement. If a party elects not to comply with an order under Rule 26.2(a) to deliver a statement to the moving party, at the detention hearing the court may not consider the testimony of a witness whose statement is withheld.

Rule 47. Motions

An application to the court for an order shall be by motion. A motion other than one made during a trial or hearing shall be in writing unless the court permits it to be made orally. It shall state the grounds upon which it is made and shall set forth the relief or order sought. It may be supported by affidavit.

Rule 48. Dismissal

(a) By Attorney for Government. The Attorney General or the United States attorney may by leave of court file a dismissal of an indictment, information or complaint and the prosecution shall thereupon terminate. Such a dismissal may not be filed during the trial without the consent of the defendant.

(b) By Court. If there is unnecessary delay in presenting the charge to a grand jury or in filing an information against a defendant who has been held to answer to the district court, or if there is unnecessary delay in bringing a defendant to trial, the court may dismiss the indictment, information or complaint.

Rule 49. Service and Filing of Papers

(a) Service: When Required. Written motions other than those which are heard ex parte, written notices, designations of record on appeal and similar papers shall be served upon each of the parties.

(b) Service: How Made. Whenever under these rules or by an order of the court service is required or permitted to be made upon a party represented by an attorney, the service shall be made upon the attorney unless service upon the party personally is ordered by the court. Service upon the attorney or upon a party shall be made in the manner provided in civil actions.

(c) Notice of Orders. Immediately upon the entry of an order made on a written motion subsequent to arraignment the clerk shall mail to each party a notice thereof and shall make a note in the docket of the mailing. Lack of notice of the entry by the clerk does not affect the time to appeal or relieve or authorize the court to relieve a party for failure to appeal within the time allowed, except as permitted by Rule 4(b) of the Federal Rules of Appellate Procedure.

(d) Filing. Papers required to be served shall be filed with the court. Papers shall be filed in the manner provided in civil actions.

Rule 50. Calendars; Plan for Prompt Disposition

(a) Calendars. The district courts may provide for placing criminal proceedings upon appropriate calendars. Preference shall be given to criminal proceedings as far as practicable.

(b) Plans for Achieving Prompt Disposition of Criminal Cases. To minimize undue delay and to further the prompt disposition of criminal cases, each district court shall conduct a continuing study of the administration of criminal justice in the district court and before United States magistrate judges of the district and shall prepare plans for the prompt disposition of criminal cases in accordance with the provisions of Chapter 208 of Title 18, United States Code.

Rule 51. Exceptions Unnecessary

Exceptions to rulings or orders of the court are unnecessary and for all purposes for which an exception has heretofore been necessary it is sufficient that a party, at the time the ruling or order of the court is made or sought, makes known to the court the action which that party desires the court to take or that party's objection to the action of the court and the grounds therefor; but if a party has no opportunity to object to a ruling or order, the absence of an objection does not thereafter prejudice that party.

Rule 52. Harmless Error and Plain Error

(a) Harmless Error. Any error, defect, irregularity or variance which does not affect substantial rights shall be disregarded.

(b) Plain Error. Plain errors or defects affecting substantial rights may be noticed although they were not brought to the attention of the court.

Rule 53. Regulation of Conduct in the Court Room

The taking of photographs in the court room during the progress of judicial proceedings or radio broadcasting of judicial proceedings from the court room shall not be permitted by the court.

Rule 54. Application and Exception

(a) Courts. These rules apply to all criminal proceedings in the United States District Courts; in the District Court of Guam; in the District Court for the Northern Mariana Islands, except as otherwise provided in articles IV and V of the covenant provided by the Act of March 24, 1976 (90 Stat. 263); and in the District Court of the Virgin Islands; in the United States Courts of Appeals; and in the Supreme Court of the United States; except that the prosecution of offenses in the District Court of the Virgin Islands shall be by indictment or information as otherwise provided by law.

(b) Proceedings.

(1) Removed Proceedings. These rules apply to criminal prosecutions removed to the United States district courts from state courts and govern all procedure after removal, except that dismissal by the attorney for the prosecution shall be governed by state law.

(2) Offenses Outside a District or State. These rules apply to proceedings for offenses committed upon the high seas or elsewhere out of the jurisdiction of any particular state or district, except that such proceedings may be had in any district authorized by 18 U.S.C. § 3238.

(3) Peace Bonds. These rules do not alter the power of judges of the United States or of United States magistrate judges to hold to security of the peace and for good behavior under Revised Statutes, § 4069, 50 U.S.C. § 23, but in such cases the procedure shall conform to these rules so far as they are applicable.

(4) Proceedings Before United States Magistrate Judges. Proceedings involving misdemeanors and other petty offenses are governed by Rule 58.

(5) Other Proceedings. These rules are not applicable to extradition and rendition of fugitives; civil forfeiture of property for violation of a statute of the United States; or the collection of fines and penalties. Except as provided in Rule 20(d) they do not apply to proceedings under 18 U.S.C., Chapter 403—Juvenile Delinquency—so far as they are inconsistent with that chapter. They do not apply to summary trials for offenses against the navigation laws under Revised Statutes §§ 4300–4305, 33 U.S.C. §§ 391–396, or to proceedings involving disputes between seamen under Revised Statutes, §§ 4079–4081, as amended, 22 U.S.C. §§ 256–258, or to proceedings for fishery offenses under the Act of June 28, 1937, c. 392, 50 Stat. 325–327, 16 U.S.C. §§ 772–772i, or to proceedings against a witness in a foreign country under 28 U.S.C. § 1784.

(c) Application of Terms. As used in these rules the following terms have the designated meanings.

"Act of Congress" includes any act of Congress locally applicable to and in force in the District of Columbia, in Puerto Rico, in a territory or in an insular possession.

"Attorney for the government" means the Attorney General, an authorized assistant of the Attorney General, a United States Attorney, an authorized assistant of a United States Attorney, when applicable to cases arising under the laws of Guam the Attorney General of Guam or such other person or persons as may be authorized by the laws of Guam to act therein, and when applicable to cases arising under the laws of the Northern Mariana Islands the Attorney General of the Northern Mariana Islands or any other person or persons as may be authorized by the laws of the Northern Marianas to act therein.

"Civil action" refers to a civil action in a district court.

The words "demurrer," "motion to quash," "plea in abatement," "plea in bar" and "special plea in bar," or words to the same effect, in any act of Congress shall be construed to mean the motion raising a defense or objection provided in Rule 12.

"District court" includes all district courts named in subdivision (a) of this rule.

"Federal magistrate judge" means a United States magistrate judge as defined in 28 U.S.C. §§ 631–639, a judge of the United States or another judge or judicial officer specifically empowered by statute in force in any territory or possession, the Commonwealth of Puerto Rico, or the District of Columbia, to perform a function to which a particular rule relates.

"Judge of the United States" includes a judge of a district court, court of appeals, or the Supreme Court.

"Law" includes statutes and judicial decisions.

"Magistrate judge" includes a United States magistrate as defined in 28 U.S.C. §§ 631–639, a judge of the United States, another judge or judicial officer specifically empowered by statute in force in any territory or possession, the Commonwealth of Puerto Rico, or the District of Columbia, to perform a function to which a particular rule relates, and a state or local judicial officer, authorized by 18 U.S.C. § 3041 to perform the functions prescribed in Rules 3, 4, and 5.

"Oath" includes affirmations.

"Petty offense" is defined in 18 U.S.C. § 19.

"State" includes District of Columbia, Puerto Rico, territory and insular possession.

"United States magistrate judge" means the officer authorized by 28 U.S.C. §§ 631–639.

Rule 55. Records

The clerk of the district court and each United States magistrate judge shall keep records in criminal proceedings in such form as the Director of the Administrative Office of the United States Courts may prescribe. The clerk shall enter in the records each order or judgment of the court and the date such entry is made.

Rule 56. Courts and Clerks

The district court shall be deemed always open for the purpose of filing any proper paper, of issuing and returning process and of making motions and orders. The clerk's office with the clerk or a deputy in attendance shall be open during business hours on all days except Saturdays, Sundays, and legal holidays, but a court may provide by local rule or order that its clerk's office shall be open for specified hours on Saturdays or particular legal holidays other than New Year's Day, Birthday of Martin Luther King, Jr., Washington's Birthday, Memorial Day, Independence Day, Labor Day, Columbus Day, Veterans Day, Thanksgiving Day, and Christmas Day.

Rule 57. Rules by District Courts

(a) In General

(1) Each district court acting by a majority of its district judges may, after giving appropriate public notice and an opportunity to comment, make and amend rules governing its practice. A local rule shall be consistent with—but not duplicative of—Acts of Congress and rules adopted under 28 U.S.C. s 2072 and shall conform to any uniform numbering system prescribed by the Judicial Conference of the United States.

(2) A local rule imposing a requirement of form shall not be enforced in a manner that causes a party to lose rights because of a nonwillful failure to comply with the requirement.

(b) Procedure When There Is No Controlling Law. A judge may regulate practice in any manner consistent with federal law, these rules, and local rules of the district. No sanction or other disadvantage may be imposed for noncompliance with any requirement not in federal law, federal rules, or the local district rules unless the alleged violator has been furnished in the particular case with actual notice of the requirement.

(c) Effective Date And Notice. A local rule so adopted shall take effect upon the date specified by the district court and shall remain in effect unless amended by the district court or abrogated by the judicial council of the circuit in which the district is located. Copies of the rules and amendments so made by any district court shall upon their promulgation be furnished to the judicial council and the Administrative Office of the United States Courts and shall be made available to the public.

Rule 58. Procedure for Misdemeanors and Other Petty Offenses

(a) Scope.

(1) In General. This rule governs the procedure and practice for the conduct of proceedings involving misdemeanors and other petty offenses, and for appeals to district judges in such cases tried by United States magistrate judges.

(2) Applicability of Other Federal Rules of Criminal Procedure. In proceedings concerning petty offenses for which no sentence of imprisonment will be imposed the court may follow such provisions of these rules as it deems appropriate, to the extent not inconsistent with this rule. In all other proceedings the other rules govern except as specifically provided in this rule.

(3) Definition. The term "petty offenses for which no sentence of imprisonment will be imposed" as used in this rule, means any petty offenses as defined in 18 U.S.C. § 19 as to which the court determines, that, in the event of conviction, no sentence of imprisonment will actually be imposed.

(b) Pretrial Procedures.

(1) Trial Document. The trial of a misdemeanor may proceed on an indictment, information, or complaint or, in the case of a petty offense, on a citation or violation notice.

(2) Initial Appearance. At the defendant's initial appearance on a misdemeanor or other petty offense charge, the court shall inform the defendant of:

(A) the charge, and the maximum possible penalties provided by law, including payment of a special assessment under 18 U.S.C. § 3013, and restitution under 18 U.S.C. § 3663;

(B) the right to retain counsel;

(C) the right to request the appointment of counsel if the defendant is unable to obtain counsel, unless the charge is a petty offense for which an appointment of counsel is not required;

(D) the right to remain silent and that any statement made by the defendant may be used against the defendant;

(E) the right to trial, judgment, and sentencing before a district judge, unless:

(i) the charge is a Class B misdemeanor motor-vehicle offense, a Class C misdemeanor, or an infraction; or

(ii) the defendant consents to trial, judgment, and sentencing before a magistrate judge;

(F) the right to trial by jury before either a United States magistrate judge or a district judge, unless the charge is a petty offense; and

(G) the right to a preliminary examination in accordance with 18 U.S.C. § 3060, and the general circumstances under which the defendant may secure pretrial release, if the defendant is held in custody and charged with a misdemeanor other than a petty offense.

(3) Consent and Arraignment.

(a) Plea Before a United States Magistrate Judge. A magistrate judge shall take the defendant's plea in a Class B misdemeanor charging a motor-vehicle offense, a Class C misdemeanor, or an infraction. In every other misdemeanor case, a magistrate judge may take the plea only if the defendant consents either in writing or orally on the record to be tried before the magistrate judge and specifically waives trial before a district judge. The defendant may plead not guilty, guilty, or with the consent of the magistrate judge, nolo contendere.

(b) Failure to Consent. In a misdemeanor case—other than a Class B misdemeanor charging a motor—vehicle offense, a Class C misdemeanor, or an infraction—magistrate judge shall order the defendant to appear before a district judge for further proceedings on notice, unless the defendant consents to trial before the magistrate judge.

(c) Additional Procedures Applicable Only to Petty Offenses for Which No Sentence of Imprisonment Will be Imposed. With respect to petty offenses for which no sentence of imprisonment will be imposed, the following additional procedures are applicable:

(1) Plea of Guilty or Nolo Contendere. No plea of guilty or nolo contendere shall be accepted unless the court is satisfied that the defendant understands the nature of the charge and the maximum possible penalties provided by law.

(2) Waiver of Venue for Plea and Sentence. A defendant who is arrested, held, or present in a district other than that in which the indictment, information, complaint, citation or violation notice is pending against that defendant may state in writing a wish to plead guilty or nolo contendere, to waive venue and trial in the district in which the proceeding is pending, and to consent to disposition of the case in the district in which that defendant was arrested, is held, or is present. Unless the defendant thereafter pleads not guilty, the prosecution shall be had as if venue were in such district, and notice of the same shall be given to the magistrate judge in the district where the proceeding was originally commenced. The defendant's statement of a desire to plead guilty or nolo contendere is not admissible against the defendant.

(3) Sentence. The court shall afford the defendant an opportunity to be heard in mitigation. The court shall then immediately proceed to sentence the defendant, except that in the discretion of the court, sentencing may be continued to allow an investigation by the probation service or submission of additional information by either party.

(4) Notification of Right to Appeal After imposing sentence in a case which has gone to trial on a plea of not guilty, the court shall advise the defendant of the defendant's right to appeal including any right to appeal the sentence. There shall be no duty on the court to advise the defendant of any right of appeal after sentence is imposed following a plea of guilty or nolo contendere, except that the court shall advise the defendant of any right to appeal the sentence.

(d) Securing the Defendant's Appearance; Payment in Lieu of Appearance.

(1) Forfeiture of Collateral. When authorized by local rules of the district court, payment of a fixed sum may be accepted in suitable cases in lieu of appearance and as authorizing the termination of the proceedings. Local rules may make provision for increases in fixed sums not to exceed the maximum fine which could be imposed.

(2) Notice to Appear. If a defendant fails to pay a fixed sum, request a hearing, or appear in response to a citation or violation notice, the clerk or a magistrate judge may issue a notice for the defendant to appear before the court on a date certain. The notice may also afford the defendant an additional opportunity to pay a fixed sum in lieu of appearance, and shall be served upon the defendant by mailing a copy to the defendant's last known address.

(3) Summons or Warrant. Upon an indictment or a showing by one of the other documents specified in subdivision (b)(1) of probable cause to believe that an offense has been committed and that the defendant has committed it, the court may issue an arrest warrant or, if no warrant is requested by the attorney for the prosecution, a summons. The showing of probable cause shall be made in writing upon oath or under penalty for perjury, but the affiant need not appear before the court. If the defendant fails to appear before the court in response to a summons, the court may summarily issue a warrant for the defendant's immediate arrest and appearance before the court.

(e) Record. Proceedings under this rule shall be taken down by a reporter or recorded by suitable sound equipment.

(f) New Trial. The provisions of Rule 33 shall apply.

(g) Appeal.

(1) Decision, Order, Judgment or Sentence by a District Judge. An appeal from a decision, order, judgment or conviction or sentence by a district judge shall be taken in accordance with the Federal Rules of Appellate Procedure.

(2) Decision, Order, Judgment or Sentence by a United States Magistrate Judge.

(a) Interlocutory Appeal. A decision or order by a magistrate judge which, if made by a district judge, could be appealed by the government or defendant under any provision of law, shall be subject to an appeal to a district judge provided such appeal is taken within 10 days of the entry of the decision or order. An appeal shall be taken by filing with the clerk of court a statement specifying the decision or order from which an appeal is taken and by serving a copy of the statement upon the adverse party, personally or by mail, and by filing a copy with the magistrate judge.

(b) Appeal From Conviction or Sentence. An appeal from a judgment of conviction or sentence by a magistrate judge to a district judge shall be taken within 10 days after entry of the judgment. An appeal shall be taken by filing with the clerk of court a statement specifying the judgment from which an appeal is taken, and by serving a copy of the statement upon the United States Attorney, personally or by mail, and by filing a copy with the magistrate judge.

(c) Record. The record shall consist of the original papers and exhibits in the case together with any transcript, tape, or other recording of the proceedings and a certified copy of the docket entries which shall be transmitted promptly to the clerk of court. For purposes of the appeal, a copy of the record of such proceedings shall be made available at the expense of the United States to a person who establishes by affidavit the inability to pay or give security therefor, and the expense of such copy shall be paid by the Director of the Administrative Office of the United States Courts.

(d) Scope of Appeal. The defendant shall not be entitled to a trial de novo by a district judge. The scope of appeal shall be the same as an appeal from a judgment of a district court to a court of appeals.

(3) Stay of Execution; Release Pending Appeal. The provisions of Rule 38 relating to stay of execution shall be applicable to a judgment of conviction or sentence. The defendant may be released pending appeal in accordance with the provisions of law relating to release pending appeal from a judgment of a district court to a court of appeals.

Rule 59. Effective Date

These rules take effect on the day which is 3 months subsequent to the adjournment of the first regular session of the 79th Congress, but if that day is prior to September 1, 1945, then they take effect on September 1, 1945. They govern all criminal proceedings thereafter commenced and so far as just and practicable all proceedings then pending.

Rule 60. Title

These rules may be known and cited as the Federal Rules of Criminal Procedure.

Appendix D

PROPOSED AMENDMENTS TO FEDERAL RULES OF CRIMINAL PROCEDURE

[These amendments to the Rules were approved by the Supreme Court and submitted to Congress on April 17, 2000, and will take effect on December 1, 2000, unless Congress takes contrary action. Underlined language is to be added; lined through language is to be deleted.]

Rule 7. The Indictment and the Information

* * * * *

(c) Nature and Contents.

* * * * *

(2) Criminal Forfeiture. No judgment of forfeiture may be entered in a criminal proceeding unless the indictment or the information ~~shall allege the extent of the interest or property subject to forfeiture~~ <u>provides notice that the defendant has an interest in property that is subject to forfeiture in accordance with the applicable statute.</u>

* * * * *

Rule 31. Verdict

* * * * *

~~**(e) Criminal Forfeiture.** If the indictment or the information alleges that an interest or property is subject to criminal forfeiture, a special verdict shall be returned as to the extent of the interest or property subject to forfeiture, if any.~~

Rule 32. Sentence and Judgment

* * * * *

(d) Judgment.

* * * * *

(2) Criminal Forfeiture. <u>Forfeiture procedures are governed by Rule 32.2.</u> ~~If a verdict contains a finding that property is subject to criminal forfeiture, or if a defendant enters a guilty plea subjecting property to such forfeiture, the court may enter a preliminary order of forfeiture after providing notice to the defendant and a reasonable opportunity to be heard on the timing and form of the order. the order of forfeiture shall authorize the Attorney General to seize the property~~

~~subject to forfeiture, to conduct any discovery that the court considers proper to help identify, locate, or dispose of the property, and to begin proceedings consistent with any statutory requirements pertaining to ancillary hearings and the rights of third parties. At sentencing, a final order of forfeiture shall be made part of the sentence and included in the judgment. The court may include in the final order such conditions as may be reasonably necessary to preserve the value of the property pending any appeal.~~

* * * * *

Rule 32.2. Criminal Forfeiture

(a) Notice to the Defendant. A court shall not enter a judgment of forfeiture in a criminal proceeding unless the indictment or information contains notice to the defendant that the government will seek the forfeiture of property as part of any sentence in accordance with the applicable statute.

(b) Entry of Preliminary Order of Forfeiture; Post Verdict Hearing.

(1) As soon as practicable after entering a guilty verdict or accepting a plea of guilty or *nolo contendere* on any count in an indictment or information with regard to which criminal forfeiture is sought, the court shall determine what property is subject to forfeiture under the applicable statute. If forfeiture of specific property is sought, the court shall determine whether the government has established the requisite nexus between the property and the offense. If the government seeks a personal money judgment against the defendant, the court shall determine the amount of money that the defendant will be ordered to pay. the court's determination may be based on e4evidence already in the record, including any written plea agreement or, if the forfeiture is contested, on evidence or information presented by the parties at a hearing after the verdict or finding of guilt.

(2) If the court finds that property is subject to forfeiture, it shall promptly enter a preliminary order of forfeiture setting forth the amount of any money judgment or directing the forfeiture of specific property without regard to any third party's interest in all or part of it. Determining whether a third party has such an interest shall be deferred until any third party files a claim in an ancillary proceeding under Rule 32.2(c).

(3) the entry of a preliminary order or forfeiture authorizes the Attorney General (or a designee) to seize the specific property subject to forfeiture; to conduct any discovery the court considers proper in identifying, locating, or disposing of the property; and to commence proceedings that comply with any statutes governing third-party rights. At sentencing–or at any time before sentencing if the defendant consents–the order of forfeiture becomes final as to the defendant and shall be made a part of the sentence and included in the judgment. The court may include in the order of forfeiture conditions reasonably necessary to preserve the property's value pending any appeal.

(4) Upon a party's request in a case in which a jury returns a verdict of guilty, the jury shall determine whether the government has established the requisite nexus between the property and the offense committed by the defendant.

(c) Ancillary Proceedings: Final Order of Forfeiture.

(1) If, as prescribed by statute, a third party files a petition asserting an interest in the property to be forfeited, the court shall conduct an ancillary proceeding but no ancillary proceeding is required to the extent that the forfeiture consists of a money judgment.

(A) In the ancillary proceeding, the court may, on motion, dismiss the petition for lack of standing, for failure to state a claim, or for any other lawful reason. For purposes of the motion, the facts set forth in the petition are assumed to be true.

(B) After disposing of any motion filed under Rule 32.2(c)(1)(A) and before conducting a hearing on the petition, the court may permit the parties to conduct discovery in accordance with the Federal Rules of Civil Procedure if the court determines that discovery is necessary or desirable to result factual issues. When discovery ends, a party may move for summary judgment under Rule 56 of the Federal rules of Civil Procedure.

(2) When the ancillary proceeding ends, the court shall enter a final order of forfeiture by amending the preliminary order as necessary to account for any third-party rights. If no third party files a timely claim, the preliminary order becomes the final order of forfeiture, if the court finds that the defendant (or any combination of defendants convicted in the case) had an interest in the property that is forfeitable under the applicable statute. The defendant may not object to the entry of the final order of forfeiture on the ground that the property belongs, in whole or in part, to a codefendant or third party, nor may a third party object to the final order on the ground that the third party had an interest in the property.

(3) If multiple third-party petitions are filed in the same case, an order dismissing or granting one petition is not appealable until rulings are made on all petitions, unless the court determines that there is no just reason for delay.

(4) An ancillary proceeding is not part of sentencing.

(d) Stay Pending Appeal. If a defendant appeals from a conviction or order of forfeiture, the court may stay the order of forfeiture on terms appropriate to ensure that the property remains available pending appellate review. A stay does not delay the ancillary proceeding or the determination of a third party's rights or interests. If the court rules in favor of any third party while an appeal is pending, the court may amend the order of forfeiture but shall not transfer any property interest to a third party until the decision on appeal becomes final, unless the defendant consents in writing or on the record.

(e) Subsequently Located Property; Substitute Property.

(1) On the government's motion, the court may at any time enter an order of forfeiture or amend an existing order of forfeiture to include property that:

(A) is subject to forfeiture under an existing order of forfeiture but was located and identified after that order was entered; or

(B) is substitute property that qualifies for forfeiture under an applicable statute.

(2) If the government shows that the property is subject to forfeiture under Rule 32.2(e)(1), the court shall:

(A) enter an order forfeiting that property, or amend an existing preliminary or final order to include it; and

(B) if a third party files a petition claiming an interest in the property, conduct an ancillary proceeding under Rule 32.2(c).

(3) There is no right to trial by jury under Rule 32.2(e).

Rule 38. Stay of Execution

* * * * *

(e) ~~Criminal Forfeiture,~~ Notice to Victims, and Restitution. A sanction imposed as part of the sentence pursuant to 18 U.S.C. ~~3554,~~ 3555 or 3556 may, if an appeal of the conviction or sentence is taken, be stayed by the district court or by the court of appeals upon such terms as the court finds appropriate. The court may issue such orders as may be reasonably necessary to ensure compliance with the sanction upon disposition of the appeal, including the entering of a restraining order or an injunction or requiring a deposit in whole or in part of the monetary amount involved in the registry of the district court or execution of a performance bond.

* * * * *

†